From Social Democracy to Neoliberalism

The Consequences of Party Hegemony in Spain 1982–1996

Sebastián Royo

St. Martin's Press
New York

ISBN 0-312-22390-0

Library of Congress Cataloging-in-Publication Data
Royo, Sebastián, 1966-
    From social democracy to neoliberalism : the consequences of party
hegemony in Spain, 1982–1996 / by Sebastián Royo.
        p.   cm.
    Includes bibliographical references and index.
    ISBN 0-312-22390-0
    1. Labor policy—Spain.   2. P.S.O.E. (Political party)   3. Unión
General de Trabajadores de España.   I. Title.
HD8588.R69   2000
331.1'0946—dc21   99–41530
                                                                      CIP

Design by Letra Libre, Inc.

First edition: February, 2000
10 9 8 7 6 5 4 3 2 1

To my wife, Cristina

Contents

Acknowledgments

This book is an outgrowth of my doctoral dissertation, written in the Political Science Department at Boston University. It would not have been possible without the help and inspiration of a number of people. I would like to thank the members of my dissertation committee for their support during the researching and writing of the project. I am particularly indebted to my primary advisor, Professor Sofía Pérez, who painstakingly read several drafts of this undertaking and helped me with every aspect of this research project. Without her encouragement and inspiration none of this would have been possible. I am also grateful to Professors David Scott Palmer, Edouard Bustin, David Mayers, and Paul Manuel for their guidance, wisdom, and support.

The list of persons who assisted in my field research in Madrid includes a large number of former socialist cabinet members, union leaders, employers' association leaders, scholars, and administration officials who were involved in the concertation process. All of them were extremely generous with their time and interest. I am particularly grateful to my father José Royo, Professor Emilio Ontiveros, and Fernando Gimeno, who not only provided valuable insightful information but also encouraged me during all the stages of my research. They were also instrumental in helping me get access to relevant policymakers, union and business leaders, and scholars. Without their generous support and encouragement none of the interviews that I conducted in Spain would have been possible. I am forever indebted to them. I also thank my colleagues in the Government Department at Suffolk University for providing a cordial and receptive research environment.

On a more personal note, I would like to thank Anne Stich, who was extremely helpful in polishing my English and editing my dissertation, and to an anonymous reviewer for St. Martin's Press, who helped in the final revision of the manuscript. This book would not have been possible without the strength derived from my family: my parents José Antonio and María del Valle, with their unquestioning love and support, who have fostered the best that I have achieved; my twin brother José Antonio and his wife Sue, who helped with the editing of the book and were always there offering their support and encouragement; my mother-in-law Paloma, who stuck by me and offered her unconditional support; my brother and sister, Borja and Rocío, for enlightening the way; and my daughters Andrea and Mónica, who were born during the elaboration of this project and made it so much fun. My deepest gratitude is reserved for my wife, Cristina. Without her love, commitment, time, patience, and encouragement this project would have never been completed. I dedicate this book to her.

Sebastián Royo
Boston, Massachusetts

Preface

Political scientists have long been interested in examining the effects of political institutions on the efficiency and performance of economies. This research project seeks to push forward this theoretical concern by examining an empirical puzzle that to this day has received little attention in the comparative politics literature: the failure of the Socialist government that held tenure in Spain from 1982 until 1996 to combat unemployment in that country. This policy failure is explained in terms of the characteristics of Spain's political and economic institutions.

This book considers the Spanish Socialist government's experience in light of various arguments developed in the recent literature on European political economy, none of which are found to offer a fully convincing explanation of the Spanish case. Interviews with policymakers, business and union leaders, and Spanish scholars, along with an extensive review of the secondary literature are used to support an alternative hypothesis: that the institutional dependence of the main labor union, the General Confederation of Workers (UGT) on the Spanish Socialist Workers Party (PSOE) led the Socialist government to default repeatedly on promises made to the union. Since the Socialist government's economic strategy hinged on the cooperation of the union, this breakdown in their relationship ultimately doomed the success of their policies. The main contribution of this research project to the literature is therefore to highlight the critical importance of an institutional factor that has not been given serious attention by other scholars, namely, the autonomy or lack thereof of labor unions from governing parties.

List of Tables

List of Figures

List of Abbreviations

ABI	*Acuerdo Básico Interconfederal* (the Basic Inter-confederation Agreement)
AD	*Alianza Democrática* (the Portuguese Democratic Alliance)
AES	*Acuerdo Económico y Social* (the Social and Economic Agreement)
AI	*Acuerdo Interconfederal* (the Inter-confederation Agreement)
AMI	*Acuerdo Marco Interconfederal* (the Framework Interconfederation Agreement)
ANE	*Acuerdo Nacional de Empleo* (the National Agreement for Employment)
AP	*Alianza Popular* (the Popular Alliance)
CAP	*Confederaçao da Agricultura Portugueses* (the Confederation of Portuguese Agriculture)
CCOO	*Comisiones Obreras* (the Workers' Commissions)
CDS	*Centro Democrático y Social* (the Democratic and Social Center)
CDS	*Partido do Centro Democratico e Social* (the Portuguese Democratic and Social Centre party)
CDU	*Christlich Demokratische Union* (the German Christian Democratic Party)
CEOE	*Confederación Española de Organizaciones Empresariales* (the Spanish Confederation of Business Enterprises)
CEPYME	*Confederación Española de Pequeñas y Medianas Empresas* (the Spanish Confederation of Small and Medium Size Businesses)
CES	*Consejo Económico y Social* (the Economic and Social Council)
CFDT	*Confédération Française Démocratique Du Travail* (the French Democratic Confederation of Workers)
CGIL	*Confederazione Generale Italiana del Lavoro* (the Italian General Confederation of Workers)
CGT	*Confédération Générale du Travail* (the General Confederation of Workers)
CGTP	*Confederaçao Geral dos Trabalhadores Portugueses* (the General Confederation of Portuguese Workers, or *Intersindical*)

CIG	*Confederación Intersindical Gallega* (the Galician Intersyndical Confederation)
CIP	*Confederação da Indústria Protuguesa* (Confederation of Portuguese Industry)
CIS	*Centro de Investigaciones Sociológicas* (Center for Sociological Investigations)
CISL	*Confederazione Italiana Sindicati Lavoratori* (the Italian Condeferation of Worker Unions)
CiU	*Convergència i Unió* (Coalition of Convergència Democràtica de Catalunya and Unió Democràtica de Catalunya)
CNS	*Central Nacional Sindical* (the Central and National Syndical)
CNT	*Confederación Nacional del Trabajo* (the National Confederation of Workers)
COBA	*Scomitati di base* (rank-and-file committees)
COPYME	*Confederación de la Pequeña y Mediana Empresa* (the Confederation of Small and Medium Enterprises)
COS	*Coordinadora de Organizaciones Sindicales* (the Coordinator of Syndical Organizations)
CPCS	*Conselho Permanente de Concertação Social* (the Permanent Council for Social Concertation)
CPI	Consumer Price Index
CSIF	*Confederación Sindical Independiente de Funcionarios* (the Confederation Syndical Independent of Civil Servants)
CSU	*Christlich Soziale Union* (the Bavarian Christian Democratic Party-a sister party to the CDU)
DC	*Democrazia Cristiana* (the Italian Christian Democracy Party)
DGB	*Deutscher Gewerkschaftsbund* (the West German Trade Union Confederation)
DM	Deutsch Mark
EC	European Community
ECB	European Central Bank
ECU	European Currency Unit
EFTA	European Free Trade Association
ELA-STV	*Solidaridad de Trabajadores Vascos* (the Solidarity of Basque Workers)
EMS	European Monetary System
EMU	European Monetary Union
ERM	European Rate Mechanism
EU	European Union
FDP	*Frei Demokratische Partei* (the German Free Democratic Party)

FN	*Front National* (the National Front)
FNT	*Fomento Nacional del Trabajo* (the National Foundation of Work)
FO	*Force Ouvrière* (Workers Force)
FT	*Financial Times*
GAL	*Grupos Armados de Liberación* (the Armed Groups of Liberation)
GDP	Gross Domestic Product
GHK	*Gewerkschaft Holz und Kunststoff* (the German Wood and Plastic Union)
GTB	*Gewerkschaft Textil-Bekleidung* (the German Textile and Clothing Union)
IG Metall	*Metallindustriarbetareförbundet* (the German Metalworkers Union)
IMF	International Monetary Fund
INEM	*Instituto Nacional de Empleo* (the National Institute of Employment)
INTG	*Intersindical de Trabajadores Gallegos* (the Inter-syndical of Galician Workers)
IU	*Izquierda Unida* (the Unified Left)
LO	*Landsorganisasjonen i Sverige* (the Swedish Trade Union Confederation)
LOLS	*Ley Orgánica de Libertad Sindical* (the Union Freedom Act)
MS	*Moderata Samlingspartiet* (the Swedish Moderate Unity Party)
MTSS	*Ministerio de Trabajo y Seguridad Social* (Ministry of Labor and Social Security)
NATO	North Atlantic Treaty Organization
ÖAKT	*Österreichischer Arbeiterkammertag* (the Austrian Central Chamber of Labor)
OECD	Organization for Economic Cooperation and Development
ÖGB	*Österreichischer Gewerkschaftsbund* (the Austrian Trade Union Confederation)
OS	*Organización Sindical* (the Syndical Organization)
ÖVP	*Österreichische Volkspartei* (the Austrian Peoples Party)
PCE	*Partido Comunista de España* (the Spanish Communist Party)
PCF	*Parti Communiste Française* (the French Communist Party)
PCP	*Partido Comunista Portugues* (the Portuguese Communist Party)
PDC	*Pacte Democràtic per Catalunya* (the Catalan Democrats)
PNV	*Partido Nacionalista Vasco* (the Basque Nationalist Party)
PP	*Partido Popular* (the Popular Party)
PS	*Parti Socialiste Française* (the French Socialist Party)

PS	*Partido Socialista* (the Portuguese Socialist Party)
PSD	*Partido Social Democrático* (the Portuguese Social Democratic Party)
PSI	*Partito Socialista Italiano* (the Italian Socialist Party)
PSOE	*Partido Socialista Obrero Español* (the Spanish Socialist Workers Party, or the Socialist Party)
RPR	*Rassemblement pour la République* (the Movement for the Republic)
SACO	*Sveriges Akademikers Centralorganisation* (the Swedish Confederation of Professional Associations)
SAF	*Svemska Arbetsgivareföreningen* (the Swedish Confederation of Professional Associations)
SAP	*Swedish Sveriges Socialdemokratiska Arbetarparti* (the Swedish Social Democratic Party)
SOV	*Solidaridad Obrera Vasca* (the Basque Worker's Solidarity)
SPD	*German Sozialdemokratische Partei Deutschlands* (the German Social Democratic Party)
SPÖ	*Sozialistische Partei Deutschlands* (the Austrian Social Democratic Party)
TCO	*Tjästemännens Centralorganisationen* (the Swedish Central Organization of Salaried Employees)
TUC	Trades Union Congress
UCD	*Unión de Centro Democrático* (the Democratic Center Union)
UDF	*Union pour la Démocratie Française* (the Union for the French Democracy)
UDP	*Unión Democrática de Pensionistas* (the Democratic Union of Pensioners)
UGT	*Unión General de Trabajadores* (the General Confederation of Workers)
UGT	*Uniao Geral de Trabalhadores* (the Portuguese General Workers' Union)
UIL	*Unione Italiana del Lavoro* (the Italian Union of Workers)
UK	United Kingdom
UNIPYME	*Unión de la Pequeña y Mediana Empresa* (the Association of Small and Medium Enterprises)
USA	United States of America
USO	*Unión Sindical Obrera* (the Syndical Union of Workers)
VAT	Value Added Tax

Note: Billion is used throughout this book to mean a thousand millions and not a million millions, as is the Spanish usage.

Introduction

This research project seeks to address a fundamental issue that Western society faces today: How to achieve a balance between economic and social needs. It also explores some of the questions that have attracted the interest of political scientists for the past several years: Are social democratic (SD) policies still feasible in a period of free movement of capital and increasing economic interdependence? Is the decline in *social concertation*—that is, centralized agreements between business and labor organizations, often with the participation of the state, on wages and other social goals[1]—an irreversible trend? If so, is there a feasible SD policy that can balance the interests of labor and capital? What are the conditions under which such a policy can be implemented?

In answering these questions, political scientists have been among the first to focus attention on the possible effects that domestic institutions have on the efficiency and growth rates of economies. In this research project, I seek to push forward this theoretical concern by studying the economic strategies pursued by successive socialist governments in Spain since 1982 with a view toward explaining the collapse of concertation after 1986. This is a critical factor because the collapse had important macroeconomic and social consequences in Spain and resulted in the abandonment of the traditional option by the social democrats to tackle inflation—voluntary incomes policy, a set of domestic processes that seek to influence wage settlements directly such as agreements to limit permissible wage increases. In this book I attempt to analyze the Spanish experiment with concertation, using it empirically to evaluate recent theories that have tried to account for the failure of incomes policies and concertation schemes in the Western world.[2]

The literature on concertation has mostly focused on economic institutions and structural factors to explain the success or failure of concertation processes. I argue, however, that these factors fail to account for developments in Spain. This literature omits other important considerations that also influence the decisions of social actors. It does not consider the impact of political relationship on the willingness by unions to participate in and of governments to abide by agreements. Interviews with policymakers, business and union leaders, and Spanish scholars, along with an extensive review of the secondary literature are used to support an alternative hypothesis: That the institutional dependence of the main labor union, the Unión General de Trabajadores (UGT, or the General Confederation of Workers) on the Partido Socialista Obrero Español (PSOE, or the Spanish Socialist Workers Party)[3] led the socialist government to default repeatedly on promises made to the union. Since the socialist government's economic strategy hinged on the cooperation of the union, this breakdown in their relationship ultimately doomed the success of its policies. The main contribution of this book to the literature is, therefore, to highlight the critical importance of an institutional factor that has not been given serious attention by other scholars, namely, the autonomy or lack thereof of labor unions from governing parties.

The analysis of the Spanish experiment with concertation confirms that the link between changes in the international economic environment and the process of domestic policymaking also depends on domestic political factors. The domestic environment, in addition to the global and institutional context, provides its own set of incentives for domestic actors to entertain certain political strategies. This book, therefore, stresses the pivotal role of domestic political and economic institutions in informing the success (or failure) of concertation schemes and economic policies.

The main empirical puzzle addressed—the failure of concertation in Spain—represents a historical outcome. It therefore requires an exploration of the origins of concertation in Spain and the political context under which concertation flourished and collapsed. The next section therefore, offers a summary of this historical context.

Historical Background (1975–1982)

Concertation in Spain emerged in the late 1970s, at the time of the transition to democracy. Spain had remained under the rule of Francisco Franco, the dictator, for about forty years (1936–1975). He kept control of the political machinery almost unchallenged. On November 22, 1975, two days after Generalísimo Franco passed away, Juan Carlos de Borbon, the designated successor, was proclaimed King. This development initiated the democratization process. The foundations for real democracy were laid through legal reform. The existence of solid institutions permitted the regime to initiate political reform from within as well as to accommodate pressures from below and from the international community.

King Juan Carlos and President Adolfo Suárez were successful in negotiating with the opposition and convincing them to accept their plan of reform from above. Several factors fostered the convergence among the competing political forces: (1) Francoist regime factions did not have the cohesion or strategy to take leadership in government. Internal struggles, consequently, weakened their position. (2) The Armed Forces had been relegated to a secondary role throughout the final years of Francoist rule. (3) Pressures from governments and political forces from the international community that sought a truly democratic outcome in Spain. The lack of strength of the various involved parties to impose their will, joined to a commitment for democracy from King Juan Carlos I, carved out a space for accords that permitted political pluralism to flourish. The fear of a return to the Civil War discouraged rupture, bringing parties and interest groups together to the negotiating table.

Pressure from the working class was fundamental to a negotiated transition. When Franco died, the labor movement was represented within Spain by the two illegal organizations that had emerged during the dictatorship, Comisiones Obreras (CCOO,[4] or the Workers' Commissions), and the Unión Sindical Obrera (USO, or the Syndical Union of Workers). The end of the authoritarian regime, however, accelerated the return of labor organizations that had been in exile, such as the UGT and the anarchist union, the Confederación Nacional del Trabajo (CNT, or the National Confederation of Workers), as well as the Basque nationalist union, the Solidaridad de Trabajadores Vascos (ELA-STV, or the Solidarity of Basque Workers)[5] in the Basque Country. These syndicates endorsed the cause and became extremely active soon after Franco's death. Labor mobilization contributed to the achievement of the goals set by the left—legalization of political parties and labor unions, amnesties, and elections with democratic guarantees—and forced the Right to break definitively with Francoism and its institutions.

The negotiation among democratic institutions was first implicit and tentative and became gradually more explicit. Although at first the government defended the interest of the ruling elites, the final agreement granted demands from the opposition, particularly the legalization of the two main political parties of the Left, the PSOE and the Partido Comunista de España (PCE, or the Spanish Communist Party); the formation of a new centrist party under Suárez's leadership, the Unión de Centro Democrático (UCD, or the Democratic Center Union); the self-dissolution of the Francoist Courts; and the convocation of direct elections. A popular referendum endorsed and legitimized the reform plan.

The emergence of a democratic regime in Spain resulted in the emergence of over 150 political parties. The first electoral contest, which took place in 1977, clarified the political spectrum. From 1972 until late 1982, the party system was dominated by two moderate political parties—the conservative UCD, and the socialist PSOE. The UCD won the 1977 elections with 34 percent of the vote, and the PSOE finished second with 29 percent of the popular vote. Other political parties such as the rightist Alianza Popular (AP, or the Popular Alliance), and the communist PCE, gained seats in Parliament. The regional nationalist parties, the Pacte Democràtic per

Catalunya (PDC, or the Catalan Democrats), later Convergencia i Unió, (CiU, or the Union and Convergence), and the Partido Nacionalista Vasco (PNV, or the Basque Nationalist Party) also achieved representation. The newly elected Parliament wrote a new constitution that was approved in a popular referendum in December of 1978. In the 1979 general elections, the UCD won again with 35.1 percent of the votes and the PSOE finished second with 30.5 percent.

The approval of the constitution intensified the organization of employers' associations and unions. Employers founded in 1977 a unitary employers' association, the Confederación Española de Organizaciones Empresariales (CEOE, or the Spanish Confederation of Business Enterprises), which represents businesses from all sectors of the economy. In April of 1977, the Spanish parliament approved the Free Union Association Act, which fully legalized free unions. A large number of unions emerged at that time with no proven support from workers. Some of them were even supported by business and aimed at weakening the labor movements. The government, however, following the Italian and French models, developed mechanisms to guarantee the predominance of majority unions, and established elections to work councils as the instrument to determine the representativeness of unions. The first union elections took place in 1978 and established the superiority of the CCOO (34.5 percent of the vote), closely followed by UGT (21.7 percent), and, at a far larger distance, by USO (3.37 percent). ELA-STV received 11.6 percent of the vote in the Basque country. The CNT refused to participate in the elections. Subsequent elections confirmed the dominance of CCOO and UGT. These elections consolidated a pluralistic and competitive industrial relations setting in Spain. Table I.1 summarizes the results of the first four union elections under democracy:

Table I.1 Elections to the Work Councils, 1978–1986 (%)

Union	1978	1980	1982	1986
CCOO	34.4	30.9	33.4	34.54
UGT	21.70	29.3	36.7	40.92
USO	3.9	8.7	4.6	3.8
ELA-STV	1.0	2.4	3.3	4.60
INTG-CIG*	—	1	1.2	0.7
Other Union	20.9	11.9	8.7	10.0
Nonunion	18.1	15.7	12.1	7.6

Sources: Ministerio de Trabajo y Seguridad Social. *Elecciones Sindicales.* Various Years. Madrid. MTSS.
*The *Intersindical de Trabajadores Gallegos* (the Confederation of Galician Workers).

All these developments took place in midst of one of the worst economic recessions experienced in Spain since the 1950s. The second oil crisis, the lack of competitiveness of the Spanish economy, a wages explosion, and the international economic crisis resulted in a sharp increase in unemployment (14.6 percent by 1981), and inflation (15.5 percent by 1980). Table I.2 summarizes the main economic indicators.

The weakness of the UCD government, which lacked a sufficient majority in Parliament, prevented it from taking the necessary measures to tackle the economic crisis. The 1981 failed coup d'état became a grave reminder of the shaky foundations of the new regime. The intensity of the economic crisis, coupled with the Basque terrorist problem, and the rejection of the new regime by a minority of hard-liners, instigated the coup leaders. The majority of the Spanish Army, however, rejected it, and the coup failed.

The following year the PSOE won the 1982 general elections with almost 10 million votes (48.4 percent) and achieved an overwhelming majority in Parliament. These elections signaled the restructuring of the party system. The UCD disappeared as a consequence of internal struggles that culminated in a disastrous electoral performance, and the rightist AP (later named Partido Popular, PP, or the Popular Party) emerged as the main opposition party. The Socialists remained in power for the next thirteen years, winning three further elections in 1986, 1989, and 1993. The PP defeated the Socialists in the 1996 elections. Table I.3 summarizes these electoral results:

These institutional, political, and economic developments provided the context for the emergence of agreements between the social actors—business, unions, and the government. The political and economic crisis convinced the new democratic government of the need to implement incomes policy based on top level agreements among the two major labor confederations, the employers associations, and at times the government. This process was known as "social concertation." The purpose of these agreements was to restrain wage demands to control inflation and foster the recovery of business profits, and to contain labor militancy—which might pose a threat to the stability of the new regime by provoking the army and the extreme right. From the late 1970s until the mid-1980s, five major agreements were reached among the government, unions, and business. The government only signed two of them. While concertation took place under conservative governments (1978–1982 and again in 1997), the socialists were only able to reach two concertation agreements to cover three years (1983, 1985, and 1986). Figure I.1 includes the agreements and its signatories:

These agreements involved wages and incomes policy, plus a variety of other issues. Wage bargaining was based on the next year's forecasted inflation rate, and wages were indexed to inflation in a backward fashion. What was remarkable about the concertation process was that Spain

Table I.2 Wages and Economic Outcomes in Spain, 1977–1990 (%)

Year	National-Pact Provisions[1]	Average Wage Increases[2]	Inflation[3] (%)	Work Days Lost in Strikes[4] (%)	Unemployment[5] (%)	Growth[6] (%)	Social Expenditure[7] (%)
1977	n.p.	25.0	24.5	16,642	5.7	3.0	10.3
1978	20–22	20.6	19.8	11,551	7.4	1.4	11.9
1979	n.p.	14.1	15.7	18,916	9.1	-0.1	11.9
1980	13–16	15.3	15.5	6,178	11.8	1.2	12.3
1981	11–15	13.1	14.6	5,154	14.6	-0.2	13.7
1982	9–11	12.0[a]	14.4	2,788	16.5	1.2	13.4
1983	9.5–12.5	11.4	12.1	4,417	18.1	1.8	13.8
1984	n.p.	7.7[a]	11.3	6,358	20.9	1.8	13.8
1985	5.5–7.5	7.4[a]	8.8	3,223	21.9	2.3	14.3
1986	7.2–8.5	8.1[a]	8.8	2,279	21.5	3.3	13.9
1987	n.p.	6.5	5.2	5,025	20.6	5.5	13.8
1988	n.p.	6.2[a]	5.7	6,843	19.5	5.2	13.8
1989	n.p.	6.7	7.0	3,685	17.3	4.8	13.9
1990	n.p.	8.1	7.3	2,443	16.3	3.7	14.6

[1]Wage band included in concertation agreement. n.p. = no global pact. Adapted from: Roca 1993, Table 6, p. 187. Used with permission. Source: Ministerio de Trabajo y Seguridad Social, *Boletín de Estadísticas Laborales*. See also de la Villa, L. E. *Los Grandes Pactos Colectivos a Partir de la Transicion Democrática.* MTSS: Madrid, 1994.

[2]Average wage increases negotiated in collective agreements. [a]Prior to the implementation of revision clauses. From: Roca 1993, Table 6, p. 187. Reprinted with permission. Source: Ministerio de Trabajo y Seguridad Social, *Boletín de Estadísticas Laborales.* Data for 1987–1990 adapted from OECD, *Economic Surveys: Spain, 1992,* p. 58.

(continues)

Table I.2 *(continued)*

[3]Sources: Instituto Nacional de Estadística, *Contabiliadad Nacional de España* (Madrid: Ministerio de Hacienda, Secretaría General Técnica, various years); and IMF, various years.

[4,5]From Escobar 1995, Table 6.1, p. 159. Reprinted with permission. Sources: Instituto Nacional de Estadística, *Contabiliadad Nacional de España* (Madrid: Ministerio de Hacienda, Secretaría General Técnica, various years); Intituto Nacional de Estadística, *Encuesta sobre Población Activa* (Madrid: various years). See also Führer 1996, Table 30, p. 343.

[6]Sources: Unpublished data from the Bank of Spain and the Dirección General de Previsión de Coyuntura.

[7]Government social expenditures as percentage of GDP. Source: IGAE.

Table I.3 Electoral Results, 1977–1996

Year	Party in Government		Main Opposition Parties	
	Party	Percentage	Party	Percentage
1977	UCD	34.0	PSOE	29.9
			PCE	9.2
1979	UCD	35.1	PSOE	30.5
			PCE	10.8
1982	PSOE	48.4	AP	26.6
			UCD	6.3
			CDS*	2.9
			PSE	4.1
			CiU	3.7
			PNV	1.8
1986	PSOE	44.1	AP	26.0
			CDS	9.2
			IU**	4.6
			CiU	5.0
			PNV	1.5
1989	PSOE	39.6	AP	25.8
			CDS	7.9
			IU	9.1
			CiU	5.0
			PNV	1.2
1993	PSOE	38.7	PP	34.8
			IU	9.6
			CiU	5.0
			PNV	1.2
1996	PP	38.8	PSOE	37.5
			IU	10.6
			CiU	4.6
			PNV	1.3

Sources for the years 1977 and 1979: Ministerio de la Gobernación, Direccion General de la Politica Interior, *Elecciones Generales 1977;* and Ministerio de la Gobernación, Direccion General de la Politica Interior, *Elecciones Generales 1979. Sources for the years 1982 and 1986:* Gunther, Sani, and Shabad 1988, p. 402. *Sources for the years 1989–1996: The Economist,* December 14, 1996, p. 13.

*Centrist party, Democratic and Social Center.

**A coalition of Leftist parties, including the Communist Party, PCE, names *Izquierda Unida.*

Figure I.1 Concertation Agreements in Spain, 1979–1986

Agreements	Years	Actors
Acuerdo Básico Interconfederal (ABI)	1979	CEOE-UGT
Acuerdo Marco Interconfederal (AMI)	1980–1981	CEO-UGT-USO
Acuerdo Nacional de Empleo (ANE)	1982	CEOE-UGT-CCOO-GOVT.
Acuerdo Interconfederal (AI)	1983	CEOE-UGT-CCOO
Acuerdo Ecónomico y Social (AES)	1985–1986	UGT-CEOE-GOVT./ UGT-CEOE

lacked a tradition of concertation among democratic actors. In fact, it had no experience with the concertation agreements that had been an integral part of the industrial relations setting in many other European nations.

Concertation in Western Europe

In Sweden, Austria, the Netherlands, Finland, and Belgium, concertation had been the preferred mechanism to regulate relations among social actors after World War II. In these countries social democratic parties had remained in power for an extensive period of time and sought to implement traditional social democratic policies to achieve full employment. At the core of such policies lies a compromise between business, the state, and the organized working class in which all partners cooperate to promote what might be described as a virtuous circle of full employment, economic growth, and welfare state redistributive measures. Concertation plays a critical role in such SD experiments because it is the institutional instrument that "delivers" incomes policy, or the wage restraint that results from top-level negotiations between business organizations and trade unions. Under these agreements unions agree to wage moderation in exchange for material and political compensation from business and the state. According to the corporatist literature, the organizational prerequisites for concertation were the presence of highly centralized and encompassing unions and employer associations, and a peak-level system of wage bargaining (Schmitter and Lehmbruch 1979; Lehmbruch and Schmitter 1982; Goldthorpe 1984).

Social democratic governments have traditionally implemented policies that have given priority to the manipulation of aggregate demand. The practical formula pursued by such governments consisted of expansive fiscal and monetary policies on the part of the government to stimulate aggregate demand and create jobs, while relying on wage restraint by unions to control inflation (Scharpf 1991, 166–167). This SD strategy stresses the capacity of unions to engage in a solidaristic wage stance as the key to successful disin-flation based on social concertation. The success of this strategy, however, depends on unions' cooperation in implementing incomes policy and con-trolling inflation. Without voluntary incomes policy, SD governments are forced to implement restrictive monetary policies to control inflation. These policies, however, traditionally have had higher cost in terms of unemploy-ment and, thus, run against one of the main social democratic stated goals: full employment. The implementation of these policies in countries such as Austria, Sweden, or Germany resulted in remarkably successful comparative economic performance. Up to the mid-1980s these countries experienced lower levels of unemployment and inflation than other continental Euro-pean states, such as Italy, France, the United Kingdom, or even the United States. Table I.4 illustrates the economic performance of these countries vis-à-vis other western European nations:

The good economic performance of countries implementing SD policies based on social concertation prompted the emergence of an extensive body of literature, known as neocorporatist literature, which sought to explain the reasons behind that success. Neocorporatist authors argued that a combina-tion of social democratic parties in government, monopolistic and encom-passing unions, and a centralized/coordinated system of wage bargaining contributed to the success of concertation, and, thus, to the good economic performance of the nations mentioned above.

A comparison of these institutional factors across European countries suggests that Spain does not meet some of the institutional criteria advanced by the neocorporatist literature for the success of concertation schemes. Al-though Spain had a SD government from 1982 to 1996, a longer tenure than any other SD party in Europe during the past decade, the structure and

Table I.4 Economic Performance of Eight European Countries, 1974–1985

Nation	Inflation (Average)	Unemployment (Average)	GDP Growth (Average)
Spain	15.5	10.8	1.8
Britain	12.25	7.65	1.35
France	10.45	6.15	2.15
FRG	4.5	3.6	1.75
Sweden	9.8	2.3	1.8
Austria	5.55	2.4	2.3
Portugal	22.9	7.4	2.05
Italy	15.55	7.75	2.8

Source: OECD: *OECD Economic Outlook,* various years.

organization of Spain's economic actors, especially its labor unions, did not foresee the successful implementation of concertation in that country. Union membership rates in Spain are among the lowest in the OECD (Organization for Economic Cooperation and Development), (approximately 10 percent), and Spain does not have the monopolistic and encompassing unions that exist in other countries such as Germany, Austria, or Sweden. The labor movement is dominated by two major confederations, the UGT and the CCOO, that compete for votes in the elections to work councils. Competition among unions at the firm level, however, has been tempered by the organizational structure of the major confederations, with powers concentrated in the executive committees, and by the representation powers given by law to the major confederations. Spain, therefore, has not experienced the levels of interunion competition that has been characteristic in countries such as Britain, France, and Italy. Furthermore, the structure of collective bargaining in Spain is an adaptation of what existed under the Franco regime. The number of workers covered by collective bargaining agreements is high (68–75 percent), and the industrial relations setting is characterized by three-tier bargaining, which occurs at the central, sectoral, and firm level. Most bargaining, however, actually takes place at the sectoral level (86.5 percent in 1995). Therefore, Spain is often labeled as a country with an "intermediate system" of wage bargaining, more centralized than the one existing in countries such as France or Britain, but less so than the system prevalent in Austria or Sweden. Table I.5. summarizes the main political and institutional indicators of eight Western European countries:

This institutional setting, however, did not preclude the emergence of concertation in Spain in the late 1970s. On the contrary, the strategy based on the implementation of voluntary incomes policies through concertation to moderate wages growth and control inflation, was successfully implemented in Spain from 1979 until 1986. Nevertheless, although there is generalized agreement that the outcomes of concertation were very positive—that is, that it contributed to wage moderation, reduced inflation, lowered industrial conflict, and helped to consolidate the institutional position of the social actors—the process collapsed after 1986 under a Socialist government.

Plan of the Book

The collapse of concertation in Spain after 1986 is, thus, the central empirical puzzle of this book. In order to account for such collapse I analyze two possible explanations derived from the literature and argue for a third. First, I consider whether the institutional and structural factors emphasized by the literature—that is, the domestic institutional framework along with

Table I.5 Political and Institutional Indicators of Eight Western European Countries

Nation	SD Party in Power/Coalition*	Main Trade Unions	Concertation	System of Wage Bargaining	Interunion Competition	Union Density** 1980–1990
Spain	1982–1996	UGT CCOO	Yes, until 1986	Sectoral	Yes	25.0–11.0
Britain	1997–	Over 600, 183 in TUC	No	Decentralized	Yes	50.4–39.1
France	1981–1986 1989–1994 1997–	CGT CFDT FO	No	Decentralized	Yes	17.5–9.8
FRG	1969–1983	IG Metall & 15 in DGB	Yes	Sectoral	No	35.6–32.9
Sweden	1932–1976 1982–1991 1994–	LO TCO SACO	Yes, until 1984	Centralized until 1984	No, until 1988	82.6–82.0
Austria	1949–1983 1983–	ÖGB ÖAKT	Yes	Centralized	No	59.6–57.5
Portugal	1983–1985 1995–	UGT CGTP	Yes 1986, 1987, 1990, 1991, 1996	Decentralized	Yes	60.7–31.8
Italy	1979–1993 1996–	CGIL CISL UIL	Yes 1992, 1993, 1996, 1998	Centralized 1992–1993	Yes	49.0–39.3

*The PSOE, Labour, PS, SPD, SAP, SPO, PS, and the Olivo Coalition are all social democratic oriented parties/coalitions. In Italy the PSI was for years (1979–1993) a minority party part of the CD coalition in government. In many cases the parties in government had coalitions with other parties. In France the PS (F. Mitterand) retained the Presidency from 1981–1995.

**Percent membership/employed workers. Sources: Blanchard et al., 1995, p. 120 (reprinted with permission); and Ferner Hyman, eds., 1992, pp. 119, 285, 545.

constraints imposed by technological changes and the increasing internationalization of economies—are sufficient to account for the collapse of concertation in Spain. I argue that these explanations are not sufficient, and I offer a third explanation—that is, the collapse of concertation was rooted in party-union relations.

The literature on comparative politics has attributed the collapse and failure of concertation to two main factors: The domestic institutional framework and structural changes in the international economic environment. According to the neocorporatist literature, which supports the institutional framework hypothesis, concertation has been successful in countries characterized by strong and monopolistic unions, social democratic parties in government, and centralized/coordinated wage bargaining. Under this explanation, union fragmentation and decentralized collective bargaining hinder social concertation by intensifying rivalries among unions and by forcing unions to compete for members. The structuralist literature, on the other hand, attributes the collapse of concertation to three main structural changes within the international economic environment: the decline of the dominant production paradigm (Fordism, or mass production), the emergence of new production methods, and the globalization and liberalization of capital markets. Structuralists argue that these developments have shifted the balance of power between capital and labor in favor of the former; that they fragmented and weakened the labor movement and limited the power of national governments to manage monetary and fiscal policies, and that these trends have made concertation more difficult, if not impossible, to achieve.

This book, however, argues that the institutional and structural explanations emphasized in the literature on concertation are insufficient to account for the collapse of concertation in Spain after 1986. Concertation was successful in Spain for almost eight years (1979–1986) despite an institutional framework characterized by decentralized collective bargaining, weak and competitive unions, and the strength and even dominance of the labor movement by a communist union for years. At the same time, the structural conditions faced by Spain were not less conducive to concertation than those faced by countries such as Portugal, where concertation flourished in the late 1980s and 1990s, nor were they different from those faced by the conservative government that came to power in 1996 and managed to restart the concertation process then.

The collapse of concertation in Spain can only be understood in terms of a third factor: The party-union relationship. I hypothesize that the union's weakness and its limited influence within the Socialist Party hindered concertation because it gave the government incentives to exploit that relationship and disavow its promises made to the union. The UGT lacked the institutional clout and the file-and-rank support of its northern European counterparts. The Austrian Social Democratic Party (SPÖ), the German Social Democratic Party (SPD), and the Swedish Social Democratic Party (SAP) all have a significant union base; union activists have representation in the highest policymaking organs of the party and they can also influence the party's decisions through their involvement in the local and regional offices. The UGT, on the contrary, had weak representation and little institutional power in the party. It only had one nonvoting member in the PSOE's executive committee; union activists did not have representation in the highest policymaking organs of the party; and UGT representatives did not participate institutionally in the party's programmatic discussions. At the same time, while the party was strong and had received almost ten million votes in the 1982 elections, the union was weak and had less than 630,000 members. This precarious position was further reinforced by the union's lack of economic resources to finance its activities, and its weak personnel structure. This situation led government officials to conclude that they did not need the union to execute government policies and to adopt a view of the union as merely being one more instrument by which to implement its plans. Consequently, the government failed to fulfill its compromises with labor because it encountered few constraints in disregarding those promises to the union. The final rupture between the PSOE and the UGT after 1986, caused by union disappointment with the government's economic policies, gave a final blow to concertation because UGT had been the only union which took part in all concertation agreements.

In countries with longer neocorporatist traditions, such as Sweden or Austria, unions play a critical role in the economic policymaking process, and differences between unions and social democratic governments are generally worked out through discussions and negotiations between the social democratic party and the union with the aim of reaching a consensus that can be supported by both. This was not the case in Spain, where the main socialist union, UGT, lacked the institutional clout to influence the position of the government, a deficiency that led government officials to stop treating the union as a necessary partner in the policymaking process. UGT was given a subordinated role to ratify the orientation of economic policy, and was then marginalized from the economic policymaking process. At the end, this subordinate position of the union led the government to ignore the union's demands and to implement restrictive economic policies that ultimately alienated the UGT leadership.

The overall strategy pursued by the socialist government was a tight monetary policy: an appreciating currency, high interest rates, and the absence of comprehensive supply-side policies and industry-oriented measures that would be very costly for unions and workers alike. These policies endangered the crucial party-union relationship and eventually resulted in a breakdown between the UGT and the Socialist Party and government.[6] The decision to marginalize the union and abandon concertation had negative consequences because the socialists' economic strategy hinged on the cooperation of the unions. The breakdown between the party and the union ultimately doomed the success of the socialist economic policies, resulting in higher unemployment in the early 1990s—over 24 percent by 1993.

The Relevance of the Spanish Case: Contribution to the Field

The Spanish case offers insights that are relevant to the field of comparative political economy. This literature generally leads us to expect that concertation is most successful in countries with SD governments (Garret and Lange 1985). However, Spain presents a case wherein the Socialist Party was in power for over 13 years—a longer period than any other social democratic government during the last decade. From 1982–1989 they held an absolute majority and received a high enough share of the vote to allow them to pursue a long-term strategy. The Socialist Party also controlled the local government of the major cities and most of the regional governments. This fact, however, did not prevent the collapse of concertation. Second, when the party first won the elections in 1982, it had the support of one of the major labor unions—the UGT, some of the leaders of which became members of Parliament. Nevertheless, concertation only worked until 1986. Afterwards, the socialists failed to recruit the support of the union to implement their economic policies. They even witnessed, for the first time since Franco's years, two general strikes. Finally, the Spanish case offers one of the few instances in which a social democratic government remained in power for a substantial period of time, in a context markedly different from that of the small European states of Northern and Central Europe where social democratic parties had ruled for years. Hence, Spain offers an opportunity to research the impact of a different institutional setting on social democratic policies.

This book makes three major contributions to the field. By looking at an instance of a failure that has not yet been examined and by analyzing how the case of Spain adds to our knowledge of institutions, I hope to shed further light on our understanding of how the institutional setting affects economic policy. Whereas most of the literature concentrates on the ways that business and labor unions influence economic policymaking, I seek to explore the influence that the relationship between the labor union and the Socialist Party has on economic policymaking. I also hope to demonstrate the importance of that institutional factor in the ability of social democratic governments to respond to economic challenges.

This research project also focuses on an empirical puzzle that is of great significance for the literature on comparative politics, namely, the failure of the Spanish Socialist government to combat unemployment. This book seeks to shed further light on our understanding of the phenomenon of Spanish unemployment (which currently stands at almost 17 percent and is the highest in Western Europe). I hope to explain this failure in terms of the collapse of concertation. Finally, I also seek to integrate Spanish experience, which to date has been studied almost solely from the standpoint of the literature on political transitions to democracy, into the literature on European political economy.

Methodology

In order to account for the collapse of concertation in Spain, I have chosen a historic and institutional approach that considers the objectives of policymakers and the way that they interpret existing economic conditions. I have selected this approach because it allows the researcher to examine the ways institutions structure the relations among actors and shape their interests and goals, thus constraining political struggles and influencing outcomes (Steinmo and Thelen 1992, 2).

This book is based on an extensive review of the secondary literature and interviews with scholars, social actors, and policymakers. I had meetings with representatives from the Confederación Española de Organizaciones Empresariales and the Instituto de Estudios Económicos. I also conducted interviews with the leaders of the major trade unions: Unión General de Trabajadores, and Comisiones Obreras as well as leaders and representatives of the following political parties: Partido Socialista Obrero Español, Partido Popular, and Izquierda Unida. I also conducted interviews with former high-ranking officials—including four former ministers—from three state agencies: Ministerio de Trabajo y Seguridad Social, Ministerio de Economía, and Banco de España. Finally, I met with scholars and specialists in industrial relations and economics. In total, I conducted 41 interviews over the period between November 1996 and June 1997.

Organization of the Chapters

This book is divided into six chapters. In chapter one I analyze the relevance of voluntary incomes policy and concertation for a social democratic government. This chapter is largely based on a review of other scholars' work. According to some scholars, concertation is critical because without it there can be no voluntary incomes policy, and without incomes policy, there will be no social democratic full-employment policies. In the economic context of the 1970s and 1980s, which had both inflation and unemployment, incomes policy offered social democratic governments a way to control inflation while pursuing expansionary policies that were consistent with the social democratic objective of full employment. The possibility of implementing voluntary incomes policy, however, depends on the acquiescence of unions.

In chapter two I consider explanations offered in the literature as to why concertation has worked in certain countries but not in others. According to the neocorporatist literature, concertation is more likely in countries that meet certain institutional criteria: Monopolistic and encompassing trade unions, centralized or coordinated wage bargaining, and social democratic parties in power. The structuralist literature for its part has focused on new economic developments that have hindered the maintenance and consolidation of concertation schemes. In this chapter I apply these arguments to the Spanish case to determine if they are adequate to explain the collapse of concertation in Spain after 1986. I conclude that institutional factors and economic constraints are not sufficient to account for the collapse of concertation in Spain.

Chapter three is an introduction to the history of the Spanish case. I describe the concertation process that took place in Spain from 1979 until 1986 and analyze the major concertation agreements, their content, and outcomes. I close the chapter examining the consequences of concertation in Spain, and conclude that it had very beneficial consequences for the Spanish economy because it resulted in wage moderation, lower inflation, and higher business profits in the second half of the 1980s.

Chapter four analyzes the institutional barriers to concertation in Spain. I examine the Spanish framework of industrial relations, the major unions and business associations, the relationships among social actors, and the system of wage bargaining. The Spanish industrial relations setting is often characterized by weak and competing unions, and by a decentralized system of wage bargaining. These institutions are very different from the ones that, according to the literature, foster concertation. The success of concertation in Spain for a prolonged period of time, however, suggests that we cannot attribute its collapse solely to the existence or nonexistence of these allegedly critical institutional factors.

In chapter five, I outline changes in the international economic environment that have taken place in the late 1970s and 1980s and their impact on concertation in Spain. Factors such as the globalization of production, the liberalization and internationalization of capital markets, and the decline in Fordist models of production have resulted in a weaker and fragmented labor movement and have also hindered the capacities of governments to conduct economic policy. I analyze how these developments affected the

Spanish actors and economic policymaking. I conclude, however, that while the relevance of these factors cannot be denied, they cannot solely account for the collapse of concertation in Spain either, as there was a margin of autonomy that the government could have used to implement its own policies if it had chosen to satisfy union demands.

Finally, in chapter six I examine the impact of the transition to democracy in Spain on concertation, and the ways in which the relationship between the PSOE and the UGT affected concertation. The union's weakness, its lack of influence, and its position of subordination vis-à-vis the government/party allowed the government to cheat on the agreements reached with the union. Such governmental reneging on compacts with the union fueled a confrontation between the party and the union that culminated in a rupture between both organizations and gave a critical blow to the concertation process. I conclude the book analyzing the impact that the collapse of concertation had on the socialists' economic policies, and the lessons derived from the Spanish case.

CHAPTER 1

The Basis of Social Democratic Policies: Incomes Policy and Concertation

Introduction

The significance of the key question of this book, which attempts to explain the collapse of concertation after 1986 in Spain, requires that I first explain the importance of concertation for social democratic (SD) full-employment policies. According to political economists, concertation is a critical variable because it is the institutional instrument for an effective voluntary incomes policy. Since World War II, voluntary incomes policies have become very important components of any full-employment plan by social democrats. These are policies aimed at controlling the growth of wages that are the result of centralized negotiations between business organizations and trade unions (and often the state, which acts a "guarantor" of the agreements). The success of these policies, however, depends on acquiescence by unions.

In what follows, I explain the macroeconomic objectives of social democratic parties, and analyze how incomes policies help reconcile these objectives. The chapter has three sections. In the first section, I start by exploring the historic foundations of SD policies. In section two I summarize the most common macroeconomic problems and the solutions that neoclassical and Keynesian economists have proposed to tackle those problems. In the third section, I describe the limitations and negative side effects of fiscal and monetary policies, and analyze the advantages of using incomes policy as a macroeconomic instrument in the achievement of social democratic objectives. I close the chapter by discussing briefly the history of incomes policy in Western Europe and conclude that the record shows varied results.[1]

I. The Historic Foundations of SD Policies

Traditionally, SD parties in the western world have sought to defend the interests of the working class. After World War II, however, SD parties, acting as the political arm of the labor class, became convinced of the unfeasibility of abolishing capitalism, given the existing power relations. They were also aware that capitalism has proven to be one of the most efficient ways to manage resources—even though they recognized and emphasized the need for wealth redistribution and equal opportunity. SD leaders also acknowledged that one of the major components of the capitalist system was the need for capital, and this scarce resource was controlled by a minority. Moreover, if companies were to be created and workers were to find jobs it was capitalists who would have to invest. Therefore, they sought to find ways to humanize capitalism and make it more favorable for the working class, while maintaining the foundations of the system (Scharpf 1991, 22–25).

The example of the Soviet Union convinced social democrats in Western Europe of the negative results of a centralized controlled economy. The economic backwardness of Russia had became very evident during the war, and the political consequences of central interventionism were unacceptable for social democrat politicians. One of their major concerns, however, was the instability of capitalism. The Great Depression of the 1930s, with its poverty, unemployment, lack of opportunity, and rampant misery, convinced social democrats of the need to modify the capitalist system. The Depression era confirmed the inherent instability of capitalism and the weakness of the reforms achieved by labor. When the Depression hit industrialized countries, the welfare system lacked safeguard mechanisms. Despite the strength and organization of some social democratic parties and the labor movement, these groups were unable to prevent the collapse of the nascent welfare state. Given this terrifying experience, social democrats looked for alternatives that would minimize the instability of capitalism and prevent these events from happening again. The emergence of Nazism, and the polarization of the social classes in Western Europe provided another source of inspiration for leftist leaders to avoid the mistakes of the past. Therefore, they sought a middle way between the existing policies of the Soviet Union, which resulted in scarcity and dictatorship, and the prewar western conditions of labor exploitation (Scharpf 1991, 23).

The total collapse of the European economies after World War II facilitated the convergence of political views and strengthened the determination to rebuild these countries. Political and labor conflict was replaced by more cooperative relationships, and ideological differences among political groups narrowed. Some political scientists have described this period as the "end of ideology" (Bell 1965). There was almost universal unanimity among politicians from the whole political spectrum about the need to adopt mechanisms that would prevent a crisis like that of the 1930s. SD politicians throughout western Europe also agreed that the state had to play a stronger role in the economy in order to provide safeguards that would cushion the weakest stratus of society from economic dislocations. In this regard, one of the major outcomes of the postwar settlement was the consolidation of the welfare state and the implementation of reforms that favored labor (Pontusson 1992, 441).

The postwar then became a period when labor, business, and the state came together and negotiated implicit and explicit agreements that would change the balance of power in western Europe for decades. It was also a time when the state deepened its responsibilities for the conduct of the economy. The provision of social services was one of the new responsibilities (Krieger and Kesselman 1992, 41–44; Scharpf 1991, 22–24). Keynesianism offered governments—social democratic ones in particular—the tools that allowed them to build up the welfare state while minimizing the consequences of economic downturns on the economy. Economic policies in the 1950s–1960s aimed at reaching an acceptable equilibrium between unemployment and inflation. Keynesian economics provided the theoretical foundation that allowed postwar politicians to achieve these objectives.

John Maynard Keynes criticized the neoclassical assumption that market-induced price changes would always return an economy to equilibrium and full employment. Instead, he proposed using taxation and fiscal policies as macroeconomic tools to help achieve stability, growth, and full employment. He argued that deficit spending had expansionary effects, increased private incomes, and raised tax revenues. He contended that by intervening in the economy, the state would generate confidence in the economic actors and would, therefore, help the economy out of a recession. The crisis of the 1930s discredited the neoclassical approach, and Keynes' theories became widely accepted after World War II.

Keynesianism provided SD parties with the economic theories that they needed to humanize and "tame" capitalism while developing their distributive agendas. As long as events such as the Depression took place, social democrats would have little defense against their opponents on the left because such crises would confirm the inherent weakness of the capitalist system and the devastating consequences that they would have had over the working class. Keynes' ideas, however, offered social democrats the opportunity to develop economic plans to strengthen the distributional aspects of economic policy and stabilize economic cycles, while maintaining the foundations of the capitalist system. State intervention in the economy and "fine tune-ups" helped stabilize economic downturns, while fiscal intervention and taxation also offered the opportunity to generate the resources that governments needed to build up the welfare state. This way, social democracy and Keynesianism became closely associated after World War II. While it is true that even conservative governments experimented with Keynesianism, social democratic governments were the ones that pushed Keynes' proposals to extremes after World War II and tied their electoral fortunes to the success of macroeconomic interventionism. These policies helped consolidate growth, stabilize economic circles, and maintain full employment for over two decades.

The favorable economic environment of the 1950s and 1960s helped consolidate SD economic and institutional reforms and strengthened the position of labor. But that economic climate did not last forever. Keynesian policies, as we will later see, were particularly suited to deal with unemployment caused by lack of demand coupled with a deflationary fall in prices—that is, the events that characterized the Great Depression. Keynes himself, however, had warned that once the economy was out of the recession, full employment might generate inflationary pressures (Scharpf 1991, 36). The events of the late 1960s and 1970s confirmed those fears.

The trade-off between inflation and unemployment became a major subject of debate during the 1960s, when both problems resurfaced in Western Europe and the United States. It was at this time that political scientists and economists began to focus on the relationship between unemployment and inflation put forward by Bill Philips (1958), who postulated a direct trade-off between unemployment and inflation. He argued that inflation depended, at least in the short run, on the level of unemployment. Therefore, expansionist policies aimed at achieving full employment would raise inflation and would also increase the deficit of the balance-of-payments. Figure 1.1 summarizes Philips' findings.

The implications of the Philips curve were clear: Governments could reduce unemployment by tolerating a higher rate of inflation. Since leftists and social democratic parties represented workers, their main priority was the achievement of full employment. This meant that they could be expected to implement economic policies that would achieve full employment even at the cost of inflation. Conservative governments, on the other hand, focused on combating inflation to achieve higher economic growth and reduce unemployment. The experience of the 1950s and most of the 1960s shows that countries with leftist governments experienced higher inflation and lower unemployment than countries with conservative governments (Hibbs 1977).

Keynesian macropolicies, however, are not well suited to deal with macroeconomic ailments that originate on the supply side of the market. A continuation of expansionary policies under conditions caused by supply-side problems only results in further inflation. Throughout the 1950s and 1960s, SD governments tended to prioritize employment over inflation.

Figure 1.1 The Trade-off between Inflation and Unemployment

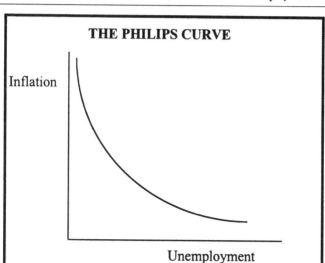

However, the emergence of high inflation and high levels of unemployment in the late 1960s and 1970s forced SD governments to reevaluate their strategies. Fiscal and monetary policies proved insufficient to tackle this combination. Only the cooperation of unions through concertation allowed SD governments to deal with inflationary pressures without resorting to restrictive macroeconomic policies that would raise unemployment. It is thus not surprising that the historic origins of incomes policy are linked to SD governments. After World War II, incomes policy became one of the most important macroeconomic instruments to be used by SD governments in Western Europe. Such a policy was first adopted in the 1950s in Austria, Belgium, and Sweden, where it contributed to the enormous growth of some of these European economies. The following two sections explain the limitations of fiscal and monetary policies and the benefits of incomes policy as an instrument to reconcile the interests of SD governments (low inflation and low unemployment).

II. Economic Foundations

The objective of this section is to show that Keynesian and neoclassic policies are ill suited to address certain macroeconomic ailments such as a combination of inflation, unemployment, and balance-of-payments deficit. The implementation of these policies under such conditions will most likely have countereffects that will worsen these problems. The cooperation of unions through concertation in order to implement voluntary incomes policy and moderate the growth of wages can, on the other hand, have a favorable impact on these macroeconomic problems.

Governments have at their disposal four principal instruments of economic policy to tackle macroeconomics problems such as unemployment, inflation, and growth: Fiscal policy, monetary policy, exchange rate policy, and incomes (or wages) policy (Scharpf 1991, 28–31).

The first instrument, fiscal policy, can be applied in two different ways. An expansive fiscal policy—that is, increasing public investment, public consumption, or cutting taxes—stimulates aggregate demand, reduces costs, and potentially increases business profits, thus stimulating consumption and investment. A restrictive fiscal policy, on the contrary—that is, reducing public investment, public consumption, or raising taxes—reduces aggregate demand, increases productive costs, and inhibits productive investment.

Monetary policy has similar effects: An expansive monetary policy enlarges the money supply, providing more credit at lower interest rates, and thus increasing aggregate demand and reducing capital costs. On the contrary, a restrictive monetary policy reduces the money supply and raises interest rates, thus increasing capital costs and reducing investment.

Finally, an exchange rate policy is used to determine the value of the country's currency. A currency devaluation results in higher import prices and lower export prices, thus increasing the demand for domestic products, but it also raises the cost for imported raw materials, goods and services, wages, and even capital. A reevaluation upward, on the contrary, reduces imports' prices and the cost of capital.

These policies, however, are very likely to have negative effects in certain circumstances and may not be able to reconcile the objectives pursued by SD governments, that is, low inflation with the lowest cost in terms of unemployment. Incomes (or wages) policy, on the other hand, helps reconcile these two objectives, and becomes useful under such circumstances because wages affect both the demand and the supply side of the economy in opposite directions. A restrictive incomes policy reduces aggregate demand and inflation while lowering productive costs, thus increasing business profitability and investment and allowing firms to maintain and create jobs. An expansive incomes policy has the opposite effects.

In order to understand the advantages of incomes policy more clearly, we need to consider the effects that each macroeconomic instrument has on common economic policy problems. Economists throughout history have advanced different solutions to tackle the macroeconomic problems of the day. Today, with the demise of the Soviet empire and the discreditation of

Marxism, there are two major schools of economic thought: Keynesianism and neoclassic economics. Each of these two schools offers different solutions to the four major sources of macroeconomic problems: Unemployment, inflation, balance-of-payments deficits, and weak economic growth. Figure 1.2 summarizes typical macroeconomic problems and their sources:

Economists also differ in their assessment of the utility of each of the policy instruments discussed above in addressing different macroeconomic problems. What follows shows that neither Keynesian nor neoclassical policies are well suited to address certain macroeconomic ailments. On the contrary, they are very likely to have negative effects in certain circumstances (see Scharpf 1991, 25–37).

Economists distinguish between two different kinds of unemployment depending on its cause: Demand side (or demand-gap) unemployment, and supply side (or investment-gap) unemployment. In the case of unemployment caused by lack of demand (Keynesian unemployment), Keynesian economists propose an expansionary fiscal and/or monetary policy. These policies increase aggregate demand, stabilize people's expectations, and foster consumption and investment. The negative side effects of these policies, however, is an increase in imports because people consume more, and it takes sometime for domestic producers to catch up with new demand. More imports will also result in a higher trade deficit and balance of payment problems. Therefore, once full-capacity utilization is reached, a continuation of these policies will result on demand-pull inflation as demand grows faster than production capacity. Further continuation of expansionary policies results in cost-push inflation because workers anticipate increases in inflation and will demand higher wages to compensate for it. Higher wages, in turn, result in higher costs and further inflationary pressures. The neoclassical solution, on the other hand, calls for tightening monetary and fiscal policies,

Figure 1.2 Economic Problems and Their Sources

Problems	Causes	
	Demand Side	*Supply Side*
Unemployment	a. Demand-gap (Keynesian)	b. Investment-gap (Classical)
Inflation	c. Demand-pull	d. Cost-push
	Foreign Trade Deficits Low Economic Growth	

From Scharpf 1991, 26. Reprinted with permission

but the implementation of such policies results in lower wages and prices, which in turn reduces consumer demand and deepens the recession. But it also increases investment as companies invest more to capitalize on lower costs. Yet there is no guarantee that lower demand will be offset by higher investment, since companies are not very likely to invest more at a time of lower demand (Scharpf 1991, 31).

In the case of unemployment caused by lack of investment, Keynesian economists favor policies that expand aggregate demand. However, since unemployment exists despite sufficient demand, the only way to create new jobs is by increasing firms' profitability. This means that prices have to rise faster than production costs. Higher prices, however, result on demand-pull inflation. The neoclassical response, on the other hand, results in declining consumer demand, and most likely, as we have seen, lower investment, as firms will be reluctant to invest at a time when consumer demand is being reduced.

When it comes to inflation caused by higher demand (demand-pull inflation), both Keynesian and neoclassic economists agree that aggregate demand has to be checked with restrictive monetary and fiscal policies. This course, however, results in companies producing less because higher interests rates will increase the cost of capital for productive investors and will result on lower profits. Lower production will, in turn, result in higher unemployment caused by lack of investment.

In the case of inflation caused by higher costs (cost-push inflation), Keynesian scholars argue that loosening the protection normally given to services such as hospitals, education, and governmental monopolies, coupled with trade liberalization and lower interest rates, will help to reduce costs. These policies, however, also have negative side effects—that is, liberalization will likely bring unemployment as traditionally protected companies struggle to reduce costs in order to be able to compete, while lower interest rates might cause inflationary pressures as people borrow and invest more. Neoclassical economists, on the contrary, favor tight monetary and fiscal policies to reduce the money supply. Reducing the money supply, however, will not reduce all costs—that is, wages do not move downward easily—and it will result in lower profits due to higher interest rates and less investment. This will later result in higher unemployment.

Finally, when it comes to foreign trade deficits, Keynesian economists' expansive policies result in lower production costs, more consumption, and a devalued currency. However, higher consumption will result in more imports, thus increasing the balance-of-trade deficit. Neoclassical authors would defend tight monetary policies to decrease consumption and imports and attract foreign capital. This will result, however, in higher costs for productive investors, lower investment, and will raise the value of the currency, thus damaging the competitiveness of domestic products in foreign markets. Table 1.1 summarizes the shortcomings of the solutions proposed by neoclassical and Keynesian scholars to address the most typical macroeconomic problems.

In conclusion, Keynesian and neoclassic recipes may not be at times the best alternatives to address certain macroeconomic ailments. The implementation of these policies have countereffects that may worsen the problems that they attempt to address. It is in this context that one can see how incomes policy may offer some alternatives when dealing with some of these macroeconomic ailments. In the 1960s and 1970s stagflation, defined below, was partially blamed on the sharp increases in real wages. Wage moderation, therefore, was seen as a prerequisite to renewed profitability and competitiveness, which in turn were critical to foster investment and growth. The cooperation of unions through concertation in order to implement voluntary incomes policy and moderate the growth of wages had a favorable impact on some of these macroeconomic problems. SD parties in government with strong links with unions and with widespread support among workers were particularly well suited to implement these policies because they could count on the cooperation of workers and unions. I will explain next the potential benefits of incomes policy.

III. The Benefits of Incomes Policy

a. The Theoretical Foundations of Incomes Policy

Monetary and fiscal policies sought to balance inflation or unemployment. In the context of the late 1960s and 1970s, however, they seemed insufficient to tackle a combination of both macroeconomic ailments. The recession of the 1970s was characterized by low growth, high unemployment, high inflation, and balance-of-payments deficits, all characteristics of what is called stagflation. These ailments confirmed the limits of relying only on fiscal and monetary policies. The new economic environment of the 1970s created a more favorable environment for the implementation of a new generation of incomes policy to address changes in the international economic environment. This incomes policy was based on concertation—that is, voluntary multilateral negotiations between unions and business, often with the participation of the government, to negotiate on economic issues, including wages—as opposed to the guidelines and bilateral negotiations that characterized the first generation of incomes policies. Social democratic parties in government were particularly concerned about inflation because it hindered the competitive situation of their economies, but they were also worried about unemployment because it affected mostly blue-collar workers—one of their traditional

Table 1.1 Keynesian and Neoclassical Solutions to Macroeconomic Problems

Economic Problems	Keynesian Solutions	Shortcoming	Neoclassical Solutions	Shortcoming
Keynesian unemployment (demand-gap): Insufficient demand	Government intervention to increase aggregate demand.	Temporary relief. Imports up and balance of payments deficit. Inflation.	Reduction of wages and prices to increase business investment.	Higher business investment is not certain. Potential recession.
Neoclassical unemployment (investment-gap): Lack of jobs	Government intervention to increase aggregate demand.	Profits up only if they rise fasters than costs. Inflation.	Reduction of wages and tax cuts to increase profitability.	Lowers investment and consumer demand. Lowers profits. Higher interest rates. Unemployment.
Demand-pull inflation: Full productive capacity/low profits	Tight monetary and fiscal policies.	Reduces aggregate demand, unemployment.	Tight monetary and fiscal policies.	Reduces real wages. Hinders consumption and investment.
Cost-pull inflation: High productive costs	To increase price competition and reduce factor costs.	Relies on wage restraint from unions to contain inflation.	Tight monetary and fiscal policies.	Reduces prices. Lowers profits, investment, and output.
Low growth	Expansive fiscal and monetary policy.	Inflation.	Flexibility and liberalization.	Unemployment.
Balance-of-payments deficits	Restrictive monetary and fiscal policies. To reduce factor costs.	Reduces aggregate demand. Increases domestic consumption. Devaluations.	Restrictive fiscal and monetary policies.	Reduces consumption and imports. Attracts foreign capital. But lowers investment and increases costs.

constituencies. Incomes policy offered a solution to that dilemma and allowed SD governments to reconcile the objective of low inflation with the objective of full employment.

The single most important argument in favor of incomes policy involves the effect that it has on demand and supply. As we have seen above, fiscal and monetary policies have proved to be more effective in those situations when inflation and unemployment are caused in the demand side of the goods markets—that is, the crisis of the 1930s characterized by demand-gap unemployment and deflationary prices. In these cases, monetary and fiscal policies are sufficient to stimulate aggregate demand and generate confidence in the economic actors' ability to end the recession. However, when a recession's causes are originated on the supply side of the goods market— that is, cost-push inflation, and/or investment-gap unemployment—fiscal and monetary policies are relatively helpless because they have simultaneous expansive and restrictive effects of the supply and demand sides of the economy. They will, therefore, result in worsening inflation and vice versa.

Political economists such as Scharpf (1991, 32–37), Flanagan, Soskice, Ulman (1983, 45); Freeman and Gibbons (1995, 345–370) argue that the limits of monetary and fiscal instruments can be redressed through incomes policy. This possibility was, however, ignored by many economists who neglected to study the situations in which a constellation of macroeconomic problems coexist. The proponents of incomes policy start from the observation that wages in the western world are determined not only by the market. Governments, unions, and collective agreements between unions and business groups also play an important role on wage determination, and they can reach agreements above or below the market price. It is for this reason that incomes policy can play such an important role in economic planning: "Incomes policy affect both the demand and supply side of the economy on opposite directions. An expansive incomes policy will stimulate aggregate demand but reduce the profitability of production and investment, and a restrictive policy will have the opposite effect" (Scharpf 1991, 34). This means that a restrictive incomes policy, for example, can be used as a means to control inflation and increase profitability—and, thus create jobs. Figure 1.3 summarizes the effects of incomes policy:

Incomes policy has been implemented in various countries as a way to sustain employment while controlling inflation. Restrictive incomes policy reduces aggregate demand while lowering productive costs, thus increasing business profitability and investment—allowing firms to maintain and create jobs. It is, therefore, a valid instrument to fight demand-gap and cost-push inflation, and balance-of-payments deficits without resorting to the negative effects of restrictive monetary and fiscal policies. It is also useful for fighting investment-gap unemployment because it allows for an increase in

Figure 1.3 The Effects of Incomes Policy

Incomes Policy	Demand Side	Supply Side
Expansive	Stimulates demand	Reduces profits
Restrictive	Restricts demand	Increases profits

business profits and, therefore, for further investment. Wage restraint is also an adequate instrument to fight cost-push inflation, balance-of-payments deficits, and demand-pull inflation. Wage restraint results in income losses for the workers and reduced consumption, but it also lowers productive costs for firms, therefore helping fight cost-push inflation and raising the profitability of productive investment. Furthermore, wage restraint also reduces aggregate demand, thus lowering consumption and imports and helping fight demand-pull inflation and balance-of-payments deficits. It also lowers productive costs and increases firms' competitiveness in foreign markets. Finally, while wage restraint does not, by itself, help fight demand-gap unemployment—that is, lower wages and consumption do not create new jobs—or investment-gap unemployment—that is, lower consumer demand and higher profits do not guarantee higher investment—a combination of incomes policy and other policy instruments will have very positive effects (Scharpf 1991, 34–35).

Incomes policy is particularly effective when used in combination with fiscal and monetary policies. A combination of restrictive incomes policy may help restore business profits and limit inflationary pressures, while an expansive fiscal policy would offset the negative effects on aggregate demand and encourage investment. Therefore, SD governments can focus on unemployment via expansionary fiscal and monetary policies—that is, lower interest rates—while inflation is controlled via incomes policy (Scharpf 1991, 34–37). Restrictive incomes policy combined with expansive fiscal policies stimulate demand and lower interest rates, thus fostering investment and reducing investment-gap unemployment. Such a combination will also help fight cost-push inflation and demand unemployment because expansive fiscal and monetary policies compensate for the demand shortfall caused by wage restraint. Incomes policy is, therefore, an adequate instrument to reduce unemployment and inflation. It is critical from a social democratic point of view because it helps reconcile the objectives of social democratic governments to fight inflation while keeping unemployment very low. In this regard, social democratic governments have traditionally been more open to the participation of unions in collective bargaining and macroeconomic policymaking. Conservative governments, on the contrary, have usually opposed—

explicitly or implicitly—attempts to increase the institutional role of unions. It is not surprising, therefore, that these policies have been mostly implemented in countries with SD governments, since they depend on the acquiescence of unions who are the critical participants in wage setting.

b. Incomes Policy and Concertation: The Role of Unions

Since wages in the western world are not only determined by the market but also by collective bargaining between unions and business associations, a successful incomes policy requires the cooperation of unions. Such cooperation is achieved through concertation, whereby labor agrees to limit wage growth in exchange for compensation from business and/or the government. Without concertation with unions there will be no wage restraint and, thus one of the key components of a successful SD policy will be missing. SD governments seeking to implement voluntary incomes policy are, thus to some degree restricted by the desire of unions to cooperate in restraining wages. Such cooperation with unions cannot be taken for granted. SD governments seeking to implement full-employment policies face four options, each depending on whether they can attain this cooperation (Scharpf 1991 170–173):

The first policy preference for SD governments seeking to achieve full employment while keeping inflation low is the policy mix described in cell (1)—expansive fiscal and monetary policies combined with wage restraint. Such a combination allows an SD government to implement expansive policies to fight unemployment while unions collaborate through moderate wage demands to keep inflation low. If unions choose not to cooperate but

Figure 1.4 Cooperation from the Perspective of the SD Government

Monetary and Fiscal Policy	Wages Policy	
	Restrained	Aggressive
Expansionary	(1)	(2)
Unemployment	Low	Low
Inflation	Low	Very high
Restrictive	(3)	(4)
Unemployment	High	Very high
Inflation	Low	Very high

From Scharpf 1991, 170. Reprinted with permission.

instead pursue aggressive wage demands, SD governments will not be able to implement expansive fiscal and monetary policies.

Failure to achieve union cooperation and concertation, however, often results in excessive wage demands and, therefore, in the implementation of policies described in cell (2)—expansive fiscal and monetary policies by the government coupled with aggressive wage demands by the unions. The outcome of such a policy, however, will be low unemployment and very high inflation because excessive wage increases will stimulate demand and raise prices. Moreover, such an outcome will be followed inevitably by the implementation of restrictive policies to reduce inflation, found in cell (4), which will only result in higher unemployment. From the point of view of any social democratic government aiming at full employment and low inflation, therefore, the optimal solution is the one in cell (1) and the worst one is the one in cell (4) (Scharpf 1991, 170–173). As seen in Figure 1.5, labor market institutions and union strategy have a very important effect on macroeconomic variables:

Unions, however, might have divergent strategies or particular short-term interests which do not coincide with the common good—that is, while unions do not necessarily represent the unemployed, their actions will affect unemployed people. Union leaders might have different points of view about the economy or different priorities than the government. For some union leaders, inflation might not even be a major threat because losses in purchasing capacity can be compensated by increases in nominal wages. Unemployment, on the other hand, is critical for unions because it affects firms and industries across the board.

Despite previous optimistic assessments about the positive cooperative relationship between SD governments and encompassing SD labor unions (Cameron 1984, 143–178), cooperation between SD governments and unions cannot be taken for granted. On the contrary, new analysis (Scharpf 1991, 171) shows that unions have limited economic purposes to cooperate with SD governments for the following reasons: Full employment is the first priority for SD governments. Therefore, these governments will implement

Figure 1.5 The Consequences of Unions' Strategies

	Consequences on:		
Unions' Strategies	Wages	Inflation	Unemployment
Cooperative	Low	Low	Low
Non-Cooperative	High	High	High

policies consistent with such an objective—that is, expansive fiscal and monetary policies—that will favor labor and unions. So long as the government implements those policies, unions have few incentives to cooperate further because their major objective—employment—is being taken care of. In this scenario, union leaders can concentrate on further wage increases and do not have to worry about job losses. This will most likely result in inflationary pressures, but inflation may not be that critical for some union leaders; hence, if inflation increases, unions will push for further nominal wage increases to compensate for any income losses. Unions, therefore, will be very comfortable with the strategy described in cell (2)—expansive fiscal and monetary policies and aggressive wage demands. Such a policy would satisfy their interest to keep unemployment low while negotiating higher wage increases that will favor their constituencies (Scharpf 1991, 170–171).

SD governments are, therefore, prisoners of their need for the cooperation of unions. Failure to get such cooperation will force a SD government to implement restrictive monetary and fiscal policies to control inflation. These policies, however, will only result in further unemployment and will run against the major objective of any SD government—full employment. Unions thus need incentives to cooperate, and they have to be compensated for their acquiescence in wage moderation. They also have to replace their individual and short-term goals with common long-term goals.

Lack of cooperation from unions helps to explain why incomes policy has failed in some countries—for example, Britain—and succeeded in others—for example, Sweden or Austria. At the same time, the effectiveness of concertation and voluntary incomes policy, where it has succeeded, has come under increasing pressure in recent decades. We have already seen how incomes policy was first implemented to reduce the dramatically high levels of unemployment that existed in Europe after the war. The first generation of incomes policy (1950s–1960s) consisted of generic guidelines that set caps on the growth of wages and prices. These guidelines usually tied raises in wages to productivity increases. While these policies were effective in limiting wage raises, they also resulted in the late 1960s in a dramatic increase of industrial conflict and wage drift. These bilateral agreements between unions and business, and price guidelines proved ineffective in this new economic environment. Sharp increases in the prices of food and raw materials, and the oil shock of 1973 worsened the situation. Union leaders and workers thought that they were paying too high a price, particularly at a time when the increase in unemployment was not followed by a reduction in inflation. Social discontent was rampant, and the general strikes that took place in France in May 1968 were soon extended to other countries. Social discontent convinced governments of the unfeasibility of applying restrictive policies that would increase unemployment (Flanagan, Soskice, Ulman 1983, 21–41).

Additional developments in the 1960s and early 1970s—that is, wage explosions, higher taxes and public expenditures, increases in nonwage costs, the international recession, raises in world prices, and a sharp increase in strikes and labor militancy—resulted in high inflation, lower profitability for firms and, therefore, in less investment, higher unemployment, and lower growth (Flanagan, Soskice, Ulman 1983, 35–38). They also had a very important impact on the existing institutions of collective bargaining. Union leaders faced sharp dilemmas. Further strikes would only have deteriorated the economic situation, but accepting the stringent wage proposals demanded by business would have resulted on the rebellion of their rank and file. Therefore, an incomes policy based on governmental guidelines was badly suited to address these problems. The new situation required a new set of responses. It was within this context that a new generation of incomes policies based on concertation—that is, tripartite agreements to moderate wage growth—emerged in certain countries, such as Sweden, Austria, and Belgium, as an instrument to reduce inflationary pressures and achieve full employment.

The success of these policies was uneven. While the northern European countries successfully fought unemployment and inflation in the 1970s by combining an expansive government monetary and fiscal policy with a restrictive wage policy on the part of the unions achieved through concertation (see Garrett and Lange 1985, 792–827), other countries such as the United Kingdom experienced these policies with disastrous results. In this regard, some authors have argued that the strategic behaviors of governments and actors in the labor market are mutually contingent (Alvarez, Garrett and Lange 1991; Garrett and Lange 1986; Garrett and Lange 1985, Garrett 1998, 33–38).[2] There is a large body of literature that seeks to explain this difference in experience with incomes policy. It is to these explanations that I turn in the next chapter.

CHAPTER 2

The Institutional and Structural Foundations of Concertation

Introduction

In the previous chapter we have seen how voluntary incomes policy is a critical component of social democratic (SD) economic strategies. The combination of cost-push inflation and demand-gap unemployment of the 1970s showed the limitations of pure Keynesianism. Demand management by itself would not be able to contribute to the fight against inflation and foster full employment when inflation and unemployment appeared together. In fact, demand management, in such a context, would only result in a wage offensive on the part of the unions to increase wages and/or increase the power of labor. Incomes policy, as we saw, offers a solution to this dilemma. It is the key factor that allows a reconciliation of SD objectives—low inflation and full employment—because it encourages the coordination of unions' moderate wage policy with government's expansive fiscal and monetary policies.

The success of incomes policy and concertation, however, has not been universal. While Austria, Sweden, Norway, the Netherlands, and Switzerland succeeded throughout the 1970s and early 1980s in fighting unemployment and inflation through the implementation of voluntary incomes policy and concertation, the United Kingdom experimented with incomes policy in the late 1960s–1970s with disastrous results. The successful countries did so by combining an expansive government monetary and fiscal policy with a restrictive wage policy on the part of the unions. The differing experiences with incomes policy gave rise to a substantial literature, starting in the 1970s.

The objective of this chapter is to examine the main findings of the literature on social concertation in order to consider the Spanish case from a comparative and theoretical perspective. This literature reflects two paradigms: The institutional and neocorporatist literature focuses on institutional variables to account for the success or failure of concertation in different countries. The structuralist literature,[1] for its part, focuses on how changes in the international economic environment and the production regime affect concertation schemes. I explore these hypotheses in order to determine whether these explanations help to account satisfactorily for the collapse of concertation in Spain.

Both paradigms are reflected in the existing literature on concertation in Spain. A number of authors such as Führer 1996, Lang 1981, and Pérez Díaz 1984,[2] have argued that the experience with social concertation that took place in Spain among unions, business associations, and the government from 1979–1986 can be analyzed at a descriptive level using the neo-corporatist paradigm. Other Spanish scholars have argued that the constraints imposed by the international economic environment and the new organization of production influenced the course of the socialists' economic policies and determined the collapse of concertation (Maravall 1995, 215–228; Boix 1996, 217). I will argue later in this book, however, that the institutional factors and the economic context variables emphasized in the literature are not by themselves a sufficient explanation to account for the collapse of concertation in Spain after 1986. Political factors—and particularly the institutional relationship of dependence by unions on political parties—also played a critical role.

This chapter has three sections. The first discusses the conditions set out by the neocorporatist literature for the success of incomes policies and concertation, focusing on two main variables: The structure of unions and the collective bargaining system. Austria has been often mentioned as the country that best epitomizes this institutional mixture conducive to the success of incomes policy. Britain, on the other hand, offers a clear-cut case where an inadequate institutional setting hindered concertation and incomes policy. In the second section I describe developments in the organization of production and the international economic environment, and their impact on concertation. I shall illustrate the impact of these developments on concertation and economic policy with reference to the Swedish and French cases. The last section analyzes whether the institutionalism and structural variables emphasized by the literature are adequate to examine the Spanish experience with concertation.

I. Institutional Conditions Favoring Concertation

The first significant body of work that focused on the institutional variables that foster the development of corporatist arrangements (or concertation) was the neocorporatist literature of the 1970s and 1980s.[3] This approach attempts to assess the impact of neocorporatist arrangements on economic and political outcomes by distinguishing between nations that are more neocorporatist and those that are less so. The concept of "neocorporatism" refers to a "system of interest and/or attitude representation, a particular modal or ideal typical institutional arrangement for linking the associationally organized interests of civil society with the decisional structures of the state" (Schmitter and Lehmbruch 1979, 8).[4] This system of interest representation is organized into a "limited number of singular, compulsory, noncompetitive, hierarchically ordered and functionally differentiated categories, recognized or licensed (if not created) by the state and granted a deliberate representational monopoly within their respective categories" (Schmitter and Lehmbruch 1979, 13). Although some authors have argued that traditional corporatism has facilitated the development of democratic neocorporatist structures in countries such as Germany, Sweden, Denmark, Finland, Norway, or Austria, it is important to point out that this new system of interest representation is markedly different from the authoritarian modalities that have existed in many countries since World War II—including Spain.[5] Neocorporatist arrangements are founded on voluntary cooperation and can be terminated at any time by any of the participating actors.[6]

According to neocorporatist scholars, neocorporatism is a "system of institutionalized wage restrain in which labor, acting 'responsibly', voluntarily participates in and legitimizes the transfer of income from labor to capital" (Cameron 1984, 146). In this view, neocorporatist pacts emerged as a response to the need by the state, first, to find consensus and to address the economic challenges of industrial societies after World War II, and second, to tackle the crisis of "governability" that was plaguing industrialized nations (Offe 1993, Wiarda 1997). In neocorporatist countries (i.e., the Scandinavian), given the complexity of issues, SD governments realized that adequate responses to the crisis could only come through voluntary coordination with other economic actors and, therefore, they sought to co-opt the support of business organizations and trade unions. At the same time, in transferring part of the responsibility over its interventionist economic policy to other social actors, the state tried to foster consensus about the foundations of its economic policies. Other authors have argued that "corporatist" arrangements emerged in countries such as Sweden from the pressures exercised by employers seeking to restrain overall wage growth to increase competitiveness (Pontusson and Swenson 1996).[7]

How does the neocorporatist literature explain variations—that is, why have some countries been more successful than others with concertation? According to neocorporatist authors such as Garrett and Lange 1989, Wiarda 1997, Cameron 1984, and Scharpf 1984, the successful implementation of neocorporatist arrangements depends on the "existence of institutional conditions, above all in the labor movement, appropriate to them" (Garrett and Lange 1989, 683). In this regard, the success of concertation in some countries has been associated with two major institutional variables: First, the strength and organizational structure of the labor movement, and second, the locus of collective bargaining. These variables are crucial because:

> If union organization is concentrated, with a limited number of "encompassing" industrial unions, and if collective bargaining is centralized at the national level, the unions will tend to consider the macroeconomic consequences of wage settlements out of rational self-interest even in the absence of government guide-lines. . . . On the other hand, if union organization is fragmented and collective bargaining decentralized, individual wage settlements are unlikely to be determined by considerations of macroeconomic management. (Scharpf 1984, 275)

In other words, the more the labor market is organized, the more incentives union leaders will have to focus on the national economy as a whole and the more likely they will be to restrain wage growth. One of the first scholars to introduce a coherent explanation of this argument was Mancur Olson (1982). He argued that the externalities associated with labor strength could be mitigated in cases where labor market institutions are "encompassing"—that is, where most of the labor market is organized into unions and power is concentrated in peak union confederations. In such a case union leaders will be willing to limit overall wage growth because they realize that high wages will only lead to higher inflation, which will constrain economic growth and increase unemployment (thus hurting workers). According to this argument, unions were more likely to accept greater wage restraint collectively and not individually. These authors showed evidence that corporatism was associated with wage restraint and low strike rates, as well as with lower unemployment and inflation than in noncorporatist countries (Cameron 1994).

Therefore, one of the first questions the neocorporatist literature concerned itself with was the institutional conditions that foster union strength. According to the authors named above, unions' strength and internal organization are important variables—and foster concertation—because they determine unions' recognition and their capacity to influence and control their members. Some of the institutional factors that influence unions' "strength" are the "level of unionization,"—that is, that which determines the support that unions receive from workers—"union jurisdiction"—that is, whether unions are organized along industry lines—which influences competition/cooperation among unions and also affects the possibility of resolving distributional conflicts among unions (i.e., blue-versus-white collar unions, and highly-skilled versus low-skilled workers); and finally, the "degree of internal centralization," which determines the capabilities of the union to negotiate agreements and enforce them (Scharpf 1991, 187–192; Golden 1993).

The theoretical argument of why centralized bargaining at the national level promotes wage restraint is that "there are important externalities in wage setting whereby the wage gains for one group of workers lower the welfare of other groups of workers" (Moene and Wallerstein 1999, 234). According to this view, the externalities may be due to the impact of wage increases on inflation (Calmfors and Driffill 1988), or the possibility that unemployed workers can find new jobs (Layard, Nickell, and Jackman 1991); or finally, the impact that wage increases in the non-tradable sector of the economy have on the tradable one (Swenson 1991).

Other authors such as Pizzorno (1978) have contended that centralization of authority is fundamental for unions leaders to be able to isolate themselves from their rank and file and to sign agreements with business and the government. According to this view, the larger and more centralized the union, the greater the ability of its leaders to isolate themselves and agree on wage moderation. Without centralization, workers would pursue their own interests—wage maximization and conflict with capital. Internal centralization is thus a key component for a successful policy of wage moderation.

Concertation was successful in the 1970s and early 1980s in countries with high levels of unionization such as Sweden and Austria (over 80 percent of the Swedish workers were organized in unions in 1982, and 60 percent of the Austrian ones). In these countries unions were organized into one large federation such as the German Deutscher Gerwerkschaftsbund (DGB, or the West German Trade Union Confederation), the Austrian Österreichischer Gewerkschaftsbund (ÖGB, or the Austrian Trade Union Confederation), and the Swedish Landsorganisasjonen i Sverige (LO, or the Swedish Trade Union Confederation). These confederations organized along industry lines do not compete for members or wages within the same branch. Finally, these unions have a high degree of internal centralization. In Austria there are no unions outside the ÖGB confederation. The ÖGB has both a financial and legal monopoly, and wage agreements are concluded in the name of the federation. In Sweden the LO confederation also had powers to conclude centralized negotiations with the employer association, the Svenska Arbetsgivareföreningen (SAF, or the Swedish Confederation of Professional Associations). In Britain, on the other hand, the level of unionization was comparatively lower—52 percent in 1982. Britain also has a fragmented union structure; unions are not organized along industry lines, and they compete for wages within the same branch or plant. Therefore, according to this view, the institutional conditions for concertation were unfavorable and the reason that concertation failed (Scharpf 1991, 185–192).

Another institutional variable emphasized by the literature to determine the success of concertation in some countries has been the level of "union concentration"—that is, the degree of competition and fragmentation within the labor movement (Golden 1993, 440).[8] According to Olson 1965, Bowman 1982, and Golden 1993, the degree of competition among unions is a critical variable because it influences the possibility of centralized or co-ordinated wage bargaining. As long as unions are competing for members, they will have incentives to engage in wage militancy to maintain and attract membership. Small unions also tend to rationalize that the settlements will probably not have any effect on the economy and will choose to ignore macroeconomic considerations. Their main objective then becomes to make certain that there are no real wage losses for their workers. If they do not compete for members, however, they have "fewer incentives to engage on wage militancy" and will be forced to take into account macroeconomic considerations (Golden 1993, 441).

According to these authors, less competition fosters concertation because collective action problems are easier to address when fewer actors are in-volved.[9] The fewer the number of unions involved in wage setting, the greater their capacity to assess each others' behavior, the easier the transmis-sion and interpretation of information, and finally, the lower the costs of reaching an agreement (Golden 1993, 440). This is so for several reasons: First, union leaders will be more willing to cooperate if there are fewer unions because they will be rewarded for their cooperation—that is, with participation in the decision-making process, welfare benefits, and solidaris-tic policies. Second, union inclusion in the system reduces labor militancy, and there is a high correlation between high union militancy and organiza-tional fragmentation of the labor movement. The higher the militancy, the greater the wage push (Cameron 1984, 143–178). Third and last, union concentration also fosters concertation because monopolistic, encompassing unions are more likely to frame their demands in the light of the conse-quences that those demands will have on the whole economy, not only on their members. The fact that the consequences of the pact will be felt throughout the whole economy eliminates the need for unions to increment their demands to take into account the inflationary pressures of other settle-ments (Scharpf 1991, 253–254).

The literature offers evidence that countries where concertation has been successful for an extended period of time have had a high degree of union concentration. In Austria the ÖGB union confederation, as we have said be-fore, has enjoyed a legal and financial monopoly. Collective bargaining agreements are legally extended to virtually the entire Austrian labor force. Moreover, there are no unions outside the federation and wage agreements are formally concluded by individual unions in the name of the ÖGB. In

Sweden the LO incorporated all blue-collar unions (Scharpf 1991, 189–190). The emergence of new confederations in the 1960s–1970s (particularly white-collar and civil servant unions) and the increasing competition between private and public sector unions led to the collapse of centralized bargaining in the mid-1980s. When the blue-collar confederation (LO) lost its monopoly over wage bargaining, the whole system of centralized bargaining collapsed. In Germany, on the other hand, despite Germany's low degree of union centralization, voluntary union coordination contributed to the effective restraint of wage increases in the 1980s (Golden 1993, 441). In Britain, as a third example, there are multiple unions competing at all levels, which hindered coordination and concertation.

Another variable emphasized by authors in the neocorporatist paradigm is "the locus of collective bargaining," that is, the level at which wage bargaining takes place. In countries such as the United States and the United Kingdom unions negotiate at the plant level. In other countries such as Sweden or Austria, they bargain at a centralized level with the business confederation and the government. Finally, in Germany, unions bargain on an industry-by-industry basis. A number of political economists have examined the benefits of centralized bargaining on wage moderation and concertation. Calmfors and Driffill 1988, Crouch 1985, Olson 1986, Scharpf 1991, Bruno and Sachs 1985, Freeman 1988, and Layard 1982 among others, have stressed that centralized bargaining induces unions to take into consideration the macroeconomic implications of their actions and to leave aside—at least temporarily—the possibility of exploiting their short term advantages in wage settlements.[10] According to these authors, centralized (or coordinated[11]) wage bargaining contributes to the success of concertation because it helps overcome the problems associated with the prisoner's dilemma of wage settlements. Under centralized bargaining the social actors are more conscious about the macroeconomic implications of their decisions and follow a cooperative strategy seeking to restrain wages and reduce inflation. Centralization then fosters cooperative relations among unions because it reduces interunion competition and encourages homogeneity in wage increases. At the same time, centralization provides an insurance effect that gives an incentive for social actors to collaborate, because already agreed-upon pacts insure workers against wage losses during recessions when firms will not be able to lower wages during periods of economic downturn. It also insures companies from upside swings of the economy, because wage settlements will still be valid through periods of economic bonanza, thus increasing business' profits. Finally, centralized bargaining also helps minimize the costs associated with local bargaining—that is, wage drift, or "wage increases over and above those stipulated by collective bargaining agreements" (Pontusson 1992, 448)—and helps internalize the costs of wage moderation, because all unions will be part of the wage settlements and, therefore, they will not be able to go out and seek new members by criticizing the agreement or blaming it on other unions (Freeman and Gibbons 1995, 349–350).

Centralized wage bargaining, according to these authors, offers a way out of the dilemma because the focus of centralized bargaining is not only the threat of job losses for current workers but also the effect of wage increases on employment levels. Under a centralized wage bargaining system, negotiators take into account the potential reaction of the government to the settlement. Therefore, they can avoid settlements that will raise unemployment levels directly—due to higher labor costs, or indirectly—the government might react to an excessive wage settlement with a tight monetary policy which will also increase unemployment (Hall 1994, 7). The implication, according to these authors, is that nations with centralized, or coordinated, wage bargaining, such as Sweden, Austria, or Germany, have been able, until the mid-1980s at least, to achieve lower levels of inflation, and at a lower cost in terms of unemployment, than countries without centralized or coordinated wage bargaining.

The main instance of failure pointed out by these authors is the case of Britain. Britain has been characterized by a very decentralized system of collective wage bargaining; there have never been wage negotiations for the whole economy, and agreements covering company branches have dominated wage setting. This system of decentralized bargaining and competitive unions fostered wage competition among unions and resulted in a dynamic that drove up wages and increased inflation in the 1970s. Individual unions were sensitive to the risk of losing members, because when one union negotiated higher wages for its affiliates in neighboring jobs in the same firm, workers from the other unions could think that their interests were not being well served and potentially abandon the union. Therefore, in the following wage negotiation round, other unions were forced to achieve even higher wages to satisfy their affiliates' demands and avoid losing members (Cameron 1984, Streeck 1992).

In contrast, the successful implementation of incomes policy in countries such as Austria or Sweden has been closely associated with their centralized system of collective bargaining. In Austria the Commission for Prices and Wages has had to give its approval before individual unions can open wage negotiations, approval that is granted based on a presentation by the ÖGB confederation in which the confederation states the negotiation goals of the individual unions. This process guarantees that there is an understanding about the macroeconomic implication of wage increases among individual unions. In Sweden from the mid-1950s to the early 1980s, the normal wage bargaining level was between the LO and the employers association nationally. In addition, the existence of regulations restricting wage differentials limited the scope of the negotiators working at lower levels (Scharpf 1991, 189–191). This system was challenged by the emergence of new unions in the 1970s, which intensified interunion rivalries and hindered centralized bargaining. Neocorporatists, thus stress the discrepancy "between a pluralistic fragmented organization and decision making structure and the pursuit of joint macroeconomic goals" (Scharpf 1991, 174).

Lars Calmfors and John Driffill (1988), and Soskice (1990a) further refined these arguments and analyzed the economic consequences of labor market institutions. They introduced a significant amendment to the neocorporatist approach by developing a "hum-shaped" model that distinguishes among three scenarios based on the level at which most wage bargaining takes place—nationally, at the industry level, or in individual firms. Calmfors and Driffill (1988) argue that the relationship between economic performance and the level of centralization of labor unions is not monotonic. According to their model, economic performance would be superior at both extremes, when trade unions are highly fragmented or highly centralized, than when they are moderately concentrated. They claim that economic performance will be better in countries where wage setting takes place predominantly at the national level, because it will mitigate wage militancy and will offer strong incentives to union leaders to internalize the externalities associated with labor power (for the reasons mentioned above). On the contrary, when wages are primarily set at the industry level, unions will act as monopolies in their industry, will not take into consideration the macroeconomic consequences of their actions (their employers can pass on the higher costs to consumers and they will not lose their jobs), and wage-push inflation will result. Finally, in countries in which wage setting is predominantly at the firm level, economic performance will be good, because individual firms cannot pass on higher costs to consumers in highly competitive markets, and therefore small groups of workers cannot challenge the market determination of wages. This is also the essence behind Lindbeck and Snower's (1988) insider-outsider theory that attributes inadequate economic outcomes to the monopolistic power of the insiders.

This hypothesis, however, has been criticized for focusing too much on the level at which bargaining takes place. In a more recent study Miriam Golden (1993), argues that the critical variable is the internal structure of labor movements—that is, the ability of union leaders to coordinate the behavior of large sections of the workforce. Golden argues that even under centralized agreements there are powerful incentives for workers and employers to provoke wage drifts. Moreover, central wage agreements may be imposed, but in the absence of concentration of union authority, their effectiveness will be undermined by wage drift. According to her, the concentration of authority in peak confederations mitigates wage drift in two ways. First, the leaders of encompassing unions have strong incentives to restrain wages to maximize employment and wages for the labor force as a whole. Second, they will also have the authority to sanction free riders.

A last variable emphasized in the literature to account for the success of concertation in countries such as Sweden, Denmark, Finland, Norway, or Austria in the 1970s and early 1980s is the partisanship of government—that is, the ideological orientation of the party in government. Political scientists such as Cameron (1984); Garrett and Lange (1985, 1986, 1989); Alvarez, Garrett, and Lange (1991);[12] and Hicks (1988) have argued that concertation arrangements work well only when SD parties are in power. These scholars claim that the participation of SD parties in government is beneficial for neocorporatist arrangements because there are important interaction effects between the objectives of the ruling party and the organization of the political economy (Schmidt 1982). According to these authors, the best scenario for concertation and the implementation of full employment policies is a combination of institutional factors, such as "a high level of unionization; a single labor confederation composed of few industry-based unions; economy-wide bargaining between labor confederations and employer associations; in which works councils and codetermination exist; and social democratic parties are in government" (Cameron 1984, 169). Such an arrangement has positive consequences because SD governments share many of the objectives of unions. Therefore, they are more willing to compensate unions for wage moderation and offer further assurances about the commitment of the government to the advancement of some of labor's traditional goals, which results in greater social expenditures and lower industrial conflict (Lehmbruch 1979, 157). Concertation, on the other hand, is difficult to achieve in countries with trade unions that have close links to communist parties because they oppose cooperative relations with the government and pursue confrontational strategies.[13]

The combination of monopolistic unions with SD orientation and SD governments in Sweden, Austria, Norway, Finland, and Germany contributed in the 1970s and early 1980s to the success of concertation agreements that resulted in wage moderation, social peace, and the support of unions for the economic policy of the SD government in exchange for institutional and legislative concessions by government and business. SD parties in power in countries such as Sweden, Austria, Norway, Finland, or Belgium pursued high growth and low inflation and unemployment using government intervention in the economy—that is, subsidies, intervention to stimulate demand, and political bargaining with labor unions. Such a policy mix, however, was not feasible under conservative governments because they rejected government intervention in the economy and relied instead on market mechanisms (Garrett and Lange 1985).[14] In these cases the absence of compensation for labor resulted in the collapse of concertation.

In sum, the neocorporatist literature has made four main contributions to our understanding of comparative political economy (Hall 1999, 138). First, neocorporatist scholars linked economic outcomes to organizational variables, helping us explain variations. Second, they focused their research on trade unions, an economic actor that has not been the center of analysis for political economists. Moreover, these authors emphasized the significance of the bargaining level to account for the success of neocorporatist incomes policies. Finally, these scholars opened up new lines of inquiry about the organization of the political economy (Cameron 1978; Katzenstein 1985), and the role of the state in maintaining corporatist structures (Lange 1984).

II. Structural Constraints to Concertation: The Organization of Production and the Globalization of Economies

As we have just seen, the neocorporatist literature focuses on institutional variables to account for the success (or failure) of concertation and incomes policy in certain countries. New developments, however, took place in the late 1980s and 1990s that had a severe impact on concertation. By the end of the 1980s it was becoming evident that a general retreat from SD policies and institutions had taken place throughout northern Europe. This was particularly salient in Sweden, where after 27 years of centralized bargaining, concertation came to a halt in 1983 when a separate agreement was signed in the metal working sector (Lange, Wallerstein, and Golden 1999). This collapse—despite the fact that Sweden had an institutional setting favorable to concertation up to the mid-1980s—led some authors to analyze the reasons behind this dramatic development.

The crisis of concertation was first attributed to low levels of growth, high unemployment, and the fiscal crisis of the state that intensified throughout the late 1980s and 1990s (Schmitter 1990, 33). These authors argue that within this context, the scarcity of resources limited the capacity of governments to reward consensus and compromise, and because of this, unions refused to share the responsibility of redistributing limited resources.[15] In this new context concertation and Keynesianism were not feasible (Scharpf 1987, 26–28; 1992, 7–12; Regini 1995, 73–85). This explanation, however, cannot account for variations.

It was in this context that a different group of scholars advanced another set of factors to account for the waning of concertation in the late 1980s and 1990s in countries such as Sweden. The long-term success of corporatist bargaining was based on two main assumptions: first, that unions would remain strong in order to be able to continue exercising control over wages to improve macroeconomic performance; and second, that most workers would remain unionized and most of the work force would continue to be exposed to market forces (Golden, Wallerstein, and Lange 1999, 195). Developments in the 1980s–1990s threatened both conditions. Today trade unions and concertation seem less durable than they did ten years ago. Unions are seen today as suffering from declining strength and influence (Visser 1992).

The literature has developed two main explanations to account for the decline in unions and concertation (Golden, Wallerstein, and Lange 1999, 196). A group of authors have focused on the impact of changes in technology on the organization of production, workplace relations, and occupational structures (Moene and Wallerstein 1993, Hernes, 1991, Streeck 1993, Pontusson and Swenson 1996). According to this explanation, technological changes have affected unions and workers in ways that have eroded the unity and strength of the labor movement. Other authors also emphasized the detrimental impact of the growing weight of public sector workers in the labor movement (Garrett and Way 1995). The second main explanation of the decline of concertation concerns the constraints imposed by transformations in the international economic system. According to this view, unions' weakness has been exacerbated by the increasing capital mobility and the potential for firms to threaten to "exit" (Regini 1995; Schmitter 1991; Scharpf 1991, 244–248; Kurzer 1993). Other authors have emphasized that increasing economic integration has also eroded the ability of unions to raise wages (Reder and Ulman 1993). A final group of scholars stressed the declining room for discretionary macroeconomic policies on the part of national governments in a globalized economy (Streeck and Schmitter 1991). In other words, these authors claim that changes in domestic socio-occupational structures or in international economic relationships have resulted in the decline of unions across advanced industrial countries that have rendered corporatist arrangements less likeable.

In sum, the conventional wisdom about the 1990s is that SD concertation has become a luxury that cannot be afforded in this new era of globalization (see Garrett 1998, xiii; Garrett 1999, 147–148). According to this view, globalization and changes in technology had two main negative consequences over economy-wide wage regulation and concertation. On the one hand, it has fragmented the working class into conflicting groups that are divided according to their position in the international division of labor, thus making SD corporatist policies based on concertation very difficult (Pontusson and Swenson 1996, Swenson 1991). On the other hand, globalization has imposed new constraints on domestic policies making it virtually impossible for leftist governments to depart from market-oriented principles

(Iverson 1996, Kurzer 1993; Scharpf 1991). In this section I analyze both arguments.[16]

a. The Impact on Concertation of Changes in the Organization of Production

By the early 1990s there was the widespread perception that unions were suffering from declining membership and influence (Visser 1992), with little power to affect wages; and that their ability to affect outcomes had been restricted to the firm level, thus making centralized bargaining more difficult. A group of authors have focused on the impact of changes in technology on the organization of production, workplace relations, and occupational structures to account for this development (Moene and Wallerstein 1993). According to this view, technological changes have affected unions, workers, and the "organization of production" (Hall 1999, 140) in ways that are detrimental to the unity and strength of the labor movement.[17]

According to these authors, changes in technology have altered workplace relations and occupational structures in ways that have eroded the sustainability of concertation and full-employment policies. In the 1980s dramatic changes took place in the organization of firms. Some authors (Piore and Sabel 1984, Streeck 1991) argued that the Fordist system of production that characterized the post–World War II period, a system based on the use of semiskilled labor to produce high volumes of standardized goods and supported by the implementation of Keynesian policies to ensure high levels of aggregate demand and a system of collective bargaining to secure labor peace, broke down in the 1970s and was replaced by new forms of production that they labeled "flexible specialization." According to this view, the traditional production paradigm, mass production or Fordism, gave way to new forms of production that required flexibility—that is, "flexible specialization" (Piore and Sabel 1984), or "flexible automatization" (Boyer 1988). These authors emphasize that new technologies based on microelectronics and robotics are displacing traditional tasks and fostering flexible production in small units and highly differentiated contexts that hinder standardized bargaining and result in further decentralization of production (Schmitter 1990, 34; Regini 1990, 17).

The impact of these changes on workplace relations and occupational structures was very detrimental to the unity of union movements and concertation for several reasons. On the one hand, while Fordist production required uniform rules, flexibility, on the contrary, requires many unique or at least specialized agreements on regulation of labor, organization, training, quality, flexible allocation of skills, mobility, flexibility of hours, and the like. In most cases, these issues cannot be properly dealt with through centralized bargaining. They can be better dealt with at the plant level, thus hindering centralized negotiations and concertation. In other words, these authors emphasize that the widespread adoption of new production technologies that place a premium on product differentiation and the flexibility to satisfy changing consumer demands, is resulting in the increasing decentralization of wage bargaining (Pontusson and Swenson 1996). On the other hand, technological changes have resulted in the emergence of a new, highly specialized group of workers who have increasing market leverage (Moene and Wallerstein 1993; Hernes 1991; Streeck 1993). These authors have also pointed to the destabilizing impact of the increased substitutability of unskilled labor by capital in the union movement. These developments have weakened the labor power of less skilled workers and increased the power of skilled ones, affecting industrial unions, whose membership is largely comprised of the less skilled ones (Rodrik 1996; McKeown 1999), and have resulted in greater fragmentation and decentralization of unions because workers have become more heterogeneous in their interests (Locke and Thelen 1995).

This literature offers evidence that the decline in Fordism has resulted in such increasing heterogeneity described above both within business and labor. Increasing heterogeneity has had two consequences on corporatist structures. On the one hand, it has resulted in further diversification of conflict of interests—that is, the traditional conflict between labor and capital is being superseded by more differentiated and specific conflicts, such as conflicts over the quality of life or the environment. On the other hand, intermediate institutions, particularly business' associations and trade unions themselves are forced to adjust, and thus have regrouped into more differentiated categories of representation (Schmitter 1990, 33). In other words, rising conflict among different groups of workers has undermined the ability of even the most encompassing labor market institutions to regulate economywide wage growth. A major consequence of these developments has been that unions and business associations now have a harder time aggregating worker and business demands, increasing the potential for sectoral conflict within labor. This has made SD corporatist polices based on concertation more difficult because workers cannot speak with one voice. New organizations have emerged to represent these interests and this has hindered concertation. Furthermore, the increasing heterogeneity of labor has hindered the pursuit of solidaristic and egalitarian objectives—that is, some workers will oppose centralized wage bargaining because it may limit their leverage at the firm level, a further factor making centralized wage bargaining and concertation more difficult.[18]

Another development that has had a significant impact in the organization of the labor movement and occupational structures has been the emergence of differentiated unions representing the increasing number of public sector workers in many countries (particularly in the Nordic countries). In this regard, a group of scholars are emphasizing the destabilizing impact of the growing weight of public sector workers in the union movement (for a summary of this argument see Garrett 1998; Lange, Wallerstein and Golden, 1995; Garrett and Way 1995). According to these authors, union fragmentation (and the collapse of concertation) has been further hastened by the potential for conflict between workers in sectors exposed to international competition and those insulated from external pressures—mostly public sector workers (Garrett 1998, 40–41). In the tradable sector, which is exposed to international competition, wage setting will be disciplined by international supply and demand. If workers push up wages beyond world market prices, they will lose their jobs. On the contrary, workers insulated from competitive pressures and sheltered from international market competition, (i.e., public sector workers), do not face such constraints. They can assume that they will keep their jobs even during economic downturns, because governments are likely to prop up public sector employment to minimize the crisis. Conflict between these workers will increase labor fragmentation, thus hindering centralized bargaining.

These authors have also emphasized the decline in the interest of business in centralized bargaining due to the changes in mass production that I described above. In this new environment wage moderation is no longer the main or only objective for business. What business now wants is to attract skilled workers and to be able to keep them. However, while some firms need flexibility to negotiate higher wages to attract highly skilled workers, others would prefer centralized agreements to keep wages down. For this reason employers, instead of supporting centralized bargaining, are promoting aggressively the decentralization of wage setting to the level of the firm (Katz 1993). This environment favors greater wage differentials, a development that runs against solidaristic wage policies that characterize concertation agreements (Schmitter 1990, 33). It is for this reason that centralized bargaining no longer satisfies the demands of heterogeneous capital. All these changes have promoted new forms of bargaining at lower levels—that is, Regini's "microconcertation" (1990, 19; and 1995)—that are resulting in the creation of flexible work rules.

In summary, the authors that focused on this conceptual approach have offered evidence that the emergence of new forms of production, further competition, and increasing labor differentiation have had a tremendous impact on concertation. A prime example cited by them is the collapse of centralized concertation in Sweden in the mid-1980s (Pontusson 1992; Moene and Wallersein 1999, 236–237). In Sweden, concertation emerged in the 1950s. The decline in the relative size of the manufacturing sector resulted in the changing composition of employment (Esping-Andersen 1999). The development of a strong public sector union in the late 1960s threatened to challenge the dominant position that the LO had exercised for years over the labor movement. Structural changes in the union movement further intensified in the 1960s and resulted in the emergence of a white-collar union. The power of this union increased in the 1970s, when it started challenging LO's traditional claim of leadership in negotiations with private employers and the government.[19] Interunion competition hastened conflict between the unions over compensation clauses and intensified disputes between private and public unions over solidaristic policies.

In Sweden, increasing interlabor disputes were further aggravated by the worldwide economic crisis of the 1970s. The Swedish government lacked the resources to satisfy union demands. At this time, changes in international markets and the emergence of new technologies shifted the bargaining power in favor of skilled and white-collar workers at the expense of the rest. The decline of the Fordist model of production for many Swedish firms competing in international markets forced business to place more importance on other factors like flexibility and productivity, which, in turn, diminished business's interest in centralized bargaining. These developments intensified wage drifts—that is, workers from companies, such as Volvo, received wage increases above those negotiated between the SAF and the LO. Wage drift, in turn, intensified industrial conflict, which reflected the failure of the system to control wages and hastened the end of concertation in the second half of the 1980s (Scharpf 1991, 250). All these factors intensified interunion competition, hindered solidaristic wage principles, and eroded the rationale for centralized bargaining. At the end, centralized wage bargaining was abandoned in 1984.[20]

Other authors, however, have recently challenged these arguments (Garrett 1998, 40–41; Golden, Wallerstein, and Lange 1999, 197–198). These authors stress that this interpretation of events rests on the assumption that the widespread and permanent weakening of unions and corporatist institutions is an empirical reality that has resulted in the transformation of the social structure of the industrialized countries. They emphasize, however, that contrary to what should be expected if the above arguments were true, we do not see today a pattern of union decline, nor we see a process of convergence among industrial relations systems toward the noncorporatist end of the spectrum (Golden, Wallerstein, and Lange 1999, 197; Hyman 1994; Traxler 1994, 1995). Golden, Wallerstein and Lange (1999) analyze changes in 12 OECD (Organization for Economic Cooperation and Development) countries along four dimensions: union density, union coverage, union concentration, and statutory authority for employers' union organizations, and conclude that union decline has not been as widespread as previously perceived. On the contrary, their data supports the view that industrial relation institutions and trade unions have proved quite resilient in the face of domestic and international pressures. They show that there have been countries—Denmark Sweden, and Finland—in which union density increased in the 1980s (1999, 198–202). They also present conclusive evidence showing that interconfederal concentration has increased in some countries (e.g., Japan) (1999, 205–213); that the rates of coverage have remained uniformly high throughout Europe (1999, 203–205); and finally, that the statutory authority of employers and unions has remained stable (1999, 213–221). They find no supporting evidence that there have been substantial changes in authority relations within labor unions and employer organizations. They conclude that "unions have retained most of the institutional based capacities for the defense of worker interests that they had prior to the 1980s" and attribute the current weakness of unions in most countries to sustained unemployment (1999, 224).

Furthermore, while these scholars recognize that the potential for intersectoral conflict is real, they argue that "labor market institutions can reconcile conflicts between employees in the exposed and sheltered sectors of the economy in ways that are consistent with competition in global markets" (Garrett 1998, 40). He argues that a wage push from workers sheltered from international competition will have negative consequences for the domestic economy as a whole because it will lead to higher deficits, higher inflation, and increasing interest rates, which in turn will push up exchange rates, thus lowering the competitiveness of the tradable sector exposed to international competition. According to him, labor leaders must ensure that economywide wage growth does not undermine the competitiveness of the sectors exposed to international competition. This, according to him, will be easier in countries in which the labor markets are organized and authority is highly concentrated within the labor movement because they will be able to limit wage militancy in the nontraded sector. The experience of Scandinavian countries in the 1930s, when business leaders supported the centralization of trade union authority to stop wage militancy in the sheltered sector of the economy renders authority to this argument (Swenson 1991, Flanagan 1983).

b. The Impact of Globalization on Domestic Policy Making and SD Corporatism

The political economy literature has also given particular attention to the impact of increased economic integration (the phenomenon termed as "globalization") on labor market institutions and domestic policies and structures. Budget deficits and accommodating monetary polices are viewed as the typical policy instruments of SD corporatism in the 1960s and 1970s. However, the collapse of the Bretton Woods system coupled with the dismantling of government exchange controls, which took place in most countries through the 1980s, the liberalization of domestic financial markets, and the development of new technologies have resulted in the integration of markets in goods, services, and, above all, capital. These developments, according to many scholars, have imposed constraints in domestic policymaking and have had a significant impact on domestic structures and institutions, leading to cuts in taxation, welfare state retrenchment, and the rollback of public services (McKenzie and Lee 1991, Ohmae 1991).

According to this view, in this new environment government attempts are doomed to fail if they extend beyond promarket measures. The combined impetuses of increasing exposure to trade, capital mobility, and foreign direct investment are forcing countries to implement neoliberal policies and abandon neocorporatist structures. In other words, globalization is considered to have rendered expansionary macroeconomic policies far less feasible. Indeed, today's international financial markets trade over $1.2 trillion per day (*Financial Times* September 20, 1995, 1), which is more than the annual budget of many countries. The consequence for SD oriented policies is clear: "unemployment and declining wages marked the 1980s. Governments could combat such situations by spending money on public programs, increasing public employment, or raising social transfer payments, but no government can afford to do this today" (Kurzer 1993, 252). In this new environment, in which governments do not have the ability to manage demand, they do not need union cooperation, and unions have little incentives to restrain wages (Streeck and Schimtter 1991). In this regard, it is particularly important to analyze the globalization thesis to account for the collapse of concertation in Spain, because some Spanish scholars have argued that the changing economic environment constrained economic policy in Spain and prevented the implementation of expansive policies that would have permitted the continuation of concertation after 1986 (see Boix 1996, 204–220; Maravall 1995, 217–228; Solchaga 1997, 36–50).

From a theoretical standpoint the globalization approach rests on the contention that governments are dependent on the willingness of owners of productive assets to invest (Lindblom 1977; Przeworski and Wallerstein 1988). This is so because economic performance depends on increasing investment. Since in democratic countries the electoral prospects of governments are strongly influenced by economic performance (Hibbs 1987), and economic expansion is necessary to finance public programs and to respond to the demands of their constituencies, governments will promote policies that bolster capital investment. On the contrary, policies that undercut the confidence of business—such as increasing tax burdens—will reduce investment and growth. Globalization, according to this view, by bolstering capital movement has increased the structural power of capital with respect to governments. In this view, governments have lost the autonomy needed to implement redistributive polices and provide public services and social rights financed through higher taxes (Steinmo 1993, Ch. 6). This is so because capital can walk away from countries that implement policies that are unfavorable to their interests (Swank 1998).[21] Therefore, in the new global economy governments have to respond to the domestic demands of business and also consider international investment climates and the relevant policies of other nations.[22]

The authors that support the globalization thesis arguments (Andrews 1994, Scharpf 1991, Cerny 1990, Gill and Law 1989, Kurzer 1993, Moses 1994, Schwartz 1994, McKenzie and Lee, 1991) contend that the integration of markets of goods, services and capital has had two main consequences on SD corporatist based policies. On the one hand, globalization has increased the "exit" opportunities of mobile asset holders, therefore strengthening the position of business vis-à-vis labor; because firms can now raise capital in foreign markets and move production abroad, thus they do not depend solely on national governments to raise capital any longer (Kurzer 1993). On the other hand, countries have lost their sovereignty over monetary policies as the result of the integration of financial markets. According to this view, efforts to run monetary polices that are more expansionary than those of other members of a exchange rate regime will fail. Capital flight will increase until interest rates rise to equal those of other members (Scharpf 1991).

The situation that seems to support this argument originated at the end of the 1970s. During the 1960s, interests rates in the United States were "negative"—that is, lower than inflation, that allowed other nations to choose the level of their own interest rates. However, the rise in interest rates that took place in the United States in early 1981 forced other countries that needed capital inflows to offset their current account deficits to raise their interest rates to attract investors. Interest rates in Europe were raised to U.S. levels to avoid capital outflows and currency devaluations. A major consequence of this development regarding SD neocorporatist-based policies was that national monetary policies lost their sovereignty over interest rates because they could not undercut the rate of return offered by the dollar. Therefore, domestic monetary policy could no longer be used as an instrument to compensate unions, and the burden had to be borne by fiscal policy (Scharpf 1991, 244–248).

High interest rates, at the same time, also limited fiscal expansion because they increased the cost of an expansive fiscal policy.[23] Under this scenario, countries were forced to implement policies to reduce their deficits. Deficit reduction, however, had negative consequences on concertation, which depends on fiscal expansion to stimulate demand and compensate unions for wage moderation. The end result was that the high mobility of capital precluded an effective control of interest rates at a national level, while investment in firms was conditioned by expensive credit and the increased profitability of financial investment (Scharpf 1991, 246).[24] The outcome of these developments, according to this author, was clear " . . . there is no economically plausible Keynesian strategy that would permit the full realization of social democratic goals within a national context without violating the functional imperatives of the capitalist economy" (Scharpf 1991, 274).

From the standpoint of SD neocorporatist policies based on concertation, the consequences of these developments were, thus, devastating. According to these authors, trade liberalization, coupled with the emergence of new competitors and the opening of new markets, has resulted in the intensification of worldwide competition, which has had dramatic consequences for industries and workers alike. Countries have had to wipe out industrial sectors which were not competitive anymore because of new competition from countries with lower production costs. This process of de-industrialization has had obvious and dramatic consequences for unions and workers. On the one hand, since most new jobs are being created in new sectors of the economy where unions do not have a strong presence—for example, the service sector—the process of de-industrialization has eroded unions' strongholds. At the same time, increasing trade has weakened the leverage of less skilled workers and increased that of the skilled ones, a transformation that has affected the largest industrial unions, whose membership largely comprises the less skilled workers (McKeown 1999). Finally, restrictive monetary polices resulted in higher unemployment, which further hindered the position of unions at a time when governments had less autonomy to compensate unions for wage moderation because interest rates were high and fiscal expansion was limited (for a synthesis of these arguments see Andrews 1994, Scharpf 1991, Cerny 1990, Gill and Law 1989, Kurzer 1993, Moses 1994, Schwartz 1994, McKenzie and Lee, 1991).

A prime example cited by these authors to show the impact of these developments on domestic policies is the failed French experiment with expansive economic policies in the early 1980s. When François Mitterrand, the French Socialist Party leader, won the presidential elections on May 1981, he sought to experiment with a Keynesian economic program similar to the one that the British Labour Party had implemented in the United Kingdom in 1974–1975, trying to expand demand and redistribute wealth.[25] This economic program, however, failed. The position of the French economy in the international system, coupled with structural changes that took place in the economy, prevented the success of these policies (Hall 1986, 196). After World War II, the French economy had become increasingly dependent on international markets to sell its products. By 1983 imports and exports accounted for 23 percent of Gross Domestic Product (GDP)—which was only 13 percent in 1953. The reflation that took place in 1981–1982 resulted in demand stimulus and a sharp increase in consumption that ignited imports. Since the economies of France's trade counterparts remained in crisis, exports could not compensate for the dramatic increase in imports. The consequence was a massive balance-of-payments crisis that pushed down the value of the franc.[26] Mitterrand decided to reduce the budget deficit in June 1982, following a new devaluation of the franc. This policy shift certified the death of the Keynesian expansionary polices in France.[27]

New empirical studies, however, challenge the globalization arguments. Some scholars have attempted to assess the claim that states are now virtually powerless to make policy choices (Garrett 1998, Garrett 1999, Weiss 1998, Swank 1998). These authors argue against the notion that increasing exposure to trade, capital mobility, and foreign direct investment are forcing countries to implement neoliberal policies and abandon neocorporatist structures. On the contrary, they claim that governments still have strong incentives to cushion the dislocations generated by increasing economic integration. These authors claim that the notion of the "powerless state" and the reports about the decline of the welfare state are fundamentally misleading for three main reasons. First, since states are very diverse and exhibit different levels of adaptability to external pressures, the effects of integration on government capacities are not uniform. Second, globalization is being advanced in some instances through the nation-state; therefore it may take different shapes depending on the interest and strategies of the leading actors. Finally, production and investment are not subject to a strong globalization strategy (Weiss 1998, 188–189). These authors emphasize that globalists have tended to exaggerate state powers in the past to explain current weaknesses while overstating uniformity of state responses. New empirical studies, however, show that governments have responded to similar market pressures in different ways, and in some cases reorganizing, rather than abandoning, control over private sector behavior (Vogel 1996). Others dispute the notion that globalization is forcing convergence of national policy models (Pierson 1996). These scholars attribute the notion of the "powerless state" rendered incapable of resisting the market forces to monetarist polices and the actions of politicians (Weiss 1998, 193).

One of the main empirical arguments of the authors who oppose the "globalist" position is that countries with large and expanding public economies have not suffered from capital flight. Garrett 1998 and 1999, and Swank 1998, among others, criticize the argument according to which, increasing exposure to trade, capital mobility, and foreign direct investment impose severe constraints on monetary policy. Garrett (1998 and 1999) challenges the prevailing notion that the running of countercyclical fiscal policies—for example, the running of budget deficits during periods of economic downturn to stimulate domestic aggregate demand, has been mitigated by integration into international markets. According to Garrett, "it is not clear that globalizations stops governments from being able to run deficits that are larger than some international norm" (1998, 44). He recognizes that increasing exposure to trade limits the benefits of deficit expansion because domestic sources of demand are less significant for overall levels of national activity. He also acknowledges that deficits may act as "a signal of fiscal recklessness in a world of integrated capital markets for which offending governments must pay a hefty interest rate premium" (1998, 43). This is so because borrowing must be repaid, and running deficits today may develop inflationary pressures in the near future, thus resulting in higher interest rate premiums on national debt. He argues however, that the empirical record does not offer much support for these arguments. Garrett emphasizes that many countries, including the United States and Belgium, have been able to live with higher deficits without paying substantial interest rate premiums. The reason for this, according to him, has been that the globalization of capital markets has created a large pool of lenders competing amongst themselves and willing to purchase and fund government debt, thus easing the monetary costs of expansionary fiscal policies. He points to Italy and Belgium as examples of countries in which their high debt burdens (over 100 percent of their GDP) have not triggered fears that the government will default on their loans and that consequently there will be a reduction in the availability of credit (Latin America would provide an opposite example).

Moreover, Garrett and other scholars challenge the conventional notion that globalization puts downward pressure on taxing and government expenditures (Garrett 1998, 44–45; Garrett 1999, 172–179; Swank 1998, 21–22). They acknowledge that globalization has given more credibility to the exit threats of mobile asset holders—that is, in the face of a large public economy they will choose to exit because government spending is inefficient and taxes are distortionary, which in turn, forces governments to cut spending and taxes. However, they challenge the notion that capital mobility is leading to a pattern of crossnational convergence. For instance, utilizing trend analysis of patterns of convergence/divergence and an econometric analysis of 1964–1993 data from 16 countries, Swank finds that international capital flows, liberalization, and financial market integration have few if any direct effects on the scope of the public economy (1998, 22–24; see also Garrett 1999 172–179). Swank emphasizes that the direction and magnitude of effects of different dimensions of international financial integration depend on the democratic institutional context, the institutional mechanisms for collective representation within interest groups, the electoral and party systems, and the organization of policy-making authority systems of interest representation. In other words, national institutions matter and governments' responses to internationalization of capital markets differ depending on national institutional contexts.

Furthermore, these authors challenge the arguments (supported by the scholars that stress the structural constraints imposed by globalization) that emphasize the constraining effects of fixed exchange rates on domestic macroeconomic policies. According to this view, governments must pursue fixed exchange rates when capital mobility is high. This led Garrett (1998, 41–45; 1999, 147–184) to challenge the above arguments. Garrett acknowledges that governments "can only insulate themselves against the damaging vicissitudes of the currency markets by participating in stable fixed exchange rates" (1998, 42). The reason for this is that real interest rates will be lower in countries with credible fixed exchange rates because they will lower prospects for future inflationary policies. He claims, however, that the empirical record is not clear regarding the costs of floating under conditions of capital mobility. He points to the breakup of the European Monetary System (EMS) in 1992 and 1993 that forced Italy and Britain to depreciate their currencies and abandon fixed exchange rates when the costs became clear. The smooth depreciation of these currencies has managed to stimulate aggregate demand in both countries without significantly increasing inflation. This example led Garrett to conclude that "one should be extremely careful and cautious when basing claims about the constraining effects of globalization on monetary policy" (1998, 43).

The scholars that challenge the globalization approach stress that government spending can additionally benefit mobile asset holders and increase their profits because they provide numerous benefits for capital. Government spending in the welfare state (e.g., income transfer programs, public social services) in education, training, and physical infrastructure, for instance, can increase productivity and competitiveness and contribute to economic growth by generating collective goods that are undersupplied by the market—such as human and physical capital or social stability. Therefore, according to Garrett (1998 and 1999), there is no a priori reason why mobile asset holders will not be willing to pay higher taxes to finance these programs as long as the benefits derived from them outweigh the costs in the form of taxes. Furthermore, Garrett claims that policies that mitigate the market dislocation caused by the increasing globalization of the economies—that is, welfare state policies, industrial subsidies, and the like—increase the incentives for the leaders of encompassing trade unions to use their power to limit wage growth, which will benefit mobile asset holders who will, in turn, be more willing to pay higher taxes to finance these polices. Finally, Garrett emphasizes that mobile asset holders will not exercise their exit options in the face of large government as long as they are convinced that public expenditures generate stable investment environments (1998, 45). In this regard he points out that numerous economists have shown that government spending contributes to social stability by reducing income inequalities, thus fostering stable investment environments and increasing the possibilities for investment and growth (Alesina and Rosenthal 1995).

In sum, the authors that challenge the globalization approach argue that globalization has few if any direct effects on the scope of the public economy. In fact, they contend that the strength of external pressures is largely determined at the domestic level, and that the effect of such pressures depends on the strength of domestic institutions.[28] According to this view, state capacity will rest on the ability of authorities to mobilize savings and investment and to promote their deployment to foster higher-value-added activities (Weiss 1998, 202). Therefore, they conclude that institutions matter: "democratic institutions and processes are more important than in the recent past in shaping national policy trajectories during the era of dramatic increases in capital mobility" (Swank 1998, 8). That is so because globalization accentuates the asymmetry between groups that can cross international borders, and those that cannot (Rodrik 1997), and it thus produces different effects on domestic economic sectors. Therefore, the ability of those actors threatened by globalization to resist changes and the domestic politico-institutional setting will shape different national policy trajectories (see Iversen 1999 for a challenge to these arguments).

Summary

Some authors contend that the increasing mobility of capital and pressures induced by technology restructuring have changed the international economic environment in the 1980s. These changes resulted in a higher demand for scarce, highly skilled labor, which in turn fostered wage differentiation and labor segmentation and shifted the balance of power between capital and labor in favor of the former. Moreover, as a result of globalization, governments lost their fiscal and monetary policy-making autonomy and were forced to implement supply side policies in order to lower taxes and industry subsidies to promote efficient market allocation. They were also compelled to redistribute scarce resources from less skilled workers to skilled ones, and from consumption to investment. In this new environment, the implementation of traditional Keynesian expansive policies would only result in higher inflation and balance-of-payment crises

(Scharpf 1991, 7–12). According to this view, increasing exposure to trade, capital mobility, and foreign direct investment is forcing countries to implement neoliberal policies and abandon neocorporatist structures.

These views, however, have been challenged by other authors who claim that "globalization and national autonomy are not mutually exclusive options" (Garrett 1998, 6–10). According to Garrett, although globalization increases "exit" opportunities for holders of mobile assets, it also increases dislocations at the domestic level among the less mobile factors (i.e., citizens) (see also Rodrik 1997, 6–7). Therefore, SD governments have the opportunity to devise polices to mitigate the collision of both factors. Garrett argues that supporters of the globalization paradigm tend to overestimate the "exit" threat and underestimate the positive externalities of government intervention in the economy, while ignoring the impact of labor market institutions on the behavior of workers. According to him, the combination of left government and encompassing labor market institutions reduces sources of inefficiency and instability generated by social programs associated with SD governments and facilitates the continuation of SD neocorporatist policies based on concertation. Garrett (1998 and 1999) and Swank (1998) show that big government, countercyclical fiscal policies, and progressive fiscal systems that have been central to SD corporatist policies in the 1960s to 1970s have remained distinctive features of SD corporatism in the 1980s and 1990s in spite of globalization (Garrett 1998, 74–105; and Garrett 1999, 172–180).

III. The Spanish Case

This book seeks to test the hypothesis advanced by the literature to account for the success/failure of concertation in certain countries. This section will explore the question of whether the experience of concertation in Spain fits the conclusions offered in the literature. How did the institutional setting affect concertation in Spain? How did the international economic environment affect full-employment policies and neocorporatist arrangements in Spain? What does the Spanish experience suggest about the feasibility of SD policies under changing international economic conditions? In this section I seek to analyze the findings of the literature examined in previous sections in light of the Spanish case, which offers an intriguing test of some of the main findings discussed earlier.

a. Shortcomings of the Neocorporatist
Explanation for the Collapse of Concertation

How do the conclusions advanced by the neocorporatist literature help to account for the collapse of concertation in Spain after 1986? As we have already seen, the neocorporatist literature has concluded that concertation is more likely to succeed in countries with strong, monopolistic, and encompassing unions; with a centralized wage bargaining system; and where SD parties are in power. The Spanish experience with concertation from 1979 until 1986 offers a fertile ground to test these hypotheses.

In the case of Spain, the Spanish Socialist Workers Party (PSOE) held power for over thirteen years (1982–1996)—a longer period than any other SD government during the last two decades. From 1982 until 1989 the PSOE held an absolute majority in the Parliament and received a high enough share of the vote to allow it to pursue a long-term strategy. The socialists also controlled the local governments of the major cities and most regional governments. Moreover, when the socialists first won the 1982 elections, they had the support of one of the major labor unions, the UGT, and some of its leaders became members of the Spanish Parliament as socialists. They had the capacity and the electoral strength to impose agreements on the economic actors and to help them to monitor and control such agreements.

Despite these propitious circumstances, however, concertation worked only intermittently in Spain until 1986. When unions and business associations agreed on pacts, they were never fully carried out and the government did not live up its role of "guarantor." After 1986 the socialists failed to recruit the support of the labor unions to implement their economic policies and were forced to implement restrictive monetary policies to tackle inflation.[29] The socialists even witnessed, for the first time since Franco's years, four general strikes; they also failed to reduce unemployment in the long run and did little to reform the institutional setting to accommodate it to their strategies.

The Spanish experience also challenges the findings of the neocorporatist literature on partisanship (or party control of the government). Concertation collapsed under the PSOE, yet it had worked in Spain before under a conservative government. Moreover, according to the neocorporatist literature left power is strongly correlated with higher union density and with fewer trade unions (Garrett 1998, 15). The Spanish case, however, shows that low levels of union density coupled with labor conflict and socialist control of government are possible at the same time. The PSOE managed to remain in power for over 13 years despite the fact that Spain has a fragmented, weak, and not highly inclusive labor movement, and in spite of strong opposition from the unions after 1989. This challenges previous neocorporatist assessments about the close linkages between concertation and the long-term domination of government by leftist parties and also the presence of a strong and monopolistic organization of labor.

At the same time, the Spanish experience also offers new insights into the role of the institutional setting. According to the literature, the relative weakness of the Spanish labor union institutions, the competitive structure of the labor movement (with two major confederations, the UGT and CCOO, striving for dominance), and the decentralization of the collective bargaining system should have hindered concertation in Spain. This institutional environment should have meant that the government could not rely on the unions to contain inflation—as the Northern European countries did—while implementing expansive countercyclical policies. Despite this unpropitious setting, however, concertation flourished for an extensive period of time (1979–1986) and cooperation between unions, business, and the government, helped to reduce inflation from 26.4 percent in 1977 to 8.8 percent in 1986. Hence, Spain offers an opportunity to research the impact of a different institutional setting on SD policies.

Furthermore, we have already seen how the neocorporatist literature concluded that concertation is only feasible in countries with monopolistic and encompassing unions that have a SD orientation and that also have close relationships with SD parties in government (Cameron 1984). Communist unions, in this regard, were viewed as counterproductive to concertation because they would oppose cooperative approaches. In Spain, however, the system of industrial relations was dominated for years by a communist union, the Workers' Commissions (CCOO) with close links to the Spanish Communist Party, yet concertation worked for an extensive period of time, and the communist union took part in two of the centralized agreements (the Acuerdo Nacional de Empleo, ANE in 1982, and the Acuerdo Interconfederal, AI, in 1983). The Spanish case, therefore, offers new ground to refute some of the conclusions of the neocorporatist literature.

Finally, a major shortcoming of the neocorporatist literature is its overwhelming focus on the small states of Europe. Since these countries—that is, Sweden, Norway, Austria, Switzerland—were very successful in coping with the economic crisis of the 1970s and were able to limit effectively unemployment and inflation, most of the literature has focused on the rationale behind these successes. The emphasis has been on cases of success and not so much on cases of failure. Few analyses, except for those of Britain, have focused on how institutions have impeded the implementation of SD policies. The Spanish case offers such an opportunity. While the SD program was fully implemented in other European countries before the crisis of the 1970s, only in the 1980s were SD parties elected in southern Europe. The Spanish experience with concertation offers one of the few instances where a social democratic government remained in power for a substantive period of time within an institutional, historical, and structural framework that is markedly different from those of the small European states.

b. Shortcomings of the Organization of
Production- and Globalization-Based Explanations
for the Collapse of Concertation

As seen earlier, some authors concluded that the globalization of economies, the internationalization and liberalization of financial markets, and the emergence of new production methods preclude the implementation of full-employment polices based on concertation. Such a policy course, according to them, would result in a run on the currency and a massive flight of capital (very much like what happened in France in 1982). The Spanish experience with concertation offers new ground to test this hypothesis.

When the Spanish socialists came to power in 1982, the country was in the midst of a sharp economic recession. This was also a time when some of the most powerful countries—the United States, Germany, Britain—were implementing restrictive monetary policies to quell the inflationary pressures that developed after the second oil shock. At this time, the failure of the French experiment with expansionary policies became also evident. These factors played a relevant role in the course of economic policies in Spain. Socialist politicians argued that within such a framework they could not implement full-employment policies (Solchaga 1997, 36–50). It was also at this time that the country's economy became fully integrated in the international economy. Spain joined the European Community in 1986 and subsequently proceeded to dismantle all trade barriers and to liberalize the financial sector. According to the view of some of the authors that we analyzed above, the integration within the international economy accelerated new developments that had severe influence on policy making and hindered the implementation of neocorporatist arrangements: The decline of Fordist structures of production; the emergence of new methods of production, based on flexibility; the heterogenization of the labor force; wage drifts; the liberalization of the financial sector; and the intensification of competition that hastened the process of industrial reconversion.

This explanation, however, does not account for the collapse of concertation in Spain after 1986. First, concertation in that country collapsed during a period well before most of the developments mentioned above, developments advanced by the some authors as destructive to concertation. Spain remained a relatively closed country until the 1990s, and Fordism was still dominant in Spain. Additionally, the liberalization of the financial sector was not completed until 1992. Moreover, the heterogenization of the labor movement did not further weaken the position of the traditional unions, nor did it result in the emergence of new unions that would threaten the position of the old ones (similar what happened in Sweden in the 1980s). On the contrary, unions regained some strength in the late 1980s, and wage drifts were not as significant as in Sweden. Despite these facts, however, concertation failed and did not resume until 1997, when a new conservative government was in power (see Conclusions).

A second issue related to the "globalization" explanation and pertaining to the Spanish case is the question of whether it may overestimate the effect of freer trade and capital flows on the established balance of power between business and labor. Although it is true that globalization has made it easier for firms to shift production overseas, this is an option that only companies operating globally have. In Spain, however, this has not been the case; the overwhelming majority of firms (60 percent) are small and do not operate in international markets and so do not enjoy such an option. Labor is still strong in Spain, and unions have regained some strength in the late 1980s and early 1990s. Moreover, Spanish business remains deeply interested in centralized bargaining.

The third issue relates to the autonomy and capacity of all national governments. The Spanish Constitution establishes a system whereby power is mostly concentrated in the hands of the executive branch; which always has a majority in the Parliament (this was particularly true throughout the 1980s when the regional governments were not yet fully consolidated, and the Socialist Party held an absolute majority in the Parliament). Despite this power and the relative closed nature of the Spanish economy up to the late 1980s, the Socialist economic team still argued that it lacked the autonomy to satisfy union demands and that the international markets precluded them from meeting those demands. This argument was subsequently contradicted when the government satisfied union demands after the great success of the 1988 general strike. How was the government able to satisfy these demands in 1989 and not in 1986? Moreover, this policy shift did not have the dramatic economic consequences predicted by the socialist government.

Finally, the case of Spain points in the direction of another shortcoming of the neocorporatist literature in that it fails to account for cases of success. Changes in the organization of production and globalization are not forcing all countries to converge toward a more deregulated and decentralized regime. On the contrary, new reports show that the deregulation of domestic markets have only taken place in Anglo Saxon economies (Garrett 1998, 11–16). In northern Europe and Japan the industrial relations system has remained well established. In these countries, organized business seeking to preserve long-term financial frameworks, cooperative skilled work forces, and research networks, (the sources of the international competitiveness), has promoted regulation in order to face the challenges of increasing globalization (Soskice 1999, 133–134).

In this regard, it is worth emphasizing that there are other countries—such as Portugal, Austria, the Netherlands, and Belgium—that faced similar economic constraints as Sweden but were still able to develop or maintain a system of labor relations based on concertation. Portugal in particular is a very interesting reference from a comparative perspective because it has an institutional structure similar to Spain's and faced comparable economic constraints. Yet Portugal developed a system of industrial relations in the late 1980s and 1990s based on concertation.

Conclusions

The success of concertation has varied significantly among countries. The objective of this chapter was to review the explanations offered in the literature for these differences. According to the neocorporatist literature, the key variable that determines the success of some countries' SD full-employment policies has been the effective implementation of voluntary incomes policy based on concertation. Its analysis of cases of success led neocorporatist authors to conclude that concertation has been possible only in countries with a certain institutional setting that involves the role played by the labor movement, its strength, and its organization, as well as the structure of wage bargaining. According to other authors, on the other hand, changes in the economic context and the organization of production imposed constraints on domestic economies, weakened the industrial relations system, and prevented the implementation of full-employment policies that would have allowed for the continuation of concertation in the 1980s and 1990s. Trade globalization, financial liberalization, and the decline of Fordism have all hindered concertation, they say, because they resulted in labor fragmentation, unions' difficulties in aggregating workers' demands, problems coordinating expansive monetary and fiscal policies with unions' restrictive wages policy, fiscal discipline and deficit reduction, the increasing power of capital vis-à-vis labor, and the weakening of unions' traditional strongholds.

I have pointed out a number of ways in which the Spanish case challenges the findings of the literature. In the chapters that follow, I shall offer a detailed description of the Spanish concertation experience, and then consider this experience against the institutional and organization of production/globalization arguments more carefully. This examination leads me to conclude that the literature overlooks the role of societal, institutional, and political contextual considerations that influence the decisions of social actors—that is, the circumstances under which competing and weak unions are willing to take part in concertation arrangements, or under which social democratic governments are willing to participate in concertation and do not defect from their agreements with unions. In this regard, a critical explanatory factor that accounts for the failure of concertation in Spain is the socialist union subordination to the political party.

CHAPTER 3

Concertation in Spain (1979–1986): A Historic Overview

Introduction

Until the end of the Franco regime, Spain lacked a tradition of concertation among democratic actors. In other words, the country had no experience with the neocorporatist arrangements that had been part of the industrial relations setting of many other European countries. However, since democracy was established in Spain in 1975, there have been various attempts to reach centralized political agreements between business and unions—sometimes with the participation of the government—on economic matters including wages. Some authors have referred to these attempts as "neocorporatist experiences" (Moscoso 1995, 17; Führer 1996, 31; Roca 1993, 159; Folgado 1989, 268). All these agreements involved wages and incomes policies, plus a variety of other issues. Wage bargaining was based on the inflation rate forecast for the subsequent year. Wages were, therefore, indexed to inflation.

From the late 1970s until the mid-1980s, five major agreements were reached between the government, unions, and business. While successful concertation took place under conservative governments (1979–1982), only during three years were the socialists able to reach agreements (1983, 1985, and 1986). After that, industrial conflict intensified. The first concertation attempt, the so-called 1977 Pactos de la Moncloa (the Moncloa Pacts), was unique because unions and business organizations were not signatories. These were political pacts negotiated and signed by the major political parties. Concertation, understood as centralized agreements with the participation of labor and business, only took place in Spain after 1979. These agreements included, first, the 1979 Acuerdo Básico Interconfederal (ABI). This was a one-year agreement reached by the employers' association (CEOE, Confederación Española de Organizaciones Empresariales) and the socialist labor union, (UGT, Unión General de Trabajadores), without the intervention of the government. This pact established a blueprint for future legislation to regulate the industrial relations setting. The second agreement was the 1980—renewed in 1981—Acuerdo Marco Interconfederal (AMI). This expanded the issues covered in the ABI and introduced voluntary incomes policies. It was a two-year agreement reached between the UGT, the CEOE and the small union USO (Unión Sindical Obrera). The third agreement was the 1982 Acuerdo Nacional de Empleo (ANE). This was a one-year agreement signed by the CEOE, UGT, and the communist union (CCOO, Comisiones Obreras), with the government formally present. It included a plan to create jobs, granted public subsides to the unions, introduced retraining schemes, and included measures to reduce overtime work. The fourth agreement was the 1983 Acuerdo Interconfederal (AI) signed by the CEOE, UGT, and CCOO, with the government formally absent. This pact reduced the working week to 40 hours, and extended vacation to 30 days per year. It also sought to bring down the retirement age. Finally, the 1985—renewed in 1986—Acuerdo Económico y Social (AES) excluded CCOO but included the government in the first round. This introduced schemes to promote job creation, and included government funds for new investment. It also extended unemployment benefits and included measures to increase labor flexibility. After a period of conflict in 1987–1989, there were two bipartite agreements between government and unions, and government and employers in 1990, the Acuerdos del 25 de Enero. These agreements, however, did not have the scope of the previous centralized ones, and 1986 is generally considered the last year of centralized concertation (Moscoso 1995, Espina 1991, Hawkesworth and Fina 1987). A summary of these agreements is below.

Figure 3.1 Tripartite Agreements, 1979–1990

Agreements	Years	Actors
Acuerdo Básico Interconfederal (ABI)	1979	CEOE-UGT
Acuerdo Marco Interconfederal (AMI)	1980–1981	CEO-UGT-USO
Acuerdo Nacional de Empleo (ANE)	1982	CEOE-UGT-CCOO-GOVT.
Acuerdo Interconfederal (AI)	1983	CEOE-UGT-CCOO
Legislative Imposition	1984	GOVT.
Acuerdo Ecónomico y Social (AES)	1985–1986	UGT-CEOE-GOVT./ UGT-CEOE
Two Bilateral Agreements (Acuerdos del 25 de Enero)	1990	CEOE-UGT-CCOO-GOVT. and CEOE-GOVT.

Although the Moncloa Pacts failed to meet some of their objectives, they established a precedent that would be followed in subsequent agreements: Wage increases were tied to next year's inflation forecast. However, these agreements were more than an attempt by the government to enforce income policies. They also included "safeguard clauses" to compensate workers for income losses when inflation grew faster than expected, and "dripping-out" clauses that allowed firms with severe losses to pay below the norm. Supplementary wage increases tied to productivity improvements were to be negotiated at the firm level. They also introduced measures to regulate collective bargaining as well as dealing with other issues. Among those provisions, they included mechanisms that sought to facilitate a better relationship between workers and firm managers, and non-pay issues, like declarations about the institutional position of unions, the individual rights of workers, and proposals to address unemployment.

By tying wage increases to productivity increases, the objective of these pacts was to establish a pattern of noninflationary wage bargaining. Despite the fact that government's inflation forecasts were invariably unrealistic, these agreements were quite successful at reducing inflation and proved to be effective instruments to tie wages to forecasted inflation while safeguarding worker incomes. Inflation receded after 1978 and only rebounded after 1988, when concertation had collapsed. It went down from 14.4 percent in 1982 to 8.2 percent in 1986—the year of Spanish entry into the European Community (EC), when the new Value Added Tax (VAT) was introduced (Moscoso 1995, 22). However, these pacts were not as successful at rewarding productivity increases.

In the first half of this chapter, I shall describe these agreements, their genesis and content. I shall then proceed to describe the end of concertation in Spain, and close the chapter with an evaluation of these pacts. The major contention of this chapter is that concertation had very positive results for the Spanish economy. It contributed to wage moderation, lower inflation, and fostered business profits and investment in the second half of the 1980s. At the same time, wage moderation and social peace were the foundation upon that the new democratic regime was consolidated. The question is: If concertation was so positive, why did it collapse after 1986? Its collapse had serious consequences for the Spanish economy and determined, in the end, the failure of the Spanish socialist government to reduce unemployment.

I. A Historic Overview of Concertation in Spain (1979–1986)

After 36 years of dictatorship, Spain started its democratic transition process when General Franco, the dictator, died in 1975. This was also a time when all industrialized countries were experiencing a sharp economic recession as a consequence of the first oil shock of 1973. That year the price of oil increased from $1.63 per barrel to $9.31. Industrialized countries reacted to this crisis with the implementation of adjustment policies to control the dramatic increase in inflation and unemployment, that resulted in a sharp decline in consumption, business profits, investment, and economic growth. In Spain, however, the Francoist leadership did little to tackle the crisis, and Spaniards continued living as if the crisis had little implications for the national economy (Bustelo 1986). Part of the reason for the absence of action was that the regime was leaderless because General Franco was ill and his political regime was nearing its sunset. Some of the regime's economists could not grasp the implications of the crisis and argued that the recession was part of the business cycle, and that countries would come out of it automatically. Others, aware of its implications, argued that, given the weakness of the Francoist political system, they could not take the measures necessary to cope with it if they wanted to avoid the risk of a social explosion (Estefanía and Serrano, 1990, 25).

The effects of the crisis were catastrophic for the Spanish economy. It resulted in a dramatic increase in unemployment and inflation, a deterioration of the trade deficit, and a sharp decline in business profits and investment. And all this was occurring at a time of increasing political instability caused by the death of the dictator in October 1975, and the lack of authority and legitimacy of his successors. One of the consequences of the crisis was the intensification of industrial conflict because workers refused to bear the burden of the economic crisis. Demands for wage increases were coupled with political demands for freedom and the establishment of a democratic regime. In 1976 alone, there were up to 350,000 strikes in one day (Díaz Cardiel, Plá, Tejero, and Triana, 1976). The negative effects of the international crisis were compounded by circumstances that were specific to Spain: The end of the emigration boom in the second half of the decade, the chronic inflation of the Spanish industrial structure, and the lack of technological development in the national economy.

By 1977 the economic situation was very worrisome. Wages had increased by 30 percent, inflation reached 27 percent, the trade deficit had increased from $8.5 billion in 1975 to $15 billion in 1977, unemployment was up to 6.3 percent of the active population, the peseta had been devalued 10 percent in 1976 and 20 percent in 1977, and the current account deficit had increased by $1 billion in one year (Estefanía and Serrano 1990, 26; Leal 1982). Another major problem was the dramatic explosion of salaries. In 1977 wages increased 26.9 percent—and inflation 24.5 percent (Roca 1993, 151–153). The collapse of the authoritarian regime resulted in the sudden strengthening of the labor movement and the intensification of industrial conflict; both factors, in turn, led to a wage explosion that accelerated the collapse of the existing economic setup. Wage increases were not justified in the light of productivity stagnation and resulted in a worsening economic condition (Sevilla 1985). The Spanish government had to take some drastic action.

The election of Adolfo Suárez as the new president gave new momentum to reform. Upon being sworn in, however, he became very concerned with the threat posed by reactionary groups. To counter it, he sought to strengthen the government by seeking to co-opt the support of potentially revolutionary groups in favor of the new system (particularly the major trade unions, the socialist UGT, and the communist CCOO). In April of 1977, the Spanish Parliament approved the "Ley de Asociacion Sindical" (the Union Association Act), legalizing trade unions. At this time unions entered in negotiations with the government to seek a social pact that would help to develop an adjustment plan. An agreement could not be reached because of the profound discrepancies between the government and the unions on most issues—expected inflation, pensions, wage increases—and the demands of the unions for fiscal reform and a new system of industrial relations. Unions were in the midst of a consolidation process, and were not yet prepared to reach agreements with the government. The government then decided to abandon this approach and sought to negotiate with other political parties (Domínguez 1990, 79).

A result of these developments was the signing of the "Pactos de la Moncloa" on October 25, 1977. These pacts have been considered, given the social and economic context and the level of negotiation, as the first concertation attempt in Spain, and this despite the fact that neither the Employer's Organization nor the unions signed it. A major peculiarity of these pacts was that they were signed by the political parties only and not by the unions and business organizations.[1] They were also approved by the Spanish Parliament. These pacts were a response to an acute political and economic crisis that threatened the stability of the new democratic regime. Therefore, they had a strong political flavor. The exclusion of other groups can be explained by the lack of experience in negotiated settlements of the Spanish social actors (business, unions, and the government), and the fact that the business organization (CEOE) had not yet established itself at the time that the pacts were signed (it was founded two months before the signing). Another reason for this development was that the government and the political parties wanted to give the impression that the pacts were a success of the democratic regime.

Most scholars, however, considered this pact as an instance of neocorporatist agreement. The presence of top businessmen in the first government after Franco's' death coupled with the close links between the Workers' Commissions and the Communist party (Carrillo was one of the signatories), and between the Socialist party and the UGT, plus the fact that the leadership of the unions did not speak against the pact (the leaders of the Workers' Commissions even carried out a campaign in favor of the pact) seems to confirm the notion that it was an instance of neocorporatism (Martínez-Alier and Roca 1986, 17).[2]

In this regard, a major objective of these pacts was the consolidation of the democratic regime. It has been argued by some scholars that the weakness of the new regime and the intensity of the economic crisis of the late 1970s helped to overcome the Spanish lack of tradition in concertation and social pacts (see chapter 6). It has been argued that the unions and the left-wing parties (including the Communist party) restrained their members in exchange for assurances on the consolidation of a democratic regime, despite the fact that the actor that represented a real threat, the Army, had no representatives at the negotiating table (Martínez-Alier and Roca 1986, 17). The social actors hoped that concertation would be an adequate instrument to deal with the crisis and would help avoid the industrial conflict that could threaten the emerging democratic institutions (Zaragoza and Varela, 1990, 54). In the Pactos de la Moncloa, the main political parties agreed on certain measures to guarantee the success of the transition process. They introduced a stabilization plan for the Spanish economy that included provisions to implement incomes polices, as well as moderate fiscal and monetary policies to reduce inflation. In exchange for incomes policy, the government accepted the responsibility to take steps to reform the education, fiscal, social security, and housing systems.

An additional peculiarity of these pacts was that despite the fact that unions and business were not signatories, they would be the ones that would have to enforce one of the pacts' major components: incomes policy. Obviously, at the heart of the agreements was an attempt to control a rather loose political and economic context, with the government trying to impose its economic targets upon the economic actors. The reaction of unions was ambivalent. Both Nicolás Redondo and Marcelino Camacho, the secretaries general of the two major union confederations, UGT and CCOO, were representatives in Parliament and voted in favor of the pacts (Roca, 1985, 4). However, while the CCOO, influenced by its close links with the Communist Party, one of the signatories of the pacts, declared them "a historic agreement" and a necessary instrument both to consolidate the democratic institutions and to contribute to the overcoming of the economic crisis, the socialist union, the UGT, and the other unions did not feel as enthusiastic and accepted them only reluctantly. They resented the fact that they had been left out of the negotiation and emphasized the lack of provisions to strengthen the role of the unions and reform the industrial relations setting. They also questioned the commitment by the government to fulfill its promises (Domínguez 1990, 78).

At that time the strategies of the UGT and CCOO were closely associated to those of the parties with whom they had links, the socialist PSOE (Partido Socialista Obrero Español), and the communist PCE (Partido Comunista de España) respectively. One of the priorities for the new leaders of the PSOE during the transition to democracy was to extend their control over the labor movement. Given the important role that the Communist Party had played during the dictatorship, the socialists believed that the communists had dominated the trade union movement during the late 1960s and early 1970s. Socialist union leaders coming from exile did not know the degree of support that they had within the rank and file, but they knew that the Socialist Party would be accepted into the new political framework. Therefore, thinking that confrontation would bring more workers to their side, they sought to stimulate labor conflict in order to extend their control over the labor movement (see Fishman 1990). The communists, for their part, believing that they had the upper hand in the labor movement but unsure about what role—if any—that the Communist Party would play in the new regime, followed an opposite strategy and implemented moderation and restraint in the activities of their trade union (CCOO), trying to gain recognition by the new regime. In the end, the communist leaders offered restraint by workers in exchange for a party role in the transition period. The result of this strategy was the communist support for the Pactos de la Moncloa in 1977. The UGT, in a weaker position and lacking a similar political motivation (the PSOE was already a player in the transition process) tried to capitalize on worker discontent and strengthen its position among the rank-and-file, and thus did not explicitly endorse the pacts. The UGT also had another challenge; it had to respond to attacks from the CCOO that it was a "transmission belt" from the employers and the conservative government (Moscoso 1995, 61). The strategies of these unions were to be shortly reversed.

As mentioned before, the Moncloa Pacts pegged, for the first time, wage increases to expected inflation (as opposed to past inflation). This mechanism was to be replicated in successive agreements. In the period up to 1977, gross real wages grew by and large as quickly as productivity (between 1964–1977 wages effectively increased 6.69 percent while productivity grew 5.08 during the same period) (Martínez-Alier and Roca 1986, 19, 31). In 1977 the government issued a decree that set wage increases for the following year, 1978, between 20–22 percent. They also included provisions to punish firms that accepted wage increases beyond 22 percent with the loss of fiscal benefits (Espina 1991, 335–336). In 1978 inflation increased "only" 16.56 percent by the end of the year, proving the efficacy of these mechanisms (Iglesias 1990, 148). The pacts lasted a year and a half.

The first elections to the work councils took place in 1978. They validated the supremacy of the communist trade union, with 37.8 percent of the elected representatives, followed closely by the socialist union, with 31 percent. The elections also confirmed the concentration of the vote in those two major unions. Only ELA-STV (Solidaridad de Trabajadores Vascos) in the Basque country was able to surpass the large unions. These elections, however, also confirmed that the gap between the socialist and communist unions was not as large as previously thought. The UGT's strength was reinforced by the strong electoral performance of the Socialist Party in the general elections of 1979 and the dismal results of the Communist Party. These electoral results had an enormous impact on the position of unions towards concertation.

As a consequence, the communist leaders realized that they did not have as much support among the rank and file as they thought and started to adopt a more confrontational and militant strategy that would last until the failed coup d'état of 1982. It has also been argued that CCOO was "manipulated" by the Communist Party. According to Moscoso (1995, 66), the electoral decline of the Communist Party in the general elections of 1979 confirmed the weakening of the PCE and the strengthening of the PSOE. Consequently, the UCD (Unión de Centro Democrático) conservative government abandoned the preferential treatment it had given the PCE at the beginning of the transition process. Within this context communist leaders thought that a "more militant labor movement could be used as an effective threat to force UCD's government to rescue the preferential relation it used to have with the PCE since it was declared lawful" (Moscoso 1995, 65). Moreover, despite the fact that the CCOO won the elections to the work councils, its worse-than-expected performance (34.7 percent of the votes) might have also influenced the position of the union leadership that saw how its presumed hegemony within the labor movement was slipping. Both factors might help to explain the decision to leave the negotiations with the government on the Estatuto de los Trabajadores (the Workers' Statute) in 1979, and not to sign the first two centralized bilateral agreements between UGT and the business organization, CEOE (Confederación Española de Organizaciones Empresariales)—the Acuerdo Básico Interconfederal (1979), and the Acuerdo Marco Interconfederal (1980–1981). According to this view, CCOO leaders thought that a more combative stance would retrieve some recognition for their organization. By refusing to negotiate, they expected to encourage the militancy of their affiliates, challenge the government's policies and, therefore, force the government to back off and offer them a more relevant role. This strategy failed because the CCOO lacked the strength within the labor movement to make a credible threat, a fact that had been already determined in the 1978 elections to the work councils but that the leaders of the union chose to ignore. Wage increases did not surpass the pay norm established by the government in 1978 despite more strike activity (Moscoso 1995, 66).

The socialist union (UGT), on the other hand, surprised about its good electoral results in the 1978 elections for work councils, and more confident about the support from the rank and file, decided on a more conciliatory stance. At the same time, given the fact that by 1979 the CCOO had adopted a more confrontational approach, the UGT leaders felt that the union risked a dilution of its own personality if it decided to follow the CCOO's aggressive strategy. Therefore, the UGT's leaders rejected this option and adopted a more conciliatory strategy to expand the influence of the UGT. In this regard, one of its major stated goals was to become a union confederation that would mirror its Swedish and German counterparts and become a critical player in the economic policymaking process. Therefore, its leaders looked for strategies that would allow the union to play a role in the political and economic structure of the system (Paramio 1992, 528–530). Concertation offered them such an option. The UGT leaders reached the conclusion that a confrontational approach would result only in further political and economic uncertainties and would thus damage the reputation of the union as a reliable partner. Concertation, on the other hand, would offer the union an opportunity to play a role in economic policy while reinforcing its position as a reliable actor and consolidating its role within the labor movement by capitalizing on any positive results that might come out from the agreements. Consequently, the UGT played a critical role during the negotiations of the next two centralized agreements. This strategy proved to be successful. In the following elections for work councils, the UGT gained almost 8 percent points compared its percentage with 1978, while CCOO lost 4 percent points (Fishman 1990, Moscoso 1995, 62).

In summary, UGT's decision to support the process resulted in the negotiation and signing of five centralized agreements. CCOO participated only in two of these agreements—the ANE and the AI. The content of these pacts is shown below (from Moscoso 1995, Espina 1991, and Hawkesworth and Fina 1987, 64–83).

The ABI (1979)

Despite intense maneuvers by the government—for example, the 1978 *jornadas de reflexión* or "meditation days"—organized by the UCD government to try to reach an agreement with unions and business organization, there was no agreement in 1979. The discussions showed the differences among the social actors. While the communist union preferred political pacts with the

Figure 3.2 The Content of Concertation Agreements

Issues

ABI: CCOO and UCD government excluded. Declaration and proposals about the institutional position of the social actors, workers rights.

AMI: CCOO and UCD government excluded. Pay norm between 13–16 percent for 1980 and 11–15 percent for 1981; reduced the working week to 42/43 hours; measures to reduce absenteeism; mechanisms to guarantee union recognition; mechanism for coordination of collective bargaining; dropping out clauses for firms in trouble; wage increases linked to productivity.

ANE: CCOO and UCD government included. Pay norm between 9–11 percent for private sector and 8–9 percent for the public sector—2.5 percent below inflation; safeguard clauses to guarantee that wages would rise at least 2 percent below inflation; job creation mechanisms; public subsidies to maintain confederations; measures to reduce overtime; framework to negotiate retirement schemes; retraining plans; bargaining system.

AI: PSOE government excluded; pay norm between 9.5–12.5 percent with an expected inflation of 12.2 percent; mechanisms to reduce overtime; retirement age; 30 days of holidays; reduced working week to 40 hours; new structure to coordinate sectoral bargaining.

AES: PSOE government included and CCOO excluded; pay norm between 5.5–7.5 percent for 1985 and 90–107 percent of expected inflation for 1986 with an expected inflation of 7 percent for 1985 and 6 percent for 1986; government funds for investment; solidarity funds to create jobs; measures to increase labor flexibility; extension of unemployment benefits to 48 percent of the unemployed; negotiations to structure sectoral collective bargaining.

participation of the government, the UGT defended bilateral social and economic pacts between the unions and the business organization without the government. These strategies were closely related to the preferred options of the political parties to that both unions were closely allied (Führer 1992, 356).[3] Given the lack of agreement, the government unilaterally developed its own wage provisions for 1979, and established wage increases between 11 percent and 14 percent for 1979 with an expected inflation of 10 percent. These rules were mandatory for public firms and recommended guidelines for private ones—which were threatened with losing fiscal benefits and public loans if they did not follow them. Inflation, however, grew beyond expectations, reaching 15.6 percent at the end of 1979 (Estefanía and Serrano 1990, 29).

The high levels of inflation and unemployment (8.6 percent), further reinforced the will of the conservative minister of economics, Fernando Abril

Martorell, to foster some kind of agreement between unions and the business organization. In the spring of 1979, the leaders of the trade unions and the CEOE held several meetings to try to reach an agreement. The CCOO leaders decided to abandon the negotiation because of disagreements with the UGT about the proposed law that would regulate the industrial relation setting (the Estatuto de los Trabajadores). For their part, the leaders of the UGT and the CEOE reaffirmed their interest in reaching a bilateral agreement, and intensified their contacts in the summer of 1979 to conclude it. They rejected the participation of the government to emphasize a departure from the state intervention that had characterized Spanish industrial relations up to that time (Domínguez 1990, 81). At the same time, leaders of both organizations saw a bilateral agreement as a great opportunity to promote and strengthen their individual organizations. After intense negotiations, on July 10, 1979, they signed an agreement, the Acuerdo Básico Interconfederal (ABI). The signatories, however, emphasized the programmatic character of the agreement and refused to consider the ABI a "social pact."

The ABI was the declaration of principles that would be the foundation for future agreements. It was also an attempt to rationalize the existing fragmented and outdated industrial relation setting and included recommendations to the government as to how to proceed with the reform of the industrial relations setting, as well as also including extensive discussions about the system of collective bargaining. As a result of the ABI, the Socialist Party modified its intention to introduce in Parliament an alternative to the government's Estatuto de los Trabajadores. The ABI also contained clauses that introduced the figure of the "union delegate" from individual firms and specified the position's functions and rights. Finally, the ABI also included recommendations on how to deal with the unemployment problem and suggested the participation of the unions and business organization in the management of state agencies (that is, the National Institute of Employment, INEM). It did not include income policies.

The AMI (1980–1981)

In September of 1979 the UGT presented a proposal to CCOO and the CEOE, inviting their leaders to negotiate a centralized bilateral agreement that would cover such economic and industrial relations issues as unemployment, wages, productivity, and unions rights. This proposal was motivated by the UGT's conviction that in "situations of crisis it was necessary as an exercise of responsibility" (Domínguez 1990, 82, my translation). In 1979, however, CCOO had exploited the nonfulfillment by the government of some of the clauses of the Moncloa Pacts to intensify worker protests. The union leaders thought that such a strategy would pay off in the long run and refused to change it. Therefore, although they took part in the AMI negotiations, they decided to abandon them at the end of the year. The UGT and CEOE continued negotiating, and the Acuerdo Marco Interconfederal, AMI, was signed by the leaders of both organizations on January 5, 1980. Another minority union, USO, subscribed to it later on. The AMI was published in the Boletín Oficial del Estado (the State's Official Bulletin) on January 14, 1980. It was valid for two years, 1980–1981.

The AMI was very significant because it was the first time in Spanish industrial relations history that business and trade unions had signed a bilateral agreement about economic and industrial relation issues that included incomes policy without the participation of the government. It was very different from the ABI. It had 14 chapters that covered various issues. It included provisions dealing with the industrial relations setting that were later incorporated to the Workers' Statute. After several meetings between the social actors and representatives of the political forces in Parliament, the new Workers' Statute was approved in March of 1978. It covered the individual rights of workers.

The AMI also included provisions that dealt with several other issues: The autonomy of the social actors, naming the actors who have legitimacy to participate in negotiations; the need to rationalize the number of collective agreements; the individual rights of workers: the right of public functionaries to collective negotiations; the need to handle productivity and absenteeism, security and hygiene; the need to establish mechanisms of arbitration; and the role and rights of union delegates (de la Villa 1984, 79–98). Some of these clauses foreshadowed the 1985 Union Liberty Act.

The AMI also established that the yearly number of working hours would be reduced from 2,006 hours in 1980 to 1,880 in 1982. As mentioned before, the agreement introduced incomes policy. Expected inflation was set at 15.3 percent for 1980, and the agreement established a range for increasing wages of between 13 percent and 16 percent in pacts negotiated through 1980. The AMI also contemplated a so-called "safeguard clause"— that is, if after six months inflation rose more than 6.5 percent, the pact allowed for a revision of already negotiated wage increases—and a "dripping-out" clause that allowed firms that could prove that they had losses in 1978 and 1979 to negotiate wage increases below those established in the pact. Despite the fact that the CCOO did not take part in the agreement and actively opposed it in firms, the AMI was successfully implemented in subsequent low-level negotiations, and wages increased an average of 15.33 percent in 1980. It also resulted in a dramatic decline in strikes and industrial conflict (1,351 strikes in 1980 versus 1,789 in 1979). These results were a major defeat for the CCOO and confirmed the workers' support of the moderate strategies followed by the UGT (Führer 1996, 360; Iglesias 1990, 152–153; Domínguez 1990, 83).

Elections to the work councils took place again in 1980. They confirmed the supremacy of CCOO (31 percent) and the advance of the UGT (29 percent). In February of 1981, the UGT and the CEOE closed the negotiations to renew the AMI and established a negotiation range for wage increases of between 11 and 15 percent with an expected inflation of 13 percent. The AMI revision also included clauses allowing firms with duly certified losses to increase wages by less than 11 percent, and clauses to revise wage increases in case of higher inflation after six months. Wages grew in 1981 by 13.2 percent and inflation by 14.5 percent.

The ANE (1982)

Two events had tremendous influence in the negotiations that led to the Acuerdo Nacional de Empleo (ANE): First, the failed coup d'état of February 1981, and, second, the results of the elections to the work councils of 1980. On February 23, 1981, a group of seditious militarized civil guards occupied the Spanish Parliament. Fortunately for the new democratic system, the coup failed when most military commanders refused to support it. This event, however, had a tremendous impact on the minds of the social actors. The failed coup confirmed, in case anyone had doubts, the fragility of the new democratic institutions.

A few days after the coup, the new Prime Minister, Leopoldo Calvo Sotelo, during his acceptance speech, invited the social actors to open negotiations to conclude a pact that would contribute to the strengthening of the democratic institutions and help overcome the current economic crisis (Calvo Sotelo 1990). Unions and business accepted the invitation and opened negotiations that concluded on June 9, 1981, with the signatures of the government, the UGT, the CCOO, and the CEOE ratifying the Acuerdo Nacional de Empleo (ANE)—also known as the "pact of fear."[4] The negotiations were very complicated and almost broke down on several occasions. One of the consequences of the disputes among the participating actors was that the ANE included at least two "secret" clauses—one about financial compensation to unions, and the other one about limits to temporary contracts—that undermined its implementation.

The major significance of this agreement was that for the first time in the new democratic regime, the government recognized the social actors as equal partners, signed an agreement with them, and was fully engaged in the pact's negotiation and implementation. Unions, for their part, reluctantly accepted negotiations with the condition that they would also include not only incomes policies but also measures to tackle some of the most challenging problems of the time: unemployment, the institutional neglect of unions, and the increasing expansion of the underground economy (Domínguez 1990, 85). Unions were fully satisfied with the outcome. The ANE gave real power to the social actors through membership on commissions that were created to follow up on the implementation of the agreement. It confirmed the participation of the social actors in economic policymaking, and their institutional role in the political system. Some analysts have even talked about a "power in the shadows" to emphasize that no other pact gave so much power to unions and business organizations over the actions of the government as did the ANE (Estefanía and Serrano 1990, 35).

Another major feature of the ANE was that for the first time, the communist union, CCOO, agreed to sign a centralized agreement. The disappointing results in the 1980 elections to the work councils (the union received "only" 31 percent of the elected representatives) forced communist leaders to reevaluate their strategy. It has been argued that "the ascendancy of UGT over CCOO was not the result of a movement from the political field to the unions, but it was based substantially on a strategic policy matured to respond to the crisis. In face of this strategy, the confrontational approach pursued by CCOO could only lead to a disaster" (Paramio 1982[5]). A conference of communist workers that took place in 1980 decided that the CCOO had to shift course and participate in subsequent agreements. Moreover, the fact that the government—absent in the previous two bilateral agreements—also took part in the ANE provided a good excuse for the communist leaders, who argued that they always wanted to negotiate directly with the government. This strategic change, however, took place too late. The UGT had already consolidated its position among workers and had also capitalized on the good results that derived from the implementation of the ABI and AMI. The 1982 elections for work councils would confirm the electoral decline of the CCOO (Moscoso 1995, 67).

The ANE had eight chapters (de la Villa 1984, 208). It included provisions allowing union and business organization members on the board of many public institutions (the National Institute for Employment, the National Institute for Social Security, the Health Institute, and others). It also introduced incomes policy by establishing a wage range for 1982 between 9 percent and 11 percent. The agreement also incorporated "safeguard clauses" that would apply in six months if inflation increased more than expected (6.04 percent). While the average wage increase negotiated in pacts for 1982 was 11.3 percent, the incapacity of the government to control inflation led to an inflation of 14.4 percent at the end of the year, that forced the renegotiation of wages, and they increased another 3.4 percent (Iglesias 1990, 157).

The ANE also incorporated provisions about public servants' wage increases (9 percent); pension increases (10 percent); the minimum wage; the expansion of unemployment benefits to cover more people and longer; the establishment of a fund of 15 billion pesetas to address situations of extremely high unemployment to be administered by unions, the business organization, and the National Institute for Employment; and the expansion of health benefits for the unemployed who had no benefits. The ANE also included a whole chapter dealing with unemployment, supplying proposals to foster job creation. It established fiscal advantages for firms that hired long-term unemployed workers (it exempted them from paying 90 percent of social security tax); punished firms that encouraged overtime; offered compensation to foster early retirements (100 percent retirement if the firm hired a new worker); and established new types of temporary contracts to promote youth employment (the number of these contracts was limited, however, by one of the secret clauses incorporated in the agreement). The ANE also contained clauses that criticized the existing fragmentation of collective bargaining and advocated the full autonomy of the social actors to introduce changes to the system. The government also committed itself to implement an economic policy that would maintain the same number of job for 1982, a commitment that meant the creation of 350,000 jobs.

The agreement also established a commission to study the reform of the social security system, which led nowhere, and another commission to oversee the carrying out of the agreement. This commission oversaw the actions of the government; its reports served as basis for opposition parties and unions to attack the position of the government continually. This contributed to the final collapse of the conservative government in the elections of 1982 (Estefanía and Serrano 1990, 37). The worsening economic situation and the rapid disintegration of the conservative UCD hindered fulfillment of the agreement. Disputes among the signatories intensified throughout 1982. The business organization was interested mostly in the implementation of incomes polices, while the unions sought to implement the other parts of the agreement, and the government was unable to carry out its legislative compromises—it did not have enough votes in Parliament. In October 1982, the business organization left the commission using as a reason the deterioration of economic conditions (inflation had reached 14.4 percent; and unemployment, 2 million people; the economy grew less than 1 percent), and the breach of promises by the government, particularly regarding the reform of the social security system. The CEOE also emphasized its refusal to sign another tripartite agreement with that particular government. The UGT, given the proximity of the 1982 elections and the prospects of the electoral victory of the Socialist Party, also sought to leave the hands of the incoming government free and so favored bilateral agreements.

Two major events took place before the end of 1982: the elections to the work councils and the overwhelming victory of the PSOE in the general elections of October. The elections to the work councils confirmed the electoral decline of CCOO and the triumph of the UGT. For the first time, the UGT won the elections with 36.71 percent of the elected representatives, followed closely by the CCOO with 33.4 percent. These results confirmed that the moderate strategy pursued by UGT leaders was supported by a relative majority of the workers. At the same time, the Socialist Party got 10 million votes in the 1982 general elections. Both the party and the union had confirmed their supremacy in electoral arenas.

The AI (1983)

Shortly after becoming prime minister on January 4, 1983, the socialist leader Felipe González met separately with the leaders of the unions and business organization to discuss the possibility of a social pact for that year. The government sought an agreement because it did not wish to start the legislature with disputes and social conflict. The negotiations, however, at first did not go very well.[6] The major point of dispute was wage increases, with the CEOE seeking to increase wages less than the expected inflation. The government then tried to convince unions and the business association about the value of tackling the economic crisis through negotiations and social pacts. In the end, the UGT, CCOO, and the CEOE signed the Acuerdo Interconfederal (AI), on February 15, 1983. It lasted one year and covered all Spanish employers and workers regardless of their affiliation.

The government was not a signatory of the agreement but participated actively in the negotiations. The business organization, CEOE, wanted to involve the government in the agreement in order to force the socialists to negotiate its economic policies (since it opposed the electoral program of the PSOE). Unions, however, rejected the participation of the government because they considered that such participation would tie the latter's hands by forcing modifications to the socialist electoral program. In the end, the government did not sign the agreement.

The CEOE decided to sign the pact to show the willingness of business to work with the new socialist government. It would have been difficult for the organization to reject a pact when the UGT had been willing to conclude agreements with and under a conservative government (Estefanía and Serrano 1990, 38; Domínguez 1990, 89). While the UGT had reasons to be part of the agreement (it had strengthened its position by participating in the previous pacts, and this strategy reinforced its ultimate goal of taking part in the economic policymaking process), it was surprising that the CCOO also chose to do so, particularly given the fact that the government did not formally take part. Some authors have argued that the CCOO was compelled to sign it because the union leadership was not able to react otherwise to the stunning electoral victory of the socialists (Paramio 1992, 526). Others have argued that, given the loss of support experienced by the CCOO in the previous elections, it could not impose its views on the other social actors, and could not afford a confrontational approach toward the socialists and the UGT (Moscoso 1995, 67). Moreover, the ANE was implicitly supported by the government despite its formal absence, and the CCOO would have had a hard time trying to justify to the union voters and affiliates—most of whom had voted for the Socialist Party in the general elections—the union's refusal to cooperate with the new government.

The AI had nine chapters. Many of the clauses are taken from the AMI (de la Villa 1984, 100–113)—for example, unemployment measures and clauses about productivity, security, and hygiene in the working place; absenteeism; productivity; and the institutional position of unions. Wage increases were established between 9.5 and 12.5 percent. The pact also included a "safeguard clause" in case inflation surpassed the level expected (9 percent) in nine months (instead of the traditional six). Wages increased at the end of the year by 11.5 percent and inflation by 12.5 percent. The agreement also reduced annual working hours to 1,826 hours and 27 minutes, and introduced a proposal to create a National Consultative Commission that would be later implemented by the government (December of 1983). The retirement age was reduced to 64 years. Finally, the AI also included a chapter devoted to unemployment, with measures to create jobs, allowed retirements with full compensation if companies hired unemployed people, as well as the prohibition of extra hours and multiple employment. The AI also replicated the clauses contained in the AMI about collective bargaining; it criticized existing fragmentation and encouraged the social actors to introduce changes in all aspects of the system.

1984

The failure to reach an agreement for 1984 has been attributed to three major factors: First, the backlashes caused by the process of industrial restructuring, which started in 1983; second, the disputes that emerged between unions and the business organization about the enforcement of the new law approved by the government (August, 1984) reducing the working week to 40 hours; and finally differences about wage increases (Führer 1996, 367; Domínguez 1990, 91). Given the desperate competitive situation of many firms, the government could no longer postpone the process of industrial restructuring. While it is true that in most cases it tried to reach agreements with unions, the intensity of the crisis and the high costs that the process had for workers (over 80,000 jobs destroyed) caused the relationship between unions and the government to deteriorate.

In August 1983 the government issued a new law reducing the working week to 40 hours. This reduction had already been agreed upon in the ANE. A dispute, however, arose when the unions tried to enforce the law that same year. The business organization argued that it was a mistake by the government to issue a law at that particular time because it interfered with the principle of autonomy of the signatories, introduced confusion, and increased labor costs for firms at a time when most collective agreements had already been signed. Unions, however, tried to enforce the reduction immediately, and some businesses refused to accept it, arguing that it would increase the firms' costs after their budgets had been closed. The result was that some firms accepted the reduction while others did not, causing disputes among them. The Supreme Court later ruled that the law had to be applied immediately and forced firms that challenged it to pay their workers for the extra hours worked (Domínguez 1990, 91; Iglesias 1990, 158).

Wage increases were also the source of another dispute among government, unions, and business. The government and its Minister of Economics, Miguel Boyer, announced a reduction in inflation for 1984 of 4 points (or 8 percent). In order to achieve this objective, Boyer proposed that salaries should not increase beyond 5–6 percent. Unions refused to accept this proposal and demanded increases of 8 percent, plus a "safeguard clause" to protect salaries in case of unexpected inflation. The business organization, on the contrary, agreed with the government, and argued that, given the high levels of inflation (12 percent) and unemployment (17.8 percent), coupled with the dramatic increase in wages (unitary wage costs had multiplied by 5 in Spain between 1973 and 1982, whereas in the EC they had increased by only 2.43 points), they could not accept union demands to increase wages above expected inflation. On the contrary, if business wanted to reduce unitary wage costs, then salaries could not increase more than an average of 6.5 percent (Iglesias 1990, 159). Unions and the CEOE could not reach a compromise. Some authors have also argued that the business organization wanted to weaken the government and force the hand of the UGT, that had traditionally accepted compromises (Domínguez 1990, 92).

Given the lack of agreement, the government applied a restrictive monetary policy that some unionists interpreted as supporting the position of business. This policy, coupled with the disagreements among the UGT, the government, and the PSOE about the application of the 40-hour week, opened the first wounds in the party-union relationship. The lack of agreement also resulted in further industrial conflict (49,205549 hours lost in 1984 versus 38,762,560 hours in 1983). What was remarkable, however, was that despite the lack of a formal agreement, all the social actors voluntarily adopted incomes policies. In 1984 average wages grew only 8 percent, and inflation 9 percent. This shows that union leaders were fully aware of the importance of incomes policies as an instrument to foster economic recovery.[7]

The AES (1985–1986)

Negotiations between the government, unions, and employers associations resumed again in 1984. Despite the modest increases in wages, the economic situation had deteriorated. Unemployment had increased by 400,000 people, and inflation had also exceeded the government's forecast. Given this worsening situation, the socialist government decided to take the initiative and push in favor of a pact. The initial demands of the participants were not very promising. The CCOO wanted the government to create a solidarity fund financed with 300 billion pesetas to extend unemployment benefits, a reindustrialization plan, reduction of the work week to 38 hours, large increases in public investment, further control of the financial sector, and the reform of the Workers' Statute. The business association demanded more resources for firms, reform of the social security system, abolition of the administrative authorization required to make mass dismissals, further flexibility of the labor market, and complete liberalization of financial markets. Finally, the UGT demanded that the agreement should meet three major conditions: Measures to foster the creation of employment, labor market flexibility in exchange for wage moderation, and further institutional participation of unions in economic affairs (Domínguez 1990, 93; Iglesias 1990, 161–163).

At the end of 1984, the government introduced the budget for 1985 with the objective of reducing inflation to 7 percent and the public deficit by half a point, while increasing investment but reducing state expenditures and maintaining taxes. Given this restrictive budget, the CCOO decided to abandon the negotiations, arguing that signing an agreement would give support to the restrictive and antisocial politics of the government (Estefanía and Serrano 1990, 44). The CCOO leaders thought that they could help change the course of the government's policy with a more confrontational strategy. They maintained their opposition to the agreement after it was signed, arguing that it was very detrimental for workers' interests.[8]

Given these grim prospects, Felipe González decided to intervene and met separately with the leaders of the UGT, Nicolás Redondo, and the CEOE, José María Cuevas, to try to achieve consensus. Two major issues hindered the conclusion of the agreement: The demand by the CEOE to eliminate the required administrative authorization for mass dismissals and the inclusion in the agreement of a clause stating that the government should align the Spanish legislation on dismissals with the European Community's (Domínguez 1990, 93). Finally, the participants worked out an ambiguous formula of this clause that was accepted by the UGT.[9] The Acuerdo Económico y Social (AES) was signed by the government, the UGT, and the CEOE on October 9, 1984. It would last for two years (1985–1986).

The AES had two different parts (de la Villa 1984, 221–254). The first part contained a declaration from the government on economic issues and the tripartite agreements between the government, CEOE, and the UGT dealing with investment, taxes, wages in the public sector, unemployment benefits, and the creation of funds to promote investment and employment. The government stated the economic objectives for the next two years: An economic growth of 3 percent for 1985, and 3.5 percent for 1986; inflation of 7 percent for 1985, and 6 percent for 1986; and a public deficit of 5 percent for 1985 and 4.5 percent for 1986. The government also declared its intention to create 25,000 jobs in the public sector, and made a commitment to extend unemployment benefits to 43 percent of the unemployed by 1985, and to 48 percent by 1986 (Estefanía and Serrano 1990, 41–42). There were also clauses dealing with reform of the social security system and the retraining of workers. The agreement also included provisions to extend the participation of business and unions in certain public institutions, as well as a compromise by the government to develop a law that would allow for the return to unions of the resources that had been expropriated by the Franco dictatorship. The most controversial aspect of this section was, as mentioned above, the introduction of Article 17, which stated the need to reform the Spanish industrial labor system to align it with the norms of the other European Community countries.

The second half of the agreement included the bilateral pacts between UGT and CEOE. The content of this part of the agreement is similar to the Acuerdo Interconfederal of 1983. It included clauses establishing wage ranges between 5.5 percent and 7.5 percent for 1985, and between 90 percent and 107 percent of expected inflation for 1986. There was also a "safeguard clause" in case inflation increased more than expected, which would came into play after 12 months. The clauses dealing with productivity, absenteeism, employment, and collective bargaining were similar to the ones introduced in previous centralized agreements. One of the major features of the AES, however, was that the signatories agreed to develop several commissions to interpret, implement, and follow up the AES provisions. The effectiveness and success of these commissions varied, depending on their resources and the controversy of their specific functions.

The implementation of the pact was difficult. Disputes soon emerged about the interpretation of some of the clauses. The CEOE argued that the government had to apply Article 17 and bring into line Spanish industrial laws with the EC's—which meant, according to them, introducing more flexibility to dismiss people and ending the need for administrative authorization for mass dismissals. The UGT refused this interpretation and argued that EC's legislation respected domestic laws when the latter were more beneficial to workers. The Socialist Minister of Labor, Joaquín Almunia, sent a letter to UGT's Secretary General, Nicolás Redondo, in July 1985, confirming that the Spanish legislation was adequate and did not need reform to bring it into line with the EC's, thus giving support to the UGT.[10] The business organization did not accept this interpretation (Iglesias 1990, 176–177).

The reform of the social security system was also a very controversial issue. Article 13 of the AES stipulated the creation of a commission with representatives from the signatories to develop a plan to do this. The government developed its own proposal, the so-called Orange Book, that, according to UGT leaders, reduced and worsened existing coverage because it tightened the conditions for receiving benefits while reducing the amount of future pensions (Domínguez 1990, 97). The varied interpretations of the government's proposal resulted in intense disputes between the government and the union, and even within the union, with some members of its board supporting government positions.[11] It resulted in the first major confrontation between the party/government and the union. For the first time, the union took its opposition to the streets, organizing a rally to oppose the law in 1985.

The UGT leaders were also disappointed by the failure of the government to extend unemployment benefits. The government expanded those benefits to only 42 percent by 1986 (the AES had set an objective of 48 percent for that year). UGT discontent with the AES' results, however, was tempered by the fact that the pact allowed for the participation of the union in economic policymaking, thus strengthening the position of the union (Domínguez 1990, 98). The CEOE did not like the results either. It emphasized the nonfulfillment of critical aspects of the pact, particularly the reform of the social security system—it thought that the government's reform was insufficient—and the refusal by the government to bring into line Spanish laws with the EC's. This non-fulfillment led to business' decision to abandon the commission in charge of following up the implementation of the AES in mid-1985 (Iglesias 1990, 170–175).

The public assessment of the AES, however, was very positive. Wages increased 7.4 percent in 1985 and 8.13 percent in 1986, and inflation was reduced to 8.1 percent in 1985, but grew slightly in 1986 (8.3 percent), partly due to the introduction of the Value Added Tax, which forced the government to change its preliminary inflation objective from 6 to 8 percent. There was also a dramatic decrease in the number of strikes (6,357 in 1984, and 2,803 in 1985). This good performance, however, was tempered by some bad results: Unemployment remained high (2,731,505 people remained unemployed in 1985, or 20.4 percent), and inflation, despite its reduction, continued very high compared to that of Spain's neighbors—the average inflation in the EC was 3.7 percent in 1986 (Führer 1996, 343; Iglesias 1990, 174–175).

II. The End of Concertation in Spain

One of the major impetuses behind the concertation process had been the desire to come up with mechanisms that would help consolidate the new democratic regime. Concertation was viewed as a way to mitigate labor conflict and thereby placate the most extremist sectors of the right and the military (Forewaker 1987, 61). When the socialists won the elections of 1982 with an overwhelming majority, the change in power was viewed as the cornerstone of the transition process.[12] During the second half of the 1980s three major developments had an impact on the concertation process: The approval of the Union Freedom Act, the process of re-industrialization, and the 1986 elections to the work councils.

In August of 1985 Parliament approved the new Ley Orgánica de Libertad Sindical (LOLS, the Union Freedom Act), which finally institutionalized the role of trade unions in Spain. Many of its provisions have been included previously in the centralized agreements. This law finally established the framework that regulated industrial relations in Spain and was fully consistent with the stipulations included in the 1978 Constitution. It also established the legal framework under that unions would operate and outlined a system of guarantees and rights for union representatives in firms. One of the most important aspects of the law was that it introduced the concept of "most representative union," that established a system based on powerful union confederations and hindered the survival of weak and small unions, thus preventing the atomization of the labor movement. The approval of this law was followed by the return to unions of goods and properties expropriated by the Franco regime. Both factors contributed to a period of good relationships between the government and the unions—particularly UGT. It would not last long, however.

The year 1985 also witnessed the intensification of the process of industrial rationalization. The Ministry of Industry approved a "White Book" on the topic, that was followed by the approval in Parliament in December of 1985 of the Industrial Rationalization and Re-industrialization Law. The UGT contributed to the development of the law. It included provisions that established the continuation of contracts for workers in firms affected by the process. The law also introduced provisions to develop "promotion funds" that would provide financial resources to compensate workers who accepted early retirements. The CCOO, however, refused to participate in the law's development, demanding the creation of alternative industries prior to the implementation of any rationalization plan in any firm or sector in order to make certain that the laid-off workers would have new jobs.

Elections to the works councils took place again in the second half of 1986. These elections raised high expectations because they were the first that took place within the new legal framework. At the same time, there was interest in seeing the reaction of workers to the policies of the PSOE and the cooperative strategy followed by the socialist union, the UGT. The results confirmed the dominance of the UGT (40.5 percent), closely followed by the CCOO (34.1 percent). These elections, however, influenced the rounds of negotiations that started in mid-1986 to try to negotiate a new agreement for 1987. Despite the fact that the UGT had won the elections, the union had seen how support among workers from larger firms (strategic for the union) had dipped vis-à-vis the CCOO. In firms with more than 1,000 workers, the UGT had elected only 28 percent of the representatives, while the CCOO's candidates exceed 37 percent (Ministerio de Trabajo y Seguridad Social 1987, 127). Many people within the union considered these results a strategic defeat, (that they attributed to the union's moderate stance), and feared further losses in future elections if the policy of concertation was continued.[13]

The budget for 1987 established an inflation target for 1987 of 5 percent and applied this figure to various budgetary items, for example, civil service wages and pensions. In return, the socialist government expected the UGT to accept wage demands of 5 percent in the next centralized agreement. The union, however, refused to accept that target. Emphasizing the positive economic prospects for 1986, the fact that social concertation had resulted in a fall in real wages for workers, and, further, that unemployment had not been reduced, the UGT and CCOO refused to restrain wages. Unions did not accept, either, the government's plans to restructure much of the outdated public industrial sector in exchange for a vague promise of economic recovery and more jobs. Therefore, the CCOO and UGT decided to demand higher wage increases to compensate workers for previous real income losses; they argued that wage improvements should be introduced across the board and should not be tied to productivity gains. In making this latter demand, the UGT departed from one of the major foundations of concertation, namely, the link between forecasted inflation and wage increases. Instead, in order to restore workers' real wages, the UGT and CCOO asked for increases two points above the government's inflation target of 5 percent and stressed the need to boost demand and increase social expenditures to create new jobs. The government and business association refused to compromise, and negotiations failed.

Despite the fact that firms gladly accepted the recommendations of the government to increase wages up to 5 percent since the economy was picking up and demand was expanding, business negotiated higher wage increases (the average increase at the end of the year was 6.82 percent).[14] In contrast, the government stuck to its objective and raised public salaries by only 5 percent. This resulted in dramatic explosion of industrial conflict (50 million hours lost, the highest since 1979). In 1987, however, despite the lack of agreement, wages increased only 1.8 points above the governmental forecast of inflation, which was almost fulfilled; it was 5.3 percent at the end of the year. This result reaffirmed the unions' position that wages had no substantial impact on inflation—the opposite of government's position.

According to some authors, falling inflation coupled with the recovery of the Spanish economy after 1987 diluted the prospects for a social pact (Moscoso 1995, Espina 1991).[15] The Prime Minister, Felipe González, invited the social actors to negotiate a new agreement for 1988, and offered the possibility of agreement on the budget for that year. At the end, however, the negotiations went nowhere (see Moscoso 1995, 42–49). The government was adamant about the need to develop a restrictive budget to control inflation and foster an environment where business profits would flourish—which in turn would result in higher investment and more jobs. The UGT and CCOO, on the contrary, demanded the fulfillment of previous commitments (such as the compromise included in the AES to increase unemployment benefits to 48 percent of the unemployed), and the implementation of an expansive policy—that is, higher pensions and public service salaries, higher public expenditures, and wage increases beyond expected inflation (3 percent)—to stimulate domestic demand. Further disputes on other issues (fiscal policy, unemployment benefits, pensions) caused the relationship between the government and the unions to deteriorate.[16] While growth accelerated due to the increase in demand, inflation bounced back to 5.7 percent at the end of 1988, well exceeding the government's target (3 percent).

The failure to meet the inflation target undermined the government's credibility vis-à-vis the unions, and the accelerated growth of the economy, that resulted in a dramatic recovery of business profits, radicalized union strategies. Economic recovery intensified in 1987, mostly driven by the entrance of foreign capital into Spain as a result of the liberalization of the capital and real estate markets. This recovery, however, did not result in a significant improvement of unemployment. When unions realized at the end of 1987 that the business cycle was turning up, they decided that labor had suffered most of the cost of economic adjustment and that vague promises would no longer be enough to restrain wages. In other words, economic recovery caused distributional problems because unions wanted to reap its fruits and demanded compensation for the sacrifices their members had made over the past years (Espina 1991, 345). Unions argued that concertation had resulted in a loss of 10 percentage points in real wages and emphasized especially the deterioration of incomes among public sector employees due to the fact that the latter could not exercise collective bargaining. They also contended that employers had not fulfilled their part of the agreements, particularly in regard to their compromise to establish mechanisms guaranteeing that wage increases would be tied to productivity gains. The reluctance of the employers to implement these clauses had resulted in little increase in purchasing power—that is, 0.3 percent in 1985 and 0.8 percent in 1986 (Moscoso 1995, 22 and 43; Espina 1991, 346). As a result of these conditions, the unions decided to escalate their wage and benefits demands. Industrial conflict intensified in 1987 when unions decided to call additional strikes to force the hand of business and government.

The situation further deteriorated in 1988 when the unions called a general strike to oppose the government's Plan de Empleo Juvenil (the Youth Employment Plan).[17] The overwhelming success of this strike led to new negotiations between the unions and the government. The results were the so-called Acuerdos del 25 de Enero (the Agreements of January 25), which bound the government to accept collective bargaining in public enterprises. They also included safeguard clauses for public sector wages, the retroactive indexing of such wages, raises in pensions to compensate for past incomes losses, and increases in unemployment benefits (the same demands of the unions during the 1988 general strike). Union leaders, however, emphasized that these new agreements did not mean a return to centralized tripartite bargaining and declared that the era of concertation was dead (Redondo 1990, 19). They also refused to take seriously the government's proposed "Competitiveness Pact" of 1990 to prepare Spain for the Common Market. Union leaders saw it as a disguised attempt to implement incomes policies.[18] The government, for its part, emphasizing that inflation depended on collective bargaining, was forced to choose monetary instruments to quell inflation (Moscoso 1995, 45).

All this occurred at a time when the other western European countries were entering a severe recession. As the recession swept through Europe, the unemployment situation deteriorated even further in Spain. The new policy course, which was based on very restrictive monetary policies, meant that the government could not use the deficit to stimulate demand, particularly at a time when the increase in unemployment meant further outlays in unemployment benefits. When the situation further deteriorated, unions and the government exchanged accusations and refused to cooperate with each other. Unions blamed the recession on the government's so-called neoliberal polices.[19]

The socialist government, for its part, insisted that the failure of concertation had to be attributed to the unions. It accused them of irresponsible wage demands and attacked them for defending very limited interests: Those of current workers with indefinite contracts and relatively high salaries and benefits. Unions for their part blamed the government, arguing that it had failed to deliver on its promises. For unions, concertation was also an instrument of solidarity and income redistribution. The union leaders rejected the government accusations, and emphasized that they also defended the interests of the less-favored and the unemployed. The CCOO and the UGT approved jointly the *Propuesta Sindical Prioritaria* in October of 1989—the trade unions' plan's priorities. This proposal meant that for the first time since Franco's death, unions had come up with their own alternative economic plan that included not only subjects relevant to collective bargaining and industrial relations, but also social demands to help the less favored. This plan included proposals to enhance working conditions, to create jobs, to extend social and unemployment benefits, to develop a "social salary," to enhance conditions relating to the access of health care and housing, as well as measures to foster income redistribution—such as progressive fiscal policies—and better wages for pensioners and public employees. The plan also proposed the creation of investment funds following the Swedish model and the increasing participation of workers in business decisions (Roca 1993, 264).

The government reacted to this plan with its own proposal to renew social concertation. The Minister of Economy, Carlos Solchaga, introduced in 1991 the *Pacto Social del Progreso* (the Social Pact for Progress).[20] In this pact the government sought to gain the collaboration of unions to address the unemployment problem. After several meetings, however, the negotiators failed to reach a compromise. The government accused the unions' of lack of interest.[21] While the government made concessions in social issues—that is, it increased expenditures in minimum pensions and unemployment benefits and established noncontributory pensions in 1990—the unions refused to moderate their wage demands. Unions viewed government calls for wage moderation as attempts to ignore the fact that wage increases were caused by productivity growth and ignored them. Consequently, wages grew an average of 8.3 percent in 1990, 8.1 percent in 1991, and 7.2 percent in 1992 (Moscoso, 1995, 45–47).

An additional factor that diluted the prospects for a pact was the fact that the economic crisis had resulted in further unemployment that, in turn, had caused a decline in social security contributions to the system and a dramatic increase in unemployment benefit outlays. The government, in order to meet its deficit targets and to limit the burgeoning deficit, as well as to avoid the collapse of the unemployment benefits system, issued the so-called "Decretazo," reducing benefits and cutting the period of coverage. The reaction of the unions was predictable. They blamed the government for the near collapse of the system of unemployment benefits and refused to acknowledge that only a cooperative relationship among themselves, the government, and business might have helped to detect and punish the fraudulent use of that system by workers, that had been a particular problem of late. The unions called a general strike for May 1992 (Moscoso 1995, 47). Its relative failure compared to that of 1988 crushed any hope for new concertation. The government, strengthened by the failure of the strike, refused to acknowledge union demands and proclaimed that social concertation was not necessary.

As a further background for the recession, it is noted that the World Exposition and the Olympic Games in 1992 had delayed the intensity of the economic crisis for a few months in Spain. When it arrived in full strength, however, it was worsened by the collapse of the European Monetary System. After the general elections of 1993—won by the PSOE with a slim majority—Felipe González named a new economic team. Pedro Solbes replaced Carlos Solchaga as Minister of Economics. The crisis, however, intensified through 1993. Unemployment increased by 500,000 people, wages increased almost two points beyond expected inflation and there was a budget deficit of 1.5 billion pesetas caused by a reduction of 1 billion pesetas in expected income, and a dramatic increase in unemployment outlays.

The government reacted to the worsening situation with a new call to the unions in the summer of 1993 to negotiate an agreement to address unemployment. Negotiations took place between July and December of 1993. The government wanted to develop a new system that would hold down wages below inflation over the following three years, as well as introduce new laws that would end fixed-term employment contracts, permit job mobility, streamline redundancy procedures, and lower severance costs, and that would replace sectoral collective wage agreements with case-by-case deals (*Financial Times,* November 25, 1998, 3). These demands were a response to the analysis that the new economic team made of the country's economic problems.[22] Negotiations between the government and the unions dragged for weeks with few results.

The government accused the unions of lack of interest when the unions' leaders refused to negotiate during the month of August because they were "on vacation."[23] By this time the relationship between the UGT and the government had deteriorated so much that the CCOO was the more receptive of the unions to the government's proposals.[24] The UGT was in the midst of a serious financial scandal that would have negative implications for its leaders. The collapse of the union's housing project, the PSV (*Plan Sindical de Viviendas,* or the Union Housing Plan)—with some funds being diverted to finance the union, as well as involving personal embezzlement—dragged down the leaders of the union. Within this context the negotiations became increasingly entangled. The government argued that it did not have financial resources to bail out the union and refused to do so (Mr. González, the Socialist Prime Minister, claimed that the main difficulty in reaching a compromise was "that the government has nothing to give—the unions—in exchange"[25]). At the same time, the union felt it had to maintain its independence and confirm that its own goals would not be compromised by the need for the government's help.[26] Simultaneously, union leaders were reluctant to sign anything with the government because it would mean an implicit support of its economics policies, which was something they adamantly opposed.[27] This was also a time when another series of economic scandals were discovered, scandals in that some former members of the economic team were implicated—that is, the president of the Bank of Spain, Mariano Rubio, became entangled in the Ibercorp case involving influence peddling, the use of privileged information, and tax evasion. Union leaders, very reluctant to sign a pact with the government from the very beginning, used these events to justify their opposition to the government. At the end the negotiations failed, and this resulted in escalating industrial unrest. The negotiations, however, were probably doomed from the start, Mr. González edged as much in an interview with the *Financial Times* (November 25, 1993, p. 3) in which he claimed:

> The great problem of (the social) pact is that . . . we are asking for an incomes policy to improve competitiveness, for changes in traditional collective bargaining procedures and for a modification of the labor market that will make it more flexible . . . this requires a cultural change in unions attitudes and this is very difficult.

The unions may have been blamed for intransigence, but the government refused to acknowledge that the deterioration of the economic and political situation had been partly the result of the breakdown of concertation and rejected efforts at further concertation with the unions.[28] It is also worth emphasizing that the labor market rigidities concerning fixed employment conditions, severance terms, and job classifications that the government was trying to modify at that time, were enshrined in a reform of the Workers' Statute that was introduced by the socialist government and approved with the support of socialist representatives in Parliament in 1984. Moreover, that government was also responsible for the inflationary spiral. During the second half of the 1980s, when the economy was expanding rapidly, the government did very little to curb inflationary wage agreements in public sector companies and forced up unit labor costs by transferring a growing social security burden on to companies. By 1993, 24 percent of Spain's social security expenditure was financed directly by companies (the average in the EU was 9.8 percent) (see *Financial Times,* Thursday November 25, 1993, 3). At this time, however, Spain was entering the second year of recession, but the unions refused to bulge. At the end, the attempt to secure an incomes policy for the following three years failed and industrial unrest escalated in response to the government's unilateral actions.

To worsen this already poisoned climate, in 1994 the government introduced a package of measures to deregulate the labor market. This included the first serious attempt since 1984 at making the labor market more flexible. Its objective was to further develop the new contracts that had been introduced in the Workers' Statute of 1980, particularly the part-time and short-term ones that offered alternatives to the traditional full-time, indefinite contracts. This proposal, however, totally alienated union leadership, that argued that the newly proposed contracts would result in a more precarious labor market wherein the temporary workers would replace full-time ones but would lack the strength to organize. The unions emphasized the fact that Spain already had the highest amount of temporary labor of the European Union, caused by the seasonal character of many jobs—for example, agriculture, tourism, fishing, and construction. The plan, however, acknowledged that fact and included measures to encourage the transformation of temporary contracts into permanent ones—that is, it gave up to a 50 percent discount on social security contributions for certain categories of workers. The unions, however, called for a new general strike on January 24, 1994, to force the government to withdraw the proposal. The strike was not as successful as the 1988 one, and the government stayed the course and refused to bend to the union demands. The law was finally approved by Parliament in May 1994. The implementation of the reform resulted in more contracts and lower unemployment but did not eradicate the unemployment problem (Moscoso, 1995, 47).

After 1995 the economy recovered but the government became increasingly entangled in several scandals, which worsened the political environment. In March of that year, the Ibercorp scandal, in that some of the members of the former economic team were implicated, came to a head and caused the resignation of Carlos Solchaga, former Minister of Economics and Speaker of the Socialist Group in Parliament. The government's position was further worsened when some former members of the government, who were implicated in other corruption scandals, and the Grupos Armados de Liberación (GAL) case—which involved death squads organized within the government apparatus in the early 1980s to combat terrorism—became public. At this time, unions also entered a period of internal conflict and dissent. The leaders of the UGT resigned in 1995 as a consequence of the PSV scandal. A new leader, Cándido Méndez, was elected as Secretary General.

He faced a strong challenge from the progovernment sector of the union that forced him to call a new extraordinary congress in 1995. As of 1999, he is now in full control of the union. In 1996 there was also a final split within CCOO, with the former Secretary General, Marcelino Camacho, being left out of the executive team. In this context of internal division and scandal, any serious attempt towards concertation was futile.

All these developments weakened the position of the Socialist government and resulted in the call for elections on March 3, 1996. These elections were won by the conservative Popular Party (PP, Partido Popular). For the first time in almost 14 years the Socialists had to leave power. The arrival of a new government fostered a new cooperative environment among the social actors that culminated last April 1997, in the signature of a new centralized pact between the employer's association and the major unions (see Conclusions). The government also reached agreements with unions to reform the pension system and the scheme to support agricultural workers.

III. Evaluation of Concertation

Concertation agreements were reached between 1979–1986. In this section, I shall evaluate their implementation and their effects both on the social actors and on the Spanish economy. I shall consider the political objectives implicit in the agreements in chapter 6.

In the previous section we have seen how the social actors had different objectives for the process of concertation. For the business organization the major objective was to control wage growth through incomes policy in order to reduce labor costs and increase profits. The government, for its part, saw concertation as a valid instrument to control inflation through incomes policy, with limited costs in terms of unemployment. Finally, unions sought to enhance the purchasing capacity of workers, or in case that was not possible, to receive compensation from the other actors—that is, increases in social outlays, extended benefits, institutional recognition, and subsidies.

I shall conclude in this section that concertation was successful in implementing incomes policy. During these years, wages grew systematically below the wage range established in the agreements, and this development helped to reduce inflation, to increase business profits, and to foster investment in the second half of the 1980s. Concertation also contributed to the institutionalization of a new system of industrial relations. After the collapse of the authoritarian regime and before concertation started in 1977, the industrial relations setting was underdeveloped. Concertation helped the unions to participate in the development of the new system. The 1979 ABI drew a partial blueprint of what would be the guidelines of this new system, and the 1980–1981 AMI contributed to define the role of union representatives in firms. Centralized agreements, therefore, served to consolidate the unions' institutional position, including participation in several state agencies. At the same time, one of the most relevant consequences of the concertation process was the consolidation of an imperfect duopoly within the union movement, with the UGT and CCOO as the powerful unions. This development was confirmed by the 1985 Union Freedom Act, which established the concept of "most representative union."

One of the most important objectives of these agreements from the standpoint of the government and business, as I have said above, was the implementation of incomes policies. Except for the ABI, all the centralized agreements included ranges of wage increases that would be later implemented in the course of collective bargaining. What is remarkable about the concertation process in Spain is that, despite the fact that only one of the major trade union confederations, the UGT, participated in all the agreements the wage suggestions for these agreements were almost universally respected. The explanation for this lies, at least partially, in the fact that the Spanish legislation authorizes that, as long as the union has an absolute majority in the negotiating commission, the resulting agreement, despite its limited applicability, can be applied to all workers.[29] The analysis of average wage increases during the period of the pacts shows that when one of the major unions took part in the agreements, average wage increases were kept within the limits stipulated in the agreement, as illustrated in Table 3.1.

Although wage moderation cannot be attributed to concertation only, it cannot be denied that concertation contributed to wage moderation. Other factors such as labor market conditions (for example, higher unemployment

Table 3.1 Final Wage Increases, 1979–1986

Year	Agreement	Negotiated Wage Increases (%)	Final Wage Increases (%)
1978	Pactos de la Moncloa	20	20.6
1979	No agreement	11–14	14.1
1980	AMI	13–16	15.3
1981	AMI	11–15	13.1
1982	ANE	9–11	10.5
1983	AI	9.5–12.5	11.4
1984	No agreement	6.5	7.7
1985	AES	5.5–7.5	7.4
1986	AES	7.2–8.5	8.1

Source: Roca 1993, Table 6, p. 187. Reprinted with permission. Data from MTSS: *Boletín de Estadísticas Laborales.* Various years.

depresses wages) also had influence in wage increases, but concertation kept collective bargaining within the parameters determined by the agreements, lowered the number of disputes—which are also linked to the growth of wages—and introduced a new system to determine wage increases based on expected inflation (as opposed to the old system based on the prior year's inflation). All these factors had a very important impact on wage increases. In those years when there were no agreements and unions opposed the government's recommendations, the objectives set by the government were not achieved—for example, in 1984 the government set the target for wage increases at 6.5 percent, unions opposed it and demanded a wage increase of 8 percent, and wages increased an average of 7.7 percent at the end of the year. When concertation collapsed after 1986, the same thing happened, as illustrated in Table 3.2:

As shown above, the absence of concertation resulted in wage increases above the objectives determined by the government except for 1994–1995 when Spain was in the midst of a sharp economic recession. This leads us to conclude that concertation was successful in implementing incomes polices and contributed to wage moderation. It is also important to emphasize, that despite wage moderation, there was a very modest growth in wages, averaging 0.4 percent from 1979–1986 (Folgado 1989, 490; Roca 1993, 221). Concertation, however, did not result in real income gains for workers. Average wage increases grew slower than prices and workers lost purchasing power as illustrated in Table 3.3.

Table 3.2 Inflation Targets and Final Wages, 1984–1996

Year	Government Inflation Objective (%)	Final Wage Increases (%)
1984	6.5	7.7
1987	5	6.5
1988	3	6.4
1989	6.8	7.8
1990	6.7	8.3
1991	5.9	8.1
1992	5.9	7.3
1993	4.6	5.5
1994	4.7	3.6
1995	4.7	3.9
1996	3.5	3.8

Source: Data from Consejo Económico y Social: *Memoria;* and MTSS: *Boletín de Estadísticas Laborales.* Various years.

Table 3.3 Purchasing Power, 1978–1990

Year	Purchasing Power	Year	Purchasing Power
1978	1.2	1985	–0.9
1979	–1.7	1986	–0.6
1980	–0.6	1987	1.3
1981	–1.5	1988	1.6
1982	–3.4	1989	1.8
1983	–1.2	1990	1.6
1984	–3.5		

Source: From *El País,* Monday November 18, 1996. Data from MTSS: *Boletín de Estadísticas Laborales.* Various years.

Another major objective of concertation was to reduce labor costs because they were among the highest in Europe. Indirect labor costs included social security contributions from workers and firms. The government had three possibilities to reduce them: First, to increase the contributions of the firms; second, to increase the contributions of the workers; and third, to shift the burden of payment to the state. The first option, however, would have meant a deterioration of the competitive position of firms. Raising workers' contributions, the second option, would have made it impossible to achieve wage moderation because workers would have sought to compensate for higher contributions with higher wage demands. The participant social actors agreed that the best option was the third, to increase the state's contribution. Therefore, these pacts introduced clauses shifting the burden to the state, that increased payments to social security from 3.3 percent in 1977 to 21.3 percent in 1985 (Roca 1993, 194–197).

Another set of issues included in the agreements were unemployment benefits and pensions. Their extension and expansion were one of the major objectives for unions. If we take into account all social expenditures including health, education, housing, and other benefits, from 1977 to 1986 there was a systematic increase in social outlays from the state. In other words, the state acted to redistribute wealth to the less favored. In this regard, concertation agreements included compromises to raise pensions, and pension expenditures (vis-à-vis the Gross Domestic Product, or GDP) increased from 7.41 percent in 1977 to 9.91 percent in 1986 (Roca 1990, 204). The ANE also introduced a new "assistance subsidy"—that is, subsidies for people who did not contribute to social security—that benefited over 100,000 people. This measure was needed because in 1980, as a consequence of the new Basic Employment Act, the number of people with the right to receive a subsidy from the state was cut. Increased state outlays, however, did not compensate for the decline in the proportion of net wages to the total national income (Roca 1990, 238). In addition, the number of people covered by the state social security system decreased between 1976 (62.2 percent) and 1988 (28.8 percent) (Roca 1993, 203). In an effort to halt the reduction of governmental subsidies to the unemployed, the Article 10 of the AES introduced a compromise to reform the existing legislation in order to extend the coverage of unemployed people from 43 percent in 1985 and 48 percent in 1986. The government did not fulfill this promise, and only after 1986 did coverage increase to include 42 percent of unemployed people.

From the standpoint of the government, the single most important objective of the concertation process was the reduction of inflation. In this regard, it has been argued that "the economic content of the pacts implied wage moderation in exchange for a moderate monetary policy, whose objective was the gradual control over inflation" (Pérez Díaz 1986, 107, my translation). Between 1964–1977 gross real wages grew faster than productivity, increasing 6.69 percent while productivity grew 5.08 percent. This tendency was effectively reversed after 1977 when gross real wages grew less than productivity (between 1977–1986, the years of concertation, wages increased an average of 1.51 percent, while productivity increased 3.51 between 1977–1984) (Martínez-Alier and Roca 1986, 19 and 31). The result was that concertation contributed to the objective to reduce inflation through wage moderation, and inflation was systematically reduced during the years of concertation—from 24.5 percent in 1977 to 8.8 percent in 1986. By 1988, inflation was at 4.8 percent and the differential with EC countries had been reduced by almost 12 points. The only exception was 1986, when inflation did not decrease, but this anomaly is explained by the introduction of the Value Added Tax (VAT), a consequence of Spain's entry into the European Community that year.

The reduction in inflation can be attributed both to the reduction in unitary labor costs, as well as by expectations that inflation would be reduced.[30] Wages grew 18.6 percent in 1979, before the AMI. This growth was dramatically altered as a consequence of concertation. In 1986, the last year of the AES, wages grew only 9.6 percent. In this regard, one of the most positive results of the concertation process was that it introduced macroeconomic considerations into collective bargaining, that made it possible for wages to behave according to inflationary objectives. As illustrated in Table 3.4 and Figure 3.3, if we compare wage growth with inflation, we see that wages systematically grew below inflation during the years of concertation.

This can more clearly be seen in graph form.

It is important to emphasize, however, that this achievement was accomplished despite the fact that the government failed to fulfill its inflation objectives. As Table 3.5 shows, inflation grew systematically above the target

Table 3.4 Final Wages versus Final Inflation, 1978–1988

Year	Final Wage Increases (%)[1]	Final Inflation (%)[2]
1978	20.5	19.8
1979	14.1	15.7
1980	15.3	15.6
1981	13.1	14.5
1982	10.5	14.4
1983	11.4	12.2
1984	7.7	11.3
1985	7.4	8.8
1986	8.1	8.8
1987	6.5	5.2
1988	6.2	4.8

Sources: [1]From Roca 1993, Table 6, p. 187. Reprinted with permission. Data from MTSS: *Boletín de Estadísticas Laborales.* Various years. The data for the years 1982, 1984, 1985, 1986, and 1988 do not include the application of revision clauses.
[2]From Roca 1993, Table 14, p. 193. Reprinted with permission. Data from: Instituto Nacional de Estadística.

Figure 3.3 Wages versus Inflation, 1978–1988

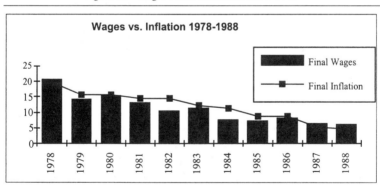

Data from MTSS: *Boletín de Estadísticas Laborales.* Various Years.

determined by the government for the following year. Part of the explanation for this could be that most agreements included "safeguard clauses" to protect workers when inflation grew beyond the government's target.[31] In those cases workers could renegotiate retroactively wage increases that further increased inflation (Roca 1993, 193). These clauses usually applied after six months.

Table 3.5 Inflation Targets, 1978–1988

Year	Expected Inflation (%)	Final Inflation Annual Average (%)
1978	22	19.8
1979	12	15.7
1980	15	15.6
1981	14	14.5
1982	12.5	14.4
1983	12	12.2
1984	8	11.3
1985	7	8.8
1986	8	8.8
1987	5	5.2
1988	3	4.8

Source: Roca 1993, Table 14, p. 193. Reprinted with permission. Data from Instituto Nacional de Estadística.

Another possible explanation for this development lies in the government's lack of credibility (see Conclusions). In this regard, one of the most important determinants of inflation growth is expected inflation, because firms determine their prices taking into account not only labor costs but also the prices of their competitors, which in turn will themselves be influenced by expected inflation (Roca 1993, 192). The fact that the government's objectives lacked credibility led both business and unions to expect higher inflation and, thus, to adjust their demands and forecasts accordingly. The government also failed to align inflation targets with those of other EC countries, and Spanish inflation was systematically higher than in the rest of Europe, eroding the competitive position of Spanish exports. The credibility of the government forecasts was further cast into doubt when the government failed to implement policies that would realistically reduce inflation. For instance, the acceleration of the public deficit on a yearly basis—that is, from 3.9 percent in 1981 to 5.6 percent in 1982—intensified pressures on monetary policies and resulted in higher financial costs for business, that in turn resulted in further inflationary pressures (Pérez 1997). This problem was intensified in the second half of the 1980s when the inflation fight was mostly left to monetary policies. The lack of congruence between monetary and fiscal policies resulted in a deterioration of macroeconomic conditions in the early 1990s. Despite these facts, concertation kept wages below inflation's growth, and this supported other economic stabilization measures, increasing investors' confidence, business' profits, and boosting investment and employment in the second half of the 1980s. After 1986,

when concertation collapsed, unions demands intensified, and wages systematically grew above inflation.

Another major benefit of concertation was the dramatic decrease in the
number of strikes. The collapse of the Franco regime intensified industrial
conflict, which in many cases involved political demands. Concertation contributed to a better canalization of industrial demands. While the decrease
in the number of strikes cannot be attributed solely to concertation,[32] as illustrated in Table 3.6, industrial conflict intensified in those years when concertation failed—1979, 1984, and after 1985 (between 1986 and 1990 the
annual average of working days lost through strikes per 1,000 employees was
647, the second highest in Western Europe after Greece). (See "Spain Survey," in *The Economist,* April 25, 1992, 14).

The major consequences of wage moderation, reduced disputes, and
lower inflation were the recovery of domestic demand and the dramatic expansion of investment in the second half of the 1980s. Business profits recovered after 1985. While it is true that other factors contributed to this
development, for example, Spain's entry to the EC and the decline of energy
costs, wage moderation had a very positive effect on business profits. Labor
costs have always been a very important component of total costs for Spanish business—no less than 60 percent in the 1970s. From 1982 to 1986,

Table 3.6 Industrial Conflict, 1978–1988

Year	Days Lost[1]	Variation (%)	Number of Strikes[2]
1977	16,641.7		974
1978	11,550.9	–31.6	1,356
1979	18,917.0	39.2	1,789
1980	6,177.5	–77.4	1,315
1981	5,153.8	–16.6	1,792
1982	2,787.6	–46.0	1,743
1983	4,416.7	46.9	1,926
1984	6,357.8	31.6	1,941
1985	3,223.5	–49.3	1,658
1986	2,279.4	–29.3	1,961
1987	5,025.0	64.7	2,576
1988	6,843.4	26.6	2,233

[1]From Roca 1993, Table 38, p. 258. Reprinted with permission. Sources: For the period 1977–
1979, Ministerio de Economía y Hacienda, 1985: *La Negociación Colectiva en 1985,* p. 207;
from 1979, Ministerio de Trabajo y Seguridad Social, *Boletín de Estadísticas laborales,* various
years. The data for 1988 does not include the general strike. Reprinted with permission. See
also Führer 1996, 343.

[2]Ministerio de Trabajo y Seguridad Social, *Boletín de Estadísticas laborales,* various years.

however, that figure was reduced by 6.4 percent and this coincided with a recovery of profits. Lower costs resulted in higher cash flow, that allowed firms to pay part of their debts and reduce their financial costs; business debt in relation to internal resources was reduced from 103.3 percent in 1982 to 53.8 percent in 1988 (Folgado 1989, 494). This reduction resulted in further profits, which increased the capacity of business to reinvest. Higher profits also increased the profitability of business investment, which expanded 7.5 percent between 1985 and 1988, and made investing in business more attractive.

Another objective pursued by unions was the reduction of working hours. Except for the AES, all pacts included working hours. The most important reduction took place with the 1983 AI, that established a maximum of 1,826 working hours per year. This agreement was subsequently followed by the approval of a law in June of 1983 that reduced the work week to 40 hours. The AES did not reduce the work week any further. Unions and business realized that the reduction agreed in the AI was substantial and before moving any further, they decided to wait and see what would be the effects of the reduction on the economy (Domínguez, 1990, 96). Table 3.7 illustrates the number of working hours established in each agreement:

In summary, the number of working hours was systematically reduced through collective bargaining, and actual worked hours grew below the maximum stipulated by the centralized agreements or legislation. Concertation contributed to this development. It encouraged negotiation, set a maximum number of work hours, and helped to foster consensus about the impact of

Table 3.7 Working Hours

Year	Agreement	Maximum Number of Yearly Hours	Actual Increase
1980	AMI	1980	1948.5[a]
1981	AMI	1930	1914.3[a]
1982	AMI	1880	1877.3[b]
1983	AI	1826	1845.2
1984	Law June 1983	1826	1798
1985	Law June 1983	1826	1793.1
1986	Law June 1983	1826	1786.8

From Roca 1993, Table 17, p. 198. Reprinted with permission. Source: Data from Dirección General de Politica Económica y Prevision (1982), and MTSS, *Boletín de Estadísticas Laborales.*
[a]Includes a sample of 300 firm and sectoral collective agreements, that affected 2,720,537 workers.
[b]It does not include data from Catalonia and the Basque Country.

reducing hours on the whole economy with a view toward encouraging job creation.

On top of these economic objectives, one of the major goals of concertation for business was to increase the flexibility of the labor market. The Spanish labor market had inherited very restrictive legislation from the Franco years. One of the economic pillars of the dictatorship was based on social peace and low wages in exchange for lifetime job security. This had resulted in one of the most inflexible labor markets in Western Europe, with high costs and bureaucratic difficulties involved in dismissals. Through concertation, employers sought to address this problem. The 1982 ANE included a secret clause wherein the signatories agreed that the government should proceed to develop the mechanisms established in the 1980 Workers' Statute to foster temporary hiring, with certain limits to avoid its overly broad use. The weakness of the UCD government, coupled with the electoral victory of the PSOE that year, delayed these reforms. As we have noted before, the AES included Article 17, which sought to bring the Spanish labor legislation into line with the EC's. The lack of fulfillment of this article by the government was one of the reasons argued by the business organization to leave the AES commission.

In 1985 the government introduced legislation to reform the Workers' Statute in order to develop new temporary contracts to foster youth employment. A major consequence was a dramatic increase in temporary contracts that resulted in the increasing duality of the labor market. By 1988, 25.1 percent of the working population was under temporary contract. By 1996—there was another reform that introduced new modalities for temporary workers in 1994—97 percent of the contracts signed that year were temporary. The inability by the social actors to reach agreements to address this problem had been one negative aspect of the concertation process.

Yet another goal addressed by the pacts was productivity. The AMI, and later the ANE, included provisions to increase productivity and to reduce absenteeism. These clauses, however, were very general because of the fact that productivity and absenteeism were greatly influenced by external factors that were particular to each sector and firm and could not be synthesized in a centralized agreement. But productivity growth was a major concern for business. One of the features of the 1960s was that wages increased on a par with productivity. However, in the early 1980s wages regularly increased less than productivity. The centralized agreements introduced clauses linking wage increases to productivity increases. These clauses were mostly ignored because employers were reluctant to implement them out of fear that unions would push for demands to control the use of excess profits—something that Swedish unions had already attempted via "codetermination." From 1979 to 1986 productivity gains grew by 3.0 percent while wages increased only by 0.4 percent (Roca 1993, 221). This resulted in lower unitary costs—between 1977 and 1988 they were lowered by 13 percent. Only after 1986, when concertation collapsed, did industrial conflict intensify and unions demand higher wage increases to compensate for previous losses in purchasing power.

Another variable to be considered is the effect of concertation on investment. Between 1979 and 1985, investment decreased an average of 1.5 percent yearly. This decline, however, cannot be attributed to concertation. Investment is conditioned mainly by two factors (Folgado, 1989, 501): The profitability of capital and the intensity of demand. From 1979–1986, both factors did not favor investment. Demand was low as a consequence of the intensity of the recession, the increasing levels of unemployment, and low business profitability. This situation, however, changed dramatically in the second half of the 1980s. In this period, concertation contributed to increasing the profitability of capital via wage moderation, lower inflation, and reduced disputes, thus fostering the re-emergence of investment in the second half of the 1980s. Starting in 1985, investment increased from 18.9 percent in 1985 to 24.4 percent in 1989. Investment growth contributed to job creation in the second half of the 1980s, and employment grew an average of 2.9 percent.

Perhaps one of the most important objectives pursued by concertation was the reduction in unemployment. Emigration, coupled with the closed nature of the Spanish economy and high economic growth during the late 1960s and early 1970s, combined to keep unemployment levels in Spain under 2 percent. However, the second oil crisis at the end of the 1970s, joined with women's entrance into the labor market and the generation of baby boomers born in the 1960s, caused a dramatic increase in unemployment. This was at a time when industrial reconversion and the emergence of new methods of production that required new skills also contributed to the increase. By 1978 unemployment had increased to 7 percent.

The fight against unemployment had been offered by social democratic governments in other countries (Sweden, Austria, Belgium) as the main argument to implement incomes policies. These governments argued that wage moderation would result in higher profits, more investment, and more jobs. Concertation in Spain also aimed at reducing unemployment. However, from 1978 until 1985, the years of concertation, unemployment increased dramatically from 7 percent to 21.5 percent. Despite general proposals in all agreements on reducing unemployment, only the 1982 ANE explicitly set a target to maintain the existing level of jobs—that meant the creation of 350,000 jobs in 1982. This objective could not be achieved, and at the end of the year, 85,000 jobs had been lost (Roca 1993, 205). The fact that concertation did not result in lower levels of unemployment was used to discredit incomes polices. Unions argued that there was no point in sacrificing wage increases if more jobs were going to be destroyed. Unions also argued that wage moderation was contributing to low consumption and demand and thus to the low economic growth of the early 1980s. They also contended that incomes policies meant that the burden of the crisis had to be borne mostly by workers and refused to accept it.[33]

Spanish scholars have offered several reasons to account for the dramatic increase in unemployment in the early 1980s (Bentolila and Toharia 1991; Moscoso 1995, 35- 41; Fernández, Garrido, and Toharia 1991, 44–93; Solchaga 1997, 159–180; Blanchard et al., 1995; Bustelo 1986, 41; De la Dehesa 1997, 41–42). High unemployment levels are mainly attributed to three economic factors: the oil crisis of 1974, the opening of the Spanish economy to international competition in the 1980s, and the policy mix when Spain joined the EMS (De la Dehesa 1997, 41–42). The oil crisis of 1973 is largely credited with the rapid deterioration of economic conditions in Spain during the 1970s. The crisis had two main consequences. On the one hand, it resulted in the deterioration of real terms of trade that reduced significantly disposable real incomes. At the same time, and due to the crisis, the standards of living of the Spanish people should have adapted downward to compensate for the increase in oil prices. This did not happen. On the contrary, hourly earnings were on the rise between 1973 and 1977 (for instance, wages increased 12 percent in 1975 and 10.5 percent in 1976). This had very negative consequences and resulted in a high rate of inflation (it shot up from 4.9 percent in 1968 to 19.8 percent in 1978) and a large balance of payment deficit. The wage explosion was further aggravated by the rapid increase of social security contributions. This situation was further compounded by the worldwide slowdown of economic growth, which had a very negative effect on basic industries (for example, shipbuilding, steel, and capital goods) that continued with their expansion plans. The result of these developments was the near collapse of the Spanish production system because its impressive growth during the 1960s had been based on the availability and cheapness of two factors: labor and energy, which were no longer cheap or abundant (Bustelo 1986, 41). This economic crisis had deleterious consequences in the labor market. Nevertheless, while most economists (Bentolila and Dolado 1994) point to inflexible labor markets and a strong insider-outsider divide as the chief reason for Spain's persistently high employment rates,[34] other scholars have claimed that the real culprit may have been the rotten timing of structural change (Marimon and Zilibotti 1996).[35]

High economic growth in the second half of the 1980s and the recovery of domestic demand proved to be insufficient to reduce substantially the number of jobless people. While 1.5 million jobs were created between 1985 and 1990 (Maravall 1992, 28), the growth of the active labor force increased the pool of labor so that, at the end of the 1980s, unemployment remained close to 16 percent. This was at a time of very high economic growth and expansion of demand. Some authors (Moscoso 1995, pp. 34–41; Palacios 1995) have argued that the fact that the unemployment rate was not reduced significantly at a time of high GDP growth and demand proves that the unemployment problem in Spain is a supply side problem. In other words, the expansion of demand proved to be insufficient to reduce unemployment.[36]

It would be unfair, therefore, to blame high levels of unemployment on incomes policies. These policies do not have an immediate effect, and it would be reasonable to argue that the effects of wage moderation would take a while to materialize (see Roca 1993, 205–206). On the contrary, I would argue that wage moderation did contribute decisively to the recovery of firm profits and fostered investment. Consequently, when the economy picked up after 1985, employment grew.

Conclusions

Attempts to establish a neocorporatist system in Spain were unstable and incomplete. Unstable because the process did not always work—there were times when the social actors could not reach agreements (1984, 1987–96). Incomplete because the unions in Spain are weak and only represent a very small percentage of the labor force (around 13 percent). Nevertheless, these pacts had very positive effects: They contributed to foster consensus and negotiation among social actors, which resulted in a lower number of disputes. They fostered wage moderation and a sharp decline in inflation (from 26.4 percent in 1977 to 8.8 percent in 1986), which very much contributed to a better allocation of resources, the increasing competitiveness of Spanish firms, and the stability of the economic system. Furthermore, concertation, by introducing macroeconomic considerations into collective bargaining, made it possible for wages to behave according to governmental objectives on inflation. Wage moderation and lower inflation resulted in higher business profits that, in turn, fostered confidence, investment, and jobs in the second half of the 1980s. Finally, concertation contributed to the integration of the social actors, unions and business organizations, to the new political and economic system, and the consolidation and strengthening of the larger union confederations.

The beneficial effects of concertation in the economy, however, were not equally shared. Concertation did not result in real income gains for workers. In five of the seven years, average wages grew slower than prices, and from 1980–1986, the purchasing capacity of workers only grew 0.4 percent. Furthermore, in the period up to 1977 the increasing rate of the salaried labor (as opposed to self-employed), coupled with the growth in social security contributions (Toharia 1981) resulted in the increased share of wage incomes in GDP—that is, the share of wage incomes as a percent distribution of GDP at factor cost grew from 47.45 percent in 1964 to 58.08 percent in 1976. However, in the period after 1977, characterized by increasing unemployment and by concertation agreements, gross real wages grew less than productivity (productivity grew 3.51 percent between 1977–1984, while wages grew only 1.51 percent between 1977–1986), and therefore, the share of wage incomes in GDP diminished (from 58.08 percent in 1976 to 49.91 percent in 1986) (Martínez-Alier and Roca 1986, 19, 31, and 32). In other words, during the concertation years, worker incomes declined as a percentage of the total national income.

Concertation also failed to address unemployment, which increased from 7 percent in 1978 to 21 percent in 1986, due to, among other factors, the intensity of the economic crisis, labor market factors, the lack of competitiveness of Spanish firms, and new demographic developments. The measures introduced in the agreements could not cope with these developments.[37] This has led some scholars to evaluate the concertation process more critically. They argue that concertation was a politically-induced restraint on economic imperatives because it delayed necessary economic adjustments and transferred tensions to the budget, thus provoking a rapid increase of the public deficit, which shot up from a 1.0 percent surplus of GDP in 1973 to a deficit of 5.6 percent by 1982 (Bustelo 1986, 39).[38] Other authors have criticized the fact that concertation facilitated the integration of working-class organizations in the setting of restrictive economic policies, thus undermining the possibilities for any working-class challenge to the status quo (Martínez-Alier and Roca 1986)

Overall, however, an assessment of the concertation process is positive. It served to consolidate the new political regime and overcome the economic crisis. Concertation resulted in social peace and wage moderation, that contributed to lower inflation and helped to restore business profits. This resulted in higher investment and employment in the second half of the 1980s. After concertation broke down, inflation regularly grew beyond government targets and reemerged at the end of the 1980s, a fact that forced the government to tighten up monetary policies, which in turn resulted in further increases in unemployment. The question, then, is why did concertation collapse after 1986? This shall be the subject of the next chapters.

CHAPTER 4

Institutional Barriers to Concertation in Spain

Introduction

We saw in chapter 2 how the neocorporatist literature has focused on institutional variables to explain the success (or failure) of concertation schemes in European countries. According to this literature, the success of concertation is based on a high level of unionization, monopolistic and encompassing unions, and centralized wage bargaining between labor confederations and employer associations[1] (Cameron 1984, 169; Schmitter 1990, 30). The Spanish system of industrial relations, on the other hand, has often been characterized as having weak and competitive unions and decentralized wage bargaining. The institutional literature then offers an a priori hypothesis to explain the failure of concertation in Spain, namely, that union fragmentation and decentralized collective bargaining hindered social concertation by intensifying rivalries among unions and by forcing unions to compete for members, while decentralized collective bargaining thwarted the implementation of centralized agreements by fostering wage competition and hindering solidaristic strategies.

In this chapter I examine the role that institutional factors played in the Spanish case. I shall explore whether the Spanish institutional framework made unions lacking in solidarity. Some authors have argued that Spanish unions were strong enough to be an obstacle, but not inclusive enough to be solidaristic. I shall argue, however, that the institutional variables analyzed by the literature are not enough to account for the failure of concertation in Spain after 1986. Relatively weak and competitive labor unions and a decentralized wage bargaining system were also features of the system from 1979 until 1986, yet concertation was successful. Other variables must, therefore, have played a role. I conclude that the neocorporatist literature with its emphasis on certain institutions ignores very important societal and political considerations that also influence the decisions of social actors. It fails to consider the circumstances under which competing and weak unions are willing to take part in neocorporatist arrangements, or under which social democratic (SD) governments are willing to participate in concertation and do not defect from their agreements with unions.

The chapter has three main sections. The first section is descriptive. I outline the Spanish industrial relations system and examine the two major confederations that have dominated the industrial relations landscape. In the second section I analyze whether the institutional variables emphasized by the literature—that is, the level of unionization, the internal organization of unions, and union jurisdiction—made Spanish unions unsolidaristic. I close the chapter analyzing the system of wage bargaining to determine whether it hindered concertation.

I. Background of the Spanish Industrial Relations Setting

Spanish Unions

The competitive structure of the Spanish industrial relations setting has been the result of a very confrontational historical struggle in pursuit of union and worker liberties. Before the Spanish Civil War (1936–1939), the Spanish labor relation setting was dominated by two major trade unions, the anarchist Confederación Nacional del Trabajo (CNT), and the socialist Unión General de Trabajadores (UGT). The strength of the anarchist union, CNT, was a specific feature of the prewar institutional setting because Spain had remained an agriculture-based country until the mid-twentieth century. The potential of Spanish anarchism, however, was eliminated by the process of industrialization which took place in the second half of the century (Führer 1996, 50).

The UGT was founded by the first leader of the Spanish Socialist Workers Party (PSOE), Pablo Iglesias, in 1888; it was oriented toward industrial workers and pursued a strategy aiming at enhancing labor conditions and increasing union and democratic rights. It also sought political influence through the socialist party (de la Villa and Palomeque 1978, 117). At the time, however, union rights were very limited and unrecognized by the government. Only after the establishment of the Second Republic in 1930 did union rights become fully recognized and union liberties guaranteed (Art. 39 of the Constitution). Subsequently, both the UGT and the CNT participated actively in the Spanish Civil War supporting the Republic. The defeat of the Republic in 1939 brought prohibition, prosecution, and, in many cases, exile for their leaders.

After the war, the Francoist regime established an industrial relations system based on institutions organized by industrial sectors, managed by the state and to which both workers and business had to be affiliated. Specifically, Franco's corporative apparatus, the Central Nacional Sindical (CNS, later the Organización Sindical, OS) was hierarchically organized by production sectors, the "sindicatos verticales" (the vertical unions). Wages and working conditions were guided by government decrees, and the hierarchical organization of firms and sectors was regulated through labor ordinances (Moscoso 1995, 154). Traditional unions were banished and prosecuted. One of the major features of the new system was the establishment in 1947 of Jurados de Empresa (work councils), in which both workers and employers participated and elected their own representatives. These work councils, however, were subordinated to the CNS. Nevertheless, they played a very important role because workers used them as instruments to elect their representatives and develop their own organizations.

The partial opening of the Spanish economy to the world markets in the late 1950s ignited a period of fast economic growth and rapid industrialization that was accompanied by migration from the country to the cities. This was followed by a certain liberalization of the industrial relations setting. In 1958 the government approved the new Work Councils Act, which permitted the negotiation of collective agreements at firm level or at a superior level through the vertical unions. The state, however, maintained its supervisory powers. Collective agreements had to be approved by the Ministry of Labor, which also influenced the process by setting content guidelines and establishing the duration of the agreements. This new framework, however, opened the door for union action and fostered the development of new worker organizations. The emergence of mining conflicts in Asturias in 1957 triggered the formation of a worker's commission elected by the miners to negotiate with employers. This practice was later extended to other conflicts and firms[2] (Vega García 1995, 28; Fishman 1990, 113). This marked the beginning of a new union movement, the communist oriented Comisiones Obreras (CCOO), which emerged in a decentralized way in firms and had no links with the traditional unions[3] (the UGT and CNT). CCOO strengthened its position in the 1960s. Unión Sindical Obrera, (USO) a socialist-oriented union, also emerged at this time.[4]

While remaining illegal under Franco, both the USO and CCOO used the facilities and instruments offered by the vertical unions to expand and solidify their position among industrial workers. They adjusted their own organization and structure to operate in such a restricted framework and were tolerated in the 1960s. In 1967 the CCOO organized its first national assembly in Madrid, which elected a group of leaders and approved a program based on the defense of worker rights as well as democratic institutions. In this assembly the members of the Spanish Communist Party, PCE, strengthened their grip over the union (Führer 1996, 78). The CCOO would continue after the end of the authoritarian regime and play a dominant role within the labor movement.

When Franco died in 1975 the labor movement was represented by the two organizations that emerged during the dictatorship, the CCOO and USO. The end of the regime, however, accelerated the return of labor organizations that had been in exile, such as UGT and CNT (as well as the nationalistic union ELA-STV, Solidaridad de Trabajadores Bascos, in the Basque country).[5] Given the strength of the CCOO and the USO at the firm level, traditional unions were forced to look for alternative ways to strengthen their positions within the labor movement.[6] At that time, CCOO leaders did not want to become a traditional trade union because they feared that such a move would trigger the development of a system based on multiple unions and insisted on remaining a sociopolitical organization. Given the control and support that they had within the labor movement, CCOO's leaders thought that they could dominate a unitary organization, and, therefore, they proposed to other unions the organization of a national assembly to replace the Francoist labor institutions to create a new unitary organization that would integrate all unions. The specific weight of each union would be determined by representatives who would have been previously elected within firms (Zufiaur 1983, 46; Almendros Morcillo 1978, 266). The final objective was to create a trade union that would monopolize worker representation and thus act as the organized representative of the entire labor movement. The Communist leaders also made it clear that they would refrain from confrontation and opt instead for the agreement of pacts with the business interests that would help build a new corporatist relationship between business and labor (Martínez-Alier and Roca 1986, 15).

This idea, however, stood little chance of success. First, the other unions resisted this proposal. While they agreed that a single organization would better serve the interests of workers, they viewed with skepticism the influence that the Communist Party had in CCOO[7] and refused to support a plan in which they could only play a limited role.[8] These rivalries among unions prevented the development of a unitary organization. Furthermore, the Workers' Commission's radical background had little in common with the European social democratic unions that had participated in such corporatist structures for decades. The union leaders themselves were concerned about an open discussion on this topic, fearing that some of its militant workers, who understood the union as a "sociopolitical" movement and opposed the bureaucratic style of the European labor organizations, would rebel against this proposal. Finally, the idea failed to take into consideration the reemergence of the other historical unions (the UGT and the CNT) (Martínez-Alier and Roca 1986, 15).

The CCOO's aspirations to unify the labor movement and to build a new corporatist relationship with business, in which the union would be the unquestioned representative of all workers, suffered a further blow when the

UGT organized its XXXth Congress in 1976 and reaffirmed its decision not to participate in a unitary organization dominated by the CCOO. The CNT, USO, and ELA-STV followed course (Führer 1996, 90). As a result of these developments the CCOO was forced to organize its own congress in 1976, wherein its leaders decided to proceed with the reorganization of the institution as a traditional union based on the support of affiliates. CCOO leaders realized that their competitors had already begun to mobilize support among workers and that their refusal to adapt their organization to the new environment would mean a lessening of power in the short term. Therefore, they concluded that the unitary objective was not feasible at that time and proceeded to organize as a traditional labor union.[9] This decision, however, caused internal dissent and conflict and culminated in the departure of several members, who then formed their own organizations.

These developments determined that there would be a pluralistic and competitive industrial relations setting in Spain. In April 1977 the Spanish Parliament approved the Free Union Association Act that recognized union freedoms.[10] The CCOO, USO, UGT, and ELA-STV were all legalized. When the government opened the Register of Union Organizations in 1977, many unions emerged with no proven support from workers. Some of them were even supported by business and aimed at weakening the labor movements. The government, however, following the Italian and French concept of "most representative union," developed mechanisms to guarantee the predominance of majority unions and established elections to work councils as the instrument to determine the representativeness of unions.[11] The 1978 election to the work councils established the superiority of the CCOO (34.5 percent of the vote), closely followed by the UGT (21.7 percent) and distantly by the USO (3.37 percent). The ELA-STV received 11.6 percent of the vote in the Basque country. The CNT refused to participate in the elections. These elections confirmed a new landscape based in the existence of a pluralistic union setting dominated by two major confederations. This system resulted in what has been denominated a "representative duopoly" (Escobar 1995, 155) with the CCOO and UGT dominating the labor relations landscape.[12] The approval of the Spanish Constitution in December 1978 formalized the legal situation of unions and strengthened union and worker rights (Arts. 7 and 28). As we will see next, subsequent elections to the work councils confirmed the supremacy of the CCOO and UGT.

II. The Spanish Industrial Relations Setting

We saw in chapter 2 how the neocorporatist literature has highlighted three aspects of the institutional setting to account for the successful implementation of solidaristic policies and concertation in countries such as Austria,

Sweden, the Netherlands, and Belgium. According to the corporatist literature, the prisoner's dilemma associated with wage restraint suggests that the more encompassing the union movement, the greater the concentration among unions, and the more centralized the authority of the peak associations, the more likely it was that wage restraint would be achieved (Golden, Wallerstein, and Lange 1999, 195). Therefore, according to this literature, the success of corporatist bargaining depends on the organization of unions.

One of the first variables emphasized by the literature has been the strength and inclusiveness of unions, which guarantees that unions are strong enough to enforce the agreements they sign and inclusive enough to take into consideration the macroeconomic considerations of their actions. This literature has concluded that concertation has been successful in countries with a relatively high level of unionization (i.e., union density refers to the proportion of employees who become union members).

A second institutional variable emphasized by the literature is union coverage which refers to the proportion of employers who are covered by collective bargaining contracts. This a very important variable because it indicates the extent to which unions affect wage levels in the economy. Declines in coverage would indicate an erosion in the capacity of unions to influence wage levels (Golden, Wallerstein, and Lange 1999, 202).

Another institutional variable highlighted by the literature involves the structure of the labor movement. According to this view, concertation has been successful in countries with a single labor confederation composed of a few industry-based unions (Cameron 1984, 169). Such a setting prevents competition among unions. A fourth set of institutional factors emphasized by the literature involve the internal organizations of unions. The more centralized the union is, the better suited it will be to pursue and enforce centralized agreements and thus to implement solidaristic policies. Cooperative relationships between trade unions and business associations and between trade unions and the government are also typical features in countries where concertation has been consolidated, because cooperative relationships between the social actors foster bargaining and consensus.[13]

The final variable highlighted by the literature to account for the success of concertation has been the structure of the system of collective bargaining—that is, the degree of coordination and/or centralization of the wage bargaining system. This variable, according to the literature, is critical to guarantee the implementation of incomes policy because it determines whether the social actors will take into account the macroeconomic considerations of wage bargaining (Scharpf 1991, 178–192; Golden 1993, 439–454).

In this section I analyze whether the (presupposed) absence of some of these institutional factors precluded the consolidation of concertation in

Spain after 1986. According to the literature, the Spanish institutional setting is inadequate for the implementation of solidaristic polices and concertation (Boix, 1996, 215–216; Maravall 1995, 221; Solchaga 1997, 146–150). Spanish unions have often been portrayed as too weak and not inclusive enough to be solidaristic, and interunion competition and a somewhat decentralized system of collective bargaining are believed to foster wage competition and to prevent unions from taking into consideration the macroeconomic implications of wage bargaining. In this section I shall dispute these arguments.

a. The Strength and Inclusiveness of Spanish Unions

According to the literature, one of the factors that determines the institutional influence of unions and their capacity to pursue and implement solidaristic policies and concertation is the level of unionization. This is so because the higher the level of unionization and the stronger the support that unions receive from their affiliates, the more influence the union has in the political process. Countries with neocorporatist traditions have unions with very high levels of affiliation. In Sweden over 80 percent of the workers were organized in unions, in Germany 85 percent, and in Austria 100 percent (Scharpf 1991, 187).

Unions in Spain are indeed weak when compared with their Northern European counterparts. During the first years of the transition process (1976–1978), affiliation was high, at around 40–45 percent of the labor force, and similar to other European countries at that time, but declined sharply afterwards.[14] In fact by 1981 union membership had declined to 20 percent (Escobar 1995, 157, Führer 1996 133–146). By 1988 that figure had been reduced to 16 percent according to a poll by the Center for Sociological Investigations (CIS). By 1990 the level of union affiliation fluctuated between 15–20 percent of the labor force (Miguélez 1995, 217).[15] More importantly, unions strongholds were still concentrated in large firms and public sector firms where the Fordist model of production was preponderant among skilled manual workers with indefinite contracts (see Führer 1996, 129). However, the growth of employment during the last decade occurred in sectors of the economy where unions were not particularly strong, such as the service sector.

This has led some authors to conclude that "small unions, mostly in the hands of 'insiders,' negotiating at the sectoral level, and imbued with a radical perception of the role of the state in the economy, could not provide the institutional basis to sustain a corporatist regime of wage moderation"; thus offering unions little incentive to "embrace wage restraint in exchange for more employment among unskilled workers" (Boix 1994, 28–29; see also

Paramio 1992, 521). Following these arguments, these authors claim that the collapse of concertation in Spain was the result of the increased weakness of the labor movement, as proved by the declines in levels of affiliation. Paramio (1992, 521–539), for example, argues that the unions' low levels of membership and the lack of commitment from their members—who do not contribute much to the union's resources—add to the weakness of unions and hinder concertation.[16] Others conclude that unions in Spain are not strong and inclusive enough to pursue solidaristic polices (Boix 1996, 215). Former Spanish socialist officials have also argued that the structural weakness of the labor movement convinced the government that an effective incomes policy was not feasible. They doubted the capacity of unions to sustain centralized agreements and to keep their rank and file under control. Therefore, the governmental economic team saw restrictive monetary policies as a more effective way to control inflation.[17]

The notion that Spanish unions are neither strong nor inclusive enough to pursue solidaristic policies, however, has to be qualified. Several factors challenge the notion that the collapse of concertation can be explained simply in terms of low union affiliation. The higher levels of membership in the late 1980s, union coverage, the overwhelming electoral support that unions have received in the elections to the work councils, as well as their capacity to mobilize workers and fulfill the agreements they sign, prove the Spanish unions' strength and refute the argument that unions in Spain are not institutionally suited to be cooperative partners in concertation schemes.

First, although union membership was low in the late 1980s—around 10 percent of the labor force (Estevill and de la Hoz 1990, 280)—new estimates show that the membership rate in the early 1990s is increasing: 14 percent in 1993 (Taboadela 1993), or even between 15–20 percent according to other estimates (Miguélez and Prieto 1991, 217; Jordana 1996, 211–220).[18] The renewed strength of unions, however, did not result in the reemergence of concertation. Seemingly, there is an inverse correlation between concertation and the strength of unions in Spain. Concertation in that country was possible even under declining union membership, but it did not resume when affiliation picked up in the late 1980s (Moscoso 1995, 33–34).

Secondly, the strength of unions cannot be determined only by the level of membership. Affiliation is just one of the criteria used in other countries to evaluate union representativeness. Other criteria such as the number of contributors (France and Italy), the electoral support and the tradition and historic experience (France); and union coverage, have been also used to determined the representativeness of unions (García Murcia et al. 1995, 251).

Union coverage refers to the proportion of employers who are covered by collective bargaining contracts. This a very important variable because it indicates the extent to which unions affect wage levels in the economy (and therefore unions' strength). According to some authors, this is a more accurate measure of the extent to which unions affect wage levels, because many employees who are not union members are still covered by collective bargaining agreements. In other words, declines in coverage would indicate an erosion in the capacity of unions to influence wage levels, while stable coverage would suggest that union still play an important role in wage setting despite low levels of affiliation (Golden, Wallerstein, and Lange 1999, 202). In Spain firms are legally required to pay a collectively bargained wage to all employees, regardless of their union status, unless they explicitly refuse to accept it. According to the Spanish Constitution, all workers are entitled to be covered by collective bargaining agreements, independently of their trade union affiliation (Art. 37.1). In Spain collective agreements have immediate and general effectiveness *(erga omnes),* which means that they are applied to all workers included within the limits of the agreement, regardless of their syndical affiliation and contractual status (the only workers excluded from this rule are the top managers). The consequence has been that although most workers do not belong to unions (as indicated above, union membership rates are among the lowest in the Organization for Economic Cooperation and Development, OECD, at 10–15 percent), very few are not covered by a union-negotiated collective agreement, and coverage rates in Spain have remained uniformly high with 68–75 percent of workers covered by collective bargaining agreements (Blanchard et al, 1995, 119–120; Roca 1993, 182; Jimeno 1997, 82). Collective agreements in Spain set sectoral minimum wages over the national minimum wage established by government decree every year, and this serves as a floor for subsequent negotiations at the firm level.[19]

As Table 4.1 shows, union coverage has remained high and stable in Spain, confirming that unions still play an important role in wage setting in Spain despite low levels of affiliation and disproving the notion of "unions in decline." This argument is further reinforced by the fact that that the most representative unions (UGT and CCOO) and the employers association (CEOE) are the bargaining partners in the overwhelming majority of the bargaining rounds to negotiate these agreements (65 and 64 percent respectively in 1997) (CES 1998, 391–392).

The argument of "unions in decline" in Spain is further challenged by the support that the two peak confederations receive in the elections to the work councils. The Spanish legislation has used unions results in the work council elections as the criterion to determine their institutional participation in certain organizations, and to give them several functions—particularly collective bargaining. There has been a high turnout in elections to work councils, and these elections have consolidated a "dual system of worker representation" in Spain (Escobar, 1995, 153).

Table 4.1 Percentage of Workers Affected by Collective Agreements (Bargaining Coverage), 1984–1997

	1984	1987	1992	1993	1994	1995	1996	1997
Firm[1]	17.2	16.1	15.0	13.5	13.6	13.7	12.9	10.6
Other[2]	82.8	83.9	85.0	86.5	86.4	86.3	87.1	89.4

Sources: Ministerio de Trabajo and Seguridad Social, Estadística de Convenions Colectivos (various years).
[1]Collective agreements negotiated at the firm level
[2]Collective agreements negotiated at a level above the firm

The first elections to the works councils took place in 1978.[20] These elections confirmed the supremacy of CCOO (34.57 percent), but the major surprise was the strong performance of the UGT (30.86 percent). The other unions followed distantly. Throughout the 1980s and 1990s turnout for these elections has been very high (over 50 percent of the workers have voted in these elections), and they have been dominated by the two major confederations.[21] Subsequent elections took place in 1980, 1982, 1986, 1990, and 1995[22] with the following results:

Moreover, the power of unions is also measured by their strong mobilizing capacity. Unions in Spain have organized strikes at three levels, by sector or firm, general strikes,[23] and demonstrations. The majority of strikes occur at the sector or firm level and usually involve disputes in collective negotiations.

Table 4.2 Elections to the Work Councils, 1978–1995

Unions	1978 (%)	1980 (%)	1982 (%)	1986 (%)	1990 (%)	1995 (%)
CCOO	34.57	30.86	33.40	34.54	36.9	37.79
UGT	21.70	29.27	36.70	40.92	42.0	34.92
USO	3.77	8.68	4.6	3.80	2.9	3.6
ELA-STV	0.90	2.20	3.30	4.60	3.2	5.74
INTG/CIG	—	1.20	1.20	—	1.5	—
Other Unions	20.80	12.20	8.70	16.10*	7.1	—
Nonunion	18.13	14.60	12.10		3.8	—

Sources: Data from the Ministerio de Trabajo and Seguridad Social. For more extensive information about these electoral results, see also: "CCOO desplaza a UGT como primera fuerza sindical y crece apoyo a los nacionalistas," in El Mundo, December 9, 1995, p. 33; Führer 1996, Table 2–4, pp. 113–114; and Escobar 1995, Table 6.4, p. 169.
*Includes both Other Unions and Nonunion.

In the late 1970s and late 1980s, Spain experienced among the highest number of strikes in the western world. In the late 1970s unions demands were also linked to political demands for freedom, and some authors have argued that in many cases strike activity was politicized during the first years of democracy (Paramio, 1992). As Table 4.3 shows, the number of strikes declined sharply during the years of concertation (1980–1983, 1985–1986):

The mobilizing capacity of Spanish unions is also confirmed by the percentage of workplaces or workers which join a strike called by unions. Since 1986 (the first year of reliable data) the percentage of workplaces that have followed unions strike calls have been above 70 percent, and 75 percent of the workers (Escobar 1995, 159–160).

These factors show that despite low levels of membership Spanish unions were stronger than previously estimated by the literature. It has been argued, nevertheless, that they were strong enough to be an obstacle to concertation but not inclusive enough to be solidaristic (Boix 1996, 215–217). Unions in Spain, however, (particularly the UGT) supported the concertation process over an extensive period of time (1978–1986) despite high unemployment, wage losses for their affiliates, and declining membership. The major reason behind this support was the defense of the general interest and the objective to contribute to the economic recovery—not only the interests of their affiliates.[24] Furthermore, new reports (García Murcia, Gutiérrez Palacios, and Rodriguez Sañudo 1995, 272–283; Jordana 1996, 211–220) are challenging the notions that Spanish unions are not inclusive and that in the 1980s they entered into an irreversible process of decline of representation and support among workers. Although union affiliation levels and electoral support have remained

Table 4.3 Number of Working Days Lost, 1976–1991

Year	Days Lost (000)	Year	Days Lost (000)	Year	Days Lost (000)
1976	12,593	1982	2,788	1988	6,843
1977	16,642	1983	4,417	1989	3,685
1978	11,551	1984	6,358	1990	2,443
1979	18,917	1985	3,223	1991	4,421
1980	6,178	1986	2,279		
1981	5,154	1987	5,023		

Source: Escobar 1995, Table 6.1, p. 159. Reprinted with permission. From Instituto Nacional de Estadística, *Encuesta Sobre Población Activa* (Madrid), various years; and Instituto Nacional de Estadística, *Contabilidad Nacional de España* (Madrid: Ministerio de Hacienda, Secretaría General Técnica, various years).

stable, new data shows that union loyalty is not concentrated solely in unions' traditional strongholds. Women, older workers, pensioners, and the unemployed increasingly became involved in unions, and the unions' capacity to attract these new constituencies in the late 1980s challenged the notion that Spanish unions were not inclusive enough to be solidaristic. Unions called a general strike in 1988 that included demands that affected the unemployed and pensioners and even developed an economic program—the Propuesta Sindical Prioritaria, in 1991—to reach new constituencies. Nevertheless, despite the fact that Spanish unions became more inclusive in the late 1980s–1990s, concertation did not resume.

Finally, it is also important to stress that unions have been recognized by the state and by the employers' organizations and this has helped strengthen their organizational capacities. Due to their cooperative behavior after 1977, the main trade unions (the UGT and the CCOO) "have been rewarded with measures that tend to make these two unions the representatives of the entire labor force, despite declining affiliation since 1978" (Martínez-Alier and Roca 1986, 17). For instance, the labor laws stipulate that no union may participate in bargaining sessions unless its members amount to 10 percent of the members of the works councils of the firms affected by the agreement, and public funds have been distributed to unions in proportion to results to work council elections or through ad-hoc measures, helping the main confederations and weakening smaller unions (Roca 1987). [25]

In conclusion, although some authors have argued that the weakness and lack of inclusiveness of unions prevented the consolidation of concertation in Spain, I have shown in this section that despite very low levels of affiliation, unions are stronger and more inclusive than previously assumed by the literature, as proved by their mobilizing capacity, union coverage, the electoral backing they receive in the elections to works councils, and the renewed support from new constituencies in the late 1980s and 1990s. These facts (and union behavior) suggest that Spanish unions could be solidaristic. Most importantly, concertation took place in Spain at a time of declining membership and supposed lack of inclusiveness, yet unions were able to fulfill their promises; however, concertation did not resume in the late 1980s and early 1990s at a time of increasing efforts on the part of unions leaders to make their organizations more inclusive.

b. The Structure of the Labor Movement

Another aspect of the institutional framework emphasized by the neocorporatist literature to determine the success of concertation and solidaristic policies is union jurisdiction. It refers to the way unions are organized—along industry lines or along lines of qualifications. This factor influences competition/cooperation among unions and also affects the possibility of resolving conflicts among unions—blue- versus white-collar unions, and highly- versus low-skilled workers. According to the literature, the critical variable to avoid interunion competition is "the demarcation of union jurisdiction and the power relations among them" (Scharpf 1991, 187; see also Golden 1993, 439–451). In countries such as Austria, Sweden, or Germany, where concertation was successful over an extended period of time, unions are organized along industry lines and do not compete for members or wages within the same branch or plant. The corporatist literature focuses on two main dimensions of concentration: interconfederal concentration (i.e., "the number of actors and their relative size at the confederate level") and intraconfederal concentration (i.e., "the number of actors and their relative size within each confederation") (Golden, Wallerstein, and Lange 1999, 206–207).

Spanish unions operate in all sectors, including the public administration, and represent both blue- and white-collar workers (and civil servants as well).[26] They are organized internally along industry lines but they compete for votes in the elections for work councils. This is a major feature that differentiates the Spanish industrial relations setting from that of other countries. In Germany, for instance, unions do not compete for members or wages within the same branch or plant. The Spanish system would be closer to Italy's or Great Britain's. Therefore, from an institutional point of view, one of the major challenges to concertation in Spain would come from the competitive nature of unions.

Along these lines, it has been argued by Paramio (1992, 525) that the existing Spanish legal framework is not conductive to solidaristic policies. According to him, since unions have to compete for ballots at the workplaces, this competition influences their behavior and wage strategies. Paramio posits that this leads Spanish workers to view unions as "instruments" to achieve some objectives and will support them as long as they provide some results. Competition for votes thus hinders concertation because it forces unions to radicalize their strategies to satisfy voters' demands and prevents them from implementing solidaristic policies. This situation, according to Paramio, is further aggravated by the fact that most union resources come from the government coffers, making unions depend on the state money for their survival. But the state grants subsidies to unions based on the results of the work councils elections, which intensifies competition among unions. The more votes, the higher the subsidies.

Other authors (Moscoso 1995, 70–71), however, consider such a view of unions-as-instruments as exaggerated. While it is true that affiliation to unions is very low and unions offer few incentives to their potential members, the high turnover in the elections to works councils supports the notion that voting is a "way of doing politics at the workplace" and not an exercise of rational maximization. Even if workers view unions as instruments, this does not mean that unions have to radicalize their strategies, and they still deliver on their promises through concertation. On the contrary, representative unions do not have to worry so much about the danger of losing their members. The UGT saw how electoral support from workers grew as a consequence of its moderation and support of concertation during the early 1980s. The CCOO, on the contrary, decided to follow a more confrontational approach and refused to sign the AMI (Acuerdo Marco Interconfederal, 1979) and the AES (Acuerdo Económico y Social, 1984) and lost electoral support in the first half of the 1980s. In other words, radicalization does not necessarily mean better electoral performance.

The coexistence of competing unions in the same branch of industry was further tempered by the fact, as we will see next, that strategic decisions, including wage strategies, were made at the top union level. Therefore, unions in Spain were able to avoid the "wage deprivation" effect—that is, higher wage increases in neighboring workplaces that foster higher wage demands in the next bargaining round in your own workplace—that had characterized other countries (e.g., Great Britain or Sweden after 1984). On the contrary, Spanish unions were able to coordinate separate bargaining levels. The fact that they represent both blue- and white-collar workers as well as civil servants also prevented the kinds of distributive conflicts that hindered wage coordination in Sweden. It thus cannot be argued that concertation collapsed because unions had to compete for votes in the workplace.

If we focus on the two dimensions of concentration analyzed by the literature and analyze changes in concentration in Spain, we see that the two main confederations (UGT and CCOO) still have the capacity to dominate decision making (for over a decade the guiding strategic principle between both confederations has been the "unitary strategy," which has led them to sign all major agreements together and present a common bargaining platform during negotiation with employers and the government; see Conclusions), which makes it easier to prevent free riding and to obtain collectively optimal outcomes (see Golden 1993). Furthermore, at the interconfederal level, the number of peak level union confederations and the distribution of members among them has remained stable over the last decade. In Spain changes in the composition of the labor force have not resulted in the emergence of new unions in which to enroll new unorganized groups of workers, (like in Sweden), and the Communist-allied union confederation (CCOO) has remained strong (unlike what happened in Italy or France). On the contrary, as proven by the electoral support in the work council elections (see Table 4.3), both UGT and CCOO remain the country's predominant peak associations for labor.

Furthermore, at the intraconfederal level, there has been a widespread tendency toward increasing concentration among union confederations. The number of unions affiliated with the main confederations has declined significantly since the late 1970s. Both UGT and CCOO have streamlined their organizations by reducing the number of affiliates and concentrating more members in their largest affiliates, as unions have responded to increasing financial pressures with mergers. For instance, between 1978 and 1984 the CCOO reduced the number of federations from 25 to 22—the final objective was to reduce them to 16—and the UGT reduced the number of federations from 21 to 15 (the most significant merger took place between the two largest federations, the metal and chemical, last year). Even today, the CCOO is trying to reduce the number of federations from 17 to 11 (see Führer 1996, 171–181). This has resulted in an increase of the share of membership held by the largest federations and has reinforced the ability of peak confederations to organize and mobilize workers. This development further challenges the widespread perception that unions in Spain are not internally cohesive and cannot dominate decision making.

Finally, it is also important to emphasize that in Spain, the wage losses that resulted from the concertation agreements did not result in the widespread discontent among skilled workers that gave rise to new unions in other countries (i.e., the *sindicati autonomi* and the COBAS, or *comitati di base,* which grew significantly in importance in Italy over the course of the 1980s). The reason was that concertation in Spain did not include the wage compression mechanisms that characterized the *scala mobile* in Italy.

c. The Internal Organization of Unions

A high degree of internal centralization of unions is another critical variable emphasized by the literature to account for the success of concertation and solidaristic policies in neocorporatist countries. According to the literature, the authority of different levels of organization in wage negotiations is a central component of corporatism (Golden, Wallerstein, and Lange 1999, 213). They focus on two main variables: statutory authority (i.e., the decisions that can be made by lower levels of union organizations without the permission of the confederation as specified by the organizations statutes, or nation law), and wage determination (i.e., the extent of confederal participation in wage setting).

Internal centralization of unions, according to some authors, is the key factor in determining the success of centralized wage bargaining (Golden 1993).[27] It includes components such as union leadership powers, control over financial resources, power over affiliates, decision-making processes, and control over strike funds. According to the literature, these factors determine the capacity of unions to implement neocorporatist agreements, because the degree of centralization within the union influences the power of its executive committee to make decisions and control its branches to mitigate wage drift. If centralized wage agreements are to be effective, they must be adhered to at lower bargaining levels.

In countries with strong neocorporatist traditions, unions are characterized by a high degree of vertical centralization. In Austria, for instance, there are no unions outside the ÖGB (Österreichischer Gewerkschaftsbund) federation. The ÖGB has a legal and financial monopoly, collects contributions from members, hires personnel for the individual unions, and collective bargaining is concluded formally in the name of the federation. In Sweden, unions also have a high degree of centralization. Up to 1984 wage bargaining for all industry branches was conducted between the employers' association and the LO (Landsorganisasjonen i Sverige) confederation (Scharpf 1991, 188–190).

In Spain unions have a dual structure, by sectors (the "vertical structure" or "professional structure"), and by areas (the "horizontal" or "territorial" structure).[28] These structures are then merged in the union leadership (named the Union or Confederation). At the firm level, union action is implemented by the "union section" (the *sección sindical*), which is elected by the union members in the workplace. Beyond the firm, the local level of the vertical structure is formed by the federation, and the horizontal structure by the area union (the *unión comarcal*). This organization is replicated at higher levels, region, province, autonomous region (the top level for unions operating within an autonomous region), and nation (Führer 1996, 151). Representatives at all levels are chosen in elections that take place in assemblies and congresses. The higher the number of affiliates, the higher the number of delegates for the provincial congress. At a national level, 50 percent of the delegates come from the federations, and the other 50 percent from the regions. The executive committees are elected by delegates from the autonomous regions in national Congresses that take place every four years[29] (for a detailed analysis of the internal organization of unions see Cabrero Morán 1997).

The organization of Spanish unions, with most powers exercised by the executive committee, has been conductive to concertation. The federations are responsible for industrial relations issues in each sector—that is, collective bargaining, decisions about strikes, resolution of conflicts, problems specific to the sector, prevention of accidents, legal support and other assistance to members, organization of the elections to works councils at firm levels, membership, fund raising, training, and union representation at lower levels. Federations thus have critical responsibilities within the unions. The confederations, for their part, are responsible for negotiations with the government, institutional representation of the union as a whole, coordination, union representation, social and political activities, and support to branches. The confederations, however, given the centralist tendencies of unions and the number of representatives that they send to congresses (50 percent), still play preponderant roles and the executive committees of the unions have extraordinary powers. They sign their own wage agreements, have their own strike funds, can veto wage agreements signed by affiliates, participate in demand formulation and wage bargaining for lower levels, and have veto powers over strikes. Moreover, federations are subordinated to the strategies and union policies defined by the confederations—which operate at the level that outlines unions' strategies and conducts negotiations with the government and the business' association. The executive committees also define the strategies regarding wage policies and wage demands. The power of the executive committees has been shown through their capacity to implement the agreements that were signed with the CEOE (Confederación Española de Organizaciones Empresariales) and the government (1980–1986). In the 1980s, as I mentioned above, in order to overcome the fragmentation of their organizations, union leaders embarked in a process that resulted in further centralization. They encouraged mergers,[30] centralized administrative and managerial responsibilities, and streamlined the organization at the regional level. Centralization was reinforced by the fact that federations are totally dependent on the confederations for their economic support. None of the federations, not even the strongest one—the metal—has the resources to self-finance its operation. This has increased dramatically the power of the confederation, and contributes further to centralization[31] (for a more detailed analysis about the power of the Federations and the Confederations, see Führer 1996, 164–167).

In Spain the concentration of authority in peak confederations whose constituents include the bulk of the workforce contributed to the success of concertation because it mitigated wage drift in two ways. On the one hand union leaders were aware that wage restraint would maximize both employment and wages for the labor force as a whole, therefore they had strong incentives to coordinate wage bargaining and push for wage restraint. On the other hand, the confederations leaders had the instruments to sanction free rider—that is, constituents who did not abide by such agreements. Concentration of authority provided labor confederations in Spain with the power to coordinate separate bargaining levels and enforce centralized wage agreements, thus avoiding the kinds of distributive conflicts that hindered wage coordination in other countries (Sweden).

In sum, in Spain central organizations exercise statutory authority over lower levels and they also actively control collective bargaining and intervene in wage setting. While unions in Spain are organized along industrial lines with strong federations that have important responsibilities, the decision-making process takes place mostly at the confederate level, and union leaders have the ability to coordinate the behavior of large sections of the workforce. Centralization was fostered by the weak economic position of the federations, unable to self-finance their activities and dependent on the confederations for funds. The confederations (mostly the executive committee) are the sources of all important decisions, the institutions responsible for external fund raising, external loans, and the ones that receive and manage subsidies from the state. These responsibilities contributed to centralization, particularly given the fact that power is concentrated mostly in the hands of the executive committees and the secretary generals. All these factors contributed to mitigate wage drift and fostered the adhesion of workers at lower bargaining levels to the centralized agreements negotiated by the confederations, which led to the successful implementation of concertation agreements in the late 1970s and early 1980s.

d. Unions' and Business' Associations

Unions relation to the employers has been another of the institutional factors pointed out in the literature as conductive to concertation and wage coordination (Scharpf 1991, 178). Countries where unions and business have close relations have been more successful in implementing neocorporatist arrangements. In Austria, for instance, such relationships between unions and the employers' association were strengthened by their shared objectives (for example economic growth). In that country the institutional setting fostered consensus because it was based on equal representation, political balance among the social actors, and unanimity in important decisions. Therefore, after World War II unions and businesses were able to develop a partnership that helped foster a common view of problems, solutions, goals, objectives, and constraints (Scharpf 1991, 179; Katzenstein 1985, 126–128). In Germany, codetermination provided unions with influence and information and strengthened the business-union partnership at the plant level.

In Spain, despite a long tradition of a confrontational relationship between unions and employers, the advent and consolidation of a new democratic regime in the 1970s changed this dynamic and fostered more cooperation between the social actors that facilitated concertation. The new democratic regime encouraged the development of institutions and processes that supported cooperative links between business and labor. Despite the fact that during the dictatorship the vertical unions had attempted to go beyond the class struggle, business and labor interests remained distant.

From the standpoint of the industrial relations setting, one of the most relevant developments that took place during the transition was the foundation in 1977 of the business association, the CEOE.[32] It represents businesses from all sectors of the economy: agriculture, industry, services, and finance (Pardo Avellaneda and Fernández Castro 1995, 157). The CEOE has over 1,350,000 businesses affiliates, which employed three-fourths of the Spanish workers in the early 1980s and up to 95 percent of the employed by 1987. The other three major business associations represent small and medium firms and are all now part of the CEOE.[33] The CEOE has a double structure; it is organized by territories and sectors, with membership defined by inclusion in both structures. Voting weight is determined by the size of the firm, with the sectoral structure having a greater weight.[34] The peak-level confederation has the power to sign its own wage agreements, participates in demand formulation, and assists in bargaining at lower levels. This representative monopoly of the CEOE favored the concertation process.

The beginning of the transition, however, did not foreshadow that a cooperative relationship would develop between the CEOE and the unions. The first years after Franco died were characterized by a very high level of disputes. The CEOE, worried about the existing industrial conflict and in agreement with the conservative government, refused to strengthen the unions' role in the system. Its stance towards them was clearly antagonistic. The CEOE blamed the political instability on the unions and accused them of supporting revolutionary strategies that were resulting in the worsening of economic conditions. It was also particularly concerned about the strength of the communist union, CCOO, and focused its actions on trying to weaken the latter's position among workers. In this regard, the CEOE and the conservative government took specific steps to consolidate the UGT when its leaders came back from exile. They viewed this strategy as a means of dividing and weakening the union movement. Consequently, they opposed the CCOO's attempts to develop a unitary labor organization that would integrate all unions. At this time, union representatives in firms suffered constant discrimination, and in most cases, they operated underground to avoid reprisals. Employers even tried to develop a Christian democratic oriented union which might balance the strength of the CCOO and the UGT. This attempt failed (Führer 1996, 233). The CEOE was able to prevent the legal recognition of union activities at the firm level until the Union Freedom Act was approved in 1985, and argued against the return of the unions' wealth confiscated by the dictatorship.[35]

The event that triggered a shift in this confrontational strategy was the 1978 election of representatives to the work councils. These elections clarified the union landscape and confirmed the supremacy of the CCOO and the UGT in the labor movement. The CEOE was forced to acknowledge these results and reassess its strategy towards unions. It began to recognize unions as valid intermediaries for the workers and realized that the development of a new industrial relations setting had to be negotiated. The organization's preference, however, was for moderate unions, and, therefore, it started a process of rapprochement with the UGT—which they considered more moderate than CCOO. The CEOE started this new strategy in 1978 with negotiations at the highest level with UGT. The consequence was the signing of the ABE that same year, the first of five centralized agreements signed by the employers association and the UGT between 1979 and 1986 (and with the participation of the government and CCOO in two of them). The CEOE viewed the concertation process as a way to consolidate its position in the system. It also sought to "reward" the moderate union. When it reached agreements with UGT in 1978 and 1980, it intensified its attacks against CCOO and accused that union of radicalization and irresponsible demands.[36]

Cooperation resulted in the institutionalization of the role of unions and business associations. Their representative position was accepted by the government, and they became recognized in the boards of several public institutions. The capstone of this process was the creation of the Consejo Económico y Social (CES, the Economic and Social Council) in 1991—an advisory board recognized by the Constitution.

III. The System of Collective Bargaining

The structure of the collective bargaining system (specifically, the bargaining unit) has also been hypothesized by the literature as one of the key factors to account for the success of neocorporatist concertation arrangements and solidaristic policies (Scharpf 1991, Golden 1993, Cameron 1984, Hall 1994). These authors have argued that within a system of centralized/coordinated wage bargaining, unions will tend to consider the macroeconomic consequences of wage settlements because of rational self-interest and, thus, individual wage settlements are likely to be determined by such general considerations. Centralized bargaining also fosters homogenized wage increases, which in turn reduce conflict and competition among unions. It also helps minimize costs associated with local bargaining—for example, wage drift—and contributes to internalize the costs of wage moderation because all unions are part of the wage settlements and, therefore, are not be able to go out and seek new members by criticizing the agreement or blaming it on other unions.

Countries where concertation has been successful are characterized by a system of centralized/coordinated wage bargaining. In Germany, the central trade union confederation, the DGB (Deutscher Gerwerkschaftsbund), is formally excluded in wage negotiations. Wage bargaining is conducted by individual unions that negotiate nationally or regionally by branches. However, IG Metall (Metallindustriarbetareförbundet, the metalworkers union) is the union which opens the first round of negotiations, and the other unions follow the guidelines adopted by it, thus fostering coordination of wage demands. This had led many authors to conclude that in Germany the strong performance of the system has been dependent on the organizational features of German unions and employers and, particularly, on the leadership position of the IG Metall and the ability of the employers' associations to coordinate the bargaining positions of their affiliates (Hall 1994).

In Austria, the Commission for Prices and Wages has to give its approval before negotiations are opened by individual unions. The trade union ÖGB (Österreichischer Gewerkschaftsbund) confederation makes a presentation to the commission stating the negotiation goals of each union. This process guarantees a certain degree of coordination, because even though the commission does not set guidelines, it ensures that wage objectives will take into account macroeconomic considerations. The result in both countries has been a high degree of wage moderation (Scharpf 1991, 189–190).

On the other hand, a system of decentralized bargaining with competitive unions, such as Britain's, encourages wage competition among unions and results in a dynamic that drives up wages and increases inflation. In Great Britain, wage bargaining is generally decentralized and takes place mostly at the firm and plant level. There have never been central wage negotiations for the whole economy, and wage restraint has only happened in exceptional circumstances and for a short period of time—for example, 1975–1978. In Sweden, the collapse of centralized bargaining in the mid-1980s hindered the implementation of solidaristic polices based on concertation because it increased wage competition among workers (Pontusson and Swenson 1996).

In this section, I seek to analyze the legal regulation of collective bargaining in Spain to determine its structure. Classifying the Spanish case is not a straightforward task. Although the legal framework is essentially neutral—that is, the decision about the level of wage bargaining was originally left in the hands of the social actors—the application of the 1980 Workers' Statute has resulted in an "intermediate" system of collective bargaining in which most of the bargaining took place at the firm level, but most workers were included in agreements negotiated at the branch or sectoral levels. This system, however, contrary to the conclusions advanced by the literature, did not result in wage explosions or wage drift during the concertation years. On the contrary, concertation took place from 1979 until 1986, and it resulted in wage moderation. The objective of this section is twofold: First to analyze whether or not the Spanish legislation favors decentralized over centralized bargaining, and second, whether wage moderation was possible under an "intermediate" system of wage bargaining.

During most of the concertation period (1979–1986) the collective bargaining system in Spain was based on the regulations established by the Workers' Statute of 1980.[37] During the dictatorship, the system of collective bargaining was characterized by decentralization, fragmentation of the bargaining process, and independence among the different levels of bargaining (Fernández López 1995, 88). This chaotic structure, coupled with the control exercised by the state, developed into a situation of instability, legal uncertainty, and the generalization of decentralized collective bargaining. The Workers' Statute sought to address these problems and established a new framework for collective bargaining characterized by predictability, stability, and legal certainty (Valdés Dal-Re 1983, 416). According to the statute, the resulting pact is law and applies to workers and employers included within its limits (Art. 82).

The collective bargaining system in Spain is mostly an open shop system[38] in which workers' representatives are elected in trade union elections organized every four years, and the representatives from the employers associations are determined based on the representative capacity of different business organizations on each sector and area in which the agreement will be applied. Based on the result of the union elections, some unions (mostly the COO and UGT) will receive the status of most representative union, which will give them the legal capacity to negotiate agreements in that particular sector (García Murcia, Gutiérrez Palacios and Rodríguez Sañudo 1995).

Furthermore, one of the most relevant aspects of the Spanish labor legislation was that the new system of collective bargaining was based on the autonomy, independence, and sovereignty of the social actors. It sought to terminate, at least partially, the state controls and interventionism of the past.[39] The system of collective bargaining was based on the following principles (Valdés Dal-Re 1994, 15–16): First, the autonomy of the parts to determine the level of bargaining. The Workers' Statute did not establish preferences in favor of certain bargaining levels. The role of the state was limited to certifying the right of the actors to negotiate at whatever level they found useful, and taking notice of the content and applicability of the agreement. Second, the "neutrality" of the system was reinforced by the fact that all collective bargains, regardless of the level of negotiation, had the same judicial value and were sources of law. Participating actors could negotiate over any of the issues included in Article 85 of the law—for example, economics, labor, employment conditions, and so on—regardless of the level of negotiation. Finally, it also established the principle that in case of conflict among several collective bargains, the oldest pact would be the applicable one (Art. 84). This clause had important consequences because it attributed preference to the oldest pact regardless of the level of negotiation. The consequence of all these principles was that the centralization or decentralization of the collective bargaining process depended on the autonomy of the social actors—that is, if the actors decide to negotiate centrally, they could choose to abolish Article 84's preference for the earlier bargain and apply the new one. The government did not take sides in this debate.[40] In conclusion, the Workers' Statute established the autonomy of the most representative social actors to decide the level of bargaining, and the resolution of conflicts among existing collective bargains. It was a neutral system that did not favor centralized over decentralized bargaining.

How did the system develop, and what determined it? Before the new law was applied in 1981, most collective bargaining took place at the firm level (65.9 percent in 1981), but the typical unit involved was higher—at the industrial level of the province, (which covered 48.1 percent of the workers).[41] After the application of the Workers' Statute, there was a dramatic increase in the number of collective agreements, which almost doubled between 1982 (3,385) and 1992 (5,009).[42] The system that developed under the statute resulted in a three-tier bargaining system at the national, sectoral, and firm level. While the number of agreements at the firm level have increased (from 64.57 percent of the total in 1982 to 72.39 in 1992),[43] the number of agreements at the sectoral level has decreased (from 28.5 percent of the total in 1981 to 25.34 percent in 1992), and the number of national agreements has remained stable. This conclusion, however, needs to be qualified. Although there has been a large number of collective bargains negotiated at the firm level, wages for most workers are negotiated at the sectoral level—that is, the overwhelming majority of Spanish workers are included in sectoral agreements.[44] Table 4.4 shows the percentage of agreements signed at different levels and the number of workers included in the agreements:

In conclusion, despite the fact that the Spanish legislation regulating collective bargaining after 1980 was "neutral"—that is, it did not favor centralized or decentralized wage bargaining—the Spanish social actors did little to reduce the fragmentation of the collective bargaining process.[45] In light of this data, Valdés Dal-Re (1995, 24) has concluded that there has not been a significant transformation of the structure of collective bargaining as a result of the Workers' Statute. The overwhelming majority of workers (82.8 percent in 1994 and 86.5 percent in 1995) are still covered in agreements negotiated at higher levels than the firm—usually at the sectoral/provincial level. The major consequence of this development was the reform of 1994, in which the government decided to

Table 4.4 Number of Collective Agreements by Bargaining Level

Year	Number of Collective Bargains	Firm (%)	Sectoral/Province (%)	National (%)	Firms: Number of Workers (000)	Superior: Number of Workers (000)
1982	3,385	64.57	28.5	—	985.7	—
1983	3,655	65	—	—	1,074.80	—
1984	3,796	66.8	—	—	1,060.50	—
1985	3,834	67.55	28.84	1.9	1,062.50	5,035.70
1986	3,790	68.28	27.99	1.95	1,092.80	5,154.30
1987	4,112	68.5	27.77	1.98	1,106.50	5,715.30
1988	4,096	68.99	27.49	2.14	1,070.40	5,766.00
1989	4,302	70.1	26.4	2.08	1,061.90	5,901.30
1990	4,596	70.81	25.65	2.12	1,132.60	6,431.00
1991	4,858	71.65	24.81	1.95	1,151.00	6,643.10
1992	5,009	72.39	24.07	1.94	1,189.50	6,706.40
1993	4,749	71	29*	—	1,045.70	6,691.50
1994	4,199	70.71	29.3*	—	855.561	6,045.40
1995	3,599	71.9	28.1*	—	818,971	5,279.90
1996	1,933	65.18	34.8*	—	—	—

Source: Own elaboration with data from Valdés Dal-Re 1995, 23; Ministerio de Trabajo y Seguridad Social, *Estadística de Convenios Colectivos*, 1993–1994; *Economía Trabajo y Sociedad*, Madrid: CES, 1996; and *El País*, December 18, 1995, 59.
*Includes all agreements negotiated above the firm level.

intervene and influence the level of bargaining. This reform had very important consequences: It fostered decentralization and some flexibility by allowing the social actors to negotiate subsequent agreements at lower levels which could differ from (and modify) previous agreements negotiated at higher levels (Fernández López 1995, 87–88).[46] The new law gives actors at the lower levels the right to withdraw from previous agreements negotiated at higher levels. Until 1996, this reform has not had great impact on the structure of collective bargaining (del Rey Guanter 1998, 352–355). Although there is still a large number of collective agreements (3,599 in 1995), most workers are covered by agreements negotiated at the sectoral level (i.e., 86.5 percent in 1995). The impact of this reform may be further tempered by new developments. In April of 1997 the UGT, CCOO and the employer association signed a new centralized agreement that sought to modify some of the reforms introduced in 1994. It sought to strengthen the collective autonomy, to reduce the existing fragmentation of collective bargaining, and to promote bargaining at the national and sectoral levels (see Conclusions).

How did the 1980 structure of collective bargaining affect concertation and the ability to implement incomes policy? The literature has argued that within a system of centralized/coordinated wage bargaining, unions tend to consider the macroeconomic consequences of wage settlements out of rational self-interest. According to this argument, in countries with such a system and cohesive labor movements, unions are believed to internalize the effects of wages on inflation, and to be willing to moderate their wage demands. The labor-market adjustment is also achieved in countries with decentralized wage bargaining and flexible labor markets—in this case the markets adjust the wages. In contrast, in countries whose wage bargaining arrangements fall somewhere in the middle, unions are believed to have a harder time internalizing the macroeconomic consequences of their wage demands because the former are not immediately obvious (Calmfors and Driffill, 1988).

Spain, with a system of wage bargaining based mostly in collective bargaining at the sectoral/provincial level, falls within the "intermediate" centralization category that is seen by the literature as less conducive to wage moderation and concertation (Garrett 1998, Calmfors and Driffill 1988, Soskice 1990, Golden 1993, Jimeno and Toharia 1994, Jimeno 1997, 83). This institutional feature has led some authors to conclude that the Spanish structure has made any attempt at income policies and concertation very difficult (Boix 1996, 216). These scholars have claimed that "the system of collective bargaining in Spain is not conductive to wage moderation typical of centralized systems, nor it is to the efficient microeconomic advantages that are derived from decentralized systems" (Jimeno 1997, 83, my translation).[47]

These conclusions, however, seem unwarranted. Although the Spanish wage-setting system falls within the "intermediate" category, it is not exactly true that this has resulted in excessive wage demands or that it hindered concertation. On the contrary, despite the fragmented structure of collective bargaining, concertation still took place in Spain for an extended period of time and wage moderation was achieved. Four of the five centralized agreements included wage ranges based on the government forecast of inflation for the following year. Despite the fact that the exact determination of wages was left to negotiations at lower levels, final wages increased less than the maximum stipulated in the central agreements, thus confirming the effectiveness of concertation to produce wage moderation despite a decentralized wage-setting system. This fact diminishes the strength of the argument advanced by the literature stating that wage moderation is not possible in countries within the "intermediate" centralization/coordination category like Spain. Table 4.5 shows that final wages grew within the margin established in centralized agreements:

Unions in Spain were powerful enough to enforce the centralized agreements despite decentralized bargaining. As long as one of the major unions took part, wages were kept within the parameters established in the wage range. Even when one of the major unions refused to take part in the agreements (CCOO did not sign the AMI in 1978 and the AES in 1984), the other major union, in this case the UGT, was able to muster support from the workers to implement the agreement.[48] Furthermore, as shown in Table 4.6, even after concertation ended in 1985 and the econ-

Table 4.5 Final Wages, 1978–1986

Year	Agreement	Wage Range (%)	Final Wage Increases in Collective Agreement (5)
1978	P. Moncloa	20	20.6
1979	No Agreement	11–14	14.1
1980	AMI	13–16	15.3
1981	AMI	11–15	13.1
1982	ANE	9–11	10.5
1983	AI	9.5–12.5	11.4
1984	No Agreement	6.5	7.7
1985	AES	5.5–7.5	7.4
1986	AES	7.2–8.5	8.1

Source: Roca, 1993, Table 6, p. 187. Reprinted with permission. From Ministerio de Trabajo y Seguridad Social: *Boletín de Estadísticas Laborales.* Various years.

Table 4.6 Purchasing Power, 1978–1997

Year	Purchasing Power	Year	Purchasing Power	Year	Purchasing Power
1978	1.2	1985	−0.9	1992	1.4
1979	−1.7	1986	−0.6	1993	0.9
1980	−0.6	1987	1.3	1994	−1.1
1981	−1.5	1988	1.6	1995	−0.8
1982	−3.4	1989	1.8	1996*	0.3
1983	−1.2	1990	1.6	1997*	1.0
1984	−3.5	1991	2.1		

Sources: El País, November 18, 1996. Developed with data from the Ministerio de Trabajo y Seguridad Social.
*From Ministerio de Trabajo y Asuntos Sociales, *Estadística de Convenios Colectivos* and *Boletín de Estadísticas Laborales.* 1997 only includes the collective bargains negotiated prior to February 28, 1998.

omy expanded, workers' incomes grew moderately despite "decentralized" bargaining.

This data challenges the emphasis placed by Spanish politicians and business on the influence that wage growth has had on inflation in the 1980s–1990s.[49] Real wage gains were very modest from 1986–1989, and unit labor costs declined in real terms until 1990 and had a moderating effect on inflation.

However, as we can see in Table 4.8, when the two major unions refused to accept the inflation guidelines imposed by the government, wages ended up exceeding those guidelines, growing faster than inflation.

Table 4.7 Labor Costs, Real Wages, and Productivity

Year	Labor Costs*	Real Wages**	Productivity***
1972–1978	5.92	5.00	4.45
1979–1981	2.09	−0.89	2.6
1982–1989	0.25	−0.33	2.12
1990–1993	1.82	1.19	2.36

Source: Blanchard et al., 1995, Table 6, p. 66. Reprinted with permission. From National Accounts.
*Mean annual growth rate of real labor cost.
**Mean annual growth rate of real net wage.
***Mean annual growth rate of productivity.

Table 4.8 Wages versus Inflation, 1984–1997

Year	Wage Increase	CPI (Real)	Year	Wage Increase	CPI (Real)
1984	7.8	11.3	1991	8.1	5.9
1985*	7.9	8.5	1992	7.3	5.9
1986*	8.2	8.8	1993	5.5	4.6
1987	6.5	5.2	1994	3.6	4.7
1988	6.4	4.8	1995	3.9	4.7
1989	7.8	6.8	1996	3.89	3.5
1990	8.3	6.7	1997	3**	2.0

Source: El País, November 18, 1996. Developed with data from the Ministerio de Trabajo y Seguridad Social.
*Last two years of concertation.
**Estimated.

This data confirms the effectiveness of the concertation process and challenges the notion that the Spanish wage bargaining system is inherently inflationary and ill suited to produce wage moderation. How can we blame the collapse of concertation on the structure of the collective bargaining system when this system helped achieve wage moderation for an extended period of time? How can it be argued that unions cannot produce wage moderation and be reliable partners of incomes polices? On the contrary, we have seen how unions could implement and enforce voluntary incomes policies and had the capacity to fulfill their agreements.[50] Wages remained moderate during the years of concertation (1979–1983, 1985–1986), and only increased beyond targets when the concertation process broke down after 1985. Afterward, wages generally increased over inflation, as illustrated graphically in Figure 4.1.

In conclusion, wage moderation in Spain was not hindered by the wage setting system. Despite an "intermediate" wage bargaining system, we find concertation and wage moderation between 1979 and 1986 (except for 1984, when there was no pact). The Spanish legislation allowed for concertation, and concertation did produce wage moderation. Only when concertation collapsed after 1986—and the system of wage bargaining remained the same until the reform of 1994—wages grew faster than inflation. This process was reversed only in 1994–1995, when the Spanish economy was in the midst of a sharp recession.

Conclusions

The literature has argued that union fragmentation and decentralized collective bargaining hindered social concertation by intensifying rivalries

Figure 4.1 Wage Increase vs. CPI, 1984–1997

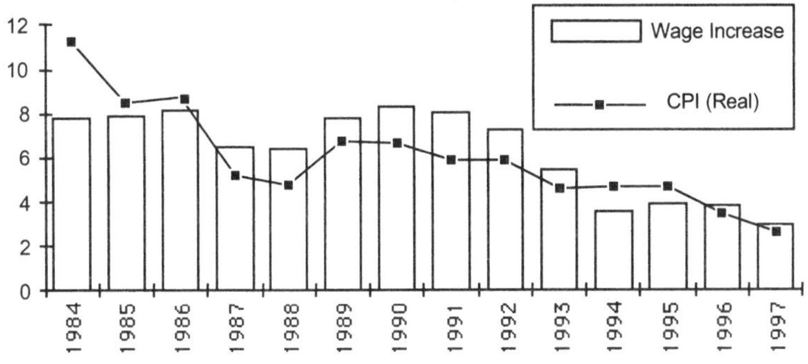

Source: Developed with data from the from the Ministerio de Trabajo y Seguridad Social.

among unions and by forcing unions to compete for members. Policymakers in Spain have also argued that concertation failed because weak unions operating within a decentralized collective bargaining system could not deliver solidaristic policies. The socialist economic team questioned the unions' capacity to sustain centralized agreements and to keep their rank and file under control in order to implement solidaristic policies, and saw restrictive monetary policy as a more effective way to fight inflation. It figured that unions would be forced to moderate their wage demands in order to avoid further unemployment. Therefore, the government would choose to apply restrictive monetary and fiscal policies to prevent aggressive wage demands.[51] These conclusions, however, seem unwarranted. In this chapter I have challenged the notion that unions and the collective bargaining setting were inadequate for concertation, and that they were ill suited to produce wage moderation and solidaristic polices.

First, despite low levels of membership, which seemed to confirm unions' weakness, concertation took place in Spain for an extended period of time. Contrary to the notion that such low levels precluded Spanish unions from pursuing solidaristic policies, these unions enjoyed a high level of support as proven by their performance in the elections to the work councils, union coverage, their mobilizing ability, their statutory authority over their members, and their capacity to implement the agreements they signed.

Secondly, the existing pluralistic and competitive structure of the industrial relations setting did not preclude the implementation and success of concertation agreements in Spain. The negative effects that such a competitive structure would have had on concertation and solidaristic policies was mitigated by the fact that the work council elections fostered the consolidation of a union duopoly, and strengthened the position of the UGT and CCOO as leaders of the labor movement.[52] Furthermore, the coexistence of competing unions in the same branches of industry was further tempered by the fact that strategic decisions—including wage strategies—had been taken at the confederate level. Finally, after the late 1980s both confederations agreed on the principle of "unitary action."

The further argument that the internal organization of unions hindered concertation in Spain is not compelling, either. In the case of Spain, unions are organized along industrial sector lines, which fosters centralized decision making, with the decision-making process concentrated at the top level. The confederation (mostly the executive committee and the secretary general) is the source of all important decisions, the institution responsible for external fund-raising, and the one that receives and manages subsidies from the state and external loans. Centralization is further fostered by the weak economic position of the federations, which are unable to self-finance their activities and are dependent on the confederation for funds. A consequence of this organization along industrial sectors has been that Spanish unions have been able to avoid the "wage deprivation" effect that hindered concertation and wage moderation in other countries (such as Great Britain or Sweden). In fact, Spanish unions have been able to coordinate separate bargaining levels. They had the strategic, tactical, and communicative experience to influence separate bargaining cycles. Finally, the fact that Spanish unions represent both blue- and white-collar workers as well as civil servants, prevented the kinds of distributive conflicts that made wage coordination difficult in Sweden.

In this chapter I have also attempted to qualify the conclusion that the Spanish system of collective bargaining was ill suited to implement solidaristic policies and concertation. I have concluded that the legislation regulating the system of collective bargaining (until the reform of 1994) was neutral—that is, it left the decision about the level of negotiation to the social actors. In the late 1970s and early 1980s there were three formal negotiation levels between unions and employers (and sometimes the government): Centralized negotiations, branch negotiations, and local negotiations between union representatives and management in individual firms. Wages for most Spanish workers, however, are negotiated at the sectoral or branch level. This "intermediate" system of wage bargaining did not result, as predicted by the literature, in an explosion of wages. On the contrary, wage increases remained moderate.

Moreover, the data that I have included in this chapter challenges the emphasis placed by Spanish politicians and business on the influence that the wage bargaining system has had on inflation in the 1980s and 1990s. Concertation resulted in wage moderation and real wage losses for Spanish workers; during the concertation period wages grew systematically below inflation, which challenges the notion that concertation was neither feasible in Spain nor able to it produce wage moderation. On the contrary, unions proved to be reliable partners. They also had the capacity (particularly the UGT) to play an adequate role in a governmental incomes policy approach. Real wage gains were very modest from 1986–1989, despite the absence of centralized bargaining and the fact that it was a period of economic expansion, and unit labor costs declined in real terms until 1990, which had a moderating effect on inflation. However, when the two major unions refused to accept the inflation guidelines imposed by the government, wages always exceeded those guidelines and wages grew faster than inflation. It was not the system of collective bargaining that prevented concertation or caused its collapse after 1985. The decision on how to negotiate wages was left in the hands of individuals and they were the ones responsible, not the structure of bargaining. When they decided to negotiate centrally, concertation succeeded and wage moderation was achieved. When they refused to do so, decentralized wage bargaining prevailed and wage moderation was hindered.

Finally, the Spanish experience with concertation confirms Golden's argument (1993) that the internal structure of labor movement—and specifically the labor confederation leaders' ability to coordinate the behavior of large sectors of the workforce—is a more important determinant of macroeconomic outcomes and the success of economywide wage bargaining than the level of wage bargaining per se. The Spanish experience confirms that the key factor in determining the effectiveness of centralized wage agreements is the ability of confederation leaders to make workers adhere to these agreements at lower bargaining levels. In this regard the concentration of union authority in peak confederations whose constituents comprised the bulk of the workforce mitigated wage drift in Spain in two ways. First, the leaders of the unions (particularly the UGT's) were willing to coordinate economywide wage restraint to maximize both employment and wages for the labor force as a whole. Second, confederation leaders had the instruments to informally sanction constituents who did not abide by such agreements.

In conclusion, it is hard to argue that the underlying structural conditions under which concertation took place in Spain were inadequate. If this was the case they would have been undermined by wage drift. This did not happen. This empirical evidence is consistent with new analyses that challenge the notion of "unions in decline" (see chapter 2). Golden, Wallerstein and Lange (1999) have analyzed changes in 12 OECD countries along four dimensions: union density, union coverage, union concentration, and statutory authority for employers union organizations, and conclude that union decline has not been as widespread as previously perceived. On the contrary, their data supports the view that industrial relation institutions and trade unions have proved quite resilient in the face of domestic and international pressures. They show that there have been countries—Denmark, Sweden, and Finland—in which union density increased in the 1980s (1998, 198–202). They also present conclusive evidence showing that: interconfederal concentration has increased in some countries (i.e., Japan) (1998, 205–213); that the rates of coverage have remained uniformly high throughout Europe (1998, 203–205); and finally that the statutory authority of employers and unions has remained stable (1998, 213–221). They find no supporting evidence that there have been substantial changes in authority relations within labor unions and employer organizations. They conclude that "unions have retained most of the institutional based capacities for the defense of worker interests that they had prior to the 1980s" and attribute the current weakness of unions in most countries to sustained unemployment (1998, 224).

If institutional factors are not enough to explain the collapse of concertation in Spain, what other factors can help us resolve this puzzle? In chapter 5 I shall focus on the economic and structural variables emphasized by the literature to explain the decline of concertation processes in the western world.

CHAPTER 5

Structural and Economic Constraints on Concertation in Spain

Introduction

If the Spanish institutional setting does not offer a sufficient explanation, the collapse of concertation might be explained as a result of changes in the international economic environment and the business cycle. Authors who focus on the first of these factors argue that developments in the international environment have limited the range of policy options available to governments and thus have intensified distribution conflicts. According to this view, increasing exposure to trade, foreign direct investment, and liquid capital mobility have limited the power of national governments to manage monetary and fiscal policies, making it more difficult for governments to meet unions' demands and compensate them for wage moderation, while strengthening the position of business vis-à-vis labor (Scharpf 1991, 244–248). Moreover, globalization, coupled with pressures induced by technology restructuring and the decline of Fordist or mass production is also said to have led to greater segmentation and differentiation of the labor market, which weakened unions and shifted the balance of power between business and labor in favor of the former. In other words, the conventional wisdom about the domestic effects of changes in the production system and globalization is that they have undermined the structural bases of corporatism by significantly weakening organized labor movements and by rendering expansionary macroeconomic policies far less feasible, prompting a policy race to the neoliberal bottom among the OECD countries. These developments have led some scholars to conclude that labor market institutions have lost their ability to tailor wage developments to external competitiveness constraints (Iverson 1996, Pontusson and Swenson 1996). Moreover, in this new economic context, centralized corporatist agreements are viewed as ineffective and even counterproductive. Negotiations at the national level are too small to have much influence over transnational developments, but they are too large to accommodate the need for flexibility and diversification required in a very volatile environment.

A number of scholars have proposed this argument to account for the collapse of concertation in Spain after 1986 (see Maravall 1995, 217–228; Solchaga 1997, 36). According to this view, when the Spanish socialists came to power in 1982, the most powerful governments (the United States, Germany, and the United Kingdom) were implementing restrictive monetary policies to quell inflation. At that time the domestic economic conditions had deteriorated sharply in Spain as a consequence of the international crisis that had magnified and intensified the inefficiencies of the economy. This period also witnessed the integration of the country into the international economy, which was completed by the entrance into the European Community (EC) in 1986. According to the structuralist argument, within this context of international integration, the socialist leaders could not cave in to union demands and had no choice but to implement restrictive policies to quell inflation and restore competitiveness. In other words, the changing economic environment constrained economic policy in Spain and prevented the implementation of expansive policies that would have permitted the continuation of concertation after 1986. Otherwise they would have suffered the wrath of the market and experienced capital outflows (as in France in 1982). The government had no room for compromise. The French example was used by the moderate fraction of the Socialist party, which took over the economic departments in 1982.

While the above argument focuses on broad structural conditions, other authors have argued that the collapse of concertation is also to be attributed to cyclical rather than structural conditions. Espina (1991) and Schmitter (1990) argue that the domestic business cycle affects concertation because it strengthens (or weakens) the position of certain actors vis-à-vis the other ones, and intensifies consensus (or distribution conflicts). According to this view, concertation is more likely in periods of economic downturn because the crisis fosters cooperation and consensus, while high unemployment weakens the position of unions. Periods of economic bonanza, on the contrary, are not propitious to concertation because they intensify distribution conflicts and augment the power of labor. The fact that the Spanish economy entered a period of rapid economic growth in the second half of the 1980s, therefore, intensified distribution conflicts and contributed to the collapse of concertation.

This chapter has two sections. First I seek to refute the argument that attributes the collapse of concertation in Spain to structural changes in the economic environment. Although the internationalization of the economy weakened the position of labor and conditioned the course of economic policy, I argue that it fails to explain the collapse of concertation after 1986 for several reasons. The government had room for compromise with unions. Furthermore, government policies in Spain have been generally attributed to international constraints, I argue that, on the contrary, they actually represented policy choices. When the government shifted direction after the success of the 1988 general strike and gave in to most union demands, Spain did not suffer the wrath of the markets and did not experience capital outflows as should have been expected according to governmental predictions. Moreover, it is difficult to maintain that the globalization of capital markets and the decline of Fordist production are the reasons for the collapse of concertation when both factors also affected countries that still have centralized bargaining—Belgium, Austria, the Netherlands, and Portugal. While I acknowledge that structural developments affected the labor movement, I also argue that they did not alter dramatically the balance of power between labor and capital in Spain. Unions are still strong in Spain, the major confederations still dominate the labor landscape, and they have been able to attract new constituencies. Two main factors help to account for this development. First, Fordism is still a dominant form of production in Spain, and second, the country has not experienced the levels of wage decompression that has damaged centralized bargaining in other countries. In the second section, I analyze the business-cycle explanation. Although economic growth intensified distribution conflicts in Spain after 1986, I conclude that the business cycle cannot provide an adequate explanation for the collapse of concertation in Spain. Contrary to what should have been expected according to the business-cycle explanation, concertation did not emerge again in the early 1990s when Spain entered into a deep recession. In contrast, it resumed in 1997 when the country was in the midst of a major economic expansion.

I. Structural Changes

The collapse of concertation in the mid-1980s in countries such as Sweden has been explained in terms of economic structural changes associated with technology restructuring, increasing trade globalization, and the liberalization of financial markets. According to this argument, the changing economic environment had two major effects on concertation: First, it weakened and fragmented the labor movement, thus strengthening the position of capital vis-à-vis labor, and second, it limited the capacity and autonomy of governments to compensate unions for wage moderation (see chapter 2).

Spanish scholars and socialist officials have also argued that these developments had an impact in the collapse of concertation after 1986. They have argued that the increasing internationalization and liberalization of the

Spanish economy limited the scope of policy responses to the economic crisis and had a dramatic impact on labor. In this regard, one of the major developments that took place in the first half of the 1980s was Spain's entry into the EC and its full integration into the international economy after 40 years of relative isolation. In 1986, just before Spain joined the EC, Spanish custom duties remained, on the average, five times higher than those in the EC. Before 1959 Franco's dictatorship had responded to international isolation by discouraging foreign trade and promoting protective measures that isolated Spanish firms from international competition. In 1959 the economic and political conditions promoted a major policy change in the orientation of economic policy, which shifted from autarchy, or self-sufficiency, to trade liberalization. Despite this, however, until 1975 the Spanish economy (along with Portugal's) was still the least competitive and most isolated in Western Europe. Therefore, the capacity of the Spanish economy to compete in international markets was questionable.[1] Access to the EC in 1986 changed this dynamic and consolidated the internationalization of the Spanish economy.[2] Throughout the 1980s the socialist government dismantled trade barriers, liberalized most economic sectors, and further opened the Spanish economy to external competition (see Solchaga 1996, 38–42). The opening of the economy to international competition, magnified by the effects of the recession, resulted in a dramatic intensification of competition, firm closures, and downsizing. Furthermore, Spain's access to the EC accelerated the process of financial reform in order to adjust the country's legislation to the EC's (Pérez 1997, 191–193). According to the structuralist explanation, the increasing liberalization and globalization of domestic economies had two major consequences: First, they caused a dramatic change in the production regime, and second, they imposed constraints on macroeconomic policy. I analyze next the impact of these two developments on concertation in Spain.

a. Impact of Production Regime Changes on Labor and Unions

Structuralists have argued that pressures induced by technology restructuring changed the international economic environment in the 1980s (Scharpf 1987, 26–28). The conventional wisdom about the domestic effects of changes in the production system is that they have undermined the structural bases of corporatism by significantly weakening organized labor movements. These changes resulted in higher demand for scarce highly skilled labor, which in turn fostered wage differentiation and labor segmentation. They also had a serious impact on concertation because they shifted the balance of power between labor and capital in favor of the latter. The emergence of large groups of highly skilled workers encouraged the development of new unions to articulate their particular demands. At the same time, the increasing wage differentials also hindered concertation because centralized bargaining did not offer enough flexibility to take into consideration particular circumstances that would justify wage differentials. In contrast, wage differentiation fosters decentralized bargaining (see chapter 2). These developments have led some scholars to conclude that labor market institutions have lost their ability to tailor wage developments to external competitiveness constraints (Iversen 1996, Pontusson and Swenson 1996).

In Spain, some authors have argued that changes induced by technology restructuring further weakened the labor movement and thus hindered concertation. According to the structuralist explanation, the emergence of new production processes, intensive competition, and industrial reconversion hit unions' strongholds and resulted in higher unemployment. Unions in Spain, however, were further weakened by three developments: First, the economic crisis of the 1970s, which resulted in high unemployment that hit unions' traditional constituencies. Second, these forces fostered wage differentiation and increased the nonunionized sector of the economy (see Moscoso 1995, 31). Finally, most new jobs emerged in sectors where unions had less influence—that is, the service sector. These developments intensified labor segmentation and weakened unions, thus hindering concertation (see Alonso 1991, 403–423; Roca 1991, 361–378; Bilbao 1991, 251–270; Boix 1994, 28–29).

At first sight, economic developments provide support to this argument. During the economic recession (up to 1985), employment was destroyed by 1.7 percent yearly (or 1,636,000 jobs).[3] After 1985 the economy recovered, and the Gross Domestic Product (GDP) grew an average of 4 percent between 1985–1989, while per capita GDP grew up to 76 percent of the EC average. Unemployment, however, remained very high (there were 2,522,000 unemployed in 1989). At the same time, during the economic crisis Spain also experienced an acute process of deindustrialization. Between 1977 and 1985, industrial employment decreased by 785,000 people, and only 231,000 of those jobs were recovered after 1986 when the economy picked up. Furthermore, most of the new employment was in the service sector—that is, between 1985 and 1989, 1,139,000 new jobs (see Recio 1991, 109; Vázquez 1991, 9–10).[4] In other words, where unions were strong, jobs were lost and where jobs were created, unions were not present. Therefore, it has been argued that given the growth of employment in sectors of the economy where unions were weak, unions had little incentive to "embrace wage restraint in exchange for more employment among unskilled workers" (Boix 1994, 28). This, according to Boix, contributed to the collapse of concertation.

The proponents of the structuralist explanation have also contended that unions were further weakened by a dramatic change in the structure of demand, with a tendency toward increasing differentiation of goods and services. These changes resulted in higher demand for highly skilled labor, which fostered wage differentiation and labor segmentation. In the 1980s in Spain there was a decline in Fordist methods of production and an emergence of new organizational and productive processes based on new technologies and managerial methods. According to some authors (Recio 1991, 103–107), the consequence of this transformation was the development of a new labor structure to limit labor costs and foster flexibility, which made concertation more difficult because labor and business heterogeneity increased the need for flexibility and differentiation.[5] Increasing labor segmentation also widened wage differentials (Roca 1993, 229; Recio 1991, 110). These developments, according to these authors, intensified interlabor disputes and hindered solidarity among workers, thus making concertation more difficult (Recio 1991, 110). The increase in temporary workers also affected unions because they are less likely to join unions due to the fear of reprisals from their employers (Bilbao 1991, 262).[6] In this context union confederations have more difficulties aggregating labor demands and centralized concertation is more difficult (Regini 1995, 77–79).

The authors cited, however, exaggerate the extent to which structural developments have affected the unions in the country. These developments do not fully account for the collapse of concertation after 1986 for several reasons. Although the Fordist system of production had been in decline, this system had lasted in Spain for a longer time than in other countries (Moscoso 1995, 30). Most firms still had not adopted new production methods, and were ill equipped to compete with more modern companies. Moreover, the process of reindustrialization that took place in the 1980s had not enhanced substantially the viability and competitive situation of most firms (Vázquez 1991, 13; Navarro Arancegui 1989, 45–69; de Quinto 1994). The consequence of this development has been that the demand for skilled labor has not been as dramatic in Spain as in other countries, and Spanish unions have not yet had to face the dramatic increases in labor segmentation that have taken place elsewhere.

Moreover, according to the structuralist argument, production changes should have resulted in wage differentials. As we have seen above, wage differentiation had been one of the major reasons why concertation collapsed in the mid-1980s in countries such as Sweden. This factor, however, was not a major issue in the Spanish concertation process, as it never became a central point of discussion in talks between the government and unions or employers and unions. The introduction of collective bargaining during the dictatorship had already resulted in wage differentiation. Union action during the transition, however, had an egalitarian effect in wages, and differentials decreased in the late 1970s. Concertation resulted in the concentration of wage increases around the mean of the wage range established in the agreements. As seen in Table 5.1, wage differentials remained stable in Spain throughout the 1980s, and differentials among workers in different professional categories grew moderately (see Roca 1993, 225–232).

At the same time, changes in the structure of demand and higher unemployment, emphasized by the authors mentioned above, have not resulted in a dramatic shift in the balance of power between capital and labor in Spain for two main reasons. First, as I showed in chapter 4, unions in Spain are not as weak as postulated by those authors, and second, businesses in Spain are mostly oriented to the domestic market and lack the ability to move their production overseas. The Spanish unions' leaders realized in the 1980s that their social base was weakening and that their traditional source of support among blue-collar Fordist workers was bound to disappear, but they took steps to attract new groups—for example, youth, public administration workers, and unemployed people. Unions put aside sectoral interests and focused on more generalized economic demands (Ortiz Lallana 1990, 136). The unions' "Propuesta Sindical Prioritaria" (1989) proved their capacity to articulate an economic alternative to the government's policies in order to attract new constituencies. It is also important to highlight, as noted before, that some of the demands that have motivated intense conflict between unions and the government involved issues that would benefit sectors of the population not traditionally associated with unions (see chapter 3). New reports confirm that new group of workers are increasingly supporting unions (see García Murcia, Gutiérrez Palacios, and Rodriguez Sañudo 1995, 273–283).[7]

Furthermore, contradicting the structuralist authors is the fact that the balance of power between labor and business has been maintained despite the increasing internationalization of the Spanish economy, which has fostered production diversification. Nevertheless, this has not resulted in a dramatic

Table 5.1 Intersector Wage Differentials, 1977–1988
(Coefficient of Variation × 100)

Year	Wages	Year	Wages
1977	23.1	1983	23.6
1978	21.2	1984	22.4
1979	21.5	1985	22.7
1980	21.9	1986	22.8
1981	22.0	1987	22.6
1982	23.4	1988	22.9

Source: Roca, 1993, Table 30, p. 227. Reprinted with permission. From INE, Salarios.

shift of power in favor of capital. The option to move production abroad depends on the level of internationalization of firms and production. While some countries—such as the United States, Italy, or Germany—are completely integrated into the world economy, and many of their firms are multinationals that operate and produce worldwide; other countries such as Spain are characterized by the predominance of domestic productive structures. The overwhelming majority of Spanish firms have less than 100 employees (the average size per establishment was 13 workers in 1986, smaller than the European standard), and the number of Spanish companies operating internationally and producing in other countries is minuscule. Therefore, it cannot be argued that internationalization has dramatically shifted the balance of power between labor and business in Spain.

Contrary to predictions, labor segmentation has not resulted in the emergence of new labor organizations dedicated to the defense of particular interests of specific workers in Spain. This fact has prevented further fragmentation within the labor movement that could have hastened the collapse of concertation, which is what happened in Sweden. On the contrary, in Spain, old forms of participation are giving way to new schemes, but this has not always resulted in the erosion of unionism. The two major confederations still receive the overwhelming support of the Spanish workers. This has been confirmed by the support that workers give unions in the elections to work councils (over 50 percent of the workers vote in these elections, 94 percent of the candidates to work councils are elected from union lists, and in 1997 both the UGT (Unión General de Trabajadores) and the CCOO (Comisiones Obreras) together received 72.87 percent of those elected to councils).[8]

Finally, from a theoretical standpoint, it is important to emphasize that new empirical evidence challenges the conventional wisdom about the domestic effects of changes in the production system and globalization—namely, that they have undermined the structural bases of corporatism by significantly weakening organized labor movements (Golden, Wallerstein, and Lange 1999). Garrett (1998, 62–69) for instance, shows that in terms of union density (the simplest measure of the strength of unions), the strength of trade unions increased significantly in the 1970s, peaked in 1980, and declined in the 1980s. He emphasizes, however, that the magnitude of the decline should not be overstated (42 percent of the workforce remained unionized in 1990 in 14 OECD [Organization for Economic Cooperation and Development] countries). According to these figures, the countries that have been more successful at maintaining the strength of the labor movements are those in which unions distribute unemployment benefits (Denmark, Finland, and Sweden). Garrett also challenges the conventional argument that attributes the collapse of social democratic (SD) corporatism to the growing divergence in the interests of labor and the decreasing ability of central confederations to resolve these conflicts (Iversen 1996; Pontusson and Swenson 1996). He shows that between 1970–1990 public sector unions became increasingly powerful, particularly in Sweden.[9] However, his empirical evidence shows that between 1970 and 1990 there was no pervasive reduction in the organizational power of peak labor confederations. His data does not support the notion of "unions in decline" (1998, 66–67).

b. The Effects of Globalization and Financial Liberalization

A somewhat different argument made in the literature postulates that the globalization and the increasing exposure to trade, liquid capital mobility, and direct foreign investment limits the effectiveness of domestic governments to implement domestic economic strategies and prompts a policy race to the neoliberal bottom and, thus the abandonment of SD corporatist strategies (Scharpf 1991, 258). According to this view, globalization is considered to have rendered expansionary macroeconomic policies far less feasible, thus eroding the prospects for concertation, because the threat of "exit" by mobile asset holders has forced governments to scrap Keynesian expansionist policies, otherwise they will move their capital and investment to less taxing and more profitable environments. At the same time, as a result of the increasing mobility of capital, governments lost their fiscal and monetary policymaking authority and were forced to implement supply side policies which lowered taxes and industry subsidies in order to promote efficient market allocation (see chapter 3). In this new environment, the implementation of traditional Keynesian-expansive policies would only result in higher inflation and balance of payments crisis (see chapter 2). These authors (Scharpf 1991; Regini 1995) have concluded that corporatism and demand Keynesianism were only successful in the context of the 1970s. Spanish government officials subscribed to this view and generally attributed the course of their economic policies to international constraints. As late as 1993 the Socialist Premier, González, still argued that "the big problem is that the government has nothing to give (the unions) in exchange (for an agreement)."[10] They argued that the liberalization and internationalization of the Spanish economy reduced the capacity of the government to compensate unions because it exposed the Spanish economy to international market forces and competition. Contrary to this view, however, there is much to suggest that the PSOE government's economic policies in fact represented real choices based on political decisions and were not imposed by the international markets.

First of all, the evolution of social policies and taxation in Spain in the 1980s and early 1990s does not support the notion that the internationalization of the Spanish economy forced the retrenchment of the public economy. On the contrary, public expenditures and taxes increased sharply between 1980 and 1992 but this was not accompanied by a deteriorating economic performance and capital flight, as should have been expected according to the globalization paradigm (see Table 5.2):

This table proves that contrary to the globalization argument, the improving macroeconomic performance of the Spanish economy in a context of internationalization was compatible with higher public expenditures (which increased from 9.2 percent of GDP in 1975 to 15.3 percent by 1991, see Table 2), the expansion of the welfare state, and increasing levels of taxation.

The socialist economic team, however, believed that the increasing internationalization of the Spanish economy did not leave much room for domestic strategies. Within the context of international integration, socialist officials argued that they could not cave in to unions' demands and had no choice but to implement restrictive policies to quell inflation and restore competitiveness. As we will see in the next chapter, despite winning the elections under a classical SD banner that supported expansion of demand, the Spanish socialist government rejected immediately the option to implement countercyclical policies to activate demand (Boix 1996, 148). Members of the economic team thought that the crisis of the 1980s was not a crisis caused by insufficient demand.[11] On the contrary, they believed that Spain's poor economic performance was mainly the result of structural factors such as inflation, the strong growth of wages, low business profits, or the fast growing public deficit, not on insufficient demand. This decision was reinforced by the French failure with expansionary policies in 1981–1982 which had a tremendous impact on the Spanish socialists (Boyer 1983, 366–368; Maravall 1995, 193–194; Maravall 1993, 95; Boix 1996, 147).[12] Therefore, the new economic team favored industrial adjustment policies and tight control of wages in order to foster investment (Paramio 1992, 530–533). These convictions led them to implement restrictive monetary policies to quell inflation and restore competitiveness, which left little room for compromise with UGT (Solchaga 1997, 43–47).

Inflation was viewed by these government officials as the core problem of the Spanish economy and the reason for its lack of competitiveness. They also believed that the process of European integration (one of the major objectives for the government) required convergence with the hard core EMS (European Monetary System) countries and this required lower inflation. In order to control inflation the socialist government had two major options. It could implement restrictive economic policies to repress wages, or it could

Table 5.2 The Evolution of Social Policies, Levels of Fiscal Pressure, and
Economic Performance in Spain

Social Policies[1]		Economic Performance and Level of Fiscal Pressure	
Social Welfare Expenditure (as % of GDP)		Economic Growth[2]	
1970	10.0	Average 1977–1985	1.5
1991	21.4	Average 1985–1992	3.7
Expenditure on Pensions (as % of GDP)		Inflation[2]	
1980	5.4	Average 1977–1985	15.3
1991	6.4	Average 1985–1992	6.5
Extent of Pension Coverage (social security and public pensioners in 000s)		Public Deficit[2]	
1975	3,404	Average 1977–1985	3.0
1992	6,859	Average 1985–1992	4.1
Expenditures Unemployment Benefits (as % of GDP)			
1980	2.7		
1991	3.7		
Extent of Unemployment Benefits coverage (in 000s)			
1975	167		
1992	1,708		
Public Expenditure on Health Care (in 000s)		Levels of Taxation[3] (as % of GDP)	
1960	2.3	1965	14.3
1992	6.4	1975	19.4
Coverage of Health Care (in 000s)			
1975	28,800	1985	28.8
1992	38,444	1990	34.4

(continues)

sign concertation agreements with unions' and employers' associations to
apply incomes polices—the latter was the preferred option for the Northern
European SD parties. At the beginning, the Spanish government favored
concertation and participated in two agreements with the unions and employers. These agreements allowed for a substantial deceleration of wage

Table 5.2 *(continued)*

Social Policies[1]	Economic Performance and Level of Fiscal Pressure
Public Expenditure on Education (as % of GDP)	
1960	1.1
1988	4.7

Source: Maravall 1997. Tables 3.3, 3.5, and 4.5; pp. 92, 100, and 179. Reprinted with permission.

[1]Comisión de las Comunidades Europeas, *La Protección Social en Europa 1993.* Brussels: European Commission, 1994; Ministerio de Economía y Hacienda, *El Gasto Público en España.* Madrid: Ministerio de Economía y Hacienda, 1989; el "Gasto Público en la democracia," in *Papeles de Economía Española,* 37 (1988).

[2]Commission Européenne, *Economie Européenne,* 54 (1993), Tables 10, 24, and 56; pp. 205, 129, and 249.

[3]Comisión de las Comunidades Europeas, *La Protección Social en Europa 1993.* Brussels: European Commission, 1994, 42; Alaain Euzéby, "La Protection Sociale en Europe: Tendances at Défis," *Futuribles,* 171 (1992), 71.

growth and inflation (cut from 14.4 percent in 1983 to 11.3 percent in 1984). After 1986, however, the socialist government failed to reach new agreements with unions and employers. It was at this stage that they decided to fight inflation with restrictive monetary policies.

The socialists' decision to ignore the unions was prompted by their determination to cut inflation, which had shot up again at the end of 1988 (6 percent). They argued that persistent inflation was rooted in the "inflation proneness" of the Spanish economy, and attributed it to wage growth (Pérez 1994, 27).[13] In July 1989, the government decided to implement a very restrictive monetary policy and accelerated Spain's access to the EMS. Economic reforms and financial liberalization produced a spurt of capital inflows chasing high rates of return. These inflows, however, led to the appreciation of the peseta and a deteriorating current account, while the spending boom financed by the foreign flows led to higher inflation. As we will see in the following chapter, these facts drove the government and UGT toward confrontation. Officials knew that such policies would alienate the unions and bring about the collapse of concertation, yet they still attributed their policies to international constraints and argued that they had no room for compromise (Solchaga 1997, 43–47).

Despite the widespread acceptance of this view, there are several factors that suggest that the government's decisions on economic policy were based on genuine alternatives, so that the collapse of concertation cannot be blamed solely on policies imposed by international markets. For instance, the course of the government monetary policy was influenced by the way that the liberalization of domestic financial markets took place. The government argued that the liberalization process was the result of constraints imposed by the increasing internationalization of the Spanish economy and by the European Community (EC) integration. The government, therefore, was left with less autonomy to compensate unions for wage moderation because interest rates were high and fiscal expansion was limited, a constraint that was further reinforced by Spain's access to the EMS[14] (Espina 1991b, 274; Bilbao 1991, 252).

Yet, the internal liberalization of financial markets was a political decision taken by the government. It was not imposed by the international markets. As Pérez (1997) shows, the decision to liberalize the system had far more to do with historical developments than with the nature of international constraints, and this was reflected in the pattern of reform. While the government lifted credit controls, it decided not to alter a critical aspect of the system and maintained an oligopolistic banking structure dominated by the banking sector. That decision was influenced by the consolidation in power after 1982 of a new economic elite anchored institutionally in the central bank that had emerged during the transition period. This new group of technocrats, led by Carlos Solchaga, Minister of Industry, and Miguel Boyer, Minister of Economics, sought an informal compact with the banking cartel to strengthen their position. This compact influenced the course of policy reform and determined the implementation of a "strong peseta" strategy that ignored a microeconomic industry-oriented perspective.[15] This strategy was based on the perceived need for continued capital inflows to satisfy the financial needs of industry and the service sector. Financial inflows, however, depended on the credibility of an overvalued peseta. Capital massively flowed into Spain as a result of the government's decision to tighten monetary policies in order to control inflation in 1987 and to join the EMS in 1989. A strong peseta was the result of the government's policies and strategies. International markets did not force the government to pursue this strategy (Pérez 1997).

This decision had important consequences for the concertation process in the sense that it increased the cost of capital for business, which, in turn, made financial investment more attractive, thus lowering productivity growth and hindering employment creation. The government, however, could have decided to increase competition within the financial sector, which would have reduced the cost of capital for business, by removing restrictions on the operations of foreign banks, restrictions that prevented them from altering significantly the price-fixing among domestic banks. Yet more evidence that proves that the government had a choice was that it delayed the liberalization of external capital flows, which was not completed until February of 1992 (Pérez 1994, 17).

Another example of policy choice was the government's decision to join the EMS in July 1989. This was prompted by the acceleration of Spanish inflation early in that year. States participating in the EMS agreed to stable exchange ratios among their currencies and monetary coordination in defense of parity, thus relinquishing monetary sovereignty (Kurzer 1993, 12). Therefore, according to the government, by joining the EMS it relinquished further sovereignty over domestic economic policies. The government, however, introduced the peseta into the EMS at the high—and controversial—value of 65 pesetas per Deutsche Mark (DM). If the government had been willing to compromise and reach a pact with unions, it could have postponed Spain's membership or negotiated other entry terms. The terms, however, were the ones favored by the government because they confirmed the government's decision to live with an already overvalued currency in order to put pressure on unions (Pérez 1994, 17–18). EMS membership, however, had little impact on either inflation or wages in Spain. The reason for this was based on the government's commitment to fight inflation at any cost, a commitment that led to large inflows of capital after 1989 from investors seeking to take advantage of the Spanish high interest rates. This choice encouraged a dynamic of resource allocation that intensified the proneness to inflation of the Spanish economy by increasing the financial costs of Spanish firms. The problem was further aggravated when unions refused to limit wage increases to resolve the contradictions of the government's "strong peseta" strategy (Pérez 1996, 17–18). The government then tried (unsuccessfully) to control wages by using an overvalued currency.

Subsequent events also confirmed that the government had had a choice. The government's decision to stick with its policy course after the collapse of the EMS and three consecutive devaluations in 1992–1993 only confirmed its commitment to the "strong peseta" strategy and the lack of interest in renegotiating the social compact with unions. This "represented a desperate attempt to rescue a policy stance that had been committed and pursued since the mid-1980s" (Pérez 1996, 19). The government had the option to abandon the EMS—as did England and Italy in 1992—to regain some sovereignty over economic policy and resolve the contradictions of the "strong peseta" strategy. In fact, it stuck to its policy and continued pursuing the objective to participate in the proposed monetary union. In accordance with the recommendation of International Monetary Fund (IMF) (1990) the government went through the motions and offered new social agreements to unions—for example, the 1990 "Competitiveness Pact" and later on the 1991 "Social Pact for Progress." These proposals, however, did not signal any policy reversal (see chapter 3). The government offered little room for negotiation, proven by its decision to reduce unemployment benefits in 1991 and to introduce further measures to increase the flexibility of the labor market in 1994, and only sought to reduce interest rates by reinstating some sort of incomes policy that would limit wage growth. The unions refused to accept.[16]

Indeed, it can be argued that contrary to the government's arguments, the internationalization of the Spanish economy opened the door for further cooperation with unions. Government officials argued that they could not increase public expenditures because of increasing constraints over economic policy imposed by Spain's integration in the world economy. Yet, while European integration limited the capacity of states to intervene in the economy in some ways, integration also increased the capacity of some states to encourage redistribution. The availability of EC/EU budget "structural funds," dedicated to the economic recovery, development, and modernization of less-developed areas and regions affected by industrial decline, and to fighting long-term unemployment, challenges the notion that the Spanish government lacked the funds to invest in social programs. Spain received 11,362 million ECUs from the structural funds for the period 1983–1993. Most of these funds, however, were spent on selective infrastructure investments. Social polices were expanded, but for the most part, only after the 1988 general strike. Furthermore, the globalization of capital markets has created a large pool of lenders competing among themselves and willing to purchase and fund government debt, thus easing the monetary costs of expansionary fiscal policies (Garrett 1998, 43). This is to say, that, contrary to the government arguments, the internationalization of the Spanish economy should have made it easier to finance expansionary fiscal policies.

The notion that the government had no room to maneuver in is further challenged by the fact that it changed its fiscal stance after the success of the 1988 general strike. How could the government dramatically increase social expenditures in January of 1989, and not before? The decision not to increase social expenditures in the 1985–1988 period was a political decision based on the government's objective to reduce the deficit at all costs.[17] Its decision not to allocate any part of the windfall surplus to social spending was motivated by its objective to build up savings and investment. The government was also influenced by the assumption that there was a strong link between budget deficits and inflation, and the conviction that by reducing interest rates and the cost of capital, inflation would decrease.[18] Yet the government refused to allocate part of the budget surplus to social spending despite high unemployment and limited social benefits, and instead allocated that money to reduce the deficit to a record low of 2.8 percent of GDP in

1989, a level well below the EC average—and the Maastricht limit, 3 percent (see Pérez 1996, 16).

The government, however, shifted course and sharply increased public expenditures after the success of the 1988 general strike, mainly for electoral reasons. In February 1989, the government reached an agreement with unions and pushed for more social spending. The government agreed to shelve the youth employment plan (see chapter 6) and to adjust pensions and public sector wages to inflation but rejected the expansion of unemployment coverage. This decision had a cost of 190 billion pesetas. Afterward, the government approved a package of measures raising minimum pensions up to the minimum wage level, establishing noncontributive pensions, and expanding unemployment benefits from 2.7 percent to 3.8 percent of Gross Domestic Product (GDP) in three years. In January 1990 the government reached a new agreement with unions, the "Acuerdos del 20 de Enero." These agreements required the government to accept collective bargaining in public firms and for public employees. They also included provisions to review public wages in order to compensate civil servants from previous income losses, and introduced safeguard clauses for such employees.[19]

The economic consequences (or lack thereof) of this policy shift suggest that the government had room to maneuver (see Table 5.2). Despite the dramatic surge in public expenditures, Spain did not suffer the wrath of the markets and did not experience the capital outflows that had been cited by the government as a reason not to accept unions demands before 1989. On the contrary, foreign capital continued flowing into the country, attracted by high interest rates. Moreover, although it is true that after 1989 the deficit surged and inflation shot up, these developments were not directly related to the government's policy shift. Inflation had already increased in the second half of 1988, before the government increased public expenditures; it did so for reasons that went beyond the orientation of fiscal policies and had more to do with the inflation proneness of the Spanish economy (Pérez 1997). Furthermore, the link between budget deficits and inflation is loose at best. The fact that other countries such as Belgium had been able to combine high budget deficits (from 1970–1996, Belgium's deficit averaged well over 6 percent of GDP) with low inflation and currency stability challenges the government argument that it could not give in to union demands and that its policy course was imposed by international markets.[20] This was, government arguments' not withstanding, a political decision. It was not imposed by the international markets. The government could have accepted union demands earlier on if it had really been interested in concertation. It was the PSOE's (Partido Socialista Obrero Español) economic team's fixation with inflation and wages, coupled with the strong peseta strategy, that prevented such an outcome. This was underlined by a shift in the government strategy toward unions after 1986. By the time that it accepted union demands in 1989, the relationship with unions had deteriorated to a point of no return, and the government had already lost all credibility as a social partner for the unions.

The fact that other European nations implemented incomes policies through concertation in the second half of the 1980s and 1990s further challenges the notion that governments are powerless and have no room for maneuver in this new globalized economy. Although centralized wage bargaining collapsed in Sweden in the late 1980s, centralization has lost no further ground in other countries like Belgium,[21] Germany, Austria, and the Netherlands. Furthermore, cooperation between governments and labor has increased significantly in the 1990s in nontraditional SD corporatist countries such as Australia, Italy,[22] Greece, the Czech Republic, and Ireland.[23] In these countries governments have solicited the involvement of their peak federations of labor and business in major economic policy decisions. Structural changes and similar constraints imposed by the international economy did not prevent those governments from reaching agreements with unions, and in many cases, from implementing incomes policies. In these countries labor leaders have cooperated to improve macroeconomic performance, which has helped to elicit support form the business sector, and have been able to transfer the support of most workers to the agreements. And all this despite the fact that labor market institutions are not so encompassing as those of the traditional SD corporatist countries (i.e., union density and collective bargaining coverage are comparatively low, and authority is not highly concentrated). As a result of these policies, these governments have experienced better economic performance.[24] In the Netherlands, for instance, the single most important factor that analysts highlight to account for the success of the Dutch economy has been a comprehensive wage bargaining system outlined 17 years ago—the Wassenaar Agreement of 1982, in which employers' organizations and unions reached a pact on wage moderation and the creation of jobs—that has contributed to wage restraint and labor peace, making Dutch success possible.[25]

Portugal is a very interesting case from a comparative standpoint. Despite an institutional framework similar to Spain's, characterized by relatively weak unions; a competitive union structure; a decentralized system of wage bargaining; and similar structural constraints; concertation was consolidated in Portugal in the 1980s and 1990s.[26] So far in Portugal, there have been concertation agreements the following years: 1987, 1988, 1990, 1992, and 1996 and an Agreement of Strategic Concertation for the 1997–1999 period.[27] This last agreement is particularly significant because its main objectives include sharing productivity gains, the promotion of competitiveness among Portuguese companies, and a policy of overall wage growth consistent with goals to achieve international competitiveness and the integration of Portugal into the European Monetary Union. This agreement includes most areas of macroeconomic and social policies, including the orientation of economic policies, incomes policies (the agreement sets a reference to cap average wages and pensions), employment policy, professional training, labor legislation, collective bargaining, social security, and the contribution to the competitiveness of Portuguese firms (Da Silva Lopes 1999, 94–96; Monteiro Fernandes 1999, 111–117).[28]

One of the most important lessons that can be derived from the Portuguese case is that in this country, and contrary to what should have been expected according to the globalization paradigm and the arguments of the Spanish socialist policymakers, Portuguese access to the EC in 1986 (the same year as Spain) and the globalization and liberalization of its economy in the 1980s–1990s (plus the fact that the conservative PSD party—not the socialist one—was in power for most of that time), did not preclude the successful implementation of incomes policies through concertation agreements.[29] On the contrary, concertation flourished and these agreements had a very positive impact on economic conditions in Portugal (see Royo 1999). By allowing for a reduction of unit labor costs, they improved the external competitiveness of Portuguese firms, contributed to the reduction in inflation from 13.4 percent in 1990 to less than 3 percent in 1999, and kept unemployment at levels well below those in other European countries (around 7 percent). Finally, they also contributed to social peace. Portugal, which as late as 1997 was considered an outside candidate for joining the euro-zone, was able to comply comfortably with the Maastricht criteria, and, in part due to the concertation process, it was able to do it in a relatively painless way. For instance, Portugal was the only country able to reduce its budget deficit to below 3 percent of GDP (the Maastricht criteria) while increasing current government spending.[30] And this stands in stark contrast with the disappointing performance of the Spanish economy after concertation failed in 1986 (see Conclusion).

Furthermore, there is increasing empirical evidence challenging the notion that SD corporatism is in decline. Recent studies (Iversen 1998; Golden, Wallerstein, and Lange 1999) have shown that the decline of corporatist wage bargaining is not as general as thought. Therefore, it is difficult to maintain that governments had no room to maneuver and that the globalization of capital markets and the decline of Fordist production prevented the implementation of concertation agreements when both factors also affected countries that still have centralized bargaining.[31]

From a theoretical standpoint, it is important to emphasize that new empirical reports have further eroded the credibility of the arguments about the domestic constraints imposed by globalization (see chapter 2), and lend further support to the arguments that I introduced in this chapter. Geoffrey Garrett (1998 and 1999) and Duane Swank (1998) have produced empirical evidence that shows that although the integration of the industrial democracies into the global economy with respect to both trade and capital mobility increased substantially since the 1960s, the institutional power of labor did not deteriorate, nor did it weaken the strong relationship between left-labor power and redistributive big government (Garret 1998, 51–73, 74–105). The bulk of this new empirical evidence focuses on the period before 1997 (1966–1994)[32]—which is the period most relevant to this study because concertation collapsed in Spain in 1986. For that period these authors introduce conclusive evidence challenging the globalization argument and showing that:

1. Globalization increased consistently throughout the period in the 14 countries studied (Garrett 1998, 53–59; Garrett 1999, 165–172).
2. The political power of the left and the strength of labor market institutions were not in secular decline (Garrett 1998, 59–69).
3. There is little empirical evidence that globalization exerted systematic downward pressure on the public sector, the welfare state, and the public service provision (Garrett 1999, 172–179). On the contrary, patterns of government spending increased with market integration. Government spending was greater in all countries with powerful left-wing parties and encompassing labor market institutions highly integrated into global markets (1998, 76–85). In other words, contrary to expectations, "the effect of partisan politics on government spending increased not decreased, the more integrated a country was into the international economy" (Garrett 1998, 75). Swank's analysis (1998, 12–14) supports Garret's findings. He shows that the coefficient of variation—the central measure of convergence—reveals that there has been no pronounced convergence in the overall size of the public economy among advanced industrial nations. On the contrary, Swank shows that increased financial integration in the 1979–1993 period is systematically related to higher social welfare spending (1998, 21). These analyses disprove the notion that there has been a clear and sustained downward movement in public consumption as a result of globalization. On the contrary, both authors prove that social corporatism is significantly and positively associated with the size of the public economy.
4. Tax revenues were more stable over time, and although there was a trend toward flatter systems of personal income, globalization did not result on any cross-national convergence in tax revenues, contrary to

what should have been expected according to the globalization argument. Furthermore, the progressivity of income taxation became stronger with the globalization of markets (Garrett 1998, 85–94; Garrett 1999, 176; Swank 1998, 24–26).

5. Market integration resulted in higher budget deficits in SD corporatist countries (Austria, Denmark, Finland, and Sweden), showing a mismatch between spending and taxation. Expansive polices, were, therefore, possible with market integration. In turn, monetary policy shows that globalization resulted in higher interest rates, which were, however, quite small. They represented the price that these governments had to pay to implement redistributive policies, but it was a price that they were willing to pay (1998, 94–102).

6. Finally, Garrett (1998) and Soskice (1999) show that the performance of SD corporatist regimes (Austria, Denmark, Finland, and Sweden) in the global economy with regards to economic growth and unemployment was better that in countries governed by rightist-oriented governments or where labor market institutions were weak (Garrett 1998, 106–128; Soskice 1999, 119–122).[33] Soskice (1999, 121) argues that once we take into consideration the effect of current-account deficits (indicative of excessive demand not sustainable in the long-term), the unemployment performance of SD corporatist countries, such as Austria, Germany, Norway, Switzerland, and Sweden, looks significantly better than that of more liberal economies (i.e., the United Kingdom, Canada or the United States). This empirical evidence proves that redistributive polices were not achieved at the cost of overall macroeconomic performance, which challenges the arguments of the Spanish socialists who claimed that they could not implement such policies because the Spanish economy would suffer the wrath of the markets and economic performance would deteriorate.

These authors also present empirical data that challenges the notion that globalization imposed constraints on redistributive big governments in the 1990s. It was after 1990, after all, that most countries liberalized their financial sectors and removed capital controls—a development that, according to the globalization argument, is considered to have rendered expansionary macroeconomic policies far less feasible. Although Garrett emphasizes that the data needed to develop the econometric methods that he used to analyze the 1966–1990 period is not available for the 1990s, using rudimentary methods he can show that: First of all, patterns of government spending increased with market integration in the 1990s. This is supported by Swank's analysis for the period before 1997 (1998, 19–22). Furthermore, even public deficits increased substantially in some SD corporatist countries

(Sweden, Finland, and Norway) and remained stable in others (Austria and Denmark). Moreover, SD corporatist countries' levels of public debt have been well within average (except for Denmark and Sweden), despite the widespread perception that they have been big spenders. Finally, Garrett shows that the levels of personal income taxation in SD corporatist countries remained somewhat higher than in other countries (1998, 136–139; Swank 1998, 24–26).[34] This empirical evidence further challenges the Spanish Socialists' arguments about the constraints imposed by globalization, and shows that redistribute policies were possible even in the 1990s.

Moreover, the globalization-based argument attributes the abandonment of concertation and the rapid increases in unemployment in corporatist countries to the removal of capital controls in the 1990s, which precipitated capital flight in these countries. According to such a view, these countries had always been inefficient and could only maintain high levels of employment under closed financial markets. This explanation, however, is also challenged by Garrett (1998, 139–144; and 1999 179–182). He argues that the direction of causality is wrong, and shows empirical evidence proving that outflows of direct investment were not higher in corporatist countries regimes (Austria, Denmark, Finland, and Sweden). On the contrary, these countries remained attractive to mobile asset holders because labor unions were able to regulate overall wage growth to promote competitiveness, thus fostering the economic, political, and social stability (Garrett 1998, 106). He acknowledges, however, that outflows of portfolio investment led the Finnish and Swedish governments to raise interest rates (1998, 141). Garrett, however, attributes this development and the deeper macroeconomic problems in Sweden and Finland—which were also the two corporatist countries that experienced the sharpest increases on unemployment—to the decline in economic activity associated with the end of the Cold War, and their attempt to move to a fixed exchange rate with Germany at the worst possible time.[35] Finally, he emphasizes that even if we focus on unemployment as the key performance variable to determine macroeconomic success, unemployment levels have remained high in some "liberal market economies"—Canada and France—and that the relatively good employment performance of the United States was achieved at the expense of higher income inequalities and lower welfare benefits (1998, 144).

Finally, these new analyses challenge the notion that capital mobility is leading to a pattern of crossnational convergence. On the contrary, Swank (1998) emphasizes that the direction and magnitude of effects of different dimensions of international financial integration depend on the democratic institutional context, the institutional mechanisms for collective representation within interest groups, the electoral and party systems, and the organization of policymaking authority systems of interest representation.

Specifically, he claims that social corporatism should facilitate the degree to which affected interests can press their claims against adverse policy changes in the face of globalization (Swank 1998, 9). According to this view, the continuing existence of encompassing labor confederations (Golden, Wallerstein, and Lange 1999, 221–225) will provide an institutional mechanism that will allow the sectors adversely affected by globalization to articulate preferences and pressure national policymakers. The influence of these groups will be reinforced by constitutional structures and institutions (i.e., the institutional mechanisms for collective representation within interest groups, the electoral and party systems, and the organization of policymaking authority) that will slow policy change in response to economic and political forces. These institutional mechanisms may allow these groups to resist adverse policy changes and will guarantee that policy change incorporates their demands. This, according to Swank, means that the impact of globalization is likely to be less pronounced in institutionally-encompassing polities and more so in fragmented polities. Utilizing trend analyses of patterns of convergence/divergence and an econometric analysis of 1964–1993 data from 16 countries, Swank finds that international capital flows, liberalization, and financial market integration have few if any direct effects on the scope of the public economy (1998, 22–24). On the contrary, his empirical analysis supports Garrett's conclusion that rises in international capital flows and liberalization are weakly associated with public sector retrenchment and market-conforming policy changes in countries with encompassing labor institutions (i.e., the Nordic nations), and strongly associated in fragmented polities (i.e., countries with pluralist and majoritarian institutional contexts and those in which decision making is dispersed, such as Canada or the United States). In the former countries "collective veto points of consensus democracy" (Birchfield and Crepaz, forthcoming[36]) favor those adversely affected by globalization, therefore the impact of international capital mobility is not associated with retrenchment of the public economy. In the latter countries, on the contrary, the mechanisms available to economic and political interests for resisting adverse policy change are relatively weak; therefore, international capital mobility is associated with retrenchment of the public economy. In other words, national institutions matter and governments' responses to internationalization of capital markets differ depending on national institutional contexts.

In sum, the evidence of this section highlights the shortcomings of the arguments that attributed the collapse of concertation in Spain to globalization and changes in the production system. According to such arguments, globalization and changes to the production regime are considered to have rendered expansionary macroeconomic policies far less feasible, and to have significantly weakened organized labor movements, therefore eroding the prospects for concertation. These arguments, however, are not conclusive. The empirical evidence that we have introduced in this section shows that despite globalization and changes to the production system, SD corporatist countries have been able to sustain their characteristic distributional policies (including higher levels of taxation), the strength of their labor market institutions, and their systems of wage bargaining through concertation. These analyses disprove the notion that there has been a clear and sustained downward movement in public consumption as a result of globalization. On the contrary, they prove that social corporatism is significantly and positively associated with the size of the public economy. Furthermore, in these countries (Austria, Denmark, Finland, and Sweden) the redistribution of wealth and social benefits was not achieved at the expense of overall economic performance (contrary to what the Spanish socialists argued). On the contrary, the macroeconomic performance of corporatist economies with regards to real aggregates vis-à-vis more liberalized economies remained better (particularly before the 1990s, and lets reemphasize that concertation collapsed in Spain in 1986). The reason for this was that labor leaders in these countries used their market power to regulate overall wage growth in ways that promoted the competitiveness of the tradable sector in exchange for benefits from the government.[37] These policies generated important collective goods that are undersupplied by markets. They increased productivity value by fostering political and social stability and the accumulation of human and physical capital, which were attractive and beneficial to the business sector and helped build popular support for the market economy, thus preventing the capital flight that was predicted by the defenders of the globalization argument (Garrett 1999). Therefore, these findings lend further support to the arguments that I introduced in this chapter that challenge the globalization explanation for the collapse of concertation in Spain.[38] Governments had room to maneuver, and arguments about the demise of national autonomy are overdrawn.

II. The Business Cycle Explanation

The argument above focuses on broad structural conditions. Other authors have argued that the collapse of concertation has to be attributed to cyclical rather than structural conditions. Proponents of this explanation argue that "there is increasing evidence that changes in the business cycle and the level of employment have a differential effect over labor and capital that makes them more or less receptive to compromise in a systematic way" (Schmitter 1990, 32, my translation).[39] When the economy is in recession, businesses have more incentives to resort to concertation in order to moderate wages. When the economy is expanding, on the contrary, unions are more interested in concertation to consolidate what they have achieved during a recession. Conflict is also more likely during the "zenith and nadir" of the business cycles, because these cycles influence the capacity of unions to convince their rank and file to accept wage restraint. If union leaders push for wage moderation during expansive periods, they might lose the support of their followers, resulting in a typical "crisis of representation" (Moscoso 1995, 54–58).

The proponents of the business cycle explanation argue that there is a high correlation between periods of economic upswing and industrial conflict, and that intensified industrial conflict hinders concertation. Empirical analyses have shown evidence that economic expansion results in increased industrial conflict because economic upswings result in wage increases and also in greater income inequality. Conflict also intensifies as a consequence of the recovery of business profits caused by the economic boom, because workers want to share these benefits. During periods of economic upswing, some workers have a stronger bargaining position because employers have higher profits and economic incentives to make concessions, and are, therefore, more likely to yield to demands. At the same time, unions see their bargaining power intensified in the workplace because employers have more incentives to make concessions to avoid strikes. This is so because during economic expansions the opportunity costs of strikes are too high for businesses and the latter would rather agree to union demands for higher wages, which are then passed on through prices, than risk a strike that might result in market-share losses. Unions, for their part, are fully aware of their bargaining leverage and intensify their demands, while strikes further reinforce the credibility of unions among workers (Moscoso 1995, 55). Finally, when the economic expansion consolidates, the threat of future unemployment diminishes (at least for people with jobs). Therefore, workers are willing at this time to stand up for their demands.

The increase in wage differentials that result from the uneven effects of the expansion, with some sectors of the economy booming faster than others, also affects concertation, according to these authors, because people working in booming sectors have more bargaining power and will push for higher wages and get better deals. This is expected to result in fragmented bargaining power and increased wage inequalities (Kaldor 1976; Dunlop 1957; Phelps 1980). The expansion of the wage structure also results in higher income inequality and further conflicts, because wage differentials result in demands for comparative increases from those with lower wages. Finally, periods of economic growth are also associated with employment growth, but newcomers are usually kept in temporary positions, intensifying labor segmentation and instability. This is so because business, particularly in those countries where the labor market is characterized by high inflexibility and high dismissal costs, is reluctant to hire workers on a permanent basis. Anticipating a future recession, it prefers to hire temporary workers, and this results in uncertainty.

At first sight, the events that took place in Spain during the second half of the 1980s seem to validate some of the conclusions advanced by the business-cycle literature. It was during the period of adjustment and reform (1979–1985) that concertation took place in Spain. At that time wage increases (22 percent between 1976 and 1980), coupled with low levels of growth, had resulted in a sharp increase in unemployment (5.6 percent in 1977 to 14.6 percent in 1981) and inflation (more than 21 percent in the early 1980s). After 1986, when Spain was experiencing a period of accelerated economic growth, inflation fell and economic problems were not perceived as urgent as before, concertation failed. This led some Spanish authors and government officials to conclude that concertation was possible during the recession, but not when the economy surged. Espina (1991, 199–212), for example, attributes the failure of concertation to the increasing levels of industrial conflict that resulted from economic upswings.[40] Government officials reached a similar conclusion and "came to believe that concertation was expensive and inefficient as well as less needed in a phase of economic expansion" (Maravall 1993, 118).

A number of events seem to confirm the business cycle argument. For instance, increasing industrial conflict after 1986 (see Table 5.24) was the result of three major developments: higher wage differentials, increased labor segmentation, and the strong bargaining position of unions.

At the same time, one of the major consequences of economic recovery was the increase in wage differentials among economic sectors, an increase that had been reduced by concertation. After 1986 wages increased more in some sectors (wood, cork, and hotel business) and less in other sectors with traditionally higher wages (automaking and shipbuilding) as seen in Table

Table 5.3 Industrial Conflict, 1985–1988

Year	Number of Strikes	Variation (%)	Number of Workers	Variation (%)	Lost Hours	Variation (%)
1985	2,029	−34.4	4,538,788	17.4	64,180,987	−47.4
1986*	2,239	10.3	1,793,187	−60.5	50,795,973	−20.9
1987	3,194	42.7	3,22,700	79.7	81,968,568	61.4
1988	2,823	−11.6	8,001,095	148.3	116,521,270	42.2

Source: Folgado 1989, p. 531. Data from Ministerio de Trabajo y Seguridad Social.
*The last year of concertation (AES)

5.4 (Roca 1993, 192, 229). This wage differentiation was fostered by the absence of a centralized agreement after 1986, because it strengthened the bargaining power of workers in booming sectors but discriminated against workers in weaker sectors.[41] Wage differentials, according to the business-cycle explanation, increase conflict among workers and hinder concertation.

According to the proponents of the business-cycle explanation, industrial conflict was further hastened by the increasing segmentation of the labor market. Between 1985 and 1998 the Spanish economy created almost two million jobs, not enough to reduce the existing levels of unemployment. It did result, however, in a dramatic segmentation of the job market for two reasons: First, given the inflexibility that characterizes the Spanish labor market and the high costs associated with dismissals, employers hired people on a temporary basis (temporary contracts increased to 18 percent of total hiring by 1987, three years after the reform of 1984 that introduced the new hiring modalities), to make it easier to reduce redundancies (excesses of the labor force) when the economy entered into recession. Second, in a context marked by higher flexibility and less contractual stability, new entrants arrived in the job market with a deep sense of job insecurity that also fostered instability (Recio 1995, 101–109).

The evolution of unions' demands, which sought to capitalize on the new cycle of economic expansion, also seem to validate the arguments advanced by the business-cycle proponents. The increase in businesses' profits (see Table 5.5) and economic expansion do seem to have hastened the employers' decision to satisfy unions' demands to avoid strikes.

Table 5.4 Intersector Wage Increases Differentials, 1981–1988

Year	Mean	Standard Deviation	Coefficient of Variation
1981 (a)	12.9	2.3	17.7
1981 (a)	11.6	1.3	11.1
1983	11.4	0.9	7.8
1984*	7.5	0.9	11.4
1985	7.8	0.6	7.4
1986**	8.2	0.5	5.7
1987	6.6	0.9	14.2
1988	6.1	0.7	11.6

Source: Roca, 1992, Table 13, p. 191. Reprinted with permission. Sources: Data from the Ministerio de Trabajo y Seguridad Social: Boletín de Estadísticas Laborales.
(a) It does not include data from the agreements that only covered Catalonia.
*No agreement.
**Last year of concertation

Table 5.5 The Recovery of Business Profits, 1983–1988

	1983	1984	1985	1986*	1987	1988
ROE**	10.7	11.0	11.2	14.3	18.0	18.7
ROA***	5.4	6.6	8.4	15.5	20.7	21.3

Source: Folgado 1989, p. 530.
*The last year of concertation (AES).
**Return on Equity = Net Economic Results/Net Assets
***Return on Assets = Net Total Result After Taxes/Net Worth

Increasing wage demands are believed to have made impossible the ne-gotiation of wage objectives similar to the ones negotiated before 1986 (Roca 1991, 369). According to scholars who support this view, while the government sought wage moderation, unions became aware that the accep-tance of such an option would most likely result in the emergence of con-flict uncontrollable by unions.[42]

There is some truth in the business-cycle argument. The various facts listed above do suggest that the development of an economic boom after 1986 played a role in the collapse of concertation. Wage differentials, cou-pled with the higher segmentation of the labor market and the stronger bar-gaining position of unions, had an unquestionable impact on concertation because they hindered solidarity among workers, thus increasing conflicts and making consensus more difficult. The collapse of concertation, however, cannot be solely blamed on the business cycle, for several reasons. First, al-though distributional conflicts have been associated typically with periods of economic expansion, high levels of conflict are not necessarily linked with economic booms in Spain. In the early 1970s, Spain was entering a sharp re-cession, but conflict was very high and the country experienced one of the highest number of strikes in the western world. Yet concertation was still fea-sible despite these high levels of conflict. In the 1980s, however, economic expansion resulted again in a high number of strikes, yet concertation was not possible after 1986.

The business-cycle approach also fails to offer a convincing explanation as to why concertation did not reemerge in Spain when the economy went into recession again in the early 1990s. Since the unions refused to accept concertation during the economic upswing (1986–1991), a concomitant re-turn to concertation when the economy entered a recession—that is, after 1992—would have been plausible (Moscoso 1995, 54). But this did not happen in Spain. In fact, what we see is a rather imperfect correlation be-tween the business cycle and concertation. The economy went into recession in the second half of 1992, but unions refused to go back to the negotiation table despite repeated pleas by the government to resume concertation.[43] Moreover, the business cycle account also fails to explain why centralized bargaining reemerged in 1997, when the economy was expanding after a protracted crisis that raised unemployment up to 24 percent (see Conclusions). According to such proponents, economic recovery should have resulted in further conflict. This was not the case. The change in government resulted in a new political climate where concertation has flourished.

Finally, although in countries such as Sweden increasing wage differentials hastened the end of centralized bargaining, in other countries, such as Austria and the Netherlands, wage differentials have not been incompatible with centralized concertation. On the contrary, concertation has worked very well in these countries because such differentials were linked to productivity. This mechanism allows for wage differentials not necessarily related to the business cycle.[44]

Conclusions

The viability and effectiveness of neocorporatist agreements is conditioned by their economic context and business cycles. These factors affect the institutional power of actors and, thus, influence policy outcomes. Structural and economic factors, however, are not enough to account for the collapse of concertation in Spain. The Spanish experience with concertation seems to corroborate the strong links between policy objectives and domestic political factors. In Spain the changing international economic environment was used by the economic team to support its deregulating agenda and to implement its economic policies. It also contributed to weaken the position of other social actors, particularly trade unions. The end of concertation coincided with Spain's entry to the EC. Within this context of international integration, socialist officials argued that they could not cave in to unions' demands and had no choice but to implement restrictive policies to quell inflation and restore competitiveness. Otherwise they would suffer the wrath of the market and experience capital outflows (as in France in 1982). I, however, have attempted to show that the government had room for compromise with unions.

Despite economic constraints, after the general strike of 1988 the socialist government gave in to most union demands, which contradicts previous statements by government officials that they had no room for compromise. This policy shift, however, did not have the dire consequences predicted by the government before 1989. In Spain, structural developments did not result in a dramatic balance shift between capital and labor in favor of the latter. On the contrary, Spanish labor unions regained some strength in the late 1980s, but concertation did not resume. Finally, it is difficult to maintain that the globalization of capital markets and the decline of Fordist production are the reasons for the collapse of concertation when both factors also affected countries that still have centralized bargaining and concertation—Belgium, Austria, the Netherlands, Finland, and Portugal.

The business cycle explanation, which links concertation with periods of economic downturn, also fails to provide an adequate explanation for the collapse of concertation in Spain. For such an explanation to be valid, concertation should have resumed in Spain in the early 1990s, when the Spanish economy entered into a deep recession. Yet, concertation did not resume. This explanation also fails to account for the reemergence of concertation in 1997 in the midst of an economic expansion.

If both institutional and economic factors do not account for the collapse of concertation in Spain after 1986, what does? In the next chapter I shall examine the role of political factors. I shall argue that the domestic political context played a critical role in the collapse of concertation. In this regard, the critical factor to account for the collapse of concertation was the relationship between the Socialist Party in government and the socialist union. The union had little influence in the government/party and played a subordinate role in the policymaking process. This relationship led to a rupture between the socialist government and the union, which had devastating consequences for concertation, because the UGT had been the only major confederation that had supported all the concertation agreements. This lack of UGT support was hastened by the overall strategy pursued by the socialist government—that is, a tight monetary policy based in appreciating currency, high interest rates, and the absence of comprehensive supply sides polices and industry-oriented measures. These policies forced the union to adopt a defensive strategy and caused the breakdown with the government. I shall conclude that the links between changes in the international economic environment and the process of domestic policymaking also depend on domestic political factors. The domestic environment, and not only the global and institutional context, provides its own set of incentives for domestic actors to entertain certain political strategies.

CHAPTER 6

The Party-Union Relationship: The Consequences of Party Hegemony

Introduction

I have concluded in previous chapters that the institutional and structural explanations emphasized in the literature on concertation are insufficient to account for the collapse of concertation in Spain after 1986. Concertation was successful in Spain for almost eight years (1979–1986) despite an institutional framework characterized by decentralized collective bargaining, weak and competitive unions, and the strength and even dominance of the labor movement by a communist union for years. The structural conditions faced by Spain were not less conductive to concertation than those faced by countries such as Portugal, where concertation flourished in the late 1980s and 1990s. Therefore, we still have to find a satisfactory answer to the puzzle of this research: How to explain the collapse of concertation in Spain after 1986? In this chapter I suggest that there are two factors that are unaccounted for by traditional explanations: The cooperation of weak and competitive unions and the behavior of the socialist party in government. I conclude that the collapse of concertation can be fully understood only in terms of the behavior of the socialist party in government. It was the government that first endangered the crucial relationship between the General Workers' Union (UGT) and the Spanish Socialist Workers Party (PSOE) because it failed to fulfill its compromises with labor. The key objective of this chapter is, thus to account for the behavior of the union and the socialist party/government.

Institutional and structural factors fail to explain the total behavior of Spanish social actors. They cannot account for the decision of weak and competitive unions to take part in concertation agreements. Generally speaking, the neocorporatist and structuralist literature on comparative politics has largely ignored the political circumstances under which the social actors are willing to participate in concertation schemes. In order to explain this behavior in Spain, some scholars have emphasized the role of the political context, specifically, the influence that the transition to democracy in Spain had in the strategies of the social actors, and, more particularly, the unions. According to this view, the concertation process was intimately linked to the transition process because one of the major objectives of all the social actors was the consolidation of the new regime, and this fostered consensus and cooperation. Once the new regime was consolidated, however, that motivation dissipated.

This argument, however, does not account for the behavior of the Socialist government. It helps to explain why Spanish unions were willing to moderate their demands during the transition to help consolidate the new regime, but it fails to explain why the Spanish socialist government failed to fulfill its compromises with labor. The PSOE's actions also cannot be adequately explained using either institutional or structuralist theories and factors. The main question of this chapter is: What is the critical aspect in the institutional and political relationship between the Socialist Party and the socialist labor union that explains the behavior of the socialist government?

In order to account for such behavior, I analyze in the second part of the chapter the institutional and political relationship between the Socialist Party and the UGT. The key aspect of the party-union relationship in Spain is the organizational structure of the Socialist Party, which sharply limited the influence of the union within it. I hypothesize that this organizational structure hindered concertation by giving the government an incentive to take advantage of any deal struck with the union and exploit that relationship. Consequently, the government chose not to fulfill its compromises with labor because it encountered too few political constraints to prevent it from defaulting on its promises to the union. The UGT's lack of influence within the party led the governmental economic team to adopt an instrumentalist view of the union and to conclude that it did not need the union to implement its economic policies. This decision brought about the rupture between the PSOE/government and the UGT and, thus, the collapse of concertation. This rupture, given the UGT's vital role in the neocorporatist process (it was the only union that had taken part in all concertation agreements), guaranteed the end of concertation. The relationship between political parties and economic actors, I argue, can be a critical variable in determining the success of economic policies, and it has not been the subject of careful examination in the literature so far.

I. The Influence of the Transition Process on Concertation

Neither the institutional nor the structural factors advanced in the literature and considered so far help to explain the circumstances under which weak and competitive unions are willing to participate in concertation. Despite unpropitious circumstances such as low affiliation, interunion competition, and a decentralized system of collective bargaining, Spanish unions were willing to moderate their demands, participate in neocorporatist agreements, and deliver wage moderation. One kind of political explanation to account for such behavior has been advanced by a number of Spanish scholars such as Linz 1981, Lang 1981, Pérez-Díaz and Rojo 1983, and Pérez-Díaz 1984. It involves the relationship between the concertation process and the process of political transition from authoritarianism to democracy that took place in Spain in the late 1970s.[1] According to this view, concertation was possible in Spain only within the specific political context that characterized the transition to democracy. This specific context provided a common objective to the social actors—that is, to consolidate the new democratic institutions—and this, in turn, fostered consensus and cooperation (and, thus, concertation). Once the new democratic regime was consolidated, however, the specific conditions that fostered consensus dissipated and concertation collapsed.

In this section, I seek to dispute this argument. Despite the widespread acceptance of the view that concertation was tied to the transition process among unions, political scientists, and others, it is questionable whether the consolidation of democracy led to the collapse of concertation. Contrary to this view, I shall argue that concertation continued beyond the point at which the democratic regime was consolidated, and that subsequent failures cannot be attributed solely to the consolidation of the democratic regime. In fact, concertation reemerged under a new conservative government in the mid-1990s. While this argument helps to understand some aspects of Spanish unions' moderate behavior, it fails to account for the socialist government's behavior and its decision to default from its compromises with labor.

As we have seen, the political and economic context in which concertation took place in Spain was markedly different from the one in which concertation took place in other countries (see Roca 1993, 255). Concertation developed in Spain at the time of the transition to democracy in the late 1970s. This democratization process influenced the perception and strategies of union leaders in Spain. Uncertainties about the consolidation of the reform process, coupled with fears about the collapse of the new regime, are said to have helped to overcome the absence in Spain of institutional factors described by the literature as conductive to concertation arrangements (Lang 1981, 252; Linz 1981, 404; Zufiaur 1985, 204; Pérez-Díaz 1984, 21). According to this view, the concept of corporatism has been applied to societies with stable institutions, where the institutional position of the social actors is consolidated and has a large tradition of bargaining—for example, Austria and Sweden (Pérez-Díaz 1984, 21). In Spain, however, a number of factors worked against successful corporatism. As we saw in chapter 4, in Spain the system of industrial relations was based on competing unions instead of an encompassing monopolistic socialist-oriented trade union, and the system of wage bargaining is decentralized and fragmented. There was also a dominant communist-oriented trade union which used to have intense ideological disputes with its socialist counterpart, and there was a historic tradition of union-supported conflict. Spain had a conservative government from 1977–1982 instead of a social democratic (SD) one, and after 40 years of authoritarian rule and intense state interventionism, a consensus-building tradition based on concertation and bargaining among the social actors was also missing. This problem was compounded by the absence of institutions that could foster negotiation and consensus-building—similar to the Conselho Permanente de Concertação Social (CPCS, or the Permanent Council for Social Concertation) in Portugal.[2] Finally, industrial and political conflict intensified dramatically during the last years of the dictatorship, thus hindering consensus and cooperation.

Despite these unpropitious conditions, concertation emerged in Spain and succeeded for an extensive period of time (1979–1986). According to the authors above, political factors associated with the transition helped to overcome the absence of adequate institutional arrangements because they fostered consensus and cooperation among the social actors. It has been argued that the unions and left-wing parties (including the Communist party) restrained their members in exchange for assurances on the consolidation of a democratic regime, and this despite the fact that the actor that represented a real threat, the Army, had no representatives at the negotiating table (Martínez-Alier and Roca 1986, 17). The threat of a military uprising was always present during the transition, and the new democratic regime was not fully consolidated. The most dramatic reminder of this fact was the failed coup d'état of February 1981, when a group of paramilitary policemen assaulted the Spanish Parliament and kidnapped the government and congressmen during a debate to elect a new premier. Despite this failure, hard liners from the old regime refused to accept the new democratic system and remained influential in certain institutions—particularly the military. Within this political context, the social actors, and particularly the unions, took into account the impact that their actions and strategies would have on the military.

The cooperative stance of unions towards concertation, according to this view, was based in fears of a return to authoritarianism and the desire to consolidate the new regime. During the transition, union leaders realized that increasing conflict might threaten the development of the new regime. This fear influenced their strategies, and union leaders decided to moderate their demands and leave aside historic claims such as limits to property rights, nationalization, and other contentious issues that would have jeopardized the consolidation of the new democratic regime (Roca 1993, 148). Union moderation was helped by the common interest shared by all the social actors in strengthening the new democratic institutions in Spain. Moreover, business, unions, and the government realized that the consolidation of the new regime required overcoming the economic crisis, and this, in turn, demanded concessions from them, real negotiations, the maintenance of social peace in firms, and the containment of confrontational strategies (Führer 1996, 305).

Interviews with union leaders confirmed their decision to moderate their demands during the transition in order to reduce industrial conflict, and to support the democratic government through tripartite agreements, which proved their commitment to the democratic process.[3] Concertation was the chosen instrument to involve all social actors in the transition process and contribute to social peace (Zaragoza and Varela 1990, 51). Unions' explicit support (particularly from the CCOO, Comisiones Obreras) for the "Pactos de La Moncloa" in 1977 was a confirmation of this approach. After the failed coup of February 1981, unions proved, once again, their willingness to reach agreements with the government to fulfill that objective and signed the ANE (Acuerdo Nacional de Empleo)—also known as the "Pact of Fear." These peculiarly unique circumstances surrounding the democratic transition, therefore, fostered concertation.[4] According to this view, "the rituals of concertation served the needs of a political class eager to bury the horrific legacy of the Spanish civil war and to shatter the Francoist myth that democracy was not possible in Spain because of inherent tendencies toward class, ideological, and ethnic conflict" (Encarnación 1997, 389). This led the above authors to conclude that once the democratic system was consolidated and these fears dissipated, concertation was bound to come to an end.

Despite this widespread conclusion among political scientists and even union leaders, it is questionable that the consolidation of democracy led to the collapse of concertation.[5] There are several reasons why the view expressed above is not a compelling explanation. The political context was unique to Spain, but as other authors have pointed out, particular political and economic conditions also played an important role in the emergence of concertation schemes in other countries. Katzenstein (1985, 35) has argued that concertation emerged in the small European states (the Netherlands, Belgium, Sweden, Switzerland, and Austria) as a consequence of the political and economic vulnerability of these countries, which in turn resulted from their small size. He links the historical experience of the 1930s and 1940s to the emergence of democratic corporatism in these countries, and attributes its permanence to the economic developments which took place in the 1950s–1960s. Therefore, the peculiarity of the Spanish concertation lies not in the way it emerged but in the fact that the concertation model was not institutionalized as in these other countries, and collapsed after 1986 (Roca 1993, 149).

Moreover, there is common agreement among historians that the transition process was completed with the PSOE's victory in the 1982 general elections (Pérez Royo 1996, 77; Montero 1996, 548). Unions also came to the conclusion that the transition process was over and that democracy had been consolidated at this time (Moscoso 1995, 67; Führer 1996, 348). Concertation, however, continued well after that year. Therefore, we cannot establish a direct causal relationship between the collapse of concertation and the consolidation of the democratic regime.[6] Collaboration among the social actors continued for a significant time after the regime was consolidated. For 1984 there was no agreement, but in 1985 the UGT, the CEOE (Confederación Española de Organizaciones Empresariales), and the government signed the "Acuerdo Económico y Social" (AES), which lasted for two years (1985–1986).[7]

Furthermore, the attempt to reach centralized agreements did not finish with the AES. Although the social actors failed to reach new agreements, the collaborative stance continued after 1986. The fact that the unions were willing to negotiate challenges the notion that concertation was not possible within a consolidated democratic system in Spain. In 1986 representatives from the government (Carlos Solchaga, the Minister of Economics), the UGT (Nicolás Redondo, the Secretary General), and the CEOE (José María Cuevas, the Secretary General) met in secret several times to negotiate a new tripartite pact. They failed to reach an agreement. The government blamed the union for not fulfilling a "secret commitment," and the union blamed this failure on the course of the socialist economic policies. Yet the unions continued to show a strong interest in the negotiation process. In 1987 representatives from the government (Alfonso Guerra, Joaquín Almunia, and Manuel Chaves, all ministers in the socialist cabinet) reached a secret pact with UGT representatives (Paulina Barrabés and Apolinar Rodríguez). The opposition to this pact from Carlos Solchaga and Felipe González prevented its final (and public) implementation (Monteira 1996, 625).[8]

The notion that concertation died with the consolidation of the democratic regime is further challenged by the fact that the arrival of a new conservative government to power in 1996 brought about the revival of concertation. Since that year, unions, business, and the government have signed five major agreements: One concerning professional training, another regulating the disappearance of labor ordinances, a third regulating an arbitration procedure to resolve conflicts, a fourth concerning the pension system, and a final one reforming labor laws and the system of collective bargaining. This last agreement was particularly significant, given its scope and the fact that unions agreed to many things that the PSOE sought; the pact demands legislative reforms to increase stability within the labor market, reduces dismissals costs for business, and also introduces measures to rationalize the system of collective bargaining.[9] I analyze the significance of these pacts at greater length in the Conclusions.

It is also important to highlight the fact that concertation collapsed precisely when the institutional framework in Spain was becoming aligned with the traditional neocorporatist model. The end of the transition coincided with the victory of a social democratic (SD) party in Spain, and the socialist union had acquired a leading position within the labor movement. Therefore, the conditions seemed fruitful for the consolidation of concertation. These institutional preconditions, however, proved to be insufficient for the consolidation of concertation.

In conclusion, the consolidation of democratic institutions is insufficient to account for the collapse of concertation. The transition process might help to explain why unions were willing to moderate their bargaining position in the late 1970s and early 1980s. It does not help to explain, however, the behavior of the socialist government. After 1986 the UGT's strategy towards concertation changed, not so much because the democratic regime was consolidated, but because of the socialist government's decision to defect from its compromises with labor. The UGT was willing to continue with concertation, but demanded that the government fulfill its promises.[10] In what follows I shall argue that the critical factor necessary to understanding the government's actions is the relationship between the party and the union. I shall examine an important variable—the impact of the relationship between party and union on policy choices and the collapse of concertation—and suggest that a critical component in explaining the collapse of concertation in Spain lies in the institutional subordination of the UGT to the PSOE.

II. The Institutional Relationship between Party and Union

All the factors that we have examined so far—that is, labor market institutional, structural, and political factors—do not help to account for the behavior of the socialist government. Despite the fact that the PSOE had won the 1982 elections with a Keynesian economic plan, the socialist government dropped the plan immediately after taking office and, instead, emphasized economic growth over curtailing unemployment (Merkel 1995, 227–325; Gillespie 1991, 431–442). The government also defected from its compromises with labor by implementing restrictive economic policies, breaking the compromises established in the previous concertation agreement, the AES, and refusing to expand social expenditures significantly. The

UGT was unable to challenge this policy shift and could not organize a strong opposition within the party to challenge the course of economic policy and force the government to fill its promises. This development led to the rupture between the PSOE and the UGT, a rupture that gave the final blow to concertation since the UGT had been the only union that had taken part in all concertation agreements. In this section I shall argue that the key factor that helps us to account for the socialist government's behavior is the organizational structure of the party, which sharply limited the influence of the union within it and, therefore, within the government.

a. The Organizational Structure of the PSOE

The PSOE's organizational structure set up a system in which most of the power was concentrated in the hands of the party leaders (López Guerra 1984, 138). Compared to other SD parties, the PSOE had a relatively small activist base and an overwhelming large and centralized power structure dominated by party leaders (Kitschelt 1994, 234). This organizational structure resulted in an unequal distribution of power that has allowed the party leadership to control activists inside the party and to shape electoral strategy and policy. Felipe González, the party's former secretary general, and his deputy, Alfonso Guerra, both controlled the party with tight reins. The PSOE leadership recruited candidates for national legislative office, so that activists needed support form their leaders to advance their political careers. This centralized power structure was compounded by the fact that the PSOE was not very democratic internally and was very much isolated from external pressures. Any challenge faced swift retaliation from the top (Koelble 1991, 20). Internal power allowed party leaders to block and control activists' and union interests, and socialist leaders were able to exclude from the party's center of power and from the policymaking process actors and groups who were most hurt by the PSOE's economic policies.

Furthermore, one of the most important organizational characteristics of the Spanish Socialist Party was its high degree of internal cohesion. The defeat of the leftist group within the party took place in September 1979 during the PSOE's Extraordinary Congress—which reelected Felipe González as its Secretary General after his unexpected refusal to run for reelection during the Twenty-Eighth Congress.[11] A significant development that took place during that Congress was the approval of an indirect winner-take-all electoral system for delegates to congresses, as well as a bloc-voting provision-that is, the heads of the delegations were the only ones who were allowed to vote during congresses (Share 1989, 56). These new rules established an indirect, strictly majoritarian electoral system that allowed the leadership to control the delegate selection process.[12] The Twenty-Eighth

Congress was followed by an Extraordinary Congress four months later, in which the new majoritarian electoral mechanisms were used for the first time. The consequence of the implementation of these rules was that the group led by Felipe González, the reelected secretary general, consolidated its control over the party. After this congress, there was not a single group within the party with the support and the clout to challenge the top leaders' positions (Gillespie 1988, 433). This combination of strong leadership by González and the use of majoritarian electoral mechanisms has been considered the key to explaining the PSOE's internal unity and high degree of cohesion (Share 1989, 125).

The centralized nature of the PSOE prevented the UGT from playing a stronger role within the PSOE government. The close historical links between both organizations, however, did not foreshadow such a development. Up to 1982 both organizations had been intimately linked.[13] From the very beginning, party and union shared leaders and strategies. These links were maintained during Franco's dictatorship, when the leaders of the party and the union were in exile. At that time, the president of the party, Rodolfo Llopis, was also the president of the union. However, this situation changed in 1974 during the PSOE's XXVIth Congress in Suresnes when Nicolás Redondo, the UGT's Secretary General, refused to accept the position of PSOE Secretary General and instead proposed Felipe González as the party leader.[14] In 1977 both the UGT and the PSOE, following the model implemented in other SD parties and unions, decided to separate the leadership positions of both organizations and their respective executive committees (Führer 1996, 94). Party and union, however, continued with strong links, and the PSOE members were required by internal law to join the UGT. It was also quite usual for the PSOE and the UGT to hold joint executive committee meetings at the local level (Share 1989, 129). In the late 1970s and early 1980s, the UGT, strongly influenced by its northern European counterparts, sought to become part of the SD project led by the PSOE and adopt principles based on the strengthening of the welfare state, increases in public expenditures, and union consolidation within a capitalist framework based in private investment (Roca 1993, 260).[15]

However, despite these strong historical links to the party, the UGT had weak representation and little institutional power there. It only had one nonvoting member in the PSOE's executive committee; union activists did not have representation in the highest policymaking organs of the party; and UGT representatives did not participate institutionally in the party's programmatic discussions. Although the UGT helped articulate workers' support for the PSOE in the 1970s and early 1980s, and some union leaders were even elected from socialist lists in the 1982 general elections, the party and the union remained distinct entities. Only Nicolás Redondo—UGT's

Secretary General—was a member of the PSOE's executive committee, but he had no voting rights. These organizational arrangements sharply limited the influence of UGT within the party. Only a minority group—Izquierda Socialista—supported the union's position within the party, but it lacked the votes to challenge Gonzalez's group. Part of the explanation for this development lies in the fact that the socialist leaders were mostly in exile during the Franco dictatorship, and therefore, were not able to establish close links with the union movement within the country (Koelble 1991, 17). Most of the union's influence was based on personal relationships. Although at the beginning union leaders were consulted and participated in some of the economic decisions, the party leadership—which coincided with the government's)—had total control over its own organization. The union, thus, had little leverage to force the hand of the government and/or the party. This organizational structure offered incentives to the government to exploit its relationship with the union.

The UGT's weak position was further eroded after the 1982 elections when Felipe González, the new socialist premier, tried to incorporate some of the UGT's leaders and cadres in to the new administration.[16] The union leadership resisted these calls because it feared responding positively could further weaken the position of the union. This fear was based on the weakness of the union vis-à-vis the party. The UGT lacked the institutional clout and the file-and-rank support of its northern European counterparts. While the party was strong and had received almost ten million votes in the 1982 elections, the union was weak and had less than 630,000 members (Führer 1996, 135). This precarious position was further reinforced by its lack of economic resources; for example, the budget for 1985 was 1.022 billion pesetas, and almost half of that amount came from state subsidies (Díaz Güell 1987, 54; Sagardoy and León 1982). The union also owes thousands of millions of pesetas to domestic and foreign banks, suppliers, and the system of social security (Führer 1996, 182). The consequence of this lack of financial resources was that the UGT had a very weak personnel structure (603 employees in 1985)[17] and very limited resources to finance its activities. Given such a precarious position, the most likely scenario, according to the UGT leadership, would be that union members working for the government would transfer their allegiance to the party (Burns Marañón 1996, 210). In other words, the UGT's weakness vis-à-vis the party prevented the participation of the unions leaders in the government as representatives of the union.

In other countries, such as Austria or Britain, union leaders participated in socialist governments, but they continued to be leaders of the union, and were able to maintain their original allegiance and defend the union's position within the government. According to Nicolás Redondo, such a development was not possible in Spain. The party was too strong and the inducements to change loyalty too attractive (Burns Marañón 1996, 155). Subsequent events confirmed the union's leadership concerns; some of its leaders who moved into the socialist administration, such as Manuel Chaves, Matilde Fernández, or José Luís Corcuera, quickly transferred their allegiances to the party/government.[18] The consequence of this development was that UGT's positions were never supported within the government (Burns Marañón 1996, 155). This lack of support, which further limited the influence of the union within the party, had negative consequences for the concertation process because it allowed party leaders to marginalize the union's views. Given the UGT's relative weakness and its lack of influence in the party, the Spanish socialist government had no need to treat the socialist union as a significant actor or one with whom promises had to be kept.

From a comparative standpoint, among the Spanish PSOE, the German SPD (the German Social Democratic Party), the Swedish SAP (the Swedish Social Democratic Party), and the Austrian SPÖ (the Austrian Social Democratic Party), the PSOE was the one whose leadership "[had] the greatest organizational independence and policy making powers and provide[d] relatively little influence to the party activists, even less to its trade union constituency" (Koelble 1991, 18; Gillespie 1988). Consequently, the party leadership had enough power to implement its own policies and the union lacked the strength to challenge the leadership positions from within the party. In other countries where concertation had been successful for an extensive period of time unions played a stronger role within the SD party. This guaranteed a greater influence in the policymaking process for trade unions and also fostered the need for consensus and cooperation.

In Sweden and Germany, for instance, the SAP and the SPD have a centralized and hierarchical organization in which policy and personnel appointments are made by party leaders. The SPD and the SAP, however, have much larger memberships than does the PSOE. At the same time, they also have a significant union base, and union activists have representation in the highest policymaking organs of the party and can also influence the party's decisions through their involvement in the local and regional offices. In other words, the SPD and the SAP have closer ties to union movements and, although their organizations are not merged (in Germany it is forbidden by law), unions leaders and affiliates are active within the party, and many of the SPD and SAP leaders and activists have union credentials. Moreover, at the local level, trade unions often form the membership of the party (Koelble 1991, 16–17).

In Sweden, the LO (Landsorganisasjonen I Sverige) has historically played a critical role in mobilizing workers' support for the SAP.[19] In

1983, about 75 percent of the SAP's 1.2 million were affiliated with the party through their unions (Pontusson 1992, 469). The party financial resources greatly depended on union member party dues, and its election campaigns were financed almost entirely by union contributions until 1965, when the government approved state subsidies. Collective affiliation was discontinued after 1987 by the SAP congress, but the weight of union representatives within the LO is still considerable because collective affiliation never involved union bloc votes at SAP congress (in contrast to the British Labour Party). LO members cast votes in precongress deliberations at the district party level. Nowadays the LO still exercises influence through their union members, who join the party on an individual basis. Moreover, in Sweden (also in contrast to the Spanish PSOE), the LO president is appointed ex officio as a voting member of the party's executive committee and LO representatives have always participated in all programmatic discussions within the SAP; SD prime ministers have often consulted with the LO leadership and appointed union officials to ministerial positions; although in these cases such officials had to resign their union offices, they have remained faithful to the union (Pontusson 1992, 469; Kitschelt 1994, 242–244).

The contrast between SD party and union relationship is even greater in the case of Spain and Austria. In Austria the union has even more influence in the party than in Sweden. The Austrian Trade Union Confederation (ÖGB) has intimate linkages with the SPÖ, which borders on an "organizational symbiosis" (Kitschelt 1994, 246). Both organizations overlap leaders and functionaries; the ÖGB chairman has been traditionally elected by the SPÖ as the speaker of the Austrian Parliament, and many union leaders have held government positions in national and regional SPÖ administrations, something that has not happened in British or Belgian socialist parties. This relationship is further reinforced by the crucial role that the union plays in the management and patronage system of the state industries (Kitschelt 1994, 245–247).

In Spain, on the contrary, the party's organizational structure, coupled with the absence of a strong and influential intraparty blue-collar interest group (and the fact that the PSOE was dominated by a single figure, Felipe González, who proved to have little attachment to traditional socialist ideals[20]) "explains the party's very rapid adoption of a vote maximizing strategy" that left aside traditional SD considerations (Koelble 1991, 26). The consequence of this organizational structure has been that the government adopted an instrumentalist view of the union. As long as it helped the government to fulfill its economic objectives, it was considered a reliable partner worth taking into consideration. When the union refused to follow up the government policies, however, it was excluded. This, as I shall show below, had dire consequences for the concertation process because it culminated in a historic rupture between party and union.

III. Impact of this Relationship on the Government's Behavior

As we have just seen, the model of union-party cooperation put into place in Spain was very different from the one established in other European states with SD governments such as Austria, Germany, or Sweden.[21] In these countries, the SD union was the institution in charge of developing the guidelines of economic policies while the party was responsible for implementing them. In Spain, on the contrary, after the 1982 socialist victory, government/party officials stopped treating the union as a necessary partner in the policymaking process. The UGT was given a subordinated role, that of ratifying the orientation of economic policy, and it was otherwise systematically neglected. The government developed its own policies and then tried to convince the union to support them. The union, given its limited influence within the party, was unable to challenge the government's positions.

How did the PSOE's organizational structure influence the government's behavior? In this section I shall argue that the organizational structure of the party, which, as we have seen, sharply limited the influence of the union within it, hindered concertation by giving the government an incentive to ignore the union's views, take advantage of any deal struck with the union, and generally exploit that relationship. I shall seek to illustrate how this attitude influenced the PSOE government's behavior. The relationship between party and union allowed government officials to adopt an instrumentalist view of the union and disregard UGT's views and demands. These facts led to a rupture between the party and the union that brought about the collapse of concertation because the UGT, contrary to the government's belief, had been a critical actor during the concertation process. While the CCOO had participated intermittently in the concertation process (it did not sign the Acuerdo Básico Interconfederal, ABI; Acuerdo Marco Interconfederal, AMI; or Acuerdo Económico y Social, AES) it had clearly jumped off the social concertation wagon in 1984; however, the UGT had participated in all concertation agreements throughout 1986. The decision by the UGT to abandon this strategy after 1986 seems to be a critical factor that helps account for the collapse of concertation.

a. The Course of Economic Policy

In the late 1970s and early 1980s, party and union worked together to lay down the foundations for the electoral victory of the PSOE in national elections. The UGT had helped draft the PSOE's 1982 electoral program and imposed the promise to create 800,000 jobs during the legislative session (Solchaga 1997, 142). Given the historical links between the union and the party, the government's reliance on the union was expected to increase when the PSOE won the general elections in 1982. It was anticipated that party and union would work hand-in-hand to implement the socialist program.[22] It was within this context that some of the UGT's leaders were elected as socialist representatives in Congress. The strategy of cooperation between the union and the party was expected to be effective given their shared objectives and goals, as well as similar constituencies. The UGT expected to capitalize on the PSOE's victory in national elections. According to the union's expectations, the socialist victory should have resulted in the strengthening of the welfare state and a favorable position towards the union, which should have led to strengthening of the union's institutional position. Concertation fit into this strategy because it would contribute to the fulfillment of those objectives. The union would help control inflation through incomes policy, while the government would compensate the union for wage moderation (Moscoso 1995, 68–69). The UGT leaders also expected to play a role in economic policymaking. Within this context of cooperation, concertation was also useful for the government because it provided political coverage for unpopular policies.

These expectations, however, were soon seen as unrealistic. Differences about the course of economic policy between party and union surfaced shortly after the electoral victory of the PSOE in the 1982 elections. The UGT leadership still favored a classic SD Keynesian strategy that favored workers and jobs, and thus advocated policies aiming at protecting their members and the union's institutional position. These views, however, never had strong backing within the government. The lack of influence of the UGT within the party/government facilitated this goal. Therefore, despite winning the 1982 elections with a classical SD Keynesian-oriented economic plan that supported expansion of demand, the socialist government dropped it shortly afterwards and became a government that emphasized economic growth over unemployment (Merkel 1995, 227–325; Gillespie 1991, 431–442).

The about-face of the Spanish socialists was facilitated by the convergence of a number of factors. Behind this policy shift was the decision by Felipe González, the new socialist premier, to name in 1982 a new economic team that had had little input in the elaboration of the original electoral program. As we have seen before, this new team was led by people who had been primarily trained in the orthodox policies supported by the Bank of Spain.[23] They held very different perspectives about the sources of Spain's economic problems and their possible remedies. Miguel Boyer, the Minister of Economics, for instance, argued that demand-oriented policies would not help to address structural economic deficiencies, and that the increasing internationalization of the Spanish economy did not leave much room for domestic strategies (see chapter 5 for a discussion challenging these views[24]). On the contrary, pointing to the historical evidence of the French experiment with interventionism, he argued that demand-boosting policy inevitably leads to inflation and balance-of-payments deficits. Boyer and his economic team were aware of the profound changes undergone by the world economy and this brought about a general critical revision of government interventionism. He thought that the crisis of the 1980s was not a crisis caused by insufficient demand (Burns Marañón 1996, 149–172; and 303–304), and believed that Spain's poor economic performance was mainly the result of structural factors such as inflation, the strong growth of wages, low business profits, or the fast-growing public deficit.

The consequence of these assumptions was that the economic team rejected immediately the option to implement countercyclical policies to activate demand—the policies favored by the union (Maravall 1995, 120; Boix 1996, 148). Rather, the new economic team favored industrial adjustment policies and tight control of wages in order to foster investment (Paramio 1992, 530–533). Behind this development was also the government's decision to favor a combination of policies aimed at as broad an electoral constituency as possible (Koelble 1991, 19). Consequently, the first Socialist government sought to harmonize an expansive fiscal policy (increased public expenditure) with a restrictive monetary policy. The objective was to expand the available per capita income by increasing foreign capital investment (Pérez 1997). The favorable international economic conditions during the second half of the 1980s—the reduction in oil prices and industrial products, coupled with a massive influx of capital investment as a consequence of Spain's entry to the EC and the appreciation of the peseta—all favored the goal of economic expansion. However, the government drive to reduce inflation through a tight monetary policy fueled the confrontation between the UGT leadership—as well as that of the CCOO—and the government. Unions resented the government monetarist policies and criticized the latter's lack of social sensitivity. The UGT's limited influence within the party/government, however, prevented the union from mounting an effective challenge to these economic views from within the party.

The major concern of the socialist government economic policies that forced the confrontation with the union was the objective to reduce inflation. As we have seen before, in order to control inflation, the socialist government had two major options. It could implement restrictive economic policies to repress wages, or it could sign concertation agreements with unions and employers' associations to implement incomes polices.

The latter was the preferred option for the Northern European SD parties. At the beginning, the Spanish government favored it and participated in two agreements with the unions and employers. After 1986, however, the socialist government failed to reach a new agreement with unions and employers, and it decided to fight inflation with restrictive monetary policies instead.

The decision by the government to disregard concertation after 1986 and implement restrictive monetary policies was driven by four major factors. First, government officials were convinced that the UGT lacked the institutional clout to challenge the government, and that the union's subordinate role vis-à-vis the party/government would prevent it from mounting an effective challenge to the economic team's views.[25] Government officials claimed that the UGT's demands after 1986 threatened the government stance against inflation and came to believe that the "costs of neo-corporatism were higher than its benefits" (Maravall 1992, 41–43). In case of a confrontation, government officials expected a split within the union, and, possibly, the triumph of the union group who supported the government.

The government policy choice was also a reaction to Franco's strategy of inflation—that is, fitting interest rates to growth objectives. This process, according to the socialists, had politicized the task of disinflation. To avoid this politicization, the socialists became convinced that they had to use monetary policy rather than collective bargaining mechanisms to discipline wages. The government had an interest in "extricating themselves from the market to avoid previous politicization of disinflation. This explains the socialist embrace of the central bank's policies" (Pérez 1997, 206). In other words, in a context of strong inflationary expectations, the goal became repressing, rather than channeling, monetary expansion.

The third factor that motivated the socialist decision to favor tight monetary policies over concertation was provided by the experience of 1984, when the absence of a tripartite agreement had not precluded wages from growing below inflation (Roca 1993, 216; Espina 1991, 274). That year the social actors failed to reach an agreement because the government sought to limit wage growth to 6.5 percent when inflation was expected to increase some 8 percent. Despite the lack of agreement, however, wages only grew 7.6 percent, a level well below inflation (9 percent). This view was further reinforced in 1987 when the absence of a tripartite agreement did not preclude a reduction of inflation by 3.5 points, down to 5.3 percent (Boix 1996, 207–208). This development further convinced the socialist economic team that they did not need union acquiescence to keep wages down.

Finally, the economic team attributed the inflation "proneness" of the Spanish economy to microeconomic labor-market characteristics, and, more specifically, to the level of wage bargaining and the power of "insiders" in the bargaining process (Pérez 1996, 20). For this reason, they viewed economic adjustment almost exclusively as a matter of limiting wage growth. Therefore, they adopted a "strong currency/low wage" adjustment strategy that sought to compensate for the lack of competitiveness among Spanish firms with increasing foreign capital inflows (Pérez 1994, 23).[26] The solution, therefore, would come via a decentralization of the wage bargaining process and an increase in the flexibility of labor laws in order to reduce dismissal costs.

This decision by the government to implement monetarist policies to tackle inflation alienated the unions. The UGT, however, was never able to muster enough support within the party to challenge these policies. Its weak position within the party/government, coupled with the centralized structure of the party and the explicit support lent by Felipe González, the party and government leader, to the economic team's policies, prevented an effective challenge to the government policies from within. In addition, the government further exploited the UGT's weakness and pursued other policies, straining the relationship between both organizations. The deregulation and flexibilization of the labor market (the government approved a law in 1984 that introduced new temporary contracts), coupled with the painful effects that the industrial reconversion process had had in traditional union strongholds, and the tight monetary stance of the government after the economy picked up in 1986 all contributed to hurt the relationship between the union and the party/government.

The government's refusal to increase public expenditures further deteriorated the relationship and fueled the confrontation. In addition, the government refused for years to allocate any part of the budget surplus to social spending. On the contrary, in order to loosen monetary policy and lower the cost of capital while freeing money for the private sector, new revenues were applied to reduce the deficit. In 1989, for instance, the government devoted the surplus to reducing the deficit to 2.7 percent of GDP. The government also enacted a reform of the social security system in 1985 that reduced benefits, shifted costs to the employees, and tried to combat persistent fraud. Part of the new revenues from taxes were also devoted to reducing the public deficit, and 83 percent of all net tax increases were applied to curtailing the deficit (A. Zabalza, "El Estado de Bienestar: Un Pacto Social," *El País,* August 8, 1994, 42). Once this objective was achieved, the new resources from tax increases were dedicated to expanding the stock of physical capital in education and training programs. Public investment rose steadily to reach 5 percent of GDP (Gross Domestic Product) in 1991 (Boix 1994). Most of it was dedicated to restore public infrastructures—mostly communication networks—and to increase productivity in health and education.[27] Between 1980 and 1986 social expenditures increased from only 18.1 percent of GDP to only

19.5 percent, well below other European countries—for example, in France these expenditures reached 28.5 percent of GDP by 1986.[28]

In conclusion, this underlined a shift in the government strategy toward unions. Government officials were fully aware that such a policy course would inevitably lead to a confrontation with the unions. However, given the UGT's limited institutional weight within the party and its similar lack of influence in the government, they were convinced that the UGT would be unable to either influence policymaking or mount a credible challenge against this new strategy. The government thus felt it had a free hand to implement its favored policies. This decision, however, led to the final rupture, because the new economic policy course intensified disputes between the government/party and the union. While the union had never been able to challenge the government's economic policies within the party, its limited influence and subordinate role became even more evident when it was not even able to force the government to fulfill the union compromises that it had made.

b. The Government's Breach of Compromises with Labor

The organizational structure of the socialist party also had an impact in the government's decision to default on its compromises with labor. The UGT's lack of influence hindered concertation by not penalizing the government for taking advantage of any deal struck with the union. The government backed off almost immediately from some of its 1982 electoral compromises, such as the commitment to reduce the working week to 40 hours and extend vacations to 30 days. It also refused to consider union demands that it had promised to follow during the reforms of the industrial sector and the pension system. The government also failed to carry out the compromises that it had signed in the last concertation agreement, the AES, such as the productivity clauses, or the commitment to increase social expenditures and unemployment benefits when the economy picked up. Finally, the government's failure to tackle the increasingly high levels of unemployment and to compensate civil servants for higher inflation was also resented by union leaders.

The consequence of these breaches was that workers were not adequately compensated for wage moderation. UGT leaders argued that the combination of the government restrictive policies and the absence of compensation mechanisms made it extremely difficult to defend concertation among their members. These developments, coupled with the government's failed attempt to try to change the leadership in the UGT, hastened the rupture between party and union. The final affront that triggered the rupture between the UGT leadership and the government was the government's youth employment plan.

The government's willingness to breach its compromises with the UGT became evident from the very beginning. After the 1982 Socialist electoral victory, one of the first decisions adopted by the socialist cabinet was to postpone the electoral compromise to reduce the working hour and to extend vacations. Nicolás Redondo and the union repeatedly expressed their dissatisfaction, but to no avail. The government did not modify its position. After this development, conflicts between the union and the party emerged almost on a "daily basis" (Monteira 1996, 627).

The PSOE government's determination to exploit the UGT's weaknesses and the latter's lack of influence within the party became evident during the industrial restructuring process. In 1983, the government approved a "White Book" with major guidelines for the industrial reform process. Although the government adopted some of the UGT's demands in a decree that regulated the restructuring process of the steel sector (i.e., the norms that regulated the cancellation of contracts), the government disavowed these compromises during the implementation of the reform. With Aceriales, one of the firms affected by the restructuring process, the government decided to rescind the workers contracts. Only the virulent response from the UGT, which included violent strikes and widespread mobilizations, forced the hand of the government. This modus operandi would become a pattern in subsequent conflicts. Only when the union was able to muster support from workers and show it in the streets did the government back off and accept the union demands.

A third instance of the government ignoring the union took place during the 1985 reform of the pension system. At this time, the government planned to approve a law that resulted in a reduction in the number of pensions through the application of more restrictive conditions to receive a pension from the state.[29] Successive negotiations between the party and the union in February and March of 1985 failed, and on April 23, UGT's executive committee rejected the government proposal and announced the mobilization of workers. The Council of Ministers disregarded the UGT threats and approved the proposal (Monteira 1996, 631). The passing of this law caused the final rupture between the UGT representatives in Parliament and the Socialist Party, some of whom resigned from their seats (Solchaga 1997, 149).[30] This fight also triggered the rapprochement between the UGT and CCOO. Although the UGT did not participate in the June 20 general strike organized by the CCOO to oppose the new law, both organized protests together and participated in several rallies—something they had not done since 1983.

The negotiations that led to the last tripartite agreement, the AES, confirmed the instrumentalist view that the party had of the union and its determination to exploit that relationship. One of the most confrontational aspects of this agreement was the bargaining about Article 17, which regulated the system of mass dismissals (see chapter 3). José Luís Corcuera (then Redondo's deputy in the UGT and later Minister of Internal Affairs) and Luís Solana had been commissioned by the PSOE to negotiate with the employer association. The CEOE sought to reform the social security system and make the labor market more flexible, and the government fully supported these objectives. The former came up with a proposal that sought to align the Spanish legislation on dismissals with that of the EC. The leader of the CEOE, José María Cuevas, recognized later that he had to "soften" the compromise offered by the PSOE to make it more acceptable to the UGT (Monteira 1996, 630). The employer association, in other words, was offering a more palatable compromise to the unions than the government. In the end, the AES was approved by the UGT despite opposition from Redondo and other UGT leaders. In this instance the group led by Corcuera within the union won the battle. It would be the last one.

UGT's weakness and lack of influence within the party also prevented the union from forcing the government to fulfill the compromises that it had signed in the last concertation agreement (the AES). The union leaders resented particularly two main breaches: The nonimplementation of productivity clauses and the decrease in unemployment coverage. These breaches by the government furthered the rupture between both organizations, and marked another instance when the subordinated role played by the socialist union and its limited influence within the PSOE hindered concertation by giving the government a chance to take advantage of any deal struck with the union (and exploit their relationship).

Starting with the AMI (1980–1981), concertation agreements had introduced clauses that included some sort of wage participation in productivity improvements. These clauses, however, were never carried out. Employers failed to meet their promise to raise wages above the agreed target, which was set in line with productivity increases at the firm level, and the government never required them to do so. UGT for its part, never had the leverage to ensure compliance with what had been promised. Wages should have increased as a result of these productivity clauses, but that did not happen. The consequence was that the workers' purchasing power only improved by 0.3 percent in 1985, and lost 0.8 percent in 1986 (Espina 1991, 346). This nonfulfillment had critical consequences. Real wages had decreased 1.2 percent between 1979 and 1986 (Roca 1993, 217), which made it very difficult for the union to defend concertation among its members—particularly in light of increasing unemployment and the absence of adequate social compensation from the government. Once the economy began to recover, workers demanded some of the benefits, and actual real wage losses made concertation, with its unfulfilled promises, unacceptable for workers over the long run. The absence of mechanisms to guarantee that workers would participate in companies' profits guaranteed their opposition to this kind of agreement, particularly at a time when such profits were recovering (See Folgado 1989, 496–497).

This situation proved that the government had failed to understand that concertation implied a "social contract" that required a distribution of costs and benefits for all the actors involved. The government, instead, viewed incomes policy as an instrument to limit wage growth. It never accepted the fact that incomes policy was also a noninflationary mechanism that could be used to redistribute benefits and compensate workers for productivity increases (Espina 1991, 216). The government views on inflation precluded such an outlook, and the lack of UGT influence within the party/government prevented the union from mounting a challenge to those views. Productivity clauses should have allowed for wage differentials, depending on the particular conditions of each firm. Their nonfulfillment had a very negative effect for concertation, increasing social discontent and real wage losses. It also incidentally made it easier for unions to demand generalized wage increases; they did not have to defend or articulate wage differentials among workers.

Another instance in which the government failed to fulfill its compromises with labor took place during the implementation of the unemployment coverage clauses included in the AES. Once again, the government took advantage of the UGT's subordinate role and defaulted on its promises. The AES included provisions to foster job creation and beef up social benefits—including the promise by the government to increase the coverage of unemployment insurance from 32 percent in 1984 to 48 percent by 1986. The government did in fact introduce measures to increase unemployment benefits coverage and the duration of coverage in 1984 and 1985. Coverage increased from 26.4 percent in 1984 to 32.4 percent in 1985. Unemployment, however, increased dramatically during those years (from 14.6 percent in 1981 to 22.2 percent in 1985) as a result of the economic crisis and the entrance of new people to the job market. Therefore, the coverage of unemployment insurance could not even keep up with 1982 levels (33.6 percent). By 1988, it only covered 28.8 percent of the unemployed (Roca 1993, 203). The government, however, side-stepped the UGT's legitimate claims for more coverage as was called for in the AES. The UGT, lacking adequate institutional presence within the government/party, once again was unable to modify the government stance. To further aggravate the situation, the government, committed to the objective of reducing the deficit, refused to increase social expenditures. This was a blatant nonfulfillment of the AES and proved, yet again, the limited influence of the UGT and how easy it was for the government to breach its compromises with the union.

The union was particularly disappointed about the increase in unemployment. Although unemployment is a variable not directly controlled by the government, union leaders perceived the government's battling it as a quid pro quo for compromises the former had made.[31] The Spanish government, however, sacrificed employment in the short term for other economic gains. In other countries (such as Sweden, Germany, and Austria), the trade-off between unemployment and wage moderation had been one of the foundations for concertation. In these countries, however, SD unions participating in the policymaking process were strong enough to make sure that the government lived up to its side of the bargain. In Spain, on the other hand, the UGT played a subordinate role in policymaking and did not have the leverage to make sure that the government would live up to its side of the agreement. Therefore, the government had an easier time ignoring the fight to consider unemployment a priority. The consequence was that in Spain wage moderation had little effect on unemployment. While such moderation contributed to the recovery of business profits in the second half of the 1980s, workers saw little compensation for their moderation. What did occur was the reduction—or stagnation—in workers' real wages—that is, between 1979 and 1986 real wages decreased 1.2 percent (Roca 1993, 217).[32] These losses, however, had little effect on unemployment, which remained very high, at 21 percent in 1985. Consequently, the coexistence during several years of high unemployment and a reduction in real wages (particularly obvious in 1982 and 1984) discredited incomes policy (Roca 1993, 205) and undermined concertation.[33]

The experience of the union was further aggravated by the government's failure to compensate public workers for the reemergence of inflation in the second half of the 1980s. In 1988 the government had set an ambitious Consumer Price Index (CPI) objective of 3 percent. Inflation, however, shot up in the second half of the year and peaked at 5.8 percent at the end of the year. Civil servants were particularly affected by this development. Although private sector workers had negotiated "safeguard clauses" that prevented income losses, public servants, pensioners, and the unemployed with incomes tied to the public budget were not as fortunate. Inflation deviations had a great impact on these constituencies' income because they did not have the clauses to protect them. This resulted in union demands for compensation. Unions developed the concept of "social debt" to refer to the purchasing power losses that these constituencies had suffered as a result of inflation deviations.

The government's strategy towards UGT became clearly evident when it attempted to change the UGT leadership in order to find a more accommodating bargaining partner. Once again, the government strategies toward the union were influenced by the UGT's institutional position. The government thought that the union would support its economic policies out of loyalty. By 1984, however, there were two groups within the union. The minority group, led by José Luís Corcuera, the union's Secretary of Syndical Action, supported the government's policies within the union and defended a close relationship with the government. The other group, led by the Secretary General Nicolás Redondo, on the contrary, increasingly resented the orientation of the government economic polices and defended the union's greater autonomy from the government and the PSOE. Government officials estimated that a confrontation between the two, given the relative weakness of the union and the presence of an influential group within it that supported the government's policies, would result in a schism in the union and the ultimate victory of the group that supported the government's position (Roca 1993, 253).[34] This assumption proved to be wrong. Supporters of the party/government within the union staged several attempts to weaken the grip that Redondo had over the organization. Corcuera himself was accused of leading a coup to remove Redondo in November of 1984 and was forced to resign to defend his innocence (Monteira 1996, 630). The collection of signatures within the UGT, organized by Manuel Chaves (a member of UGT's executive committee) to support the government's position during the NATO referendum in 1986, was another attempt by the government to weaken Redondo's grip in the union.[35] At the end, however, the group led by Redondo triumphed within the union. The government underestimated the possibility that the rupture would strengthen the position of the union and the labor movement. This is, however, what happened after 1988. Only a financial scandal brought about Redondo's resignation in the early 1990s.

The government's determination to exploit union weaknesses was reaffirmed when it tried to break the monopoly that both the UGT and CCOO had within the labor movement—and that was one of the major advantages that the unions had obtained for their participation in the concertation process. The agreements that the government signed with the CSIF (the Confederación Sindical Independiente de Funcionarios, a trade union that represents civil servants), and the UDP (the Unión Democrática de Pensionistas, a pensioners' association with no connection with the unions) in September 1988 were geared towards that objective. These agreements sought to establish wage increases for pensions and civil servants for 1989. Therefore, they questioned and challenged the representative monopoly of the majority unions, and, more specifically, the privileged relationship with the UGT (Roca 1993, 252). This attempt collapsed when those lesser organizations failed to get sufficient support from their constituencies to challenge the dominant position of the main confederations.

By the mid-1980s these breaches of agreements had convinced the UGT's leadership that the government was not willing to implement the SD policies that the union expected, and that economic recovery would not result in the expansion of the welfare state and a more expansive wage policy, which would have allowed the union to justify among workers the sacrifices that they had been asked to bear during the first half of the 1980s. The union accused the socialists of implementing monetarist policies that ignored direct redistribution of income. It also argued that the costs of modernization were being borne mostly by workers.[36] By that time it had also become very clear for the UGT leadership that the model that had been implemented successfully in other European states, where the orientation— and even the decisions—about economic issues were the responsibility of the union and the government had the role of merely implementing them, was not working in Spain. Redondo attributes this to the fact that "Felipe [González] has a hierarchical conception of power, a quasi 'Leninist' conception of the relationship between the party and the union: everything had to be subordinated to the government," (Monteira 1996, 629, my translation). The government, for its part, accused the union of lack of realism and flexibility in addressing new problems (Solchaga 1997, 147–149). González himself recognized then that he had "less trouble communicating with the citizens than he had with the unions," (Monteira 1996, 629, my translation). Earlier in the 1980s, when Redondo, who represented the union, tried to oppose the government policies in the PSOE's executive committee and asked for a vote, he was reminded that he had no right to ask for a vote because he was not an elected member of the executive committee (Monteira 1996, 628–630). These developments culminated with Redondo's decision to abandon the PSOE's executive committee in October of 1984. With this decision, the UGT was left with no voice in the party's inner circles of power, and the government had a free hand to make its own decisions.

All these developments fueled the historic rupture between both organizations, which had devastating consequences for the concertation process because the UGT had been the only union that had taken part in all concertation agreements. In fact, UGT's decision to abandon this strategy gave a final blow to concertation. The final development took place in 1988, when the government introduced the youth employment plan to facilitate the access of young people to the labor market. In this instance, however, the government underestimated the union's reaction.

Specifically, at the end of 1987, and in spite of high economic growth, youth unemployment remained extremely high at 42 percent. The socialist government feared that the persistence of youth unemployment could pose a threat for the democratic system (Espina 1991, 213) and approved a plan that introduced the possibility to hire new workers (between 16 and 25 years old) with no previous work experience and pay them the minimum wage in exchange for public subsidies and the possibility to legally extend their temporary contracts. At that time, however, the Spanish labor market was undergoing profound transformations that had resulted in higher levels of temporary workers and greater segmentation among workers. According to some authors, further consolidation of these transformations could have had profound implications for unions activities and even could have threatened their survival in the long run (Roca 1993, 261). Therefore, the introduction of the new youth scheme was viewed by union leaders as a threatening development that would further increase short term and temporary contracts and endanger the position of unions' traditional strongholds, because firms would have more incentives to hire young workers, who have less attachments to unions, or would even replace old ones with new young workers. The UGT, however, did not have the leverage within the party/government to impose its views and modify the plan. The government went ahead and approved it.

The reaction of unions was immediate and expected. This plan was the final spark that triggered the rupture between the UGT and the government. The UGT decided to mobilize its supporters and affiliates in plants and factories, and organized rallies and strikes to challenge the government plan. The rupture between the socialist government and the UGT leadership also resulted in an alliance between UGT and CCOO. This alliance culminated in a historic general strike in December 1988. This strike led to the definitive collapse of concertation (Gillespie 1990, 53). Only through its rupture with the PSOE and its tactical alliance with CCOO was the UGT finally able to force the government to attend to union demands. After the general strike the government increased social expenditures significantly; pensions rose to the level of minimum wage, public servants were compensated for previous inflation deviations, and a decree extending unemployment benefits coverage was approved. By then, however, it was too late to revive concertation and to reconstruct the relationship between the UGT and the government. Despite particular agreements between the unions and the government covering specific issues—for example, the January 25th Agreements of 1990—the general strike had marked a point of no return for the unions. It is indeed paradoxical that the UGT was able to achieve on the streets what it had been unable to accomplish within the party.[37] This is also a major lesson from the Spanish case: The subordination of the union hinders the implementation of a traditional SD strategy because it leads to the radicalization of the union that finally refuses to play a cooperative role with the government.

IV. Aggravating Factors

In this chapter I have argued that the key aspect in accounting for the behavior of the Spanish socialist government was the organizational structure of the party, which sharply limited the influence of the union within it. There were also other aggravating factors that reinforced the government refusal to accommodate the union demands and reject concertation. The overwhelming victory of the PSOE in the 1982 elections, the crisis and the underdevelopment of the welfare state, and electoral considerations all played a role in the government's behavior. These factors had an unquestionable impact on government actions. They do not explain, however, why the party defected from its agreements with the union. I argue, therefore, that the key variable in accounting for the government's behavior is the weakness of the UGT vis-à-vis the party/government.

First, it has been argued that the magnitude of the socialists' electoral victory in the 1982 elections had an important impact in the government strategies (Burns Marañón 1996, 214). The socialists won the 1982 elections with such an overwhelming majority of votes, some ten million, that they had a sufficient majority in Parliament to be able implement their own policies by themselves. This parliamentary majority was further entrenched by the PSOE's control of most of the regional governments and city councils; this reinforced the government conviction that they did not need support from other actors to implement their policies (Burns Marañón 1996, 213–214). This attitude was crystallized in the government obsession with the application of the "mandate theory"—that is, "the right and duty to carry out policies conceived in terms of the general interest" (Maravall, 1993, 118). The Spanish socialists wanted to avoid at all cost becoming prisoners of union demands (Boix 1996, 147).[38] The government's decision to abandon concertation, according to this view, was partially motivated by this objective. González sought to defend the political autonomy of the government and refused to negotiate "mortgages to the conception and implementation of our project" (González 1991, 126–127, my translation). This approach left little margin for consensus because the government refused to make concessions that seemingly would distort the main thrust of reforms.

The PSOE's overwhelming majority in Parliament, however, is not a sufficient explanation to account for the government's decision to defect from agreements with unions. Other SD parties had ruled with an overwhelming majority—such as the Swedish SAP—but this had not prevented them from cooperating with unions. In fact, unions played a critical role in economic policymaking. What is peculiar in the Spanish case is the position of the UGT vis-à-vis the party/government. If the UGT had had a stronger base and more representation in the party's organs of policymaking, then the government would not have been able to marginalize the union and ignore its demands. The problem in Spain was that the parameters that would govern the relationship between both organizations once the party was in power had never been clearly established. As we have seen, part of the explanation for this development lies in the fact that both organizations emerged from illegality to power in a very short period of time.

It has also been argued that the decision by the government to neglect the union was reinforced by the difficulties that the PSOE encountered while trying to implement a SD program in Spain, difficulties due to the extended economic crisis (Roca 1993, 254–255). According to this view, the implementation of SD programs had taken place in other countries, such as the Northern European states or Germany, during the years when rapid economic growth and the dramatic expansion of national income contributed to the establishment and consolidation of SD-oriented policies that were based on the expansion of the welfare state and concertation (Aguilar and Roca, 1990). Roca (1993, 255) argues that the starting point was very different in Spain. The union and the party had to work to build the welfare state during the crisis, not just to maintain it. Therefore, although the socialists dramatically increased public expenditures in pensions, health, and education (4.1 points of the GDP between 1982 and 1992), public expenditures in social services lagged behind those of other European nations— for example, in 1994 Spain still spent 87.6 percent of what France, the United Kingdom, Germany, and Italy spend in pensions, unemployment, health, education and housing (A. Zabalza, "El Estado de Bienestar: Un Pacto Social," *El País,* August 8, 1994, p. 42). A larger welfare state that would have satisfied unions would have required increasing public expenditures and higher wages (when the economy recovered). Therefore, according to this view, difficulties in fostering a welfare state that was underdeveloped, especially during an economic downturn that led to a lack of resources in accommodating union demands, contributed to the rupture between both organizations (Roca 1993, 255).

The government's difficulties, however, still cannot completely explain its repeated decisions to default from its compromises with labor. Other countries, such as Portugal, faced similar constraints, yet concertation succeeded and the government made strenuous efforts to satisfy union demands. In Spain, however, the socialist government refused to go the extra mile (at least until the 1988 general strike). In Spain, the socialists argued that both the backwardness of the welfare state and the intensity of the economic crisis of the first half of the 1980s prevented a sharp increase in public expenditures. Following such a program would have brought about a relocation of public expenditures and an increase in taxation that would have been incompatible, it said, with the recovery of business profits. The reality, however, was that in Spain, the recovery of business profits took place through the transfer of income from wage earners to non-wage earners and through the deepening of wage differentials (Roca 1993, 255). Even more importantly, the dramatic recovery of business profits gave further room to the government for compromises on public expenditures or monetary policy, but the government, fixated on its inflation views, refused to take advantage of this factor.

Electoral considerations were also important. The electoral triumph of the socialists throughout the 1980s was based on a coalition of blue- and white-collar workers and young urban professionals. The socialists had adopted a "vote maximizing strategy" to satisfy all these groups. Further tax increases would have alienated urban professionals and/or reduced business profits. A relocation of public expenditures to accommodate union demands, they said, also would have alienated some of the constituencies that supported the government. At the end, however, the impossibility of accommodating all these demands and balancing conflicting interests eroded the electoral support for the PSOE.

Political considerations also played a role in the UGT's behavior and influenced the union's decision to abandon concertation. Although the UGT had been effective at controlling its rank and file,[39] the strategic electoral defeat of the union in the 1986 elections had a profound impact on the UGT leaders. In these elections the UGT lost votes in major strategic firms. Consequently, it reached the conclusion that the costs of economic adjustment were becoming to high to bear for the union. Redondo himself had argued that "this was the result of signing so many pacts with a government that is ruining us" (Monteira 1996, 632, my translation). Increasing labor market segmentation and temporary hiring were also dangerous developments that threatened the union. The UGT leadership feared that continuing support for concertation might further erode union support among workers, and that the CCOO would then be able to capitalize on workers' discontent. Therefore, it decided to strengthen its bargaining position and demand the fulfillment of all the previous compromises. When the government refused to comply with the UGT demands, the latter abandoned concertation. The UGT then felt it had to seize the initiative and ride the crest of the emerging discontent to strengthen its position and to retrieve some political leverage (Moscoso 1995, 76–78). This argument, however, fails to explain why the UGT was able to gain votes in the previous electoral contests, when the union supported concertation. Moreover, a policy of confrontation did not restore the UGT's dominance. On the contrary, this strategy resulted in diminishing recognition. CCOO is today the number one union in term of votes in Spain.

Conclusions

In this chapter I have concluded that the PSOE's organizational structure, which sharply limited the influence of UGT within it, hindered rather than supported concertation in Spain by giving the government an incentive to take advantage of any deal struck with the union and generally to exploit that relationship. When the PSOE came to power, the UGT's lack of influence within the party led government officials to adopt a view of the union as merely its instrument and to conclude that they did not need it to execute its policies. Consequently, the government repeatedly failed to fulfill its compromises with labor.

The decision to ignore the union, as was mentioned before, was motivated by the lack of influence that the union had in the party. In other European countries with a long-standing neocorporatist tradition, such as Sweden or Austria, the SD unions played a critical role in the policymaking process, and their views were taken into consideration. In these cases, however, unions had strong linkages with the SD parties, a powerful support base, and union leaders and affiliates played an influential role within both the party and government. In Spain, on the contrary, the UGT was weak and had limited influence within the party. Therefore the government, which was composed of the same people as the party, relegated the union to playing a subordinate role.

I have also concluded that it was the government, with its fixation on inflation, that first endangered the crucial relationship between party and union. Differences between both did not lead to discussions and negotiations in search of a consensus that could be supported by both organizations (this would have been the approach in countries with longer neocorporatist traditions). In Spain, on the contrary, the union lacked the institutional clout to influence the position of the government/party. Consequently, the socialist government defaulted on its compromises with the union and implemented economic policies aimed at modernizing the economy, which proved to be very costly for workers and unions alike. These policies endangered the crucial relationship between the party and the union and resulted in a breakdown between the UGT and the socialist party/government. This rupture was a significant basis for concertation's failure because the UGT had been the only union that had participated in all major concertation agreements.

CONCLUSIONS

Limits to Social Democratic Policies in Spain

Introduction

This research project has sought to integrate the Spanish experience with social democratic (SD) policies into the contemporary literature on European political economy. By focusing on an institutional factor that has not been given serious attention, namely, the autonomy, or lack thereof, of labor unions from the governing party, this book is one of the few attempts to analyze the relationship between political parties and economic actors as a critical variable in determining the success of economic policies.

I have examined in this study the roles of institutional and structural factors emphasized in the literature to account for the success (or failure) of concertation processes. These factors, however, fail to explain developments in Spain. Concertation was successful in that country for almost eight years (1979–1986), despite an institutional framework characterized by decentralized collective bargaining, weak and competitive unions, and the strength and even dominance for years of the labor movement by a communist union (the Comisiones Obreras, CCOO). The structural conditions faced by Spain were not less conducive to concertation than those faced by countries such as Portugal, where concertation has flourished in the late 1980s and 1990s (see chapter 5). Throughout this book, I have argued that the literature leaves aside very important societal and political contextual considerations that also influence the decisions of social actors.

Institutional and structural explanations fail to consider the circumstances under which competing and weak unions are willing to take part in neocorporatist arrangements. In order to account for this behavior, I have analyzed the role of the political context, and, specifically the influence that the democratic transition process in Spain had on the strategies of the unions. Some scholars have argued that concertation was intimately linked to the transition process because one of the major objectives for all social actors was the consolidation of the new regime and this fostered consensus and cooperation. Once the new regime was consolidated, however, that motivation dissipated and unions did not have such an incentive to pursue concertation according to these scholars.

I have argued, however, that this explanation does not satisfactorily account for the behavior of the Spanish socialist government. It helps us understand why Spanish unions were willing to moderate their demands during the transition to help consolidate the new regime, but it fails to explain why the government failed to fulfill its compromises with labor. I have concluded that the collapse of concertation can only be fully understood in terms of the behavior of the Spanish Socialist Workers Party (the PSOE) in government. It was the government with its actions that endangered the crucial relationship between the socialist labor union (the Unión General de Trabajadores, UGT) and the Socialist Party because it failed to fulfill its compromises with labor.

In order to account for the PSOE government's behavior, I have focused on the nature of the relationship between the PSOE and the UGT in Spain. I have shown that the organizational structure of the PSOE sharply limited the influence of the union within it. Analysis of the Spanish experiment with concertation confirms that the UGT institutional subordination to the PSOE allowed the government to believe it could default on the promises made to the union. This behavior led to a break between the party and the union. This rupture was a significant factor in the failure of concertation, because the UGT had been the only union that had participated in all major concertation agreements. Moreover, since the socialist government's economic strategy hinged on the cooperation of the union, this rupture in their relationship ultimately doomed the success of its policies. The Spanish experience with concertation confirms that the structure of the relationship between party and union, and not only the global and domestic institutional context, provides its own set of incentives for domestic actors to entertain certain political strategies. Having concluded that SD corporatist policies are feasible in a global economy, I close this chapter with some ideas about the future of social democracy.

a. The Spanish Puzzle

Between 1979 and 1986 Spanish unions, business, and, in two instances, the government, signed five centralized agreements. Four of them included incomes policy. On balance, the final assessments of these agreements is very positive. There is generalized consensus that concertation contributed greatly to the consolidation of the new democratic regime. It fostered consensus and facilitated agreements over the content of the new Constitution. Concertation also contributed to the development of new laws regulating the industrial relations framework and helped mitigate industrial conflict. Social peace provided the foundation on which the transition process was consolidated. Concertation also contributed greatly to the institutional consolidation of the unions and their recognition as the legal representatives of workers. All these objectives played a critical role in the unions' strategies toward concertation. They subordinated other objectives to achieve these goals.

At the same time, concertation resulted in social peace and wage moderation, which contributed to lower inflation and helped to restore business profits. Moreover, by introducing macroeconomic considerations into collective bargaining, concertation made it possible for wages to behave according to inflationary objectives. Wage moderation and lower inflation (which was reduced from 26.4 percent in 1977 to 8.8 percent in 1986) resulted in higher business profits which, in turn, fostered confidence, investment, and jobs in the second half of the 1980s. Finally, it helped to encourage consensus and bargaining among the social actors and contributed to the integration of the social actors, unions, and business organizations into the new political and economic system.[1] After concertation broke down, wages grew beyond government's inflation targets on a regular basis, and the latter reemerged particularly strong at the end of the 1980s, which forced the government to tighten up monetary policies, which in turn resulted in further increases in unemployment. The question then is, why did concertation collapse? This has been the puzzle that I have sought to explain in this research project.

I have argued in this book that domestic institutional factors and the influence of changes in the economic structure (the focus of the literature) are not by themselves a sufficient explanation to account for the collapse of concertation in Spain after 1986. Although I acknowledge that events in Spain (as in other countries) were strongly influenced by the economic context and the problems faced by the Spanish economy, I have shown that these are not sufficient explanations to account for the failure of concertation.

The conventional wisdom has attributed the collapse of concertation in the mid-1980s in countries such as Sweden to economic structural changes associated with technology restructuring, increasing trade globalization, and the liberalization of financial markets. According to this argument, the changing economic environment had two major effects on concertation: First, changes in the production system undermined the structural bases of corporatism by significantly weakening organized labor movements. These changes resulted in higher demand for scarce highly-skilled labor, which in turn fostered wage differentiation and labor segmentation that weakened and fragmented the labor movement, thus strengthening the position of capital vis-à-vis labor. Second, increasing exposure to trade, foreign direct investment, and liquid capital mobility limited the effectiveness of domestic governments in implementing domestic economic strategies and rendered expansionary macroeconomic policies far less feasible. This eroded the prospects for concertation because the threat of "exit" by mobile asset holders forced governments to scrap Keynesian expansionist policies, thus limiting the capacity and autonomy of governments to compensate unions for wage moderation.

The socialists came to power in Spain at a time (1982) when some of the most powerful governments (in the United States, Germany, and the United Kingdom) were implementing restrictive monetary policies to quell inflation. At that time the international crisis had magnified and intensified the inefficiencies of the Spanish economy. Consequently, a few days after winning the elections, the new socialist Economic Minister, Miguel Boyer, developed a very restrictive adjustment package that included a sharp devaluation of the peseta. It sought to restore the macroeconomic conditions of the Spanish economy but ignored the socialist electoral program of 1982. Integration into the international economy was completed with Spain's entry into the European Community (EC) in 1986, which definitively opened the Spanish economy and exposed its inefficiencies. According to the structuralist argument, within this context of international integration, the socialist leaders could not cave in to union demands and had no choice but to implement restrictive policies to quell inflation and restore competitiveness. In other words, the changing economic environment constrained economic policy in Spain and prevented the implementation of expansive policies that would have permitted the continuation of concertation after 1986. Otherwise they would have suffered the wrath of the market and would have also experienced capital outflows (as did France in 1982).

In this book I have introduced empirical evidence that challenges these arguments. First, changes in the production system in Spain did not undermine the structural bases of corporatism by significantly weakening organized labor movements. In terms of union density (the simplest measure of the strength of unions), the strength of trade unions increased significantly in the 1970s, peaked in 1980, and declined in the 1980s. I have shown, however, that the magnitude of the decline should not be overstated. I have also challenged the conventional argument that attributes the collapse of concertation in Spain to the growing divergence in the interests of labor and the decreasing ability of central confederations to resolve these conflicts. I have shown that that between 1970–1996 peak confederations became increasingly powerful, and their dominant position was not challenged by the emergence of new unions (not even in the public sector). On the contrary, the empirical evidence shows that between 1970 and 1996 there was no pervasive reduction in the organizational power of peak labor confederations. In conclusion, the data that I introduce in this book does not support the notion of "unions in decline" in Spain. This data seems consistent with more extensive studies about the strength of unions in OECD (Organization for Economic Cooperation and Development) countries in the global economy (see Garrett 1998, 66–67; Moses 1998; Golden, Wallerstein, and Lange 1999).

Furthermore, the evidence introduced on chapter 5 highlights the shortcomings of the arguments that attributed the collapse of concertation in Spain to globalization. The empirical evidence shows that despite globalization and changes to the production system, some SD corporatist countries (Austria, Norway, and Germany) have been able to sustain their characteristic distributional policies (including higher levels of taxation), the strength of their labor market institutions, and their systems of wage bargaining based on concertation (Swank 1998). Furthermore, in these countries the redistribution of wealth and social benefits was not achieved at the expense of overall economic performance (contrary to what the Spanish socialists argued). On the contrary, the macroeconomic performance of corporatist with regards to real aggregates vis-à-vis more liberalized economies remained better (particularly until the 1990s, and let's reemphasize that concertation collapsed in Spain in 1986) (Soskice 1999). The reason for this was that labor leaders in these countries used their market power to regulate overall wage growth in ways that promoted the competitiveness of the tradable sector in exchange for benefits from the government (see Garret 1998). These policies generated economic growth and political and social stability that were attractive and beneficial to the business sector and prevented the capital flight that was predicted by the defenders of the globalization argument.

The argument that attributes to globalization the collapse of concertation in Spain also fails to account for the events that followed the general strike of December 1988, when the government gave in to most union demands. In 1989 it spent over 2 billion pesetas to beef up social services. This decision, however, did not have the dramatic macroeconomic impact that it should have, according to the government's expectations—that is, mobile asset holders did not exercise the "exit" threat; on the contrary, they invested massively in Spain, attracted by high interest rates and the liberalization of the Spanish economy—thus, confirming my thesis that the government earlier had room for negotiating with unions. I asked, in other words: If the international economic context made concertation in Spain impossible in 1986, how was the government able to satisfy union demands after 1988? At the latter time, the Spanish economy was even more integrated into the world economy and faced more constraints—that is, the process of capital liberalization had only just began in 1986. Even after joining the European Monetary System, the government had some fiscal leeway, and fiscal policy was expansive until 1993. Finally, it is difficult to maintain that the globalization of capital markets and the decline of Fordist or mass production are the reasons for the collapse of concertation, when both factors also affected countries in which cooperation between government and labor increased significantly in the 1980s–1990s and even had distinctive corporatist features—for example, the Netherlands, Portugal, Belgium, Greece, Australia, Ireland, Italy, the Czech Republic, and Austria.

In this book I have also analyzed the domestic institutional setting in Spain to challenge the arguments that attribute the collapse of concertation to inadequate labor institutions that could not be encompassing enough to produce overall wage moderation. Although I acknowledge that Spain has a system of industrial relations based on competitive and relatively weak unions and decentralized wage bargaining, which did not facilitate the kind of neocorporatist agreements that have been typical of other European countries, I have argued that institutional factors were not enough to account for the failure of concertation in Spain. On the contrary, weak labor unions and a decentralized wage bargaining system were features of the industrial relations system from 1979 until 1986, yet concertation still took place and was extremely successful in moderating overall wage growth, and centralized bargaining reemerged in Spain under a conservative government in 1996.[2] Therefore, these factors by themselves cannot account for the failure of concertation. Other factors must have played a role.

I have acknowledged that political factors helped explain the collapse of concertation. They seem to account for the behavior of Spanish unions. In this regard, some authors (Lang 1981, 252) have argued that the critical explanatory factor in the collapse of concertation in Spain was the changing political context. According to this argument, the objective of consolidating the emerging democratic institutions facilitated consensus among the social actors and paved the way for centralized agreements. Specifically, when the socialist came to power in 1982, Spain had a very fragile democratic system. In 1981 there has been a failed coup d'état. According to this view, within that fragile environment trade unions were willing to make concessions in order to contribute to the strengthening of the new regime. Once the new regime was consolidated, however, consensus was more difficult and concertation collapsed. Unions were not willing to make the same concessions that they had made before. In this new political scenario, unions focused mostly on economic compensations, particularly at times (in 1986) when the economy was picking up and union leaders wanted the workers to share the benefits of economic expansion.

Nevertheless, although the objective to strengthen the new democratic regime played a critical role in the strategies of unions, I argue that the consolidation of the democratic regime was not the only cause behind the collapse of concertation. The massive electoral triumph of the socialists in 1982, coupled with their fast grip of power, and the entrance of Spain to the European Community fully consolidated the democratic system. By 1985 few people questioned the strength of the regime. Yet the socialist government signed a tripartite agreement with one of the major unions (the UGT) and the business association for 1985–1986. In addition, the more recent centralized agreement of April 1997 confirms that concertation continues to be possible. Finally, I have argued that while the explanation above may help to account for union moderation, it fails to explain why the Spanish socialist government defaulted on its compromises with labor. The PSOE's actions cannot be adequately explained, either, using traditional institutional and structuralist factors.

In order to account for the government's behavior, I have concluded that a key factor was the organizational structure of the Socialist Party, which sharply limited the influence of the union within it. I have hypothesized that the PSOE's structure hindered concertation by giving the government an incentive to take advantage of any deal struck with the union and to thus exploit that relationship. Consequently, the government failed to fulfill its compromises with labor and encountered few political constraints in defecting from its promises to the union. The UGT's lack of influence within the party led the economic team to adopt an instrumentalist view of the union, and to conclude that it did not need the union to implement the government's economic policies. This decision brought about the rupture between the PSOE government and the UGT and, thus, the collapse of concertation. Three main factors drove a confrontation between the PSOE and UGT: The breach of electoral compromises, the course of the government's economic policies (particularly the fixation on inflation), and the infringement by the government of compromises included in centralized pacts. These developments culminated in the rupture between the socialist party/government and the union.

At the end, the Keynesian pact that had characterized the concertation processes in other countries—that is, wage moderation in exchange for compensation—broke down in Spain as a consequence of the restrictive policies pursued by successive socialist governments. Unions became merely spectators of the new process and intensified conflict in order to show their rejection of the government's economic policies. In fact, it was the government's fixation on inflation and the implementation of restrictive monetary policies that first endangered the crucial relationship between the party and the union. The UGT's weakness and its lack of influence within the party prevented a challenge to the economic team views and allowed the government to disavow its promises to the union. This was compounded by the fact that the government had an overwhelming majority in Parliament to carry out its own policies and felt that it did not need the support of the union. Consequently, after 1986 the government leadership decided that the costs of concertation were too high to bear, and that it did not need unions to achieve its economic objectives. It decided to implement policies aimed at modernizing the economy that proved to be very costly for workers. While the means of these policies were interventionist in nature, their objective was simply the promotion of capitalism and not socialism. This policy course caused a breakdown between the UGT and the socialist party/government.

This outcome could have been prevented. The recovery of business profits in the second half of the 1980s offered some fiscal leeway to the government. It could have used it to compensate unions for wage moderation. Alternatively, it could have chosen to offer nonmonetary inducements and to expand significantly the power of unions in return for wage restraint. The PSOE government, however, refused to increase unions' institutional position. On the contrary, the socialists did very little to strengthen labor vis-à-vis management in the private and public sectors. The UGT was then forced to seize the initiative and ride the crest of the emerging discontent to strengthen its position and to retrieve some political leverage. The UGT leaders were also afraid of losing further ground vis-à-vis its traditional competitor, the CCOO. The 1986 work council elections were considered a strategic defeat of the UGT, and its leaders feared that continued support for concertation would further erode its position in the labor movement. This strategy, however, resulted in diminishing recognition and greater reliance on the rank-and-file's more extreme demands, and this led to a confrontational stance against the government.

This book, thus, highlights the relationship between political parties and economic actors, a factor that has not been given serious attention by other scholars as a critical variable in determining the success of economic policies. The neocorporatist and structuralist literatures, with their emphasis on labor market institutional and economic factors, overlook the manner in which the behavior of unions and government parties are affected by this relationship. These explanations overlook the political and institutional factors that make concertation possible in certain circumstances. The analysis of the Spanish experience with concertation shows that the domestic political context played a critical role in the collapse of concertation.

b. Peculiarities of the Spanish Concertation Model

The Spanish concertation model was characterized by several specific features. The primacy of political considerations over other objectives, strong state intervention, a unique institutional setting, specific goals related to the existing political and economic framework, and unions' subordination to political parties all configured a concertation process markedly different than the one that took place in other countries, such as Sweden, Austria, and the Netherlands.

Political considerations had a tremendous impact throughout the concertation process in Spain. Concertation emerged in Spain at the time of the transition to democracy. In other countries, such as the northern European states, concertation emerged within well-established political regimes. This was not the case in Spain. In that country, economic and political demands that would spark conflict and potentially threaten the emerging democratic regime were left aside in favor of political arrangements that favored social peace and consensus. Concertation emerged in this landscape as an instrument that would contribute to consensus, moderation, and the consolidation of the new regime. These political objectives played a very relevant role in the Spanish concertation process. As Roca (1993) has suggested, motivations such as the institutional benefits that unions received from participating in concertation, or the benefits that unions expected to extract from their affiliates, acted more like "substitutes than complements" of the benefits that usually guarantee support for concertation in other countries. In other words, "in Spain the political exchange between union leadership, business associations, and the state replaced the incentives that unions in other countries receive from below—a high level of affiliation—and the identity incentives, which decreased as a consequence of centralization and the acceptation of the 'social pact'" (Roca 1993, 149, my translation).

Moreover, although in Spain, as in other countries, the concertation process was influenced by the economic crisis, at the beginning political factors were the dominant reason why such pacts were important. Spanish unions did not enter into negotiations with a guarantee to maintain full employment—the typical situation for their northern European counterparts throughout the 1960s–1970s—or in exchange for further social benefits and the expansion of the welfare state. By the time that concertation started in 1980, unemployment was already high (11.8 percent) and union leaders were fully aware of the cost that modernization would have to the Spanish economy. At the same time, the welfare state in Spain was underdeveloped in the early 1980s by European standards and its starting point was, therefore, very different. All this took place within a domestic context of budget discipline and restrictive monetary policies in place to control inflation. These factors, however, did not prevent the emergence of concertation, because they were replaced by political considerations. As we have already seen, at the beginning Spanish unions favored concertation as a means of contributing to the consolidation of the new democratic regime and of supporting the political and electoral goals of the political parties with which they were affiliated.

The Spanish unions' subordination to political objectives had important consequences. Once political considerations were removed and the political system was entrenched, union leaders could not justify any longer, as they did during the transition, that workers had to sacrifice to "contribute to the consolidation of democracy and to foster economic recovery." When the economy picked up in the second half of the 1980s, it became clear that the greater beneficiaries were businesses. Concertation had resulted in moderate wage losses for workers, but the socialist economic policies favored the adoption of supply side strategies that did not result in a decline in unemployment. At the same time, employers invested little, and when they did, they preferred to invest in capital intensive (not labor-oriented) processes. These developments, coupled with the lack of fulfillment by government and business of some of the AES provisions, left unions with few arguments favoring concertation.[3]

Intensive state intervention was also a main feature of the concertation process in Spain. Although the Spanish government did not always sign the agreements, it participated actively in the development of the pacts. Government participation in tripartite agreements was not unusual in other countries, but the Spanish government played a very prominent role in concertation. The reason for the state's active participation was that at the time that concertation emerged, the institutional position of the social actors was not fully consolidated. Therefore, the government not only acted as a mediator and guarantor—the typical role played by SD governments in Sweden, Austria, or the Netherlands—but also as an instigator, in promoting negotiations and forcing unions and employers to reach an agreement.

One of the main aspects of concertation in all countries using this process was the inclusion of incomes policy. Some of the other typical objectives, such as the moderation of social conflict, the development of industrial laws, or the increasing flexibility of the labor market, were also included in centralized agreements in Spain, where they had even more relevance, given the newness of the post-Franco political and institutional context and the intensity of the economic crisis. As we have seen, concertation was one of the main instruments for the institutionalization of union and employer associations and for overcoming the economic crisis. In Spain, workers' moderation and austerity was presented as the key to reducing unitary labor costs, which would contribute to the recovery of business profits.

Moreover, in Spain the institutional position and the number of signatories to centralized agreements, along with the subjects covered in the pacts, were different. Unions started with a major disadvantage: The political system was not consolidated and the unions' institutional position was not defined, either vis-à-vis the government/party or their own constituencies. In other European countries, such as Sweden, Austria, Denmark, Finland, and Norway, centralized agreements were characterized by the political/economic exchange between actors whose positions in the system are fully institutionalized and defined. These agreements often result in the participation of the social actors (unions and business associations) in the direction and management of economic and social policies. As we have seen, in the case of Spain, the position of the social actors was not fully institutionalized, and, up until to the AES (1985–1986), one of the major objectives of these agreements was the consolidation of the political regime and the definition of the new framework that would govern the industrial relations setting. The government, however, was never really interested in the participation of the social actors in developing economic and social polices.

The political and institutional context also helps to establish other important differences between the concertation processes that took place in Spain and those in other countries. In Spain, unions and parties on the left also had strong historical links. However, these links, coupled with the relative weakness of unions vis-à-vis political parties, determined the subordination of unions to political parties. In other countries—Sweden, Austria—unions had their affiliates, and they helped to articulate the support to political parties of the left. In Spain, however, low levels of affiliation, as well as the limited influence of unions within party structures, determined the subordination of unions' strategies to those of the political parties with which they were affiliated. At the beginning they accepted a political exchange: Moderation for political participation and the consolidation of the new regime. The rupture between the unions and the parties in the second half of the 1980s, however, led to increasing union autonomy, the development of unity of action between the major labor confederations, and the radicalization and politicization of disputes.

Unions' subordination to political parties had a critical influence in the concertation process. Specifically, I have argued that the subordinate role of the UGT vis-à-vis the PSOE government allowed the party leaders to default on their promises, ignore the union, and neglect the latter's views. In countries where concertation was successful for an extended period of time, such as Sweden or Germany, unions were stronger and had intimate links with SD parties. These latter institutional arrangements allowed union leaders to play a critical role in economic policy making and to act as representatives of the union within the government. In Spain, given the UGT's relative weakness and its lack of influence within the PSOE, such a development was not feasible and the UGT was marginalized. At the end, increasing differences between both organizations caused the rupture between the party and the union and culminated in a historic general strike on December 1988.

In general, the unions' subordination to political parties limited their autonomy and prevented the development of strategies based on the interests of the organization and its affiliates. They could not develop coherent and autonomous strategies in defense of their own interests and those of their constituency. As we have seen, one of the major considerations behind their support for concertation was political—that is, to consolidate the new political regime and/or to support the electoral strategies favored by their political parties. When this motivation disappeared, they lacked alternative rationales that would have allowed union leaders to defend concertation among their affiliates. For instance, the UGT did not question the pacts of the early 1980s. The union leadership merely wanted the government and the business association to fulfill their commitments and have workers receive some compensation for wage moderation. It also sought compensation for the deleterious effects that the modernization process had on unions' traditional mass-production strongholds. Modernization resulted in the segmentation and diversification of the labor movement. Union leaders though that through concertation they would participate in economic policy making and would be compensated for their moderation. These expectations did not materialize, and compensation in the form of indirect income or deferred wages did not take place. At the same time, unions saw themselves operating in a context of increasing hostility from the government and business. This led to a rupture with the PSOE government that resulted in the increasing politicization of conflict after 1987, when union leaders decided to enter the political arena, at least in terms of mobilizing public support, to achieve what they could not obtain through traditional internal mechanisms.

c. From Social Democracy to Neoliberalism: The Consequences of the Collapse of Concertation

Some authors (Solchaga 1997, Maravall 1993, De La Dehesa 1994, Boix 1996) have argued that the socialist economic policies were successful in enhancing the competitive position of the Spanish economy vis-à-vis its European counterparts. Inflation was reduced, the budget deficit was controlled, foreign investment increased dramatically—which was a major factor in the modernization of the productive structure—the industrial sector was restructured, trade liberalization was completed, and the labor market was reformed. These policies, combined with the entrance of Spain in the EC in 1986—with the financial transfers that it represented—promoted rapid economic recovery in the second half of the 1980s.

Yet economic growth was accompanied by mediocre performance in the area of employment. During the last years of the dictatorship, the closed nature of the economy and its fast economic growth had combined to keep unemployment below 2 percent. Unemployment, however, was already rapidly rising during the transition to democracy; from 1974 until 1982, average unemployment was 8.4 percent compared with 5.6 percent in the European Community, and by 1982, it had reached 16.2 percent; and it got much worse under the socialists. By 1985, just before Spain joined the EC, unemployment was 21.9 percent. At the height of the economic boom unemployment remained very high, at 16.3 percent, and this despite the fact that the participation rate actually decreased from 1976 through 1985 and recovered only modestly in the second half of the decade. When the recession hit Spain in the early 1990s, unemployment increased dramatically, reaching 24.3 percent of the active labor force by 1994, compared with 10.9 percent in the European Union (EU).[4] In other words, the socialist economic policies failed to address one of the most fundamental challenges of democratic Spain: Unemployment. Continued concertation should have helped to address some of the internal inconsistencies of the socialist policies. In contrast, the collapse of concertation had three major effects on the course of the socialist government's economic policies: It forced the government to implement restrictive monetary policies to quell inflation (mostly unsuccessfully), it distracted the government from its policy objectives, and finally, it hindered the capacity of the government to reduce the budget deficit.

When the socialists first came to power in 1982, there was agreement within the economic team that classic deficit-financed polices to stimulate demand could no longer be implemented at a time of increasing internationalization of capital markets. While income redistribution was still a stated goal, the team realized that it would need a good macroeconomic performance to fulfill its redistribution goals. Economic efficiency, a lower inflation, and a lower public deficit became the priorities. Accordingly, the socialist government acted to bring down public expenditures to reduce the deficit but, at the same time, increased social outlays—57.6 percent in real terms between 1982 and 1989.[5]

The socialist government was convinced that in order to strengthen the macroeconomic framework of the Spanish economy and increase business competitiveness it had to reduce inflation. Fighting inflation became particularly important for the government because of the higher inflation rates experienced by Spain compared with those of with its European neighbors. Furthermore, from an economic standpoint, the success of the supply side policies pursued by the socialist government required control of inflation to guarantee macroeconomic stability and investment. As we have seen, the predominant view within the economic team was that the new international economic environment constrained the scope of monetary options available to national governments to implement domestic economic policies. Under these assumptions, the internationalization of the Spanish economy meant that a monetary policy aimed at controlling inflation while maintaining a favorable environment for Spanish exports was no longer feasible.

The government felt it had two alternatives to control inflation: It could try to develop cooperative relations with unions and reach centralized agreements to limit wage demands—the traditional northern European SD strategy—or if concertation failed, it could resort to restrictive monetary policies. At the beginning, concertation was the preferred alternative because it offered the government political cover for unpopular measures while allowing for inflation restraint. Until 1986 the government, convinced that wages were the major reason behind inflationary pressures, sought to reach social concertation with the unions and employers in search of wage restraint. These attempts, as we have seen, failed after 1986, a fact that had critical consequences. The failure to achieve social concertation after 1986 damaged the chances of controlling inflation without resorting to high interest rates and restrictive monetary policies. In other words, "the end of concertation meant that the government had to forfeit the possibility to introduce consensual economic policies and the option to use inflation targets as a guideline for wage increases" (Boix 1994, 30). When concertation failed, the only option available to control inflation was the implementation of restrictive monetary policies. This, in turn, hindered productive investment and damaged employment.

The breakdown of concertation, contrary to governmental expectations, did not result in increased flexibility and decentralization of wage bargaining, which would have allowed for moderation and wage differentiation. On the contrary, wage bargaining remained highly centralized (Espina 1991, 218). This, coupled with continued deviations from government inflation objectives, resulted in a vicious circle in which unions systematically asked for wage increases 3–4 points above the government's target, which in turn further increased inflation. The consequence of these developments was an increase in workers real wages of 1.3 points between 1986 and 1988 (Roca 1993, 217), which rendered the objective to reduce inflation impossible to achieve.

Another major consequence of the collapse of concertation was that it hindered the government's attempts to meet its policy goals. After the success of the 1988 general strike, unions intensified a campaign in opposition to the government's economic policies and, in order to avoid further conflict and sustain electoral support, the government was systematically forced to accommodate union social demands. These demands diverted economic resources that were planned for further investment in education and other public services. However, while the government was forced to make concessions in social issues, unions refused to return to concertation or to moderate their wage demands. They viewed government calls for wage moderation as attempts to offset wage increases by productivity growth and disavowed them. By then unions were totally disenchanted with the course of economic policies.

Furthermore, some authors have emphasized that the failure of the socialist government to rein in the budget deficit was one of the major shortcomings of the socialists' economic policies (Boix 1994, 30–33; Fuentes Quintana and Barea 1996, 109; Gadea 1996, 164–166). The socialists had powerful reasons to control the deficit. When they first came to power, the high deficit was believed to be the major reason behind the anemic lack of investment. High inflation had forced previous governments to apply restrictive monetary policies to quell inflation, thus raising interest rates and hindering investment. A balanced budget, therefore, was seen as a powerful instrument in building up savings and promoting investment. Finally, plans for having economic conditions converge with the EU core countries and for joining the monetary union were also seen as adding pressures to the need to control the deficit.

The government's determination to carry through its fiscal consolidation drive, coupled with the accelerated rate of economic growth experienced in Spain during the second half of the 1980s, contributed to a significant reduction of the deficit from 7 percent of GDP in 1985 to 2.7 percent in 1989, a level well below the EC average. This reduction, however, proved to be temporary and not the result of budgetary discipline or structural reforms. The fast growth of the economy during the late 1980s caused a surge of demand that increased inflationary pressures and a higher trade deficit. When economic growth decelerated in the early 1990s, the deficit accelerated again and reached 5 percent of the GDP (Gross Domestic Product) in 1991. The challenge to reduce the deficit was compounded by the transfer of resources and managerial responsibilities to the country's geographical autonomous regions, because the latter implemented loose fiscal polices that contributed to the expansion of the deficit. From 1984 to 1995 the debt of the territorial administrations was multiplied by 3 points as a percentage of GDP (from 0.3 percent to 1.8 percent of GDP between 1988 and 1992) (see Solchaga 1997, 316). Since the late 1980s expenses systematically grew faster than revenues.

The government worsened this situation by giving in to unions' demands in an effort to ameliorate its electoral losses in the 1986 and 1989 elections. As a result of the general strike of December 1988, the government was also forced to make concessions to unions, thus increasing public expenditures to expand social benefits. In 1989 it spent over 2 billion pesetas to increase social services. The systematic expansion of unemployment benefits and pensions after 1988 diluted any effort to achieve fiscal restraint. The fiscal year became characterized by a pattern of accelerated expenditures during the first half of the year, and fiscal restraint and ad hoc measures, including new taxes, during the second half to compensate for the excesses of the first half. These cuts, however, were always insufficient, and since the government refused to raise taxes too much, out of fear of alienating an important part of the electorate, budget expenditures always grew faster than planned (Boix 1994, 31–33). This resulted in the erosion of the government's credibility, and hindered its investment plans. At the end the combination of a high deficit and restrictive monetary policies resulted in high interest rates, an overvalued peseta, and budget overruns. Consequently, the failure of the socialist government to rein in the deficit affected its capacity to reduce inflation, sustain public investment, and maintain economic growth, pushing the government to rely on a restrictive (but inadequate) monetary policy to implement its agenda.

The lack of congruence between fiscal and monetary policy contributed to an inflationary spiral. Tight monetary policy remained the only instrument available to quell inflation, but it proved to be insufficient. Inflation accelerated after 1987, hastening the government's decision to harden monetary policy. In 1989 interest rates were raised up to 15 percent—5 percentage points above Germany's. This anti-inflationary commitment was reinforced by the decision to join the European Monetary System (EMS) in July 1989, a year ahead of schedule, coupled with the objective to be part of a projected European Monetary Union (EMU), with is tight economic requirements.

The persistence of inflation, which, despite high interest rates, increased from 4.8 percent in 1988 to 6.8 percent in 1989 and reached 5.9 percent in 1991, has been generally imputed to wage growth that, in turn, has been attributed to the institutional characteristics of the Spanish labor market, namely, a system of centralized bargaining at the sectoral level, backward looking wage indexation, and a high level of dismissal costs that prevented high unemployment from placing downward pressure on wages (Blanchard et al., 1995; Jimeno and Toharia, 1994).

This explanation, however, fails to take into account the fact that wage moderation did contribute to the steady decline of inflation through 1987, and that inflation reemerged after 1987, well before wages accelerated. As stressed in chapter 4, concertation resulted in wage moderation and helped to kept real labor costs virtually stagnant (they only grew an average of 0.25 percent from 1982 through 1989, a level well below productivity), which contributed to a steady decline in unit labor costs through 1990 and a continuous decline in workers' real wages. It was only in 1990 that real wages accelerated and turned positive, and only in 1991 and 1992 that labor costs outpaced productivity growth. Therefore, the resurgence of inflation in 1988 cannot solely be attributed to wage acceleration. Moreover, a labor center explanation also fails to take into consideration the fact that labor laws were reformed in Spain to increase the flexibility of the labor market. Temporary contracts were introduced in 1984 (30 percent of total workers by 1991). Increasing flexibility, however, did not result in a significant improvement of the inflation and unemployment problems.

The insufficiency of the labor-market-centered explanation to account for developments in Spain prompted other scholars (Pérez 1997c, 5–7; and Pérez 1997b, 173–82) to argue that the failure of the Spanish Socialists to tackle inflation and unemployment is rooted in the costs and terms at which Spanish firms have been able to raise investment finance. According to this explanation, the manner in which financial liberalization took place in Spain limited competition in the supply of corporate finance and placed extraordinary costs on Spanish firms during the 1980s and early 1990s. This resulted in a bias against productive investment and in favor of a relocation of resources toward sectors and activities that could better absorb higher financial costs (Pérez 1997b, 187).

According to Pérez (1997c, 5), the financial costs borne by Spanish firms in the 1980s were very high by international standards and were also high in relation to the average return on capital in Spain. These high costs represented a disincentive against investment in productive capacity. The high financial costs, according to Pérez, were rooted in the structural features of the Spanish financial market and on the course of macroeconomic policies. At the end of the 1980s the Spanish market for corporate finance was still dominated by a small number of banks that enjoyed extremely high interest and profits margins, and the Spanish capital markets played a very limited role (23 percent of the external financing) as a source of investment finance. These structural conditions resulted in high financial costs for Spanish firms and a negative leverage effect (i.e., a negative difference between the average return on capital and the average cost of financing), which in turn resulted in a dramatic reduction in the recourse of external debt by Spanish firms in the 1980s (Pérez 1997c, 5–7).

The negative consequences of this oligopolistic structure were further compounded by the socialists macroeconomic policies, because they resulted in very high interest rates and the appreciation of the peseta (Pérez 1997c, 7). As we have already seen, the PSOE's macroeconomic policies were influenced by the belief that the economic crisis was a supply side crisis that required wage moderation (see chapter 5). Therefore, the government rejected countercyclical polices and concentrated on monetarist policies to cut inflation. These policies resulted in a substantial disinflation in the first half of the 1980s (inflation was cut from 14 percent in 1982 to 4.8 percent in 1988). Concertation contributed to this development. As noted before, the decision by the government to forgo the collaboration of unions in its fight against inflation was based on the assumption that wage growth could be better curtailed by pursuing an even tighter monetary policy and the appreciation of the peseta (see chapter 5).

Spanish high interest rates in the late 1980s have often been attributed to the fact that monetary policy was forced to compensate for the lack of fiscal restraint (Ayuso and Escrivá 1997, 101–103). According to this view, high interest rates were the result of a risk premium imposed on the peseta and related to public debt and inflation. The strong record of deficit reduction by the socialist government, however, challenges this interpretation. The socialist policies resulted in a significant fiscal consolidation (the deficit was cut from 5.6 percent in 1982 to 2.8 percent in 1989, averaging 3.6 percent from 1987 to 1991, a level lower than the European average). The level of the public debt was also comparatively low (47 percent in 1991). This reduction, however, was not accompanied by an easing of monetary policy. Moreover, other countries had higher deficits and public debt levels than Spain (Italy or Belgium) but their interest rate differentials were lower (Pérez 1997b, 175; Garrett 1998, 43–44). The decision by the Spanish Socialists to pursue a strong currency strategy based on high interest rates and forgo the option to fit monetary policy to the pace of fiscal consolidation, suggests that the government stressed tight monetary policy as an instrument with which to place pressure on the unions (Pérez 1997c, 12).

In Spain, high interest rates were part of the strong currency strategy pursued by the socialist government. They were aimed at curbing inflation, moderating wage demands, financing the deficit, and sustaining the exchange rates. In other words, high interest rates were assigned the strategic role of curbing wages and waging battle against inflation, while attracting the necessary foreign capital inflows to finance the resulting current account deficit (Pérez 1997b, 177–78 and 187). Given this current account deficit, high interest rates were necessary to encourage capital inflows to compensate for the deficit, and to bolster the peseta's value in order to cheapen imports. However, they penalized productive investment and contributed to the appreciation of the peseta, which went up 44 percent from 1983 to 1992. This appreciation was not matched by gains in productivity, thus damaging the competitive position of Spanish firms in foreign markets. An overvalued currency, however, was viewed by government officials as an accompanying instrument to prevent domestic producers from relying on a weak currency to increase their competitiveness. According to this view, a strong peseta would facilitate cheap imports, which in turn would foster wage moderation and higher productivity and efficiency, because low wages had to compensate for the higher financial costs and for the lower profitability that higher costs entailed. In other words, "the government was willing to incur a heavy loss of competitiveness in order to break the will of the unions in wage negotiations" (Pérez 1997, 12).

This tight monetary policy stance, however, did not prevent the reemergence of inflation in 1989 (the Consumer Price Index rose from 4.0 percent in March to almost 6 percent by the end of the year), and this in spite of very high interest rates. In 1989 inflation rose to 6.9 percent. Furthermore, contrary to governmental expectations, this policy course also failed to restrain wages. Unions were able to extract higher wages from employers; wage increases averaged 8.3 percent in 1990, 8.1 percent in 1991 and 7.2 percent in 1992. Successive attempts by the government to reach agreements with the unions (such as the "Competitiveness Pact" of 1990, or the "Social Pact for Progress" of 1991) failed.

As noted above, despite the widespread belief that the reemergence of inflation after 1987 was linked to higher wage demands on the part of the unions, it was only after 1989 that Spanish unions pushed aggressively for higher wages to recoup some of the income losses that workers had experienced during the previous years. The initial resurgence of inflation was driven by two developments over which the unions had little influence: First, massive short-term capital inflows of direct investment that sought to take advantage of the undervaluation of Spanish industrial stocks and the relatively skilled and cheap labor, and second, a shift of financial resources from competitive sectors of the economy toward less exposed activities and consumer credit (Pérez 1997c, 10; 1997b, 188).

Spain's entry into the EC resulted in very large inflows of long-term direct investment that sought to take advantage of the undervaluation of Spanish industrial stocks and the relatively skilled and cheap labor. This long-term investment was followed after 1988 by short-term portfolio investment driven by Spain's high real interest rates and the rising value of the currency, which were the result of the government's macroeconomic policies. Massive capital inflows had a strong inflationary impact, which forced the Central Bank to tighten credit and raise interest rates to compensate for the inflow of external liquidity. Yet these measures encouraged further short-term capital inflows and promoted a vicious circle that resulted in restrictions on capital inflows in 1989 (Ayuso and Escrivá 1997, 97). This development was further aggravated by EMS membership (July 1989), which produced a massive influx of short-term capital that pushed the peseta up against its upper band limit despite relatively high inflation (2 points above the ERM average) and the deterioration of the current account.

The resurgence of inflation after 1987 was also driven by the rapid expansion of the service sector vis-à-vis the tradeables sector of the economy.

This shift was driven by the appreciation of the peseta after 1987 and the oligopolistic situation in the financial sector (Pérez 1997c, 11). The high financial costs borne by Spanish firms and the appreciation of the peseta, (which appreciated by 30 percent in real terms from 1987 through 1991), encouraged resources to flow into those sectors of the economy that were better able to pass on their costs to consumers such as utilities, services, construction, and real state. The consequence of this shift, however, was that it intensified the sectoral inflation-proneness of the Spanish economy. While the inflation rate of manufacturers converged with the EMS average in the late 1980s, it increased in the service sector exceeding that of manufacturers by 7 percent (Pérez 1997c, 11) (even today—1999—the price differential in services between Spain and the EMU average remains at 1.4 percentage points proving that the liberalizing policies of the Partido Popular-PP-conservative government have been insufficient, particularly in sectors such as telecommunications, postal service, transportation, house rentals, and insurance; see *El Pais,* June 19, 1999). This shift of resources from competitive to sheltered sectors was exacerbated by the massive restructuring of Spanish banks' portfolios, which shifted credit to those users who were less sensitive to higher credit rates, seeking to maintain their oligopolistic margins. The result was the disappearance of long-term credit to industry. The banks' strategy was feasible because they operated in a highly oligopolistic environment that had been perpetuated by a process of financial reform that failed to reform substantially the oligopolistic structure of the Spanish financial market (Pérez 1997b, 187; and Pérez 1997c, 13). Figure C.1 summarizes this argument graphically.

In this oligopolistic context, the government's strategy to use monetary policy and an overvalued currency to fight inflation and to place pressure on

Figure C.1 Macroeconomic and Financial Sources of Spanish Inflation

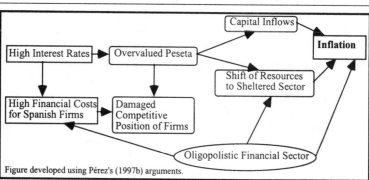

Figure developed using Pérez's (1997b) arguments.

the unions was bound to backfire. Particularly in a context in which wage bargainers were not responsive to threats from the fiscal and monetary authorities, interest rates only had a limited impact on inflation because they fostered the appreciation of the peseta and encouraged the resource allocation that intensified the inflation-proneness of the Spanish economy (Pérez 1997b, 187). In other words, the wage moderation that resulted from concertation was undermined by consumption and a shift toward sheltered sectors, which reactivated inflation and exacerbated the inflation-proneness of the Spanish economy. The outcome of these policies became evident during the crisis of the EMS (1992–1993), which had dramatic consequences for the Spanish economy (Pérez 1997b, 184). The turmoil in the EMS in 1992, coupled with the weak position of the peseta, forced 3 devaluations of the peseta, (which lost as much as 30 per cent in nominal terms), in 1992–1993, and cuts in public consumption (down to 1.6 percent of GDP in 1993, the lowest level since 1969). This crisis also resulted in higher unemployment (up from 18 percent in 1991 to 24 percent in 1994). This crisis placed the burden of adjustment on the productive sector, yet it offered some relief to the economy. It reduced the balance of payment and current account deficits, and imposed a low wage and price equilibrium that brought the external balance back into line and reduced inflation (4.6 percent by 1993). Unemployment, however, remained extremely high. At the end, the confrontational approach favored by the socialist government delayed Spain's economic convergence with the EU core. See Table C.1 for a summary of current economic indicators.

In summary, concertation resulted in decreased wage push and inflation, recovery of investment, less conflict, and electoral support for the Socialist Party. The end of concertation after 1986, on the contrary, as we have seen, had disastrous effects on the economy, the labor unions, and the well-being of the working class in general. The socialists saw how their parliamentary majority was eroded and their position isolated, and this contributed to their final electoral defeat in 1996. Confrontation with unions also helped to isolate several socialist cabinets and fostered a critical view in the citizens towards the socialist economic policies. While the socialists were able to renew their mandate in 1989 and 1993, despite consecutive general strikes in 1988 and 1992, deteriorating relations with the unions, coupled with social and industrial unrest and the emergence of major corruption scandals, resulted in an erosion of their electoral support.

At the end, disputes with the unions, coupled with the divergence between monetary and fiscal policies and the fixation on wages as the source of inflation, determined the failure of the socialist economic policies to address the unemployment problem and fight inflation. As we have seen, the collapse of concertation resulted in excessive wage settlements because

Table C.1 Main Economic Indicators, 1996–1999

	1996	1997	1998	1999**
Total GDP ($bn)	583.0	532.0	554.7	—
Real GDP growth (annual % change)	2.1	3.5	3.8	3.3
GDP per head ($'000)	—	13.5	14.1	15.07
Domestic demand*	1.8	3.2	5.0	4.9
Inflation (annual % change in CPI)*	3.2	2.0	1.4	2.1
Investment (as % of GDP)	21.9	22.2	23.3	24.4
Saving (as % of GDP)	21.9	22.6	23.0	23.6
Average hourly earnings (annual % change)	5.5	2.9	2.6	—
Industrial production (annual % change)	3.3	6.9	5.4	—
Unemployment rate (% of workforce)	22.2	20.8	18.8	16.8
Money supply, M3 (annual % change)	4.7	4.5	8.2	—
Government expenditure (% of GDP)	43.1	41.6*	—	—
Central government balance*	–3.5	–2.0	–1.4	–1.2
Government balance (% of GDP)*	–4.5	–2.6	–1.8	–1.6
Structural primary balance (% of GDP)*	1.7	2.6	2.5	2.4
Gross general government debt (% GDP)*	68.5	67.6	65.6	65.0
Current account balance (% of GDP)	0.0	0.4	–0.2	–0.8
Merchandise exports ($bn)	101.4	104.5	109.4	—
Merchandise imports ($bn)	–117.5	–117.8	–129.4	—
Trade balance (% of GDP)*	–2.6	–2.	–3.2	–4.6
Three-month interbank rate (annual average)*	7.5	5.44	4.2	2.6
10 year bond yield (annual average)	8.8	6.4	4.8	4.2

Source: Data for 1996 from: *Financial Times,* May 27, 1997, 11. Data for 1997 and 1998 from: *Financial Times,* "Annual Country Report." May 20, 1999. Sources: Economist Intelligence Unit; Datastream/ICV. Date for 1999 and * from IMF's *Public Information Notice* (PIN) No. 99/65. "IMF Concludes Article IV Consultation with Spain," July 30, 1999. **IMF staff projections.

unions sought to compensate for the wage losses that workers experienced in the first half of the 1980s. Since wages are a critical factor in productive costs, higher wages resulted in increasing inflationary pressures. The government's restrictive monetary policies, however, proved to be insufficient to reduce inflation. On the contrary, the PSOE's strong currency strategy fostered the appreciation of the peseta and encouraged the resource allocation that intensified the inflation-proneness of the Spanish economy (Pérez 1997b, 187). This situation was further exacerbated by the fact that the combination of restrictive monetary policies and expansive fiscal policies raised doubts about the government's objective of reducing inflation and resulted in higher wage demands on the part of workers, who did not believe the government inflation objectives. The final consequence was higher inflation, lower growth, and more unemployment. Figure C.2 summarizes this argument graphically.

The erosion of the socialist electoral support in 1993 and the loss of the elections in 1996 have proved the difficulties of balancing an economic strategy that fails to gain the unions' assent to rein in inflation, while at the same time, accommodating the social demands of part of the electorate. This failure also had an important cost in terms of unemployment. Now that the socialists are out of power, they will have to rethink their agenda and seek new options. The establishment of a partnership once more with unions seems to be the most feasible option to implement an agenda. Yet electoral considerations might prevent such a development.

Unions, for their part, saw how their strategy was not translated into workers' support, and how their negotiating position vis-à-vis the government and business eroded. The failure of concertation, at the same time, resulted in internal divisions within the unions and, thus, their institutional weakening. The strategy to call a general strike every three years proved to be futile and had little electoral impact. Internal friction within the CCOO and the breakdown caused by a major economic scandal within the UGT, which forced the resignation of its top leaders, further deteriorated the institutional position of the unions. Confrontation also resulted in a worsening of

Figure C.2 The Institutional Foundations of Unemployment in Spain

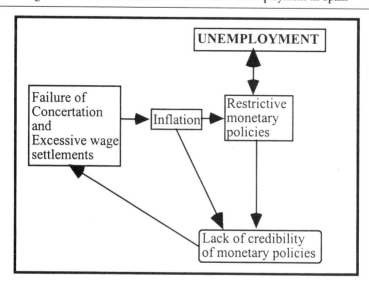

economic conditions—at a time when concertation was much needed. Union leaders failed to recognize the dramatic changes taking place in the world economy and did not react to them in a timely and creative manner. The increasing deterioration of the labor market worked against their mass-production strongholds, but it is hard to see how the end of concertation might have helped the unions to regain those strongholds or penetrate new ones. Union leaders failed to react to these developments and today have not yet developed strategies that would allow them to penetrate growing sectors of the economy, such as services. The consequence was a devastated labor market, diminished recognition for unions, and increased radicalization of demands among the rank-and-file. Only the change in government in 1996 fostered a new environment; unions have taken the initiative to regain their position and signed several agreements with the government and business association.

d. Lessons

The most important conclusion that can be derived from this book is that the institutional subordination of SD unions to SD governing parties has a negative impact on concertation because it leads governments to default on promises made to the union. The Spanish experience with concertation illustrates the difficulties in implementing an SD program based on unions engaging in a solidaristic wage stance as the key to successful disinflation, when the relationship between SD unions and parties is not conductive to this strategic capability. This broad generalization requires further testing against a broader empirical terrain. A preliminary comparative analysis, however, shows that in countries (Sweden, Austria) where concertation has been successful, unions had close institutional links with SD parties; they are not subordinated to the parties; and they play a critical role in the policy-making process. These conditions were missing in the Spanish case.

The analysis of concertation in Spain also challenges the conclusions advanced by other authors (Cameron 1984, Linz 1981, Schmitter 1981), who have argued that the success of concertation depends on the organization of the social actors. On the contrary, the Spanish case seems to confirm that the consolidation of concertation does not depend solely on the organization of the actors, but also on the interests of the social actors themselves—government, unions, and business associations. These interests will be the result of previous experiences, the ideology of the organization leaders, the economic and political situation, and the nature of the ruling coalition in those organizations. Their strategies will also be influenced by the incentives attached to concertation and by the relationship among the actors. It is for this reason that I have argued that political and institutional variables such as the party-union relationship, and not just the global and domestic institutional context, provide their own set of incentives for domestic actors to entertain certain political strategies.

Furthermore, the experience with concertation in Spain seems to confirm that concertation schemes depend on two main conditions: That there are benefits for all the actors involved, and that there is a commitment by the signatories to fill their promises. The absence of these conditions leads inexorably to the failure of concertation. Concertation implies limitations for all the actors involved and, in many cases, costs for their constituencies—that is, incomes policy constrains wage growth. Therefore, a critical component of concertation should be the inclusion of compensation mechanisms. Unions will be willing to participate in these schemes and moderate wage demands only if they are adequately compensated for such wage moderation. That moderation contributes to economic recovery and higher profits for business. Unions also will want to reap benefits from economic recovery. The failure to compensate them will only result in the rebellion of their affiliates. Therefore, the government and business must be willing to compensate unions for wage moderation in periods of economic expansion if concertation is to succeed. Compensation can take different forms. It can include institutional mechanisms that strengthen the role of unions within the political system. Governments can also introduce direct compensation that will guarantee an equitable distribution of costs among all the actors.

The analysis of concertation in Spain seems to confirm that participation rights in particular are critical to guaranteeing the stability of concertation schemes. Participation increases the influence of unions and helps them to strengthen their position among workers. In Spain, however, the government's institutional support of unions and their participation in economic policy making during the concertation process was very limited. In fact, the PSOE government exploited the UGT's weakness and its lack of influence within the party to marginalize the union. This decisively hindered the union's trust in the government. After the 1988 general strike, the government attempted on repeated occasions to revive the concertation process, and in many cases it was willing to accommodate union demands. The union, however, became convinced that under a socialist government they could never participate as equal partners in the policymaking process and refused to attend the government calls.

Moreover, participation could have contributed to consolidating the institutional position of the social actors. Although it is unquestionable that concertation in Spain was the result of very specific political and economic circumstances, the former being the transition to democracy and the latter the economic recession, the emergence of new conditions in the second half of the 1980s should not have necessarily resulted in the collapse of the process. Concertation could have survived if it had been institutionalized, but the consolidation of the position of the social actors in the system was a necessary prerequisite. The fact was, however, that the government refused to recognize and strengthen the role of unions in the system, and this ultimately destroyed concertation. Unions never had the perception that they participated in economic and social policymaking; they always felt they were outsiders.

Furthermore, one of the major difficulties inherent in any concertation process is the fact that the actors are exchanging short-term compromises for long-term ones—that is, wage moderation today for higher wages tomorrow, when the economy recovers. This means, however, that it is critical to fulfill the latter agreements when the economy expands. Failure to do so only results in the ultimate collapse of concertation. Unions will only be willing to negotiate if and only if they have the guarantee that they will receive some sort of compensation in the future. In Spain, the government and business failed to live up to their side of agreements, and this alienated unions. In the end, the latter did not trust the other actors and refused to negotiate with them.

Specifically, concertation in Spain resulted in a reduction of wages as a percentage of GDP, and this reduction was not compensated for by the government. On the contrary, the government, exploiting the UGT's weak institutional position and acting under the impression that it did not need unions' acquiescence to implement its policies, failed to come up with attractive proposals to satisfy unions demands. The PSOE government failed to implement fiscal changes that would have compensated workers for their lower income, did not increase unemployment benefit coverage to diminish the costs of adjustment for certain groups of workers, and did not even improve the conditions to receive public pensions. On the contrary, socialist politicians continued to insist on their drive to reduce the public deficit and even introduced new measures to make labor markets more flexible, which resulted in an increasing segmentation of the labor market and further weakened the position of unions. These developments contributed to the breakdown between the unions and the government and the collapse of concertation. Finally, the business association viewed concertation as an instrument to limit wage growth, reduce conflict, and increase its influence over the labor movement—that is, through bilateral agreements it helped strengthen the UGT's and weaken the CCOO's grip over the labor movement. The positive experience of 1984, when there was a reduction in real wages despite the lack of agreement, strengthened the position of business groups who opposed concertation and supported decentralized bargaining.

Spanish concertation confirms that the consolidation of neocorporatist agreements depends on a combination of political, economic, and institutional factors. Institutional arrangements such as strong and noncompetitive unions or centralized wage bargaining systems can help internalize the costs of concertation. As we have seen, the lack of these factors, however, was not critical enough to account for the collapse of concertation in Spain. Concertation worked reasonably well for years despite interunion competition, and the UGT was certainly able to fulfill its side of the agreement. Other institutional factors, such as the centralized organization of the union, or a strong relationship between the party and union, can compensate for those institutional weaknesses.

In this regard, the lack of a consensus-building tradition and the overwhelming parliamentary majorities for the socialists seemed to hinder the consolidation of concertation processes, particularly in the absence of institutional mechanisms that would have guaranteed the participation of the social actors in economic policymaking. The PSOE's overwhelming victory in the 1982 elections, coupled with the fact that it was able to renew that victory easily in the following two elections, hindered concertation because the government leaders became increasingly convinced that they did not need external support to implement their program. This problem was compounded by the lack of articulation both within the party and within the government of the socialist union's role. In other countries SD unions and parties bargain from positions of similar strength.

In Spain, the linkages between unions and parties influenced decisively the strategy of unions towards concertation. For years unions subordinated their strategies to the interests of their affiliated parties. Nevertheless, and contrary to expectations, when the PSOE won the elections in 1982, the strong historical links between the UGT and the PSOE hindered the consolidation of concertation because the government/party was strong enough to exploit the relationship and to use its allied union as an "alibi" for its policies. The UGT's relative weakness unquestionably contributed to the view that the government had of the union as merely an instrument of its policy. For successful concertation the critical aspect of that relationship is that it has to be based on parity.

The creation of formal institutions that foster consensus and understanding among the social actors may be able to contribute to the consolidation of the concertation process. In Portugal the Conselho Permanente de Concertação Social, (CPCS or Permanent Council for Social Concertation) has played a critical role in bringing business, the government, and unions together (Monteiro Fernandes 1999, 111–118; Da Silva Lopes 1999, 87–96). This condition, however, is not sufficient. The creation in Spain of the Economic and Social Council in 1992 did not result in the resurgence of concertation. Only new political conditions after the electoral defeat of the socialist party in 1996 facilitated the reemergence of concertation.

The Spanish experience seems to confirm that not only formal institutions, but also informal processes play a critical role in the consolidation of neocorporatist schemes The consolidation of concertation requires the institutionalization of informal processes that play critical roles in consensus-building, such as the establishment of bargaining mechanisms, flexibility during the bargaining process, and confidence in the other actors. In this regard, the breakdown of bargaining, the increasing animosity among social actors, the establishment of bad negotiating habits—that is, maximalist strategies—and the failure to fulfill compromises, coupled with the unwillingness of the government to consolidate and strengthen the role of the other actors (particularly the unions) in the system, doomed the possibility of institutionalizing concertation in Spain. In that country, the failure to institutionalize these processes meant that when the democratic system was consolidated and the economic recovery materialized during the second half of the 1980s, concertation collapsed.

Moreover, the model of economic management also affects the perception that the government has about unions. A model based on demand expansion will view unions as positive contributors to the economic process. Concertation is more likely in such a context. A model based on supply expansion, on the contrary, views unions with increased negativity. In Spain, the socialist economic team developed an agenda for reform that was determined to carry through its fiscal consolidation drive in order to cut inflation. The decision to adopt a model based on supply expansion led the economic team to ignore the unions, believing that monetary policy, rather than collective bargaining, would be a more efficient mechanism to discipline wages and reduce inflation. Later events proved the mistake of this assessment, when inflation continued to accelerate rapidly after 1988.

Finally, the Spanish experience shows that for voluntary incomes policy to work, both business and government have to support a system with the following characteristics (see Espina 1991b): Wage increases tied to inflation targets, the inclusion of safeguard clauses to guarantee workers' incomes in cases of inflation deviations, flexibility, and the establishment of specific and complementary compensation mechanisms tied to productivity increases. This last condition is critical to guaranteeing that wage drift will be justified so that it will benefit workers from firms that have achieved higher levels of productivity. These conditions will prevent the emergence of deprivation effects—that is, workers from one firm becoming jealous because workers from neighboring firms have received higher wages—and will guarantee that workers are paid for their performance. Firms could be fiscally penalized if they do not meet the government guidelines. The implementation of such a system, however, depends on prevailing domestic conditions.

e. The Reemergence National Social Bargaining in the 1990s

The electoral defeat of the socialists in the 1996 general election and the victory of the conservative Partido Popular in Spain brought about an unanticipated development: the resurgence of national-level bargaining between the government, business, and labor unions on diverse regulatory items. I have argued throughout the book that this development further challenges the conventional wisdom about the undoing of corporatist institutions by the pressures of international market competition and integration. This resurgence was particularly surprising given the perception of Spain as lacking encompassing labor market institutions. In this section I want to summarize briefly the content of some of these new agreements and examine the reasons behind the resurgence of national-level bargaining in Spain.

In Spain, although there has not been a return to incomes policy negotiated centrally at the national level,[6] there has been a return to national-level social bargaining in the 1990s. Since 1994 cooperation among the bargaining actors has been very significant. In 1994 the business confederation, Confederación Española de Organizaciones Empresariales (CEOE) (and the Confederación Española de Pequeñas y Medianas Empresas, CEPYME), and the two major union confederations (CCOO and UGT) signed the "Interconfederal Agreement to Regulate Labor Ordinances and Labor Regulations." The main objective of this pact was to regulate the passing-out of the old Labor Ordinances established during the Franco regime that governed the industrial relations system (including professional and wage structures and the disciplinary regime) for most economic activities. In 1996 the same actors signed the "Tripartite Agreement for the Extra-Judicial Resolution of Labor Conflicts," which developed a new system to resolve labor conflicts that may emerge between workers and employers. The main goal of this agreement is to avoid the formalization of these kind of conflicts in labor courts. In 1996 unions and the conservative government negotiated an agreement on pension reform. In 1997 the unions and employer organizations signed a "Tripartite Agreement on Professional Training" to foster cooperation between unions and employers to train workers. The most significant agreement, however, was negotiated between the two largest confederations and the employers' association in 1997 to limit employers' liability to high redundancy costs and to restructure the collective bargaining system. This reform has focused on four main aspects (De la Dehesa 1997, 45):

1. The agreement has eliminated some forms of temporary contracts and has introduced limits to additional costs for existing temporary contracts.

2. It has introduced a new indefinite contract with lower redundancy costs (from the existing 45 days and 42 months, to a maximum of 33 days and 24 months) and has reduced social contributions to incentive indefinite contracts over temporary ones.

3. It has reformed article 52-C of the Workers' Statute that regulates the termination of contract for objective reasons to facilitate its implementation by labor courts.

4. Finally, the reform attempts to rationalize the existing collective bargaining system. The agreement calls for a clearer articulation of the levels of collective bargaining, stipulating that it would be desirable to reserve some items, including wage increases, for national-level sectoral bargaining.

This agreement constituted an important milestone, not only because it was a negotiated pact, (as opposed to the previous two reforms of 1984 and 1994 that were introduced by the socialist government) but also because dismissal costs were one of the most contentious issues between employers and the unions.[7]

The return to national social bargaining has been the object of analysis by political scientists. Pérez (1998, 14–23) argues that these agreements reflect the inability of Spanish producers to control costs and the failure of the government to achieve macroeconomic policy objectives after the collapse of concertation in 1986. According to her argument, governments in Spain failed to restrain wages by relying on a tight monetary policy and a strong currency stance, because employers could not control costs in a fragmented and decentralized bargaining context in which inflation was exacerbated by the overvaluation of the currency.[8] Therefore, the government and business were interested in the return to national bargaining as a way to achieve their goals.[9]

The structure and strategies of labor unions in Spain also help to understand the resurgence of national social bargaining. With these new agreements, unions seek to counter the conventional wisdom that views them as entrenched institutions that promote the interests of insiders, while helping to improve macroeconomic conditions that contribute to Spain's accession to the proposed Monetary Union. It is also important to emphasize that labor unions in Spain are relatively weak at that plant level. By promoting centralized bargaining and a new articulation of the collective bargaining system, they are making sure that peak confederations will remain significant players (Royo 1999).[10] The success (or failure) of these initiatives will determine the consolidation of this approach. The return of national social bargaining has had very positive consequences for the Spanish economy and contributed to sustained rapid growth.[11] Given the difficulties that the government and employers had in the past controlling overall wage growth without the support from unions, coupled with the erosion that further fragmentation would have on the position of the main confederations, the actors should have powerful incentives to continue this approach.

Epilogue: The Future of Social Democratic Corporatism

The standard argument on globalization is that market integration and changes in the production system render SD corporatist policies far less feasible. According to this analysis, markets now dominate policies, and there is very little that governments can do about it. This is so because transformations in the international economy have shifted the balance of power in favor of business, which can exercise exit threats at anytime, thus undermining the voices (and votes) of citizens. If this is the case, and I have been arguing throughout this book that this argument is a simplification, it means that prospects for democratic politics are doomed. For political scientists that seek to deepen democratic institutions and promote policy alternatives, this conclusion has to be resisted. As I have emphasized in this book, several factors challenge the notion that partisan politics are irrelevant in the global economy.

First, as of June 1999, SD parties rule or participate in government coalitions in 13 of the 15 EU countries (Spain and Ireland are the two exceptions). Even in countries in which conservative parties have remained in power for over a decade (the United Kingdom, Germany, Italy) SD parties have been able to shift the tide and win elections in the past few years. This development, which challenges some pessimistic analyses about the electoral prospects of social democratic parties (Kitschelt 1994), confirms that these prospects remain buoyant. Although, it is true that many of these parties have become more moderate and have accepted the importance of market principles, they have also developed supply side policies consistent with the SD corporatist agenda (e.g., the French initiatives to reduce the working week, or the German actions to revert some of the reforms of the Kohl government). The impressive electoral performance of these leftist parties proves that globalization has, to a large extent, increased the electoral appeal of the left, because these governments are expected to implement policies that redistribute wealth and address the concern of large sectors of the population that are negatively affected by globalization.[12]

Furthermore, the levels of government spending, public debt, and taxation in most of these countries have remained stable throughout the first half of the 1990s, challenging the notion that globalization is imposing policy convergence (Garrett 1998, Swank 1998, Stephens, Huber, and Ray 1999).[13] Only the adoption of restrictive policies by most of these governments in the second half of the 1990s, implemented to satisfy the Maastricht criteria to participate in EMU, forces these governments to tighten their fiscal policies. This, however, was a policy choice on the part of the governments that wanted to become EMU members. It was not imposed by the markets, and not all the countries responded the same way (e.g., Germany's tax to pay for reunification).

Thirdly, the empirical evidence does not support the conventional wisdom about a rollback of welfare state entitlements in the past two decades. On the contrary, the partisan differences on social policy that characterized the immediate postwar period have not been eliminated (Stephens, Huber, and Ray 1999, 164–193). The resilience of these programs in most European countries, despite the inevitable constraints imposed by the liberalization and internationalization of capital markets on their budget deficits and taxes, shows that the sustainability of these programs will be the result of political choices, not inexorable economic constraints.

Fourthly, some authors have emphasized the deteriorating macroeconomic performance of some SD corporatist countries as indicative of the constraints imposed by the global economy. In this book, I have argued that this analysis is a simplification of the reality. Although it is true that the employment economic performance of some traditional SD corporatist countries deteriorated in the 1990s (particularly Sweden and Finland), other studies have proven that this was mostly the result of external exogenous factors (the recession accelerated by the end of the Cold War, the German unification, the deflationary policies of the Bundesbank, the process towards EMU) than the result of capital flight precipitated by the removal of capital controls, which made it impossible for SD countries to sustain full employment (Moene and Wallerstein 1999, 253–259; Garrett 1998, 140–144; Garrett 1999, 179–182; Soskice 1999, 119–122). These counties have fared much better at the end of the 1990s, when the effects of those exogenous factors dissipated and their economies recovered. Soskice (1999, 119) argues that once we take into consideration the effect of current-account deficits (indicative of excessive demand and not sustainable in the long term), the unemployment performance of SD corporatist countries such as Austria, Germany, Norway, Switzerland, and Sweden looks significantly better than that of more liberal economies (i.e., the United Kingdom, Canada, or the United States).[14]

Finally, as I have emphasized throughout the book, cooperation among governments, labor, and business has emerged even in countries that do not have a tradition of SD corporatist policies (Ireland, Netherlands, Italy, Portugal, Greece, Australia, the Czech Republic). These policies have contributed significantly to the improved economic performance of all these countries. In Italy the 1993 tripartite agreement institutionalized incomes policies and attributed distinct roles to different levels of collective bargaining, creating a more stable and institutionalized system of industrial relations that contributed to the country's miraculous participation in EMU (Regini and Regalia 1997).[15] In the Netherlands the so-called Wassenaar Agreement of 1982, in which employers' organizations and unions reached an agreement on wage moderation and the creation of jobs, has made Dutch success possible.[16] In Ireland and Portugal, incomes policies contributed significantly to the impressive economic performance of these countries throughout the 1990s (see chapter 5). It is, therefore, inadequate to claim that globalization has rendered corporatist policies far less feasible and inefficient. What are, then, the prospects for social democracy in the new millennium? What kind of political agenda should social democrats promote?

The global economy introduces new challenges that will force SD governments and parties to adjust their policy agendas. The most important task for SD leaders will be to redefine the SD agenda in a new context that does not admit programs that oppose the market. Throughout this century SD governments have been able to develop mechanisms—such as the welfare state, the strengthening of collective bargaining—that have contributed significantly to taming some of the negative consequences of the market operations—such as the lack of provision of collective goods; the intrinsic crises provoked by the market's individualist logic, and the unequal opportunities that are caused by market access mechanisms. As I have been emphasizing throughout the book, the consequences of these policies, in terms of economic and political stability, have been remarkable. The main goal for SD politicians will be to consolidate these achievements. The new international economic context, however, demands a new impetus from SD leaders to apply the old instruments to the new realities and to regulate the market operations to make them more democratic and beneficial for society as a whole.

Individualism, democratization, competitiveness, the survival of the welfare state, fair distribution of income, and ecological problems are just some examples of the kind of challenges that SD parties throughout the world will have to confront in the next millennium. Several scholars have analyzed the future of social democracy and developed interesting proposals to redefine the SD agenda (Gillespie and Paterson 1993, Layard 1996, Giddens 1998, Iversen 1999, Hicks 1999). The key will be to develop policy proposals that address citizens' concerns and alleviate the disruptions caused by the globalization of economies while promoting an efficient and competitive economy and SD traditional values such as social justice, equality of opportunity, solidarity, and responsibility to others.[17] In this regard, there are several areas in which SD parties can contribute to the political discourse and introduce alternatives to neoliberal policies. The deepening of the democratic state, the activation of civil society, the investment in social capital, and the promotion of policies that promote the integration of excluded citizens and groups are just some examples (see Giddens 1998). Social democrats should also give further impetus to private initiatives to stimulate entrepreunership that will increase activities and benefit society.

SD parties should redefine the role of national governments in an increasingly integrated global economy and rethink the role of the state. This does not mean, necessarily, that the main goal should be the reduction of the levels of public spending. To focus on the size of government is to ignore the fact that what matters about public spending is not its size, but the way it is spent. Despite the conventional wisdom that attributes harmful effects to a large state, the empirical evidence shows that among OECD and countries there is not an obvious correlation between the size of government and economic growth (Layard 1997, 81–83). New studies are showing the important role that the state can play providing collective goods that are undersupplied by the market (health, education, professional training, infrastructure) (Garret 1998), and how state capacities for domestic transformative strategies provide a competitive advantage (Weiss 1998). Focusing on the size of the state as opposed to the way the governments operate, is not a good way to improve governments' performance.

The SD goals of reducing inequality and insecurity while promoting growth and employment remains politically salient. In this regard, a major economic challenge for European SD parties will be to improve the employment record of their countries. The proportion of the working-age population in employment in the Euro area has fallen from 63 percent in 1970 to 57 percent in 1998 (in contrast in the United States, where it has risen from 62 to 74 percent over the same period) (IMF 1999). One of the main reasons behind this disappointing performance has been the deterioration of productivity growth in the Euro area. In the 1990s, total factor productivity rose faster in the United States (1.1 percent a year) that in Europe (0.7 percent a year). The task for European governments is to end this deterioration.[18]

In this regard, it is important to emphasize that a critical way to improve productivity standards is capital investment, coupled with education and training. One of the most important consequences of technological change has been the mismatch between skills and market needs in post-industrial economies. This is one of the areas in which the supply side policies of SD parties can make a difference. Countries such as Sweden, Austria, and Finland have been implementing active market policies—placement services, training courses, wage subsidies, and temporary public employment—for decades (Moene and Wallerstein 1999, 249–251). One of the main objectives of these policies was to provide workers with the skills to improve their capacities and employment perspectives. These policies had "the advantage of providing retraining, keeping workers in the labor market, thus avoiding the deterioration of skills" (Moene and Wallerstein 1999, 250). Investment in human resources will be key to increase firms productivity and competitiveness and to foster an adequate environment that attracts investment. Social democratic governments can further these policies by promoting public and private project partnerships, and lifelong educational programs. These sorts of policies are even more necessary in a global economy in addressing the exclusion and marginalization problems caused by the integration of markets and the introduction of new technologies. These policies should gradually replace conventional benefit programs that have proven to be inefficient at incorporating excluded people into the labor markets and have promoted inadequate behavior and dependency cultures. Moreover, supply side policies should be integrated with community-focused programs to increase their effectiveness and develop social capital (Putman 1993; Hall 1999). This approach will foster formal and informal network building, one of the keys to succeeding in the global economy.

Another area that requires a new approach by SD governments is the regulation of markets. Social democrats should not oppose the market. Markets are dominant in the new global economy and most decisions are driven by market considerations, but their operations must be regulated by governments to limit negative externalities. For instance, one of the most interesting (and dangerous) developments caused by globalization has been the tendency toward increasing concentration of firms. Globalization has promoted increasing competition in all sectors. Firms and corporations have responded to the challenge with new technological, marketing, and production systems that increase productivity and competitiveness. These systems, however, require massive investments that have resulted in the consolidation and concentration of industries in search of lower costs and larger economies of scale. This is, potentially, a very dangerous development that will erode consumers' positions in the short term, and that must be resisted by national governments. One of the tasks for SD leaders will be to develop mechanisms to regulate these markets in order to make sure that they are responsive to societal demands. It is, therefore, important to emphasize that in this new global environment in which old mechanisms—such as nationalization—are no longer advocated by SD parties, and in which governments face increasing budgetary and monetary constraints, one of the most important mechanisms to control markets' operations is the establishment of rules to regulate them—that is, to limit ecological damage, to provide access to universal services, or to prevent monopolies. This does not mean that everything has to be regulated. On the contrary, overregulation was one of the reasons for the collapse of the Soviet system in the 1980s, and the underperformance of European economies in the 1990s. Those sectors that are overregulated should be made more flexible to stimulate efficiencies and increase economic activities.

From an international standpoint the guiding principle for SD parties should be that a truly global economy can function only if there are regulations to protect against market excesses and strong safety nets that help weather the storms. In this regard, SD parties should promote a global agenda that strengthens international and national regulatory standards such as labor standards (i.e., health and safety regulations, the end of child labor, and freedom of association), environmental protection, and the reform of the world financial systems to end the destructive cycles of bust and boom (see Soros 1998).

Furthermore, one of the main contributions of SD parties in Western Europe has been the expansion and consolidation of the welfare state. The graying of populations and the high levels of unemployment in these countries are stretching the ability of SD governments to sustain these regimes. Furthermore, today's economic structure is markedly different from the one under which welfare states and labor regulations originated (Esping-Andersen 1999, 47–71). Postindustrial economies are no longer dominated by industrial production with strong demand for low-skilled workers; the labor force is not as homogeneous and undifferentiated as it once was; and stable families with high fertility in which the females were primarily devoted to the house are no longer the norm in most industrialized countries. The revolution in both labor markets and households, new global economic developments, combined with prevalent low fertility, pressures for low wages, and demand for low skills present new challenges to the welfare state that must be addressed by social democratic governments. The traditional SD goals of equality and full employment may no longer be fully feasible under these circumstances.

The welfare state, however, is one of the key issues that separate conservative and SD parties. If SD governments want to maintain their commitment to the welfare state (and the promise to provide basic needs to all citizens has been one of the historical objectives of social democracy), they will have to redefine it and come up with innovative mechanisms to finance benefits and programs. The resilience of these programs in most European countries, despite the inevitable constraints imposed by the liberalization and internationalization of capital markets in most of these countries on their budget deficits and taxes, shows that the sustainability of these programs will be the result of political choices, not inexorable economic constraints (see Stephens, Huber, and Ray 199, 164–193; Esping-Andersen 1999, 170–184). The key will be to focus on ways to finance these programs and adapt them to the new economic and social realities. This includes a cost-benefit assessment of each individual program and a willingness to promote those that are effective and dismantle others that only benefit some privileged sectors of the population at the expense of the rest (see Esping-Andersen 1999, 178–184). The guiding principles leading public policies should be efficiency and equity.

Social democrats have to resist pressures to dismantle the welfare state. New empirical evidence shows that both the welfare state and the redistributive taxation system needed to pay for it may be beneficial if they encourage people to undertake risky but profitable activities (Sinn 1996). According to this view, the welfare state is an insurance device that insures people against career risks. As long as it does not hurt efficiency by encouraging people to drop out of working, the welfare system should work as a private insurance system that encourages people to take risks and penalizes those that refuse to do so.

However, it is important to emphasize that the empirical evidence shows that in those countries in which people are offered income for an indefinite period if out of work, people remain unemployed longer (Layard 1997, 58–59; Nickell 1997). This has been one of the major criticisms against the welfare state from conservatives who advocate labor market deregulation. This does not mean, however, that SD parties should promote labor market deregulation. The "equality-jobs trade-off" is questionable and the crisis of the welfare state is not universal. As Esping-Andersen (1999) shows, welfare state generosity affects who happens to be unemployed, but does not explain levels of unemployment (1999, 124–129). He introduces empirical evidence showing that the links between unemployment, wage regulation, and employment protection are blurred at best. The U. S. model, based on deregulated and flexible labor markets, essentially starves people back into work by making them accept work at any pay, which has resulted in greater inequalities. Furthermore, this so-called liberal model has not worked so well in other countries such as Canada, Australia, or the United Kingdom. Other empirical studies are also challenging the notion that unemployment in Europe is caused by structural rigidities and job protection mechanisms (OECD 1999, Esping-Andersen 1999, 124–132). Blanchard and Wolfers (1999) have examined the role of labor market rigidities (i.e., the length and generosity of unemployment benefits, the degree of employment protection, the payroll-tax burden, and the centralization of wage bargaining) in the 15 European Union countries from 1965 to 1995 and argue that these rigidities have little or no effect on overall unemployment. They conclude that tight macroeconomic policies have intensified the unemployment problem.[19] These findings are consistent with the latest OECD's Employment Outlook (1999) that concludes that job protection laws are having "little or no effect on overall unemployment" in western economies. On the contrary, the OECD claims that there is "no clear link" between employment protection laws and an increase in temporary jobs, and concludes that tight regulation ensures more stable jobs, less labor turnover, and fewer unemployed, while business-union cooperation fosters innovative and flexible working practices (see also Esping-Andersen 1999, 125–129).[20] Therefore, SD governments should disregard market deregulation per se and promote a gradualist approach that reforms inefficient programs while promoting the establishment of new ones that foster a culture of entrepreneurship and risk.

To promote these goals, the major focus of welfare programs should be the investment in human capital that enables individuals to find work with a prospect for stable employment. The goal would be for the state to ensure decent life standards for its citizens, while the individual has the obligation to use the opportunities that they are offered. As indicated above, in many cases old welfare programs have promoted a dependency culture that has provided ammunition to politicians that oppose the welfare state. In this sense, it will be critical to switch welfare spending from the old benefits programs to new ones that contribute to human capital and promote risk taking (Giddens 1998, 122; Esping-Andersen 1999, 180–184). More restrictive eligibility requirements coupled with reform of the tax structure (i.e., an increasing reliance on consumption taxes to finance these programs[21]) should be considered by these parties to fund the welfare state.

A major area in which SD governments can make a difference is in the promotion of encompassing labor institutions that will benefit the groups adversely affected by globalization (for an alternative view promoting industry- or sector-based bargaining see, Iversen 1999, 171–176). In this book I have challenged the notion that capital mobility is leading to a pattern of crossnational convergence. On the contrary, I have stressed the findings of several authors (Soskice 1999, Garrett 1998, Garrett 1999, Swank 1998, Weiss 1998, Esping-Andersen 1999) that have concluded that the effects of globalization depend on the democratic institutional context, the institutional mechanisms for collective representation within interest groups, the electoral and party systems, and the organization of policymaking authority systems of interest representation. In other words, they argue that national institutions matter, and even determine national trajectories, thus governments' responses to internationalization of capital markets will differ depending on national institutional contexts. For example, Esping-Andersen argues that "post industrial transformation is institutionally path dependent" (1999, 4, 140). According to this view, SD corporatism should facilitate the degree to which affected interests can press their claims against adverse policy changes in the face of globalization and resist moves toward deregulation. This is so because the continuing existence of encompassing labor confederations provides an institutional mechanism that will allow the sectors adversely affected by globalization to articulate preferences and pressure national policy makers to guarantee that policy change incorporates their demands (Swank 1998, 9). In countries with encompassing labor institutions (i.e., the Nordic nations) the increases in international capital flows and liberalization are weakly associated with public sector retrenchment and market-conforming policies that have been associated with globalization, because the "collective veto points of consensus democracy" (Birchfield and Crepaz, forthcoming[22]) favor those adversely affected by globalization.

These analyses confirm that SD parties interested in preventing public sector retrenchment and market-conforming policies should strengthen encompassing SD corporatist institutions. As I have mentioned throughout the book, systems of industrial relations involving encompassing unions in which authority is concentrated in either a small group of large unions or in national confederations have been one of the main reasons behind the remarkable economic success of many European countries. These polices have been successful because unions have contributed to overall wage moderation, have generated a productive and stable economic environment, and have promoted the development of collective goods that are undersupplied by the markets (i.e., training, education, infrastructure) thus increasing the competitiveness of their companies (Garret 1999). In SD corporatist countries, organized business has sought regulation (not deregulation!) in order to confront more effectively the new challenges posed by globalization, seeking to preserve for their companies the financial frameworks, training systems, and research networks that allow them to remain competitive in international markets (Soskice 1999, 134; Weiss 1998). It is for this reason that businesses have supported these polices in these countries—even those with exit options. For this approach to succeed it will be critical for nontraditional SD countries like Spain to modify the existing institutional framework (Soskice 1999, 130–133) to build a new institutional infrastructure that will foster cooperation among firms and unions (i.e., Halls' "social capital," 1999, 163).

However, the key factor in guaranteeing the success of these policies will be a public policy that promotes an adequate social organization that contributes to the strength and organization of the labor movement (see chapter 4). Therefore, in order to promote and consolidate these strategies it will be critical for SD parties to implement policies that strengthen the institutional position of peak confederations and to provide them with the capacities to negotiate and enforce encompassing agreements (something that the Spanish socialists failed to do) (for an alternative view see, Iversen 1999, 171–176). Encompassing labor market institutions are critical to coordinate the behavior of most of the labor force. Therefore, one of the key objectives for governments interested in this strategy should be fostering centralized authority within labor movements (according to Golden 1993, this is the key factor that will determine the success of encompassing agreements; see chapter 4) and promoting union density. Some of the countries that have been more successful in stemming the decline of their labor unions are Denmark, Sweden, Finland, and Austria. One of the main reasons behind this success is the fact that unions in these countries have been in charge of distributing unemployment benefits. In all these countries union density continued to increase in the 1980s (Golden, Wallerstein, and Lange, 1999, 198–202). Another possibility will be to extend collective bargaining agreements beyond the ranks of unions members (Garret 1998, 157). These are just some ways in which SD parties could contribute to the strengthening of the labor movement in their countries. In some SD countries in which competition between public and private sector unions have undermined centralized bargaining (Sweden), it may be necessary to weaken the commitment to wage solidarity and replace it with a tax-transfer system (see Garrett 1998, 130; Esping-Andersen 1999, 153). Employers will support this institutional framework because they will benefit from it. Throughout the book I have emphasized that there is little evidence of institutional change in most countries. This, according to Golden, Wallerstein, and Lange (1999, 225) may be because these institutions benefit all the actors involved (including business) who would not gain from dismantling them—or in the words of Esping-Andersen, because "institutional paths dependencies . . . derive from the prevailing nexus between households, welfare state, and labor markets" (1999, 140).

The European Monetary Union will mean further restrictions on domestic economic policies because monetary union subjects macroeconomic policy in the EMU area to a single monetary authority, the independent European Central Bank (ECB). Although some scholars have already predicted the dismissal of centralized concertation schemes, new analyses are proving the importance that incomes policy will have in the context of the monetary union (Pérez 1998). Incomes policy, with its influence on labor relations and labor costs, seems to continue to be an adequate instrument to enhance competitiveness and contribute to the convergence objective pursued by the European economies. The benefits of centralized wage bargaining, however, hinge largely on the ability of union leaders to control overall wage growth in order to avoid monetary policy measures that will result in higher unemployment. The EMU will result in the decentralization of the level of wage bargaining across the EU because overall, the most encompassing union organizations will be less inclusive, and, therefore, they may have fewer incentives to internalize the inflationary pressures of wage increases.[23] The risk will be that in the new EMU context, in which wage bargaining is relatively fragmented but there is a single monetary authority for the area, wage bargainers will be less responsive to threats from the ECB. Nevertheless, since unit labor costs will still remain a critical factor in improving competitiveness, there will be strong pressures on governments, employers, and unions to pursue national social bargaining. SD parties can contribute to this task. Confrontation did not work in the past. It is, therefore, critical to pave the way for continuing consensus and cooperation.

Finally, it is important to emphasize that there is not a single SD model. Different parties will have to adapt their strategies to their domestic institutions and economic structures. What may work in one country will not work in others. Despite all the recent rhetoric about the development of a common SD platform (see above), it has been much easier for Tony Blair, the British Prime Minister, to implement his version of the SD "Third Way"—characterized by restrictive macroeconomic policies, limited state intervention, and market-driven policy considerations—than it has been for continental SD leaders, because Britain has undergone a dramatic transformation under successive conservative governments. British Labour policies would meet fierce resistance in other European countries with stronger labor movements and different institutional settings. Under different electoral systems it is also difficult for other SD leaders to achieve the majority that Mr. Blair has in the House of Commons, therefore, they are likely to follow a more gradualist approach. This despite the fact that, notwithstanding the strengths of the continental European economies, their need for structural reforms (i.e., in areas such as labor costs, public subsidies, overregulation, public spending, aging societies, expensive pension systems) is larger than in Britain. To reform these economies will require a consistent and integrated effort over several years on the part of these governments. How should this discussion affect the Spanish's Socialists?

It is now easier to assess the Spanish socialists' tenure in government. One of their main contributions was their effort to reform the Francoist closed and outmoded economic structures. They were characterized by autarchic tendencies, lack of extensive competition, and dependence on a paternalistic and interventionist state that was organized around authoritarian corporatist structures that had been modeled on the Italian fascism. The socialists' reforms opened up and dismantled these economic structures and forced the economic agents to operate under the market rules. This will prove a lasting legacy. The erosion of the socialist electoral support in the 1990s, however, showed the difficulties of balancing an economic strategy that failed to gain the unions' assent to rein in inflation, while at the same time accommodating the social demands of part of the electorate. It seems now evident that one of their main shortcomings was their inability to conceptualize their radical (for the time) SD economic strategy. This proved to be a fatal mistake. For the most part, their political discourse and modernizing agenda were not very different from Mr. Blair's, and it would easily fit into recent discussions about new SD strategies. Yet, they failed to frame their political ideas into a new concept (the Spanish "social-liberal" way?) that would have helped them bridge the ideological differences within the party (and union) and build a new electoral coalition that would support their agenda. More importantly, they also failed to transform the institutional setting in a way that would have been more conducive to the implementation of their preferred policies. Now that they have been out of power for almost four years, they will have to rethink their agenda and seek new options. Their improving electoral performance in the 1999 European and local elections opens up brighter electoral perspectives. The establishment of a partnership once more with unions seems to be the most feasible option to implement an SD corporatist agenda along the lines that I discussed above. Yet, electoral considerations might prevent such a development.

Notes

Introduction

1. Social concertation or concertation refers to centralized agreements between leaders of unions and business associations pursuing shared macroeconomic objectives. Although this term is less common in the United States, it is used by the neocorporatist literature in Western Europe, Latin America, and the United Kingdom. In these agreements unions are willing to moderate and limit wage growth. Government's participation is not mandatory. These agreements are usually negotiated and signed by trade unions and business organizations with centralized structures and hierarchical powers and are followed (and implemented) by the majority of business and workers. They cover incomes policies and industrial relations topics, as well as other issues—such as productivity, absenteeism, working hours, training, etc. They also include provisions dealing with macroeconomic issues—that is, redistribution, inflation targets, competitiveness, etc.—and institutional issues—that is, participation of the social actors in economic policy making, participation in state institution, and so on. Social democratic (SD) governments have often participated in these agreements seeking to fulfill their economic objectives and have offered compensation to the social actors for their cooperation—such as subsidies, increases in public expenditures, public jobs, fiscal benefits, etc. In this book I shall refer to these arrangements indistinctly as "social democratic corporatism," "corporatism," "neocorporatism," or "concertation." These definitions were explored in Schmitter 1974. In Spain we prefer the term "concertation" to refer to these arrangements so as to distinguish it from "corporatism," which most scholars use to describe the Nordic system of centralized wage setting, because the term "corporatism" has connotations of fascism, anticompetitive practices, and trade protection in Southern Europe (as well as Latin America). The distinction between a corporatist system that comes from below and which comes imposed from above has led authors such as Lehmbruch (1979) to advocate the term "liberal corporatism" instead of "societal corporatism" to stress the former voluntaristic nature and the presence on an open and competitive party system (Schmitter 1981, 324). The fascist corporative system that existed in Spain during the Franco years was characterized by appointed officials, absence of freedom of association, no right to strike, and no political parties or democratic Parliament. It is for this reason that some

scholars have argued that the word "corporatism" has been embarrassing to Spanish politicians, unionists, and employers' leaders (Martínez-Alier and Roca 1986, 25; Giner and Sevilla 1984). This version of "old" corporatism compatible with fascism, in which the social partners are not freely represented, is very different from the "new" corporatism compatible with parliamentary democracy (see Maier 1975; Lehmbruch 1979). The fascist corporatist system is fundamentally different from what the literature refers to as "liberal corporatism." Under a liberal corporatist system capitalists and workers collaborate freely in a range of new institutions (such as work councils) that deal with economic and other issues including wages and work conditions, and there is an open, competitive party system into which may flow the unresolved disputes. For instance, the Nordic variety of corporatism is associated with free trade and competitiveness, and in many of these countries (Norway, Austria, Sweden, and Denmark) the centralization of wage bargaining was instigated not by the unions, but by employers seeking to restrain wage growth (see Pontusson and Swenson 1996; Moene and Wallerstein 1999, 233–234). In Spain, when writing in Spanish, some authors (for example, V. Pérez-Díaz, or S. Giner) use *corporativismo* to refer to the "old" corporatism, and the neologism *corporatismo* for the "new" corporatism. See Martínez-Alier and Roca 1986, 23–26.

2. It is not the objective of this research project, however, to analyze the factors that made concertation possible in the first place. This has been the subject of analyses by other scholars (see, among others,: Encarnación 1997; Pérez-Díaz 1981, 1984; Martínez-Alier and Roca 1986; Führer 1996; Roca 1993). The main focus of this project will be to determine the reasons for its collapse. One of the most provocative analyses has been developed by Omar Encarnación (1997). He focuses on the institutional configuration of the state and claims that state structures and institutional legacies were the critical variables in determining the successful emergence of concertation during the democratic transition. In particular, he stresses three institutional variables: "a corporate culture with a predilection for policy mechanisms of class compromise and accommodation; a bureaucratic apparatus with well established patterns of administrative capacities over both capital and labor; and finally, a framework of industrial and labor relations that embodies an institutionalized context of social control, dialogue, and representation" (390). According to him, these institutional factors helped to overcome the absence of the presupposed necessary institutional preconditions developed by the literature for the emergence and consolidation of concertation—that is, the configuration of Spanish labor and employers, and the political orientation of the first democratic government. Martínez-Alier and Roca (1986) argue that "corporatist structures have grown (in Spain) after 1977 because the Left—with the exception of the Basque Country—had long made itself ready for a tame transition out of the Franco regime" (26). They claim that post-Franco corporatist structures have developed without any of the agents adopting an explicitly corporatist ideology.

3. I will also refer to the PSOE in this book by its abbreviated name, the Socialist Party.

4. The initials are doubled in Spanish to indicate plural, and I shall continue their usage in this book.

5. This union was the direct successor of the SOV, the Solidaridad Obrera Vasca, a Christian-oriented union that emerged in the Basque region the 1930s. It operates mainly in the Basque country.

6. In this book I refer indiscriminately to the Socialist Party and the Socialist government because the leaders of the party were also the leaders of the government.

Chapter 1

1. This chapter summarizes F. Scharpf's discussion about the limitations of the instruments of economic policy at the disposal of national governments and the benefits of incomes policy. For a more detailed description of these issues see Scharp 1991, 28–37 and 170–173; and Flanagan, Soskice, and Ulman 1983, 1–40 and 660–694.

2. According to this view, the behavior of governments will be influenced by the type of labor market institutions prevalent in that country, which in turn will influence economic performance. See Garrett 1998, 33–38.

Chapter 2

1. I refer to this literature as "structuralist" because, according to these authors (who attempt to account for the decline in unions and concertation), globalization and technological changes have resulted in the irreversible transformation of the social structures of the advanced industrial economies in ways that are detrimental to the labor movement and concertation. Other authors have referred to the "structural dependence" of the state on mobile capital. See: Przeworski and Wallerstein 1988; Swank 1998, 6.

2. Pérez Díaz has argued that "[t]he central institution of this policy [of concertation] has been the agreements between the unions, business organizations and the state. . . . The objective of these agreements has been the establishment of incomes policy, and the development of an institutional framework of industrial relations and union action. . . . All these aspects allow us to talk about a 'neocorporatist' experience in Spain" (Pérez Díaz 1984, 18–19).

3. This conceptual approach is different from "new institutionalism" approach (Evans, Rueschemeyer, and Skocpol 1985; Steinmo, Thelan, and Longstreth 1992) that emerged in the 1980s. Neoinstitutionalists also argued that economic policy variations and outcomes are also affected by organizational factors. However, unlike the neocoporatists authors, who concentrated their research efforts on the organization of labor, neoinstitutionalists focused their research in the organization of the state and of capital. They argued that both the structure of the state and the institutional setting (i.e., central bank independence, or the character of wage bargaining) affect policies, and the options

available to policy makers (Hall 1986, Zysman 1983). These authors moved beyond the neocorporatist conceptual approach and emphasized the need to analyze and expand the range of organizational factors that affect economic policy, actors' behavior, and economic performance, and the interaction among these institutional factors (Hall 1994 and 1999, 139).

4. Panich has also laid out the following definition: "The corporatist paradigm as understood to connote a political structure within advanced capitalism which integrates organized socioeconomic producer groups through a system of representation and cooperative mutual interaction at the leadership level and of mobilization and social control at the mass level, can be a heuristic tool for appropriating the social reality of many western democracies" (Panich 1977, 10).

5. Lang 1981 has argued against the notion that the Francoist corporatist structures have facilitated the development of neocorporatist structures in Spain.

6. The main reason I refer in this book to neocorporatist arrangements as "concertation" is because the word "corporatism" has quite a negative connotation in Spain, since it is associated with the authoritarian and fascist "corporatist" structures that existed in the country during General Franco's almost 40 years of authoritarian rule (see Introduction). Nevertheless, concertation and SD corporatist arrangements (understood as democratic corporatism) are the same thing. Moreover, some authors prefer to use neocorporatism to refer to the democratic corporatism that has been characteristic of the Northern European and Scandinavian states, to differentiate it from the old authoritarian corporatism that was established in many European (Italy, Spain, Portugal), and Latin American (Argentina, Brazil) countries this century. In this book, however, I use both corporatism and neocorporatism (and related words) indistinctly. They both refer to democratic corporatism, unless otherwise noted.

7. Neocorporatism reached its academic zenith in the second half of the 1970s, when dramatic cross-national differences in macroeconomic performance appeared among OECD countries as a result of the first oil-shock crisis. The European Free Trade Association (EFTA) countries—Sweden, Norway, Finland, Austria, and Switzerland—were able to maintain full employment, expand the welfare state, and reduce wage inequalities (see Moene and Wallerstein 1999, 231–232).

8. Some authors (Golden 1993; Soskice 1990a; Lange 1984) have contended that the key variable to account for the success of concertation and wage moderation is concentration—or union monopoly—not centralization. Golden 1993 emphasizes the difference between *centralization* ("the degree of centralized structure and union leaders coercive powers' to impose their views on their rank and file,") and *concentration* ("the degree of competition and fragmentation within the labor movement"), and argues that the key to avoiding high wage settlements is the degree to which bargaining is coordinated across the economy, and not necessarily the centralization of the bargaining process (Golden 1993, 439–453). She argues that wage moderation can occur without centralization as long as the institutional setting facilitates coordination among unions and there are few unions that do not compete for members—that is,

"union monopoly is high" (Golden 1993, 440). According to this view, concertation and wage moderation are possible when unions have monopoly over
wage negotiations and also when competing unions are able coordinate their
strategies. This is so because the coercive control that characterizes centralized
unions—for example, the power to withhold funds—is not easily enforceable,
and does not always work. Wage coordination, on the contrary, is the key for
successful bargaining but it depends on the institutional setting—that is, the
number of unions and the degree of competition among them—not on
whether they are centralized or not.

9. Bowman has focused on the effects of increasing the number of actors in pric-
ing behavior under cartels. He has contended that an increase in the number
of actors increases "the costs of coming to an agreement on a collusive strategy." It also increases "the difficulty of transmitting and interpreting the information upon which the cooperative effort depends." Moreover, it augments
the "likelihood that the industry will contain a 'maverick' firm determined to
torpedo any effort to maintain price stability for ideological or psychological
reasons." Finally, "it diminishes each firms choice of strategies on the total outcome . . . tending to render the detection of non-cooperative behavior more
difficult" (Bowman 1982, 583). As cited in Golden 1993, 440.

10. The most important effect of centralized (and coordinated) wage bargaining
found by these authors is wage moderation. For union leaders, the threat of job
losses is the most salient problem. Inflation does not directly concern them,
but unemployment does. Therefore, the most important point in their strategic agenda is how to increase workers' incomes. In fulfilling this goal they will
take into consideration the expected inflation growth during wage negotiations. Wage negotiations, however, only determine nominal wages that do not
take into consideration inflation—as opposed to real wages. Thus, any unanticipated inflation growth will result in incomes losses for the workers. In these
cases union leaders will react with further wage demands to compensate their
constituencies for income losses. It is also common to negotiate safeguard
clauses that will protect workers from unexpected inflation growth and income
losses. Aggressive wage demands from labor will surely result in higher productive costs, prices, and inflation. See Freeman and Gibbons 1995, 349–351;
and Scharpf 1991, 188–192.

11. New analyses are also emphasizing the importance of coordinated wage bargaining. Coordinated bargaining contributes to moderate wage settlements
for the following reasons: First, the leading negotiators know that subsequent
pacts will follow their lead and do not have to worry about increments to protect real wages against other inflationary settlements that might be negotiated
later on. They know that the agreement will be generalized. Second, having
few parties in the negotiation leads to easier agreements on the economic predictions upon which the settlement will be based. Third, the lead negotiators
usually take into consideration the export sectors of the economy that are particularly sensitive to inflationary pressures (Hall 1994, 5–6). Germany is the
typical example where coordinated bargaining takes place. IG Metall (the

German Metalworkers Union) takes the lead and sets the parameters that other unions will follow in subsequent rounds of negotiations (see Golden 1993). The influence of IG Metall union has been increased by its recent merger with the 188,000-strong GTB (*Gewerkschaft Textil-Bekleidung,* the textile and clothing union), and plans to incorporate the 160,000-strong GHK (*Gewerkschaft Holz und Kunststoff,* the wood and plastic union). See "Lafontaine in Call for End to Wage Restraint," in *Financial Times,* Monday October 6, 1997, p. 2.

12. These authors, however, have also emphasized that the electoral success of SD parties depends on the organizational structure of the labor movement. The higher the inclusiveness, unity, and monopoly of the labor movement, the longer leftist parties were in power. This was so because the party was able to act as the party of labor when in power (Cameron 1984, 167; Lehmbruch 1979, 157–63).

13. These authors recognize, however, that a leftist-controlled government is not a sufficient condition to guarantee full employment and low inflation, and vice versa. Countries like Japan and Switzerland had very low levels of unemployment throughout the 1980s despite the fact that leftist parties were marginalized from power. Other countries like Denmark or Britain experienced high levels of unemployment and inflation despite having SD parties in power for extended periods during the late 1970s (Cameron 1984, 161–163). For a detailed analysis of the "hump-shaped" model that emphasizes the importance of regime coherence and describes the strategic behavior of governments based on labor market institutions see Alvarez, Garrett, and Lange 1991; Garrett 1998, 33–49. According to this model, governments are expected to pursue partisan policies (and will achieve good macroeconomic performance) only in coherent political economies—that is, in those countries where either the right confronts very weak unions, or the left is allied with encompassing trade unions. On the contrary, strong but uncoordinated labor market institutions under left- or right-wing governments will result in instability and poor economic performance. This is so because individual trade unions are strong enough to resist governments' efforts to impose market-oriented policies and not coordinated enough to restrain wages when the government attempts to implement policies beneficial to workers. Finally, in countries in which there is a clear mismatch between the government redistributive agenda and labor market institutions—that is, governments of the left in countries with weak unions, or governments of the right confronting encompassing unions, governments are likely to move away from partisan policies and this will likely result in improving macroeconomic outcomes (Garrett 1998, 33–38 and 45–49). For a critique, see Iversen 1999, 77–81.

14. Some of the authors focusing in these variables included: Pontusson 1992, Scharpf 1987 and 1991, Kurzer 1993, Freeman and Gibbons 1995, Regini 1990 and 1995, and Schmitter 1990.

15. In this book I refer to these developments as "structural" in the sense that national governments are structurally dependent on international capital to succeed (see Swank 1998, 6). Other authors have also analyzed the impact of

globalization on societal preferences. Some scholars have argued that the structure of societal preferences has changed in ways that have lessened the electoral appeal of SD parties and policies. See Kitschelt 1994. For an argument challenging that position, see Garrett 1998, 38–40.

16. The focus of this body of literature is to analyze the impact that changes in the organization of production as well as social and institutional conditions at the regional level (not only at the national level) have on the performance of the economy (Hall 1999, 140; Soskice 1999, 101–134). However, this literature is relevant to this discussion on the collapse of concertation for two reasons. First, changes in the international economic environment and the organization of production help to explain this collapse in some countries (Sweden) despite an adequate institutional setting, and second, new analyses have shown that the study of production regimes can shed further light on how systems of industrial relations have lost influence in some countries but not in others (Soskice 1999, 102–103).

17. According to these authors, the labor force seems to be increasingly segmented and differentiated and this increasing heterogeneity of labor has fostered the emergence of new unions representing new strata of workers—that is, white-collar, or public servants. These new unions have their own agenda and interests, making concertation more difficult (Regini 1990, 18). Moreover, members of the working class seem to have a variety of lifestyles. At the same time, there are new priorities for business: Competitiveness in international markets, productivity, or value added, and highly skilled workers are better positioned to take advantages of these new demands. Many of them, however, will not be willing to make sacrifices for other workers and will refuse to keep their wages down. High unemployment has also fostered labor fragmentation by intensifying rivalries between employed and unemployed workers.

18. These tensions were heightened by the intense dispute between the LO's metalworkers' union (the Metallindustriarbetareförbundet, or Metall) and the confederation's two public-sector unions over solidarity wage arrangements. Metall leaders argued that public workers were "pay parasites" and criticized their "irresponsible wage demands." According to them, the automatic indexing of pay in the public sector when raises took place in the private one meant higher taxes and/or higher public deficit. Metall leaders opposed this. See Swenson, 1992, 45–76. The attempt of the Swedish Trade Union Confederation (LO) to establish codetermination and increase worker participation in profits further deteriorated the situation when employers reacted aggressively against these demands. See Pontusson 1992b, 186–219.

19. In 1990 SAF disbanded its negotiating division and announced that it would not accept centralized collective bargaining anymore. Business argued that a model that sought to set wages at the central level to maintain the competitiveness of Swedish products in world markets would not be affordable under new market conditions. See Swenson 1992, and Pontusson, 1992b.

20. In the last twenty years, North America and Europe have benefited from the internationalization of production, since they control 78 percent of investment.

In 1995 alone, 40,000 multinational corporations, which produce 8 percent of the world gross product and have over 30 million workers, have shifted their production location. See Estefanía, Joaquín, "Los que no dudan de nada," *El País,* January 26, 1997.

21. This, according to Swank (1998, 5–6), leads to a prisoner's dilemma for national policymakers, because they face incentives to engage in competition for investment. They will respond presumably by lowering welfare transfers, public services, and the tax burdens to a "lowest common denominator."

22. Some authors have argued that high interest rates have been the principal cause of weak growth in Western Europe in the 1980s. See Fitoussi 1996, 41–64. They point out that high interest rates have reduced investment in firms because credit became more expensive.

23. High interest rates also raised the opportunity costs of saving, because the return on investment in production firms had to increase if capital was to continue investing in firms and not in international financial markets. Profits, therefore, had to go up or investment in firms would decrease. In the 1980s, however, profits could not keep up with the high level of interest rates, and, consequently, investment in firms decreased. At the same time, increases in compensation per employee in the European Union (EU)—which had risen 60 percent since 1970—coupled with the reduction in demand caused by the crisis, further hindered profits; thus, investors preferred to invest their money in more profitable financial ventures. Even when profits recovered in the late 1980s—for example, in France the share of operating profits in national income has risen by 5.5 percentage points since 1982—this increase has not resulted in further investment. Wolf, Martin, "Reasons to be Cheerful," *Financial Times,* October 1996, p. 14.

24. The French Socialist government adopted a series of measures that combined redistributive policies, Keynesian demand stimulus, and state interventionism in industrial policies. Operating under the widespread assumption that the world economy was about to expand at that time, Pierre Mauroy, the Prime Minister, sought to stimulate the French economy by increasing substantially social expenditures, family allowances, pensions, and health benefits. The government also increased minimum wages 15 percent, extended the legal period of paid vacation by establishing a fifth week, introduced a new (and generous) early retirement program to boost employment, and shortened the working week from 40 to 39 hours. These policies had an effect both on demand and supply. On the demand side, these measures stimulated consumption and resulted in a sharp redistribution of income that favored the working class and people with lower income. The government also implemented an interventionist industrial policy that resulted in the nationalization of a larger part of the banking sector, six of the largest industrial holdings, the metal industry, and two firms that manufactured weapons and planes. These measures also sought to increase the control of the state over the economy and use public investment in the nationalized industrial sector as the engine to reactivate the French economy. See Hall 1990, 152; and Hall 1986, 193–226.

25. This problem was compounded by the fact that France was also dependent on foreign resources (oil) to satisfy its energy demands (80 percent), and price variations (paid in dollars) on these imports affected dramatically the balance of payments. Currency devaluations would, therefore, result in a higher import bill. At the same time, France monetary autonomy was also impaired by European Monetary System (EMS) membership. Any franc devaluation had to be negotiated with Germany. The Germans agreed to two devaluations in 1981 and 1982 but demanded a reduction in the French deficit, which would mean a reduction in public subsidized programs and public investment. The alternative would be the abandonment of the EMS and the establishment of protectionist measures to limit the trade deficit and stop the run against the currency. Such a decision, however, would have also implied the abandonment of the European project. See Hall 1990, 154.

26. In March of 1993 the French government introduced a new austerity plan that raised taxes and slashed public spending. The government plan sought to limit the public deficit to 3 percent of GDP. It included measures to reduce public spending, freeze wages and social security contributions, lower corporate taxes by 10 percent, and reduce family allowances.

27. Weiss claims that states are acting in many cases as "facilitators" rather than victims of globalization, assisting firms to adjust effectively to the new environment by "internationalizing" state capabilities (1998, 204–207). She argues that we are witnessing not a diminution of state power but a reconstruction of power around the consolidation of domestic and international linkages (1998, 209). She emphasizes, however, that states' responses have varied according to politico-institutional differences.

28. The course of the Spanish Socialist economic policies also seems to challenge previous assessments by the neocorporatist literature concluding that leftists governments would not be able to adopt conservative policies and/or co-opt the policies of their conservatives adversaries in countries with weak and decentralized union movements because of the opposition from their own supporters, the fear of entry by new parties and attacks from existing parties, and the lack of credibility (Garret and Lange 1989, 684–85). This was not the case in Spain. The Spanish socialists were able to stay in power for an extensive period of time and implement conservative monetary policies despite opposition from unions.

Chapter 3

1. These pacts were signed by the leaders of all political parties with representation in Parliament after the general elections of 1977: Adolfo Suárez, Felipe González, Joan Raventós, Josep María Triginer, Manuel Fraga Iribarne, Enrique Tierno Galván, Juan Ajuriaguerra, Miguel Roca, Leopoldo Calvo Sotelo, and Santiago Carrillo.

2. Martínez-Alier and Roca (1986) argue that electoral considerations played a role in this consideration. Parliamentary elections had taken place in June

1977, just three months before the Pact was signed. In that election the left-wing parties had spoken against a social pact; therefore the leaders of the parties tried to avoid labeling it as a "social pact."

3. I analyze this issue at greater length in chapter 6.

4. In the course of interviews that I conducted with representatives of the UGT and CCOO in December 1996, Antonio Gutiérrez, Secretary General of CCOO, and Nicolás Redondo and Sergio Santillán from UGT, emphasized the strong impact that the failed coup had in their strategies. The CCOO, for the first time, agreed to sign a pact.

5. This quote appeared in the newspaper *El País,* December 2, 1982 (my translation).

6. On January 28, 1983, unions and the business organization announced the rupture in the negotiation process. Alfonso Guerra, then vice president of the government, took the initiative and convinced José María Cuevas, the president of the business organization, to conclude an agreement (Estefanía and Serrano 1990, 38).

7. Another important development that took place in 1984 was the reform of the Workers' Statute. The socialists introduced modifications to the law in August 1984 to include new types of contracts to foster temporary hiring.

8. During my interview with Antonio Gutiérrez in December 1996, he emphasized the fact that Article 17 of the AES opened the door for free dismissals in Spain.

9. During my interviews with Nicolás Redondo, former secretary general of the UGT, and with Fernando Moreno and Fabián Marquez from the CEOE in December 1996, they all emphasized that this clause was the most important point of dispute between the UGT and the CEOE. They also stated that the interpretation of the article was one of the major reasons behind the CEOE's decision to repudiate the agreement later on, and the employers' association's decision to reject the possibility of reaching new agreements with UGT in 1987.

10. Joaquín Almunia confirmed this point to the author during the meeting we had in December 1996. Nicolás Redondo and Sergio Santillán from the UGT and Fernando Moreno and Fabián Marquez from the CEOE confirmed during our interviews that this article was one of the major reasons that led to the breakdown of the AES. The CEOE used the failure of the government to reform the law as an argument to abandon in mid-1985 the AES Commission in charge of following up the fulfillment of the agreement.

11. This disagreement, among other factors, caused the resignation of one of UGT's leaders, the Secretary of Union Action, José Luís Corcuera, in 1985. Nicolás Redondo and Antón Saracibar, two of the union leaders, opposed the law in Parliament. They also resigned from the PSOE's parliamentary group. I shall delve more deeply into this topic in chapter 6 when I talk about the rupture between the party and the union.

12. I shall analyze in chapter 6 the impact of the transition process on concertation.

13. I shall analyze this issue at greater length in chapter 6.

14. Fernando Moreno, Director of Industrial Relations of the business organization CEOE, confirmed during my interview in December 1996, that his organization had a lot more trouble trying to influence the bargaining position of its affiliates at times of economic expansion. During recessions, employers do not have much of a choice and follow the CEOE's guidelines. They know that their competitors cannot afford high wage increases in a situation of decreasing demand and lower profits. During expansive periods, on the contrary, firms have better prospects and often consent to union demands. They figure that it is better to raise wages than face strikes at a time of rising demand. They are also afraid that their competitors might decide not to follow the CEOE's guidelines and raise wages on their own. See chapter 5.

15. See chapter 5 for a detailed analysis of this argument.

16. In this book I shall talk about the socialist government and party (PSOE) interchangeably. Even though they were independent entities, the locus of power was concentrated in the same group of people.

17. See chapter 6 for a detailed account of the events that led to the 1988 general strike.

18. This point was confirmed by Nicolás Redondo and Sergio Santillán from the UGT, and Antonio Gutiérrez from CCOO in my interviews with them in December (1996).

19. These arguments were emphasized by N. Redondo (UGT) and C. Solchaga (PSOE) during the interviews that I held with them in December 1996. See also Solchaga 1997, 148–149, and Burns Marañon 1996, 145–173 and 199–219.

20. José Juan Ruiz, Chief of Staff of Carlos Solchaga, told me during our interview in December 1996 that he named the pact Pacto Social del Progreso, PSP, to make its initials coincide with the unions' Propuesta Sindical Prioritaria, PSP. This match, as well as the fact that the government tried to include some of unions' demands in the pact were not sufficient to attract the support of the unions.

21. José Juan Ruiz, who was in charge of this plan, told me that in August of 1990 there were no meetings because union representatives were on vacation. This proved, according to him, the lack of interest by the unions.

22. This strategy can be deducted from a set of questions that Mr. Solbes posed to the audience in a meeting of businessmen in Barcelona that year: Mr. Solbes wondered: "Why does our economy only create jobs when it is growing by more than two percent? Why, even when we are booming, do we have unemployment levels of 16 percent? How is it that in the midst of a recession, wage increases are above our inflation level and above those in the other countries that are better off than Spain?" *Financial Times,* November 25, 1993, p. 3. He attributed these problems to labor market rigidities that led the government to push for the reform of the labor market.

23. Pedro Solbes, the former Minister of Economics, confirmed this point during our meeting in December 1996. In an interview with the *Financial Times* he claimed that "rarely have I attended such long meetings with so little to show for them." Thursday, November 25, 1993, p. 3.

24. Pedro Solbes told me during our meeting that he thought that an agreement was possible with CCOO. Antonio Gutiérrez, Secretary General of CCOO, confirmed this point. They both emphasized, however, that internal divisions within CCOO made the pact impossible. At that time, there were two factions within each union. In UGT the hardest stance was lead by J. M. Zufiaur, who adopted maximalist demands, and the "softer" demands were made by Apolinar Rodríguez. Nicolás Redondo, the Secretary General, was in the middle. In the CCOO the hawkish stance was adopted by the group led by its Secretary General, Marcelino Camacho, and the "softer" ones by Antonio Gutiérrez. At the end, the hardest line triumphed and an agreement was impossible.

25. See "Sober after the feast," in *Financial Times,* Monday October 11, 1993, p. 28. In this interview Mr. González claims that "we have to remove and eliminate all the obstacles to the creation of employment," referring to the objective to set a plant-by-plant wage bargaining system, and less onerous hire-and-fire regulations. He emphasizes, however, that he will force through the measures whether he gets the agreement with the unions or not. The government set a November 30 deadline on the talks, and threatened to approve emergency legislation on December 3. This does not seem like a very flexible stance to guarantee a fruitful bargaining process.

26. Nicolás Redondo argued during our meeting in December 1996, that the government used this scandal as a means to weaken his grip on the union.

27. This point was confirmed by Nicolás Redondo and Antonio Gutiérrez during our meetings in December 1996.

28. Pedro Solbes, former Minister of Economics, is fully convinced that the unions had no interest whatsoever in negotiating with the government. He emphasized this point during our meeting in December 1996.

29. If some workers decide not to accept the agreement negotiated by one of the major unions, then the wage raise agreed upon in the pact will not affect them. This is not very likely, however, because in the absence of other agreements, it would mean that the workers who reject the pact will not have any raise, which is highly undesirable.

30. There is also a clear relationship between declining inflation and wage behavior—which, in turn, determines unitary labor costs—so consequently, concertation, by moderating wage increases, contributed to the low rates of inflation of the mid-1980s.

31. In 1988 53.2 percent of the workers had "safeguard clauses" in their collective agreements.

32. Other factors, such as labor market conditions, also have strong influence on the level of conflict.

33. These arguments were all emphasized by Antonio Gutiérrez and Nicolás Redondo during the interviews that I had with them in December 1996.

34. They claim that Spain's incapacity to eradicate mass unemployment has its roots in the monopolistic power of the insiders. The theoretical underpinning of this position was advanced by Lindbeck and Snower 1988.

35. Although this debate goes beyond the scope of this discussion, it is worth emphasizing that in the 1970s, the economic crisis was compounded by the following factors: First, changes in the social structure favored the entrance of more people to the labor market—that is, the entrance of women to the labor market dramatically expanded the pool of labor in the late 1970s and early 1980s. This problem was aggravated by the fact that many of the new workers did not have adequate skills and could not be hired. At the same time, the obsolescence of the industrial structure meant that it was not ready for the opening of the Spanish economy to foreign competition; when the opening occurred, it resulted in the closure of many firms and businesses. Finally, the lack of an entrepreneurial culture prevented the creation of a strong domestic industry and thus hindered job creation.

36. The recession that swept Europe in the early 1990s also reached Spain and resulted in a further deterioration of the unemployment problem. In 1993 alone, half a million jobs were destroyed, and Spain had only 3.6 million jobs. Unemployment benefits to two million jobless and the existence of safety nets—such as the family—prevented social unrest. The problem is particularly dramatic among young people and women who bear the burden of high unemployment rates. Women have more precarious jobs and less pay for the same work. The consequence of these developments has been that there is now in Spain a segmented and dualized labor market along generation and sex lines, and this is at a time when employed workers see how their real income rose in the 1980s, and when workers in the public sector have gotten job security and higher wage increases than their private counterparts (see Moscoso 1995, 36–40). For another perspective on this issue see Blanchard, et al, 1995.

37. Some other important provisions included in the agreements were not fulfilled. This diminished the credibility of the concertation process. The creation of the Economic and Social Council, CES, and the Advisory Council to the Prime Minister, did not materialize. The CES was created many years later in 1991, but has never fulfilled its expected functions. Finally, some structural objectives introduced in the agreements did not materialize either—for example, social security reform or labor market flexibility. I shall analyze these issues at greater length in chapter 6.

38. Bustelo recognizes, however, that concertation made it possible to dismantle the entire institutional framework of Francoism and to build a new democratic system (Bustelo 1986, 39).

Chapter 4

1. The explanation offered by this literature has been that concertation requires "a relatively high level of unionization; a single labor confederation composed of relatively few, industry-based unions; a considerable amount of collective bargaining power vested in the labor confederations; economy-wide bargaining between labor confederations and employer associations; and in which works councils and codetermination schemes exist" (Cameron 1984, 169).

Schmitter has argued that "the most reasonable hypothesis would be that concertation cannot take place without monopolistic associations, hierarchically organized, officially recognized, and clearly delimited; therefore, once concertation is established, it will stimulate the development of these properties" (Schmitter 1990, 28, my translation).

2. At first, the commissions were disbanded after the conflict was resolved. During the 1960s, however, these commissions extended to industrial sectors and became an organized entity.

3. The supporters of the traditional union that still remained in Spain did not join CCOO because they viewed with skepticism its close links with the Spanish Communist Party, PCE.

4. The USO was founded in 1960 in Bilbao. It opposed the CCOO and emphasized its socialist ideology and independence from political parties. USO also used the *"sindicatos verticales"* and the elections to works councils as a ways to strengthen its position and influence workers. It never reached the strength of CCOO because it lacked the organizational support of a political party. It became the third union far behind the UGT and CCOO after the death of Franco. A very important group of leaders and affiliates, led by its Secretary General, José María Zufiaur, left the USO and integrated into the UGT in 1977.

5. For a more detailed description of these developments see Burns Marañón, 1996. See particularly the interviews with Redondo, Juliá, and Simón.

6. It has been argued that the UGT received extensive support from the new democratic government (Roca 1993, 31). The UCD government, led by the Labor Minister Fernando Abril Martorell, viewed with fear a labor movement monopolized by a communist union, CCOO, and offered support to the UGT. For instance, when the UGT celebrated its XXth Congress in 1976 the government did nothing to impede it despite the fact the UGT was still an illegal organization. When CCOO celebrated its National Assembly shortly afterwards, the government declared it illegal. See Sagardoy Bengoechea and León Blanco 1982, 95. Businesses also viewed CCOO dominance with skepticism and tried to strengthen the UGT as a way to divide (and weaken) the labor movement. The UGT systematically received preferred treatment in the course of negotiations with business. This was reinforced by the bilateral centralized agreements that the UGT and the CEOE signed at the end of the 1970s. This point was emphasized during my interviews with representatives from the business organization, CEOE. Redondo, the UGT's Secretary General, argues the opposite. See interview with Redondo in Santos Juliá et al, 1996, 636.

7. Before the First National Congress, which took place in 1976, the board of CCOO had 26 members, and 24 of them also belonged to the Communist Party. After the Congress, out of the 42 members who took part in the executive committee, 37 also belonged to the PCE. See Guinea, 1978, 167–169.

8. This debate was further strained by the differences between socialists and communists. Events that took place during the Second Republic caused a perma-

nent schism within the socialist family. Forty years later resentments still lingered. The leaders of the Socialist Party also feared that they would be left aside to play a limited role in the new labor organization, because the communist leaders controlled CCOO while they only played a limited role in the UGT (Almendros Morcillo 1978, 266). The Socialist Party leaders also realized that they needed the support of the working class if they wanted to win the elections and refused to collaborate in a project that would strengthen the position of its major competitor within the left, the Communist Party. The other unions, USO, CNT, and ELA-STV in the Basque country, also rejected CCOO's proposal because they did not want to be absorbed by the communist union. At that time, the development of a unitary organization would have meant the dominance of CCOO, given its support among workers and the extensive structure that it had built during the dictatorship (the other unions, except for the USO, had remained mostly in exile and had only played a token role during the dictatorship, thus lacking infrastructure). Another factor that also played a role in the failure of CCOO's unitary initiative was the Spanish workers' preference for a system based on multiple unions (Führer 1996, 89). See also Pérez Díaz 1980, 258.

9. Three unions, the CCOO, UGT, and USO, were still able to create a coordinating organization, the Coordinadora de Organizaciones Sindicales (COS), in July of 1976 in which they were all represented. This institution sought to coordinate the activities of the three unions. Its main objective was to establish a democratic regime where unions' and workers' rights would be recognized. It also sought to reclaim from the government compensation for the union goods that had been confiscated by the dictatorship after the Civil War. Once union freedoms were recognized by the government, the UGT abandoned the COS in 1977, and the organization was shortly disbanded. The role of the unions during the transition process has been extensively researched. See Fishman 1990, Führer 1996.

10. The government also issued two decrees clarifying the rules of industrial relations. One of the decrees regulated collective bargaining and the right to strike, and the other one established worker representation through work councils and the rules for the first democratic elections to the work councils.

11. For instance, in the elections for the work council in workplaces with more than 50 workers, voters have to choose between lists, not candidates, and each list includes only candidates from the same union. This system gives great power to the union, which is the one that nominates the candidates. While groups of workers registered as unions do not need to collect any signatures, independents do need to obtain a certain number of signatures from their coworkers to become candidates. This system makes it very difficult for independent workers to run. The consequence of this system, however, has been that there is a significant number of council members elected on union lists who are not union members. See Escobar 1995, 168–169, and Bouza 1989. Bouza reports that in a survey of members elected on union lists, 24 percent of the councilors confirmed that they were not members. Before the elections,

unions attempt actively to recruit independents for their list, even among personnel delegates, and offer the legal support of the union if candidates decide to run under the union flag. I had this experience when I first ran as a personnel delegate in Control Data Spain in 1990. I had meetings with representatives from the CCOO and UGT, both of which offered strong enticements to induce me to run as their candidate.

12. The consolidation of the labor movement was reinforced in 1977 when some of the USO leaders, led by its Secretary General, José María Zufiaur, and convinced that there was no space for two socialist unions, defected from the USO and joined the UGT. This development definitely strengthened the position of UGT. The CNT failed to recover the support that it had before the Civil War. Within the new economic context and after 40 years of dictatorship, the Spanish workers did not support revolutionary movements. The CNT was later divided into two unions, and it never regained the power it once had. Finally, the ELA-STV, with strong links with the Basque Nationalist Party, PNV, reorganized in the Basque Country and eventually became the strongest union in that region.

13. In this chapter I will only focus on the relationship between unions and business associations. The government-union interaction will be the subject of chapter 6.

14. The sharp increase in affiliation of the late 1970s has been attributed to the euphoria associated with the transition to democracy and the wish by most Spanish workers to participate in public life and contribute to the consolidation of the new regime. The disappearance of the Francoist official union, the Organización Sindical (OS), also had an impact, because it motivated workers to join new unions which could help them articulate their demands. At that time, unions were already playing a political role in the transition process and were highly visible (see Fishman 1990). It has also been argued that high levels of affiliation were also the result of the ideological attraction that unions exercised over workers, at a time when public life was highly politicized as a consequence of the political context (See Miguélez 1995, 217).

15. After the height of the transition period, unions failed to live up to the expectations of their affiliates and were not able to reach agreements favorable to their members. They also failed to develop services to affiliates that would have made membership more attractive. Therefore, once the transition euphoria dissipated, workers decided to cancel their memberships. The economic crisis, increasing unemployment, growth of the service sectors, and underground economy, as well as emerging new forms of business organization wherein traditional blue-collar unskilled workers were no longer dominant, have been mentioned as some of the reasons for this development. For a sociological study of why workers do not support union activity more, see Fishman 1990, 203. In 1978 42 percent of industrial workers were not affiliated with a union. The level of affiliation reached its bottom in the mid-1980s. The success of the general strike of 1988, coupled with the economic recovery of the mid-1980s, ignited new affiliations to unions. Between 1986 and 1989 affiliation increased

44 percent for the UGT, and 33 percent for the CCOO Escobar, 1995, 158. See also Pérez Díaz 1985, Fishman 1990, Führer 1996, Moscoso 1995, Miguélez 1995.

16. The weakness of Spanish unions is also evident in their organization. They lack adequate facilities and infrastructure. They do not have enough financial resources—dues are low to avoid further losses of membership—and they are mostly dependent on state subsidies to survive. They have few employees—the UGT, the largest union, reported less than 100 employees in 1989—a situation that obviously hinders their capacity to serve their affiliates. It has also been argued that the low number of elected officials, coupled with the scarcity of full-time workers and the poor training of their activists, have hindered unions' efficiency. See Escobar 1995, 158.

17. This argument was emphasized during the interviews that I held with Carlos Solchaga, Pedro Solbes, Joaquín Almunia, and José Juan Ruiz, in December 1996.

18. These new reports challenge the pessimistic thesis of union decline and show that in spite of high unemployment, union membership in Spain increased significantly from 1986 to 1993. Jordana attributes this development to the effect of democratic consolidation, as well as to complex union dynamics in the labor market. See Jordana, 1996.

19. Only in special circumstances can sectoral bargaining units approve conditions below the minimum (the *clausulas de descuelge*). The government has also the power to influence bargaining coverage through the use of extension rules, which allow for the extension of sectoral or firm agreements beyond their original scope to firms or sector with similar features. See Blanchard et al. 1995, 121–122.

20. The government approved a decree in December 1977 that temporarily regulated the elections to work councils. The Workers' Statute approved in 1980 (Art. 69–76) replaced that decree and included the electoral procedure for work councils elections. It also includes the rights conferred to works councils—information, consultation, legal action, negotiation, the management of the firm's social funds, and the right to strike. The work councils are elected by the entire workforce of the firm. The number of council members depends on the size of the workplace. The representatives were first elected for two years. A new law approved in August 1984 modified the Workers' Statute and extended the mandate to four years. The law divides the election into two separate groups for firms with more than 45 workers: One group for administrative staff, and the second for unskilled workers in order to assure proportional representation for each group. In workplaces with less than 50 workers, voters can vote for between one and three candidates. In larger workplaces, voters choose between lists. In Spain these elections are called the "union elections." They refer to the ballots to elect the representatives of workers in workplaces. Work councils are legally defined as unitary bodies for the representation of workers at the workplace. They are elected to represent their fellow workers in the work council. In Spain, these elections play a critical role because the state yields to

unions all the rights to represent workers, on the basis of the results of the elections to the work councils. In other words, the electoral results determine the legal representative powers of unions. The unions that receive the most votes in these elections are declared "most representative unions" and are allowed to take part in public institutions that play a role in issues that affect workers and/or unions—such as the Institute of Unemployment, the Health National Institute, or the National Institute for Social Services. Finally, in 1985, the socialist government began to support unions financially in proportion to the numbers of representatives in the works councils which they held (i.e., between 1986–1989 the UGT received 2.127 billion pesetas from the government). The law also acknowledges the unique structure of the Spanish state and includes specific articles that regulate the situation of unions that mostly operate within an autonomous region.

21. This data shows that the Spanish model of industrial relations is based in biunionism and is characterized by the supremacy of two organizations (the UGT and CCOO have always won almost 80 percent of the vote), with the exception of two autonomous regions: the Basque country where ELA-STV (a Christian democratic union with strong links to the Partido Nacionalista Vasco, PNV) won more than 37 percent of the seats in 1990, and Galicia, where a leftist union, the Intersindical de Trabajadores Gallegos, INTG (now CIG) won more than 23 percent. Both the CCOO and UGT represent between 70–80 percent of the delegates in the work councils in the agricultural and industrial sectors, and 60 percent in the service sector.

22. In December of 1995 the government changed the law, eliminating electoral periods and establishing a new system where elections to the work councils take place permanently. Unions and the socialist government agreed to change the laws regulating the work council elections. One of the major decisions adopted was to end the official periods for elections. Since 1996 they have become a permanent process. Now each firm can call its own elections whenever it wants or whenever the mandate of their delegates expire. The results are then given to the Ministry of Labor, which is in charge of establishing the representativeness of each union. In 1997 the CCOO is still the leader and has 85,713 representatives (37.87 percent) elected in the work councils, 6,481 more than the UGT—with 79,232 representatives (35 percent). There is still a 2.87 percent differential between both unions, the same percentage that separated them in 1995 after the sixth "union elections" of the democracy. In 1995 the CCOO had 5,822 representatives more than UGT, but there were less representatives elected. The rest of the unions have 61.392 representatives, or 27,13 percent of the total. See *El País,* July 7, 1997.

23. Unions have organized six general strikes since the beginning of the transition. In 1976 the CCOO organized a strike in support of democracy, freedom and amnesty. The UGT, CCOO and USO called another general strike in 1977 against the referendum for political reform and in support of leftist parties. The CCOO called a third one in 1981 in support of the democratic regime and to oppose the failed coup d'état of February 1982. In 1985 the CCOO alone

called a fourth general strike in opposition to the socialist reform of the pension system. In 1988 both the UGT and CCOO called a general strike to oppose the government youth plan and to demand larger social expenditures and a shift in the government economic policy. In 1992 the UGT and CCOO called a four hour general strike against a decree reducing unemployment benefits. Finally, in 1994, UGT and CCOO called, with less success, a general strike to oppose the reform of the labor market. Of all these general strikes, the one that took place in December 1988 was the most successful, and the one that proved once and for all the mobilizing capacity of unions. See Escobar 1995, 160.

24. This argument was emphasized during the interview that I had with N. Redondo in December 1996.

25. In a ranking of labor market regulations and worker job rights of 18 OECD countries, Spain is the most rigid of all countries (Esping-Andersen 1999, 22). How is it possible that a comparatively weak labor movement has been able to establish the most protective regulatory system? According to Esping-Andersen, the Spanish systems reflects the familialism in labor market management and the need to safeguard the earnings and career stability of the male-bread winner (1999, 23).

26. There is also a union in the public administration, the CSIF (the Confederation of Civil Servants), which received strong electoral support in the 1987 elections (24.9 percent) and in 1990 (20.8 percent).

27. As I indicated on chapter 3, some authors have argued convincingly that the internal structure of labor movements—and specifically the ability of central confederation leaders to coordinate the behavior of workers—is a more important determinant of the success of centralized bargaining than the level of wage bargaining (the variable the I analyze in the next section). The reason for this is that if centralized wage agreements are to be effective, they must be adhered to at lower bargaining levels. See Golden 1993; Garrett 1998, 32–33.

28. In this section I refer mostly to the CCOO and UGT unless indicated. I focus mainly on these two unions because they were the ones that became involved in the concertation process and have received an overwhelming majority of support from workers—even thought the USO also signed the AMI. The organizational structure of other unions is very similar—except for the anarchist CNT. This description applies to the concertation period, 1979–1986. For a more detailed description, see Führer 1996, 149–194.

29. The UGT elects its Confederation Executive Committee with 13 members proposed by the secretary general. This is the permanent body. UGT's Confederation Committee has 120 members with representatives from the federations and regions. It meets every six months. CCOO also elects an Executive Committee with 50 members which meets monthly—and it elects a permanent Executive Council. The other unions have a similar organization (INTG similar to the CCOO's, USO similar to the UGT's, and the ELA-STV a mixture of both). See Führer 1996, 150–153, for a more detailed description.

30. This was a very unpopular measure, and there was strong resistance within the organization. The CCOO, given its large infrastructure and the fact that it also

had to close down offices in many places, faced the stronger resistance. Antonio Guitiérrez mentioned during the interview that I had with him in December 1996, that within the existing economic and functional constraints it is not feasible to sustain such a large organization. The low levels of membership, coupled with the lack of sufficient economic resources, hindered the maintenance of large infrastructures. See also Führer 1996, 171–181.

31. In June 1981 the government and the most representative unions reached an agreement about subsides to unions that was triggered by the failed coup d'état of February of that year. This agreement established that the government would give subsidies to unions (at first of 800 million pesetas) and include them in the budgets for 1982, 1983, 1984. Subsides were linked to the devolution by the state of the unions' wealth confiscated by the Franco regime after the war. See de la Villa 1984, 254. Later on, the Spanish Constitutional Court established that the state had to give subsides to all the unions that had representatives elected in the elections to the work councils and not only to the "most representatives unions." Finally, the socialist government approved a law in 1985 and returned the confiscated wealth to unions. For state subsidies to unions see Díaz Güell 1987, 56, and Führer 1996, 183.

32. Business organizations during the dictatorship were integrated into the *sindicatos verticales*. After Franco's death most business organization transferred directly from the vertical unions to the CEOE.

33. The CEPYME (the Confederación Española de Pequeñas y Medianas Empresas) is the most significant one and still maintains its own structure and statutes within the CEOE. It was integrated into the CEOE in March 1980. The other two, the Confederación de la Pequeña y Mediana Empresa (COPYME), and the Unión de la Pequeña y Mediana Empresa (UNYPIME), also represent medium and small firms.

34. In the CEOE Congress of 1982, 314 delegates came from the sectoral structure, 183 from the territorial, and 83 from the CEPYME. The larger groups of representatives came from metal (46 representatives), construction (39), and the chemical sector (18). The most important territorial organizations are the Basque and the Catalonian (represented by the Fomento Nacional del Trabajo—FNT—one of the oldest business organizations in Spain, dating from 1771). The weight of the Catalonian organization was proven by the fact that its president, Carlos Ferrer Salat, was elected as the first president of the CEOE. The CEOE is dominated by larger firms who contribute the most to the organization and have the larger number of votes. The banking sector is particularly influential. See Führer 1996, 229–231. Later on, with the delegation by the state of powers to the autonomous regions, the CEOE intensified a process of decentralization. See Pardo Avellaneda and Fernández Castro 1995, 162.

35. What was paradoxical, given this approach, was business' response to unions' wage demands. During the first years of the transition, there was a dramatic explosion in wages. For the first time, wages increased above productivity. Business' acquiescence, however, cannot be interpreted as a tolerant position

towards unions. On the contrary, businesses were concerned about the shaky political context and accepted unions' demands to avoid further confrontations that would worsen the already poisoned political climate. They preferred to increase prices, than face the wrath of workers. The consequence was a sharp increase in inflation. See Pérez-Díaz 1984, 40.

36. F. Moreno, F. Jimeno, E. de la Lama, and J. Iranzo confirmed these points to the authors during the interviews that I had with them in December 1996.

37. Since the focus of this book is the concertation period (1979–1986) I shall discuss the collective bargaining system in force at that time based on the Title II of the Workers' Statute approved in March 1980. This is the first law that systematically regulated collective bargaining in Spain.

38. An *open shop* system is one in which workers can choose among various unions and the employers bargaining with the representatives from the unions, in a way in which the results of the bargaining process are applied to all workers regardless of their union affiliation. This system is different from a *closed shop,* in which the agreement is only applied to the workers affiliated to the union, which is typical, for instance, in the United States. See Jimeno 1997, 79.

39. However, the absence of a preexisting democratic framework of collective bargaining forced the legislature to adopt some rules: Collective bargaining was subordinated to the law; it could help create the law but could not oppose the controlling statutes (Martín Valverde 1987, xxx). The Workers' Statue, thus, sets up a system based both on interventionism (i.e., it regulates the actors who can take part in the bargaining process), and industrial democracy (i.e., the actors have autonomy to regulate their relationship, and the structure of the bargaining process). This dichotomy was based on the interest of the lawmakers to develop a system that would foster stability, but would also introduce new areas to autonomous collective bargaining. It thus took a middle position between the old (interventionism) and the new (autonomy of the actors). See Martín Valverde, 1987.

40. Other authors, however, dispute this conclusion. There is a debate among Spanish scholars about the legal framework. Martín Valverde (1985, 80–81), for instance, has argued that the fact that the oldest collective bargain has preference over a new one fosters, indirectly, negotiations at a higher level and centralization. This is so, according to him, because in centralized agreements the actors have complete freedom to negotiate and do not face restrictions. If they close an agreement, it will be applicable immediately and will cover all the issues not regulated by preexisting lower collective bargains. At a lower level, however, negotiators will face the limitations imposed by preexisting collective bargains, and will have to wait until the expiration of those pacts. According to Martín Valverde, the fact that the application of a new negotiated agreement has to be postponed until the expiration of any preexisting one, will act as a deterrent to open new negotiations at a lower level. Other authors (Rodríguez Piñero 1983, 137) have even talked about a "hierarchic relationship" among collective agreements. According to this view, Article 84 of the Workers' Statute limited negotiations at lower levels if they were not authorized by collective agreements

negotiated at higher levels as specified in Article 83. This article prevented "un-hooking" from existing agreements. A final group of authors (Valdés Dal-Re 1994, 18) have argued, on the other hand, that although it is true that the higher the level of negotiation, the less limitations the bargainers will face because the collective agreement will be larger in scope and will cover many issues not covered by preexisting agreements, it is also true that, regardless of the level of negotiation, collective bargains will always be limited by preexisting pacts and can only be applied to issues not covered by them. According to him, negotiators at higher levels will also be deterred in opening negotiations if they know that many of the issues on the table will not be applicable because there are preexisting bargains that already cover those issues. The tendency towards centralization can be, thus, balanced by decentralized impulses.

41. After Franco's death, however, there was a tendency toward fewer agreements at the provincial level, and more at the national level. This was due to the fact that the Francoist legislation forbade agreements at the national level, and old sectoral agreements, which applied to all workers, were renamed and became national agreements. See Valdés Dal-Re 1995, 22.

42. This tendency was reversed after 1992. In 1993 there were 4,749 collective agreements; in 1994, 4,199; and in 1995, 3,500.

43. During the interviews that I had with Nicolás Redondo, Sergio Santillán (UGT), Antonio Gutiérrez (CCOO), and Fernando Moreno (CEOE), in December 1996 they all agreed that part of the reason behind the increase in the number of agreements at the firm level was the application until 1995 of the preexisting Labor Ordinances, which predated the democratic regime. These ordinances regulated many issues that should have been covered by collective agreements at higher levels. They were abolished in 1994.

44. This development was reinforced by the fact that the Workers' Statute establishes that agreements at the sectoral or the sectoral/provincial level apply to all workers in firms in the sector or province (Art. 82.3). Over the period 1984–1991 more than 80 percent of Spanish workers were covered by sectoral/province collective bargains, 13 percent by firm level agreements, and 7 percent by agreements negotiated at the national level. See Blanchard et al. 1995, 120; Pérez 1996.

45. One of the stated objectives of the concertation process was precisely to rationalize the decentralization and fragmentation of the collective bargaining system. The fact that unions and employers were willing to negotiate centralized agreements in the late 1970s and early 1980s confirms this objective. The five centralized agreements, however, did not help foster centralization. Between 1979–1986, the years of concertation, unions and business negotiated more than 3,000 agreements per year (too high a number for a centralized system). Several reasons have been offered to account for this development. On the one hand, inertia. Decentralized wage bargaining has been a common practice in Spain since the late 1950s. It was seen as a way by unions and business to circumvent the strict regulations imposed by the dictatorship. Moreover, after a long period of time characterized by strong state interventionism in industrial relations, the so-

cial actors valued very strongly their newly-acquired autonomy and refused to let the state make decisions for them. Furthermore, a critical factor was the fact that the Worker's Statute had not abolished the old Labor Ordinances, which regulated labor relations in most sectors during the dictatorship. This hindered any interest on the part of the social actors to regulate themselves on those issues covered by the ordinances—which the Workers' Statute allowed them to do. On the one hand, unions wanted to open negotiations with the ordinances as a starting point because they considered some of the provisions contemplated in the ordinances as good for the workers. Business, for its part, considered many of those rights outdated and wanted to start the process anew. Furthermore, most of the issues included in the ordinances, given their complexity and scope, would have had to be negotiated at least at the industry level, but this was becoming increasingly difficult given the new political structure of Spain, with emerging unions in the autonomous regions that refused to give up their power and consent to centralized negotiations. When some of the business sectors (i.e., the chemistry sector in the early 1980s) took the initiative and signed agreements with unions to replace the ordinances, some other business sectors reacted against this development (i.e., metal and hotel business). Finally, there was an absence of a negotiating tradition among Spanish business and workers, and in this context it was far more comfortable for them to continue adopting the rules that had been imposed by the state, and that they have been applying for years than negotiate new rules. In general both workers and employers prefer rules rather than agreements. I confirmed these conclusions during my interviews with leaders of the CEOE (F. Moreno, F. Marquez, F. Jimeno) and unions (S. Santillán, N. Redondo, A. Gutiérrez) in December 1996.

46. In the 1990s and despite the fact that there seemed to be common agreement that one of the major caveats of the Spanish collective bargain structure was its excessive decentralization, the government somehow was convinced that the Workers' Statute had not resulted in the necessary flexibility and decentralization of collective bargaining. The new Law of November 1994 prevented framework agreements negotiated at higher levels from defining the levels under which negotiation was possible (Art. 84.2)—a common practice in the past. The reform also modified the resolution of conflicts among agreements, attributing preference to latter pacts negotiated at a lower level (Art. 83.2), thus breaking the old principle *prior in tempore*. The social actors also lost the autonomy to decide the content of the agreements and the issues that could be left for negotiation at lower levels—the new Article 84.3 includes a list with the issues that cannot be negotiated or be left out for negotiation at lower levels, thus introducing rigidities and increasing the state's interventionism in the negotiating process. One of the major consequences of the reform was that by giving actors at lower levels the right to withdraw from previous agreements negotiated at higher levels, the new law hindered negotiations at higher levels—particularly at the national level. What is the point of negotiating a centralized agreement when any actor at a lower level can repudiate it and negotiate another pact that opposes it? This development had even worse consequences, given the fact that

the new law also established the abolition of the still-existing Francoist Labor Ordinances that regulated important sectors of the economy. It is still too early to evaluate the consequences of the reform. What is even more puzzling is the fact that neither unions nor business agreed with the direction of the reform. The UGT, CCOO, and the CEOE signed a bilateral agreement in April 1997 that sought to rationalize the collective bargaining process and limit its fragmentation. See Fernández López 1995.

47. The consequences of this system, according to these authors has been that there is an excessive union pressure, particularly in favor of less qualified workers, that has resulted in higher unemployment because unions have been particularly effective at pushing for higher wages for this category of workers. See Dolado, Felgueroso, and Jimeno 1997. These authors defend the elimination of the general efficacy of collective agreements negotiated above the firm level, the modification of the clauses of representative capacity to negotiate collective agreements above the firm level, and the articulation of collective bargaining at the territorial level. See Jimeno 1997, 85.

48. Part of the reason for this development is explained by the fact that the Spanish legislation attributes "limited efficacy" to agreements signed only by one of the major unions without absolute majority in the negotiating commission (i.e., they cannot be applied to all workers, only to those who adhere to the pact), but in reality most workers prefer to adhere to those agreements because if they are left out, they will not receive the wage increases included in the pact. Spanish courts have stated repeatedly that in these cases workers have the right to reject the agreement and return the extra money that they had received as a result of the increase negotiated in the collective bargain. This is an option, that, for obvious reasons, few workers choose. See Roca 1993, 184.

49. See Pérez 1996, and Blanchard et al. 1995, for an evaluation of the impact of the wage bargaining setting on wages and unemployment.

50. This challenges the argument later used by the government that argued that it did not need the unions to achieve wage moderation. The fact that wages grew moderately in 1984 despite the lack of agreement convinced the socialist economic team that they could produce wage moderation without concertation and without the unions. Later, events proved the lack of foundation for this assessment. I shall deal with this point more extensively in chapter 6.

51. This was argued by several people from the socialist economic team in government. In the course of my interviews with C. Solchaga, J. J. Ruiz, and P. Solbes in December 1996, they all expressed this idea in different ways. See also Escobar 1995.

52. For a detailed analysis on the effect that the union system of representative criteria had on the Spanish industrial relations setting, see Garcia Murcia, Gutiérrez Palacios, and Rodríguez Sañudo 1995.

Chapter 5

1. The relatively closed nature of the Spanish economy was reflected by the fact that imports of manufactured goods in 1986 were equivalent to 11.0 percent

of Spain's GDP and industrial exports were only 10.9 percent of GDP. In the EC the averages were 14.4 percent and 27.7 percent of GDP, respectively; see Hine 1989, 7.

2. The degree of openness of the Spanish economy (i.e., exports and imports of goods and services relative to GDP) was 26.4 percent in the 1971–1974 period, 40.3 percent from 86–90, and reached 61.1 percent by 1995. See CES 1996, 68.

3. During the crisis, the Spanish economy moved back 17 years: per capita GDP was 72.1 percent of the European average in 1985, the same level that it was in 1968. See Fuentes Quintana, 1989, 22–25.

4. This development meant that the service sector increased its participation in the Spanish economy from 42.3 percent to 54.4 percent of GDP between 1977 and 1989. This occurred at a time when the process of agricultural restructuring had intensified (only 12.5 percent of the active population worked in the agriculture sector by 1989). Between 1977 and 1989, the percentage of people working in the industrial and service sectors evolved from 27.4 and 42 percent to 23.7 and 54.4 percent of the total active population, and 85 percent of new jobs were created in the service sector. Although this process of deindustrialization also took place in other Western European countries—for example, between 1981 and 1985, the yearly rate of industrial employment destroyed in France was 1.8 percent, 1.2 percent in Italy, 2 percent in Germany, and 2.6 percent in the United Kingdom—this process was more intense in the Spanish case (4.6 percent). The reason was the lack of competitiveness of the Spanish industrial structure (the consequence of decades of protectionism), and the generalized absence of systematic responses to address the impact of new technologies in productive processes.

5. According to this view, labor differentiation and segmentation were further hastened in Spain by the reform of 1984, which introduced the possibility of temporary hiring. In 1987 only 15.8 percent of the workers were temporary; by 1992 this figure had reached 33.5 percent of the workers. There was another reform in 1994 which introduced new hiring modalities. This has resulted in yet more temporary workers—34 percent had such contracts in 1997. Spain now has the highest levels of temporary workers in Western Europe.

6. Union leaders decided that the high levels of temporary contracts could threaten the activities of their organizations (Roca 1993, 261). The fact that they called a general strike in 1988 over a government's project to beef up temporary contracts seems to confirm these fears. The governmental "youth employment project" would have allowed firms to hire workers and pay them the minimum wage, with the only condition that the newly hired were between 16–25 years old, and that they would not have worked in the past. Through these contracts, firms would have obtained important public subsidies and would have been able to extend the period under which they could have a person under a temporary contract. See Recio and Roca 1988–1989, 169–187.

7. What is paradoxical about the Spanish case, as noted in chapter 4, is that, contrary to expectations, concertation took place in Spain precisely during the period (1978–1986) in which the data suggest that Spanish unions were

becoming weaker and losing members. Since 1986 new studies are reporting a recovery in the levels of membership (Miguélez 1995, 216). Therefore, the Spanish case seems to show an inverse correlation between unions' strength and concertation (Moscoso 1995, 24–26). When unions membership was declining (1978–1986) concertation took place. When membership recovered after 1986 concertation collapsed. This sequence also took place in Italy in the early 1980s. Between 1980–1988, after the period of *"Solidarietá Nationale,"* unions lost over 1 million members, but concertation resumed in 1983 when the government and the social actors signed a centralized agreement to reduce inflation through incomes policy (Liso 1990, 99; Regini 1991, 125–137). At the same time, unions' affiliation increased in the early 1990s in Spain and other countries, but renewed union strength did not result in the reemergence of concertation until 1997, when a new conservative government was in power.

8. It is also important to highlight that, given unions' scarce support in small firms, it is in their best interests to negotiate at higher levels. Decentralization would only mean the exclusion of the big confederations. They lack the infrastructure to gather information about conditions in small firms. Therefore, centralized bargaining seems like a better way to improve the situation of their affiliates by negotiating at a higher level, where unions are stronger (Moscoso 1995, 52). In the course of my interviews with union and business representatives in December 1996, they all favored centralized agreements with flexibility to set particular issues at lower levels.

9. As I indicated above, some authors have argued in the 1990s that labor market institutions lost the ability to tailor wage developments to external competitiveness constraints (Iverson 1996, Pontusson and Swenson 1996). Garrett argues, however, that although public sector strength has become a significant obstacle to optimal wage setting in Scandinavia, because it is not subject to competitiveness constraints, the experience of Austria, where there are legal restriction of public workers rights, offers potential solutions to this challenge. Alternatively, Garrett proposes to reduce public sector employment and unionization, or to weaken the commitment to wage solidarity and replace it with tax transfers like in Austria (1998, 148–149).

10. See interview with Felipe González "Sober after the Feast," *Financial Times,* Monday, October 11, 1993, p. 28. During the interviews that I conducted with José Juan Ruiz, Chief of Staff of the Minister of Economics; Carlos Solchaga, Minister of Economics; and Pedro Solbes, the successor Minister of Economics (1993–1996); they all argued that Spain's access into the EC and its integration to the world economy eroded the autonomy of the government to select macroeconomic policies because the Spanish economy had become increasingly exposed to international forces. They also mentioned the influence that France's failed experimenting with demand polices had in their strategies.

11. See Burns Marañón, 1996; particularly see interviews with Solchaga, 149–172, and with Boyer, 303–304.

12. The option to implement expansionary policies was further constrained, according to socialist policymakers, by the severity of the Spanish economic cri-

sis as proven by extremely high levels of inflation, unemployment, and public and trade deficits. The existing levels of unemployment—over 16 percent in 1982, twice the average of the other European nations—coupled with the growing public deficit, the widening income gap with other industrialized nations, and the worrisome levels of capital investment were seen as the main challenges for the new government. The magnitude of these problems, according to government officials, prevented the implementation expansionary policies, particularly at a time of international crisis when the most important central banks, the U.S. Federal Reserve and the German Bundesbank, were implementing restrictive economic policies. See Boix 1996, 147.

13. The government refused to acknowledge that unions had contributed to wage moderation, and wages had fallen short of inflation in every year except 1987, while real unit labor costs had also decreased (Roca 1993, 234). This decline resulted in a 5 percent reduction in the share of salaried workers in national income. In spite of these facts, the government refused to accept that the resurgence in inflation had less to do with wage growth, and more with short-term capital inflows that resulted from high interest rates and from the oligopolistic character of the financial sector, which was seeking to expand profits at the expense of productive investment. See Pérez 1994, 27.

14. This argument was emphasized by Carlos Solchaga, former minister of Economics, during our interview in December 1996.

15. Spanish monetary policy in the late 1980s was characterized by the government's attempt to protect sovereignty in the financial sector and the reliance on foreign investment to satisfy the financial needs of the industry and service sectors. This policy was based on high interest rates and an overvalued currency to limit wage growth and attract foreign investment. The tight character of monetary policy was the result of the emphasis placed by the socialist economic team on the inflationary dynamics of the Spanish economy. Inflation was viewed as the core problem of the Spanish economy and lack of competitiveness thereof. European integration required convergence with the hard core countries, and this meant that low inflation was the highest priority, and that wage restraint was the instrument to achieve it. They viewed economic adjustment almost exclusively as a matter of limiting wage growth, and saw EMS membership as a way to foster convergence with Spain's European counterparts and to reinforce their commitment to reduce inflation and discipline wages. Therefore, they adopted a "strong currency/low wage" adjustment strategy that sought to compensate the lack of competitiveness of Spanish firms with foreign capital inflows (Pérez 1994, 23). For a more detailed analysis of these policies see chapter 6.

16. Unions at this time had reached a point of no return in their relationship with the socialist government. Despite the fact that the government had acknowledged many of their demands, union leaders adopted a maximalist position and refused to accept the government's terms.

17. The decision to reduce the deficit was presented as the best mean to build up savings and investment. A low deficit would also help to contain inflation

because it would help to reduce interest rates and the cost of capital (Boix, 1994, 30).

18. Therefore, the deficit decreased from 6.9 percent of GDP in 1985 to less than 3 percent in 1989. The deficit reduction, however, was the consequence of the spectacular growth experienced by the Spanish economy and an increase in tax base, not the result of fiscal discipline. Therefore, when the recession hit Spain in the early 1990s, the deficit surged—5 percent in 1991—and it spiraled out of control when the government agreed to satisfy unions' demands after 1988.

19. As a result of these developments, both social expenditures and public investment increased dramatically after 1988. The consequence was that state expenditures rose from 23.2 percent of GDP in 1990 to 26 percent of GDP in 1992 (2.9 points over the initial budget), and the public debt increased from 43.7 percent of GDP in 1989 to 48.2 percent in 1992.

20. New reports are emphasizing that the link between budget deficits and inflation is much weaker than previously anticipated. These reports emphasize that there is little relationship between monetary stability and fiscal rectitude. For 20 years Belgium, for instance, averaged a deficit of 6 percent of GDP, yet its exchange rate increased. Sweden and Finland, on the contrary, had balanced budgets (or even surpluses) but their currencies depreciated. These reports conclude that deficits matter as prove that the governments are observing their commitments. See Samuel Brittan, "Cloud over the Euro," *Financial Times,* Thursday, September 11. See also article by Paul de Grauwe, in the *Financial Times,* July 11, 1997.

21. Aside from interruptions in periods of economic crisis, centralized agreements have been regularly concluded in Belgium since 1960. Every two years, these central bipartite pacts shape the agenda for industrial relations and social policy and, as such, they are seen as a focal point of the Belgian system. The last agreement for 1995 and 1996 was concluded on December 7, 1994 by the major employers and trade union organizations. See the *European Industrial Relations Review,* April 1995.

22. In Italy trade unions and employers reached agreements in 1992 and 1993, which sought to prevent the devaluation following the EMS crisis from turning into an inflationary spiral (Regini 1995).

23. One of the building blocks of the recent Irish and Danish economic successes has been the signing of social pacts among the social actors exchanging tax cuts for moderate wage demands. These pacts have helped to restrain inflation, boost competitiveness, and provide foreign companies with a clearer investment horizon. See "Green is Good," in *The Economist,* May 17, 1997, pp. 21–24. See also John Murray Brown, "Will Miracles Never Cease?," *Financial Times,* Tuesday, June 10, 1997; and John Murray Brown and Robert Chote, "Too Much of a Good Thing," *Financial Times,* Thursday, June 10, 1999, p. 15. According to this last article, incomes policies have been one of the main reasons behind the good performance of the Irish economy, which has surged ahead at around 9 percent a year since 1997 (comparatively, economic growth across the euro-zone has averaged a disappointing 2.5 percent a year in the

same period). Incomes policies in Ireland have helped to keep inflation relative low (1.4 percent), and have contributed to a more sustainable level of growth, According to the authors a successful negotiation between management and unions on a replacement for the current three-year wages pact, which ends this year (1999), could prove critical to sustain Ireland's high levels of growth with low inflation.

24. New studies are lauding the role of centralized bargaining in economic performance. In recent years the Netherlands have been used as an example of structural reform. Dutch economic growth has been faster in the past five years than either the French or German. The Netherlands also had a very good inflation performance and has reduced the deficit below the 3 percent Maastricht criterion, and all this within an economic system based on consensus and centralized guided wage bargaining—which has produced a marginal fall in gross real wages from 1991–1996. The Dutch, however, have been able to maintain high social benefits and redistributive policies through high taxes (60 percent top personal tax rate), while reducing public expenditures and cutting corporate taxes. See Brittan, Samuel, "New Role Models for Old," in *Financial Times,* February 28, 1997, p. 10. Other reports, however, emphasize the difficulties in extending this model to larger countries. According to Thomas Mayer of the *Goldman Sachs European Economics Analyst,* the smaller the country and the more equal the existing income distribution, the greater the possibility to introduce adjustment through consensus and centralized bargaining. He points out the case of Austria and Norway. See Mayer, and Grillet-Aubert, 1997. New economic studies are also challenging the conclusion that centralized bargaining and corporatism are dysfunctional in modern economies. According to them, modern economies face three major challenges: "prisoner dilemmas, coordination games, and bargaining games." For each one of these problems, unions and concertation can help. See Hargreaves Heap, 1994.

25. Münchau, Wolfang, and Gordon Cramb, "Debunking the Dutch Myth," in the *Financial Times,* Thursday, September 18, 1997, p. 13.

26. The institutional similarities between Spain and Portugal are striking. In Portugal the two main labor confederations are the General Confederation of Portuguese Workers (CGTP) with strong links to the Communist party, and the General Union of Workers (UGT) with links to the Socialist and Social Democratic parties. Union density in Portugal is also comparatively low. From the business standpoint the situation is even less favorable to concertation. Business is divided into three main organizations, one representing industry, another one the trade and service sectors, and a last one the agricultural one. See Monteiro Fernandes 1999, 113. There are also strong parallelisms in the concertation processes in both countries. In Portugal concertation emerged in the context of the deep economic recession of 1983–1985, characterized by instability and the pessimism of the economic actors; concertation emerged in an environment characterized by the absence of an adequate institutional framework (like in Spain, the definition of the framework was one of the main objectives of the concertation process) the concertation process was initiated and

instigated by the government; some of the years the social actors failed to reach agreements, and one of the labor confederations, the CGTP, has only participated in two of the agreements (the 1991 complementary agreements about security and hygiene in the workplace); the Confederation of Portuguese Industry, the CIP, refused to sign the 1988 agreement, and the Confederation of Portuguese Agricultural Sector, the CAP, did not sign the 1990 one. One of the key differences was the presence of the Permanent Commission of Social Concertation, an autonomous organization of the Economic and Social Council with representatives from the social actors in charge of facilitating the process. For an evaluation of the agreements see Da Silva Lopes 1999, 94–96. For challenges to the process see Monteiro Fernandes 1999, 115.

27. In 1991 the social actors signed two complementary agreements regulating professional training, hygiene, and security in the workplace.

28. The agreement also includes the establishment of a commission to follow up and guarantee the fulfillment of its provisions integrated by representatives from the signatories.

29. Da Silva Lopes (1999, 95–96) attributes the success of concertation in Portugal to a combination of factors: an adequate economic and political climate; the ability of the social actors to reconcile their differences and reach consensus; the power of peak confederations to enforce the agreements at the lower levels; the ability of the social actors to incorporate the demands of other groups not represented in the negotiations; and the ability of the social actors to reach agreements flexible enough to respond to changing competitive, economic, and technological conditions while allowing for productivity and regional differences that exist in any country.

30. See *Financial Times,* Wednesday, March 31, pp. 11–13.

31. Some authors are emphasizing political and ideological variables—such as conservative governments in power or business opposition to unions as a result of the adoption of liberal principles—to account for the decline of centralized bargaining and concertation. See Freeman 1992, 377–398.

32. Garrett focuses on 14 OECD countries: Austria, Sweden, Finland, Denmark, Norway, Italy, Germany, Belgium, Netherlands, United Kingdom, Japan, Canada, United States, and France. He uses the best available data and the most appropriate econometric techniques to test the empirical validity of his arguments about the relationship among globalization and domestic politics, policy, and performance. Swank focuses on 16 advanced democracies (Garrett's plus Australia and Switzerland).

33. Garrett recognizes, however, that inflation rates were higher under more encompassing labor market institutions (1998, 117–120). He attributes this development to several factors: a simple Phillips curve explanation; the dynamics of the wage-setting process in countries with encompassing labor market institutions; and the strategies of leaders of encompassing unions who seek to further their interest in wage restraint and income inequality. For these leaders it is easier to generate real—rather than nominal—wage restraint (1998, 124–125).

34. Garrett shows, however, that social democratic (SD) corporatist countries have been forced to cut corporate tax rates. Nevertheless, he emphasizes that corporatist regimes historically have generated less revenue from corporate income taxes than other countries. He argues that corporatist countries were forced to reform their corporate tax structures because investment incentives proved susceptible to abuses by firms.

35. According to Garrett, the Nordic recessions of the 1990s were precipitated by the end of the Cold War and exacerbated by the economic consequences of the German reunification. According to him, the German Bundesbank reacted to the irresponsible economic policies of the Kohl government after reunification (particularly his decision to convert *ostmarks* one-for-one, and to transfer millions of DM to the East without raising taxes) by sharply increasing interest rates. The interest rates, according to Garrett, were then passed on to the EMS countries, exacerbating the recessions in these countries. This, as we saw above, resulted in the effective dismantling of the European Rate Mechanism (ERM). This development was particularly devastating for Sweden and Finland because they had decided to join the EMS at that time and to commit to a hard money strategy to apply for EMU membership. Both governments stuck to their hard currency strategy until short-term interest rates became untenable and their foreign currency reserves were exhausted. This strategy had devastating macroeconomic consequences for these two countries and help to explain the sharp increase in unemployment (Garrett 1998, 142–143).

36. As quoted by Swank 1998, 10.

37. Garrett argues that SD corporatist economies can provide numerous benefits to capital that will elicit mobile asset holders to remain in these countries and not exercise their exit threat. According to new growth theory, government spending can increase competitiveness by generating collective goods that are undersupplied by the market—for example, education, training, physical infrastructure—that contribute to growth. Asset holders will be willing to pay higher taxes in exchange for these benefits as long as the costs in forms of taxes do not outweigh the benefits. Moreover, welfare state policies, industrial subsidies, and policies that attempt to mitigate market dislocations increase the incentives for leaders of encompassing labor market institutions to restrain overall wage growth to increase competitiveness, which will be beneficial for mobile asset holders. Finally, he argues that government spending contributes to social stability by reducing income inequality, which in turn increases investment and growth (1998, 44–45).

38. Even when the balance sheet was not all positive for SD corporatism—in the 1980s it experienced higher public sector deficits, interest rates, and inflation—these costs should be weighed against the benefits of SD corporatism: reduced inequality, faster growth, and lower unemployment (Garrett 1998, 133).

39. While recognizing that the business cycle might have some influence over concertation, Schmitter acknowledges that this variable will not be enough to guarantee the viability and future survival of neocorporatist agreements. Structural changes—such as the emergence of new production methods, the

internationalization of economies—also lead him to question the viability of neocorporatist agreements. See Schmitter 1990, and Schmitter 1991.

40. Espina recognizes, however, that circumstances associated with the economic cycle are not sufficient to account for the collapse of concertation. He emphasizes another three factors: The Youth Employment Plan, the relative deprivation of civil servants and people dependent from the budget, and finally, the lack of fulfillment by the employers of clauses linking productivity and wage increases (Espina 1991, 211–219).

41. MTSS, 1986, pp. 7–8. Roca (1993, 191) disagrees with this conclusion. He argues that "larger wage homogenization does not always means a reduction in wage differentials, or that they increase if collective bargaining is decentralized." According to him, decentralized bargaining can also result, under certain circumstances, in higher increases for workers in weaker sectors. This is what happened during the early 1970s.

42 The UGT leaders argued that if the union acceded to the government demands after 1986 it would result in the further electoral losses to CCOO. The UGT leaders already viewed the results of the 1986 work council elections as an strategic defeat because they lost votes vis-à-vis CCOO in large strategic firms. Moreover, union leaders argued that further wage moderation would dismantle the principle under which concertation took place—that is, workers, through wage moderation, contributed to the recovery of business profits and the economy. These sacrifices, however, would be compensated when the economic recovery materialized. In reality, the economy picked up after 1985 but workers did not receive any immediate benefits. Nicolás Redondo emphasized this argument when I met with him in December (1996).

43. As we have seen before, unions refused to back up the government's polices and viewed with skepticism any attempt of incomes policies that would impose further sacrifices to workers. Disregarding the fact that the crisis was also affecting other industrialized countries, unions affirmed that it was the result of the policies pursued by the government. Union opposition to concertation had been established long before. After the general strike of December 1988, the unions refused to enter any negotiation with the government, despite the fact that the government reacted to the strike with a generous package of economic measures that included compensation for income losses due to deviation from inflation targets, and extended unemployment benefits.

44. In Spain, on the contrary, wage drift happened after 1986, but it was not always linked to productivity. This had a wage deprivation effect that intensified conflict among workers, see Roca 1993, 225–230.

Chapter 6

1. According to Lang (1981, 252–253), the transition process fostered an extraordinary situation of equilibrium between labor and capital that facilitated the emergence of neocorporatist structures. The termination of the transition period, however, meant the end of that equilibrium and a reinforcement of cap-

ital, which resulted in the breakdown of concertation. See Führer 1996, 40–43.

2. In Spain the Consejo Económico y Social (the CES or Economic and Social Council) was founded in 1992, well after concertation collapsed. It does not yet have the institutional clout of the Portuguese CPCS.

3. This view was emphasized during the interviews that I had with union leaders in December 1996. It also finds some support in the public declarations from union leaders. They have recognized openly that the compromising attitude of unions "was born out of the goal to contribute to the consolidation of the democratic system and not from a concertation or neocorporatist strategy" (Zufiaur, 1985, 204). They have also argued that the concertation process was the consequence of "political reasons" and was also specifically developed for the transition process (Gutiérrez 1988, 121–122). It has also been argued that CCOO leaders only accepted concertation under such exceptional political circumstances like the transition to democracy (Führer 1996, 293). They only signed the ANE (after the February 1981 failed coup d'état) and the AI in 1883. It is for this reason that some union leaders argue that it is incoherent to talk about the concertation process as "an autonomous, coherent, and homogenous process" (Gutiérrez 1988, 122). According to Gutiérrez, politics came first and concertation followed it. In 1987 Nicolás Redondo (Secretary General of the UGT) stated that "the tripartite pacts, are no longer possible. They were feasible during the transition because we were looking for political legitimacy" (Estefanía and Serrano 1990, 17).

4. This view finds some support among union leaders. According to some union leaders—such as A. Gutiérrez from the CCOO—social concertation had been used as an instrument to consolidate the democratic regime but could not be used as an alibi to justify and support government policies. According to him, changing political circumstances required new approaches. Therefore they could not accept the government's position, a stance summarized by a famous phrase by Prime Minister González: "I ask for my government, at least, the same sacrifices that unions have made under conservative governments" (my translation). Antonio Gutiérrez, Secretary General of CCOO, mentioned this sentence that Felipe González, the Prime Minister, told him during the negotiations that let to the AES in 1984. The CCOO refused to accept the government's terms and did not sign the AES. See also Gutiérrez 1988, 121–122.

5. Some Spanish scholars also dispute the argument that has linked the collapse of concertation to the transition process. See Roca 1993, 246; Führer 1996, 345–349; and Moscoso 1995, 67.

6. Two months after the electoral victory of the socialists, the UGT, the CCOO, and the CEOE, signed the "Acuerdo Interconfederal." The new government was interested in starting the legislative period with social peace and supported the agreement but did not sign it. By signing the agreement, UGT, ecstatic with the triumph of its "sister" organization, the PSOE, sought to support the new government's policies. CCOO leaders, still shocked about the magnitude of the socialist victory and aware that most of its supporters had voted for the

PSOE, decided to participate in the pact. Finally, the CEOE wanted to contribute to overcome the economic crisis and sought to open up a window of collaboration with the new government (Führer 1996, 365–366; Moscoso 1995, 65–67). See chapter 3.

7. By 1984 political concerns over the strength of the new regime had dissipated. The CCOO emphasized this fact on its Third Congress, which took place in 1984 (Führer 1996, 301–302). The socialists had been governing the country for almost two years and had overcome the threats against the democratic system. The military was firmly under civilian control, many of the skeletons from the old regime had been purged, and the government had came out victorious from its confrontation with other powers—that is, the Church and some capital groups (Pastor 1996, 533–537). Therefore, by 1984, political considerations related to the strength of the democratic regime had moved to another level. Consequently, this lowered the predisposition of certain unions, particularly the CCOO, towards concertation. At this time the major consideration for the social actors was the economic crisis. Despite strong indicators that the crisis was mitigating, the social costs of adjustment were becoming evident. Unemployment remained very high (20.9 percent in 1984) public expenditures (particularly social benefits) stagnated, and there was a regression in the redistribution of income, increasing industrial conflict, and more poverty (see Alonso 1991, 409). The AES had a significant relevance for two reasons. First, it was the first time that the socialist government had participated explicitly in a neocorporatist agreement. Second, it was also the first time that a neocorporatist agreement had been signed in Spain within a political system where democratic institutions were consolidated and the social actors' position had been institutionalized.

8. After a period of intense disputes between the unions and the government, which culminated in the historic general strike of December 1988, the government attempted to reach agreements with the unions in at least four instances. These included the 1990 "Pacto de Competitividad," the 1992 "Pacto Social del Progreso," and the 1993 negotiations between Pedro Solbes, the last socialist Minister of Economics, and union leaders. Only in one instance, however, did they reach a limited agreement: The 1990 "Acuerdos del 20 de Enero" (see chapter 3). Subsequent negotiations failed because the social actors could not agree, not because the democratic institutions were consolidated after the transition.

9. Union leaders agree that with this pact, they have returned to the concertation path, which had been abandoned after the rupture between the UGT and the Socialist Party/government. The other major consequence of this agreement is that unions and business have been able by themselves to tackle one of the most difficult and controversial aspects of the labor legislation, making the labor market more flexible, without the government's intervention. Nowadays, union leaders recognize that the preponderant role of the government in the concertation process was necessary at the beginning in order to contribute to the establishment and consolidation of the democratic system. This role is no

longer necessary so now direct negotiations between business and labor have acquired a predominant role. See "El Dilema de los Sindicatos," in *El País,* June 23, 1997. Finally, it is worth highlighting that both the CCOO and UGT have taken part in the agreement, something that has not happened since 1983.

10. See article by Saracibar, A., (Redondo's deputy in UGT), in *El País,* December 13, 1988, p. 20. As quoted in Roca 1993, 252.

11. See Gillespie 1991, 379–388 for an explanation of the ideological shift of the PSOE in the late 1970s.

12. The consequence of these changes was that the critics, who were supported by as much as 40 percent of PSOE members, were only able to elect 10 percent of the delegates for the Extraordinary Congress of 1979. See Share 1989, 56.

13. For a deeper analysis of the relationship between UGT and the PSOE see Burns Marañón, 1996; see particularly Burns' interviews with Santos Juliá, Alfonso Guerra, Manuel Simón, Nicolás Redondo, and Carlos Solchaga. See also Gillespie 1991, and Juliá 1997.

14. See interview with Redondo in Burns Marañón 1996, 203–204. See also interview with Redondo in Juliá, Pradera, and Prieto 1996, 635.

15. Some scholars have argued that union leaders refused to accept that changes in the world economy would require new policies. Unions also refused to acknowledge the fact that wage increases in sectors of the economy with higher job security and better organization (the ones where unions received more support from workers) would result in a "dualization of the labor market." See Moscoso 1995, 68. This analysis seems questionable. My meetings with union leaders confirmed that they were fully aware of these developments and were also willing to make sacrifices to contribute to economic recovery. The acceptance of income policies by the UGT and CCOO in the early 1980s proved their willingness to compromise in both objectives and strategies. When the economy improved, however, they also expected compensation from the government, but the latter never materialized. On the contrary, the government used the budget surplus in 1987 to reduce the deficit while reducing pension benefits.

16. The UGT leader had served as minister of labor in a socialist cabinet in the past. Francisco Largo Caballero had been Minister of Labor from 1931 until 1933. This was one of the reasons offered by González and Guerra to promote such an arrangement in 1982. However, when they proposed José Luís Corcuera as Minister of Labor—he was one of the union leaders and the projected successor to Nicolás Redondo—the union rejected such a possibility. By 1982 the union leadership had decided that they would accept any nomination except that of minister of labor. They were afraid that a UGT leader in such a position would be faced with a conflict of interests when he/she had to adopt some of the measures demanded by the economic crisis. By then the union leadership was aware of the risk that the transfer from the union position to the government position would have on their members, who could then be considered agents of the government. See Burns Marañón 1996, 210.

17. In contrast, in the 1970s the German DGB (The West German Trade Union Confederation) had 7,000 full-time employees, and the British TUC (the Trades Union Congress) 2,500 and between 4,000 and 5,000 administrators. See Salvador and Almendros Morcillo 1972, 47–67; and Führer 1996, 178–179.

18. They had started defending the government's positions within the union even before their nominations. During the NATO (the North Atlantic Treaty Organization) referendum, Fernández and Chaves had led a campaign within the union in favor of the government. The UGT leadership opposed the government shift toward favoring Spain membership to the alliance. Chaves was named minister of labor four months after the referendum. Corcuera became a staunch opponent to Redondo in the union and was forced to resign from the executive committee in 1985, when he was accused of leading a coup against Redondo. Later on he became minister of internal affairs. See Monteira 1996, 630.

19. The LO was set up in 1898, ten years after the SAP. During that time the party coordinated union activities. Under the first LO constitution, all unions affiliated with the LO were required to affiliate their members with the party and pay party dues. This requirement was dropped after 1900, but union branches usually remained affiliated with the district party of their locality. See Pontusson 1992, 468–469 and 489–490.

20. Other authors have claimed, however, that Felipe González was a strong and vocal supporter of social pacts. Martínez-Alier and Roca (1986) claim that in 1987 Mr. González "repeatedly stated that he [was] ready to negotiate even the state budget with the Employers' Organization and with the two main unions, outside parliament, as part and parcel of a social pact" (p. 21). They also stress that Mr. González favored workers' investment funds, in the Swedish pattern, in exchange for wage restraint and the enactment of legislation to create the Economic and Social Council foreseen in the Constitution. They attribute to "conjunctural political factors" and long-term factors (i.e., the increase in unemployment, the weakness of the unions, as well as the growth of new sectors of the economy) the absence of corporatist agreements in 1979, 1984, and 1987.

21. Nicolás Redondo argued during our interview that the reason for this development was that both organizations have passed from illegality to government in just a few years, so that they did not have time to establish the parameters of that relationship. In 1984, for instance, N. Redondo was meeting with F. González, A. Guerra (the government and party's deputy), and M. Boyer (the minister of economics). At this time the Spanish economy was still in the middle of a major recession and Redondo suggested that it would be a good idea to make some kind of public investment to create jobs. Boyer's response was, "What do you offer in return?" (Burns Marañón 1996, 213). According to the union leadership, government officials had acquired the habit that every time that they made concessions, they had to ask for compensations by the union leaders, who, however, rejected this approach. They argued that the priority for

a socialist party should be the fight against unemployment, therefore the government should not always demand something in return from the union.

22. For a different opinion see Burns Marañón 1996, particularly the interview with Carlos Solchaga (pp. 151–152) and Alfonso Guerra (p. 137). Solchaga (the Minister of Industry) emphasizes that Miguel Boyer, the Minister of Economics, and himself were very clear from the beginning that governmental policy could not be conditioned by the UGT. He mentions the hurtful influence that the TUC had over the British Labour government in the 1970s as an example of what they wanted to avoid in Spain. Alfonso Guerra (p. 137), on the contrary, criticizes the position of some the "neoliberals" within the party who hated unions.

23. Some authors have stressed the elements of continuity and convergence in the basic outline of economic policy on the continuity and convergence of the teams of experts with links to the Central Bank, whose influence dates back to the 1960s. They emphasize the role played by research offices and the advisors of the economic departments of the Bank of Spain on economic policymaking. See Bustelo 1986, 44.

24. In chapter 5 I challenge the government argument that there was no room for compromise with UGT. The increase in public expenditures at the end of the 1980s and its lack of consequences delegitimized the government's argument and proved that there was room for compromise. Economic recovery and the budget surplus of the second half of the 1980s offered the government greater leeway to compromise with the UGT. The government, however, decided not to follow such a strategy until it was too late, since unions were not willing to deal with the government any longer.

25. This was confirmed during the interviews that I held with N. Redondo and C. Solchaga in December 1996. During an meeting that I had with Carles Boix in May 1997, he argued that the government acted as a rational actor because, given the institutional structure of Spanish labor, the government could not expect union moderation. I challenge this argument in chapter 4.

26. International observers also emphasized that the reduction of inflation depended very much on the course of wage bargaining (OCDE 1986, 18).

27. Expenditures in education reached 4.2 percent of GDP in 1991. It was targeted mainly toward secondary and university education and focused on hiring new teachers and extending education to more people. Grants and scholarships were increased dramatically and the number of 14- to 18-year-old students attending school went up 50 percent from 1980 to 1989. The government also revamped the vocational training system, integrating it into the education system and linking it more closely to the market. See Boix 1994 and 1996.

28. The latest data on social protection spending in the EU shows that it has fallen slightly, from 28.8 percent in 1993 to 28.6 percent of GDP in 1994. Social spending increased sharply in the early 1980s from an average 24.3 because of recession and the inclusion of eastern Germany. Since 1993, it had established or fallen slightly. Finland (34.8 percent), Denmark (33.7 percent),

the Netherlands (32.3 percent), and Austria (30.2 percent). France and Germany are the highest spenders. The lowest are Greece (16 percent), Portugal (19.5 percent), and Ireland (21.1 percent). Most of this spending goes to old-age benefits (44.2 percent) but unemployment benefits are increasing as a percentage of total spending (9.2 percent). In Spain social spending fell slightly after 1993 because of budget tightening. See "Welfare Spending Falls in EU," in *Financial Times,* Saturday, April 5, 1997, p. 2.

29. The consequence of this reform was that pensions, after increasing dramatically as a percentage of GDP during the 1970s (they represented 4.01 percent of GDP in 1970 and grew to 8.56 percent in 1980), stagnated in the 1980s (by 1987 pensions only represented 9.97 percent of GDP). See Roca 1993, 204.

30. The party-union rupture also resulted in the spectacular resignation of several UGT leaders. José Luís Corcuera, Secretary of Syndical Action, resigned on May 1985, and J. Zambrana, the Secretary of Institutional Relations, resigned in October of 1987, both in opposition to the strategies advocated by the UGT's leadership. Out of the eight UGT members of Parliament elected from socialist lists, only Redondo and his deputy, Saracibar, voted against the project. They renounced their seats in Parliament two years later.

31. This breach was emphasized by the UGT's leadership in my interviews with them in December 1996.

32. The AES had resulted in a 1 percent absolute decline in real wages (Pérez 1996, 16).

33. Some authors, however, have contended that unemployment was not the reason why the unions broke with the government (Moscoso 1995, 50; Espina 1991, 214). They argue that Spanish unions only have a formal interest in unemployment, but that it is not one of their priorities. According to them, unions have pressures from their core constituencies that are more urgent. While this analysis might be partially true—unemployed do not vote in the elections to the work councils and unions have little to win in the short run from unemployed support—the government policy course proved that unemployment was a secondary objective for the government. The government was responsible for developing the macroeconomic conditions that would foster job creation, but the implementation of restrictive monetary policies in the late 1980s and early 1990s hindered job creation. It is unquestionable that wage moderation and restrictive monetary policies contributed to the moderation of demand in the first half of the 1980s, and this had a negative repercussion in job creation. This was compounded by the introduction of new temporary contracts in 1984.

34. These "maneuvers" were confirmed by Nicolás Redondo during our interview. Mr. Solchaga denies them.

35. The collection of signatures had been organized by M. Chaves to support the government's position in the NATO referendum. The government had called the referendum to see if the Spanish people wanted to remain in NATO. After a dramatic policy shift, the government decided to support Spanish permanent

membership in the alliance. This produced a profound schism both within the party and the union. By the time that Redondo aborted Chaves' plan, Chaves had the support of one-third of the executive committee. Finally, the UGT maintained a position contrary to the government in the referendum. As a result of these developments Chaves left the UGT and became Minister of Labor four months later. See Burns Marañón 1996, 214; and Monteira 1996, 632.

36. Nicolás Redondo and Antonio Gutiérrez both emphasized these points during the interviews that I held with them in December 1996. See also the interview with Redondo in Burns Marañón 1996.

37. As we have seen in chapter 3, the union-party strife doomed the negotiations for a possible centralized agreement after 1989. The deterioration of personal relationships between union and party leaders definitely hindered future attempts to reinstate concertation. The government attempted to revive concertation in 1991 and 1993, but unions had lost all trust in the government and refused to sign a pact. The decision by the government to increase social expenditures after the 1988 general strike was tempered by its decision to unilaterally implement another reform of the labor market in 1994. The Parliament approved a law that abolished job demarcation rules in order to foster labor mobility and internal flexibility, and legalized youth apprenticeship contracts at 70 percent of the minimum wage. This decision fostered further confrontation with unions and resulted in a new general strike that year. Only the arrival of a new conservative government in 1996 paved the way for new agreements between the government and the unions.

38. This attitude was influenced by the disastrous consequences that the close links between the British trade unions and the Labour government had over Labour policies in the late 1970s. According to this view, one of the main developments that hastened the defeat and failure of Labour in Britain was that it had become prisoner of unions' demands (Burns Marañón 1996, 150–152). When the Labour government proved to be unable to meet those demands, the unions radicalized their positions and intensified industrial conflict. This brought about Labour defeat in the 1979 elections and the victory of Margaret Thatcher.

39. Part of the reason for this development has been that interunion competition in Spain for support from the rank-and-file has been lower in Spain during the 1980s than in many other countries. Spanish workers have not been compelled to break with the main unions and build alternatives to satisfy new demands. See Moscoso 1995, 73.

Conclusions

1. On the negative side, concertation did not result in real income gains for workers. In five of the seven years in which there were agreements, average wages grew slower than prices, and from 1980–1986 the purchasing capacity of workers only grew 0.4 percent. From 1980–1986 workers' income declined as a percentage of the total national income. Concertation also failed to address

the unemployment problem which increased from 7 percent in 1978 to 21 percent in 1986.

2. The fact that the conservative government was willing to move toward the policies of social democratic (SD) corporatism after 1996 confirms the strength of the labor movement in Spain. Centralized bargaining was the only way that the right in Spain could convince labor leaders that they should use their power to generate wage restraint. In this case the beneficial macroeconomic consequences outweigh the negative distributional consequences that this strategy had for part of the government's electoral constituency. The behavior of the Spanish government confirms Garrett's (1998, 49) model.

3. Another consequence of unions' subordination to political objectives was the increasing internal centralization of union organizations. The fact that union leaders played a political role as spokesmen for the workers led to the present centralization of union structures. All relevant decisions and strategies are now made by the union leadership, and the federations and territorial organizations play a limited role. Moreover, the institutionalization of unions did not result in their internal consolidation and growth. Affiliation remained (and continues to remain) comparatively low. Union focus on political objectives has distanced them from the defense of workers' interests at the primary level—that is, the workplace. This development has resulted in a further delegitimizing of unions as effective representatives of the workers' interests.

4. The Spanish literature (Maravall 1995, Boix 1996, Solchaga 1997) has emphasized the role that the growth in real wages, the inflexibility of the labor markets, low investment, changes in the occupational structure, and the reversal in the flow of emigration had in the increase in Spanish unemployment. For a contending argument see Pérez 1997b, 7–10 and Pérez 1997c.

5. Social outlays included education expenditures, which grew by 94 percent from 1982–1989. The government also extended the age of compulsory education up to 16 years, and increased the budget for grants and scholarships for university students. Pensions also increased by 55.5 percent. The government changed the provision of welfare; entitlements became universal, and the minimum pension was put at the same level as the minimum wage. Public health expenditure also grew by 30.6 percent and it also established a universal national health system in 1986 that offered nearly unlimited services at almost no cost, financed by the public budget (70 percent) and social security contributions (30 percent). See Maravall 1995, 230–237.

6. It is important to emphasize, however, that there are clear indicators that unions have actively coordinated wage bargaining at the national level as part of their new relationship with employers. The result has been significant wage moderation in 1997 (average wage increased 3 percent) and 1998 (2.5 percent). See: "Los Salarios para este ano suben el 2.5 percent, medio punto menos que en 1997," in *El Pais,* Saturday, March 7, 1998.

7. The new agreement established a new system of four year renewable employment contracts that would apply to people wanting to convert from temporary to permanent jobs, to under-29-year-olds and other groups with particular dif-

ficulties finding employment. For these contracts, redundancies made on organizational grounds, even if considered unfair by labor courts, would cost no more than 33 days' pay per year worked, with a maximum of 24 months (the compensation for standard contracts is 45 days per year worked, up to a 42-month maximum, by far the highest in the European Union). Union leaders labeled this agreement as "a clear example of social consensus in Spain," see, "All Sides Hail Spain's Job Pact," in *Financial Times,* April 10, 1997, p. 3. Unions agreed to this reduction in return for a promise by employers to convert temporary contracts into indefinite ones. The result of this reform after 2 years has been the creation of two million new indefinite contracts. However, one of the major objectives of the reform, which was to reduce the level of temporality (at 32.5 percent, the highest in Western Europe), has not been achieved. For an analysis of the consequences of the reform see: Pérez Infante 1998, 150–153. See also "La reforma laboral logra dos millones de contratos, pero la tasa de temporalidad no cede," in *El País,* Monday, May 17, 1999.

8. This development contradicts other analyses that have argued that wage moderation and employment are reinforced by central bank independence in countries with intermediate levels of centralization in wage bargaining (Iversen 1998). In Spain wage bargainers have not been responsive to threats from fiscal or monetary authorities. See Hall and Franzese 1998, Perez 1998.

9. During my interview with the leaders of the CEOE in 1996 they emphasized their preference for centralized bargaining. See chapter 4. For a clear picture of the PP strategies, see interviews with José María Aznar, the Conservative Prime Minister, in "Government Takes a Siesta," in *Financial Times,* Monday, August 3, 1998, p. 13, and in "Ode to the Common Man with a Nation at his Feet," in *Financial Times,* Weekend Edition, September 12–13, 1998, p. iii.

10. I am currently working on a project analyzing these developments and extending the scope of my research to Portugal and other Latin American countries.

11. According to Martin Wolf ("The Gain in Spain," in the *Financial Times,* Wednesday, July 7, 1999, p. 10), economic performance in the second half of the 1990s has been characterized by lower fiscal deficits, reduced inflation, and currency stability. According to the data that Wolf presents from the OECD, Spain's cyclically adjusted fiscal deficit has been reduced from 5.5 percent of GDP in 1992 to 1.6 percent in 1998, and inflation dwindled from 5.1 percent in 1993 to 2.1 in the 12 months prior to May 1999. Moreover, interest rates have fallen from 13.4 percent in October 1992 to 4.8 percent in July 1999, and employment grew at 2.9 percent in 1997 and 3.4 percent in 1998 (with growth forecast by the OECD at 2.6 percent in 1999 and 2.4 percent in 2000). The convergence process laid down in the Maastricht Treaty (public spending is only 41 percent of GDP), combined with social peace and wage moderation fostered by the return of national social bargaining, have contributed to a new virtuous circle characterized by sustained rapid growth, improving fiscal position, lower unemployment, and higher investment and productivity, which in turn will promote rapid growth. According to him, wage moderation is key to close the gap with the EU richer countries (GDP

per head in Spain is only 79 percent of the EU average) to exploit Europe-wide specialization and attract investment from its European partners (average hourly compensation in manufacturing is less than half the German level). Mr. Wolf, however, highlights the low levels of productivity growth since 1995, and warns against the risk of strong domestic demand fueled by low interest rates. Given the difficulties that the government and employers had in the past controlling overall wage growth without the support from unions, the actors should have powerful incentives to continue with national social bargaining. See also the IMF's *Public Information Notice* No. 99/65, "IMF Concludes Article IV Consultation with Spain," June 30, 1999, in which the IMF praises the Spanish government for its economic policies.

12. Garrett 1998, 31 makes a compelling argument about this.

13. Even in countries under conservative governments, the level of public spending proved to be remarkably stable. Expenditure on education as a percentage of GDP fell between 1975 and 1995 from 6.7 percent to 5.2 percent. Spending on the health sector, however, increased in that period from 3.8 percent to 5.7 percent of GDP, and spending on social security increased the most from 8.2 percent of GDP in 1974–1974 to 11.4 by 1995–1996, pushed up by higher unemployment and changes in demographic patterns (Giddens 1998, 113–114).

14. Moene and Wallerstein (1999, 259) have stressed that scholars have overstated the impact of SD policies on macroeconomic performance. They argue that both centralized wage bargaining and active labor market polices can help, but that neither is enough to prevent unemployment from rising when demand falls. They highlight, however, the success of SD policies reducing inequality, insecurity, and poverty.

15. According to the new system established in the 1993 agreement, national industry-level bargaining adjusts pay scales to the expected rate of inflation, while lower level bargaining is given the function of distributing additional productivity increases. The new system establishes two annual meetings to "define common objectives concerning the inflation rate, growth of GDP and employment and to verify the coherence of behavior by the parties engaged." It also facilitated a historic agreement between the government and the unions on pension reform in 1995. See Regini and Regalia 1997, pp. 213–217.

16. For an article challenging this argument see: Frits Bolkestein, "The High Road that Leads out of the Low Countries," in *The Economist,* May 22, 1998, pp. 75–76. For a different conclusion, see Di Tella and McCulloch 1998. They have also analyzed the consequences of labor market flexibility in 21 OECD countries and found evidence that increasing the flexibility of the labor force increases both the employment rate and the rate of participation in the labor force.

17. In June 1999, the British Prime Minister, Tony Blair, and the German Chancellor, Gerhard Schroder, issued a manifiesto entitled "Europe, the third way, die neue Mitte" defining the agenda for a "Third Way" or "Neue Mitte." This document places strong emphasis on skills, flexibility, innovation, rights, and

responsibilities. According to the authors, the new social democracy should stand "not only for social justice, but also for economic dynamism and the unleashing of creativity and innovation." Their aim is to make the old SD values of "fairness and social justice, liberty and equality of opportunity, solidarity and responsibility to others" relevant to today's world. See "Crumbs from Blair's Table," in *The Economist,* June 12, 1999, p. 52. For a critique of this document see: Martin Wolf, "Not the Right Way," in the *Financial Times,* Wednesday, June 16, 1999, p. 14. See also Jordi Sevilla, "Las Tareas de la Socialdemocracia," in *El País,* Wednesday, June 16, 1999.

18. Some of the reasons that explain this inadequate performance include: European difficulties matching the United States' progress in new information and communication technologies; the costs of an aging population; the interaction between negative macroeconomic shocks and preexisting rigidities; and the difficulties managing the transition from industry to service economies. See Martin Wolf, "Not the Right Way," in the *Financial Times,* Wednesday, June 16, 1999, 14.

19. They perform two tests. First, they assume that these countries are hit by a common shock and look at how the evolution of unemployment differs across countries according to how rigid their labor markets are. Then, they assume that these countries are affected by country-specific shocks: productivity growth, higher interest rates, and company restructuring as a result of technological change. They conclude in both cases that labor-market rigidities are magnifying the effects of shocks. See also "A Shocking Error," in *The Economist,* June 15, 1999, p. 74.

20. The report acknowledges, however, that while job protection may mean lower unemployment, those without work (i.e., younger workers, women, and older workers) may stay unemployed longer, but emphasizes that "only weak evidence exists that job protection laws have a negative effect" on those groups. See "Job Laws Not Factor in Unemployment,'" in *Financial Times,* Friday, June 25, 1999, p. 1.

21. See Garrett 1998, 153–154 for a more detailed analysis of this proposal.

22. As quoted by Swank 1998, 10.

23. A new study, "Towards a Euro Wage?" by the U.K. research institute, Industrial Relations Services, suggests that the Euro will push bargaining systems both ways, toward centralization and decentralization, depending on the regions, economic sectors, and firms. There are, however encouraging signs. In September 1998, trade unions from Belgium, the Netherlands, Germany, and Luxembourg (including Germany's IG Metall), met in Doorn (the Netherlands) to develop a common bargaining strategy. They agreed on a strategy: Future wage claims in their countries should be based on a formula consisting of the sum of the total of cost of living changes and productivity improvements. They also agreed to establish an information network to monitor the course of future bargaining. This may be a first step towards greater trade union cohesion in response to European economic integration. The main challenge will be to develop a common industrial relations model.

The recently-established European Work Councils, covering companies employing 1,000 workers with at least 150 in two member states, may lead to the establishment of strategic alliances among European unions. See "Euro Comparisons May Bring New Wage System," in *Financial Times,* October, 13, 1998, 3.

Bibliography

Aguilar, S. and J. Roca, 1990: "Epilogo: La Huelga General del 14-D," in S. Aguilar, ed., *Sindicalismo y Cambio Social en España, 1976–1988*. Barcelona: Fundació Jaume Bofill.

Alcaide, Julio, et al., 1995: *Problemas Económicos Españoles en la Decada de los 90*. Madrid: Círculo de Lectores/Galaxia Gutenberg.

Alesina, Alberto and Howard Rosenthal, 1995: *Partisan Politics, Divided Governments, and the Economy*. Cambridge: Cambridge University Press.

Almendros Morcillo, F., ed., 1978: *El Sindicalismo de Clase en España 1939–1977*. Madrid: Alianza.

Alonso, Luís, E., 1991 (1995): "Conflicto laboral y Cambio Social: Una Aproximación al caso Español," in Faustino Miguélez and Carlos Prieto, eds., *Las Relaciones Laborales en España*. Madrid: Siglo XXI.

Alvarez, R. Michael, Geoffrey Garrett, and Peter Lange, 1991: "Government Partisanship, Labor Organization and Macroeconomic Performance, 1967–1984," in *American Political Science Review*, 85: 541–556.

Alvarez, R. M., G. Garrett, and P. Lange, 1993: "Government Partisanship, Labor Organizations, and Macroeconomic Performance: A Corrigendum," in *American Political Science Review*, 87, no. 2.

Amsden, Jon, 1972: *Collective Bargaining and Class Conflict in Spain*. London: Weidenfeld and Nicolson.

Anderson, Perry and Patrick Camiller, 1994: *Mapping the West European Left*. New York: Verso.

Andrews, David, 1994: "Capital Mobility and State Autonomy: Toward a Structural Theory of International Monetary Relations," in *International Studies Quarterly*, 38.

Aragón Medina, Jorge, ed., 1998: *Euro y Empleo*. Madrid: CES.

Ayoso, Juan and José Luis Escriva, 1997: "La Evolucion de la Estrategia de Control Monetario en España," in Servicio de Estudios del Banco de España, *La Politica Monetaria y la inflacion en España*. Madrid: Alianza Editorial.

Babiano, José and Leopoldo Moscoso, 1992: *Ciclos en Política y Economía*. Madrid: Fundación Pablo Iglesias.

Barreto, José, 1992: "Portugal: Industrial Relations Under Democracy," in A. Ferner and R. Hyman, eds., *Industrial Relations in the New Europe*. Cambridge: Blackwell.

Bean, Charles, Richard Layard, and Stephen Nickell, 1986: "The Rise in Unemployment: A Multi-Country Study," in *Economica*, 53: 1–22.

Bell, Daniel, 1965: *The End of Ideology*. New York: Free Press.

Bentolila, Samuel and Luís Toharia, 1991: *Estudios de Economía del Trabajo en España III. El Problema del Paro*. Madrid: Ministerio de Trabajo y Seguridad Social (MTSS).

Bentolila, Samuel and Juan J. Dolado, 1994: "Labour Flexibility and Wages: Lessons from Spain," in *Economic Policy*, no. 18: 55–99.

Berger S., ed., 1981: *Organizing Interests in Western Europe*. Cambridge: Cambridge University Press.

Berger, S. and R. Dore, 1996: *National Diversity and Global Capitalism*. Ithaca, N.Y.: Cornell University Press.

Berman, Sheri, 1998: *The Social Democratic Moment: Ideas and Politics in the Making of Interwar Europe*. Cambridge, MA: Harvard University Press.

Bermeo, Nancy and José García Durán, 1994: "Spain: Dual Transition Implemented by Two Parties," in S. Haggard and Steven Webb, eds., *Voting for Reform: Democracy, Political Liberalization, and Economic Adjustment*. Washington, D.C.: World Bank/Oxford University Press.

Bilbao, Andrés, 1991 (1995): "Trabajadores, Gestion Económica y Crisis Sindical," in Faustino Miguélez and C. Prieto, *Las Relaciones Laborales en España*. Madrid: Siglo XXI.

Birchfield, Vicky and Markus Crepaz, forthcoming: "The Impact of Constitutional Structures and Competitive and Collective Veto Points on Income Inequality in Industrialized Democracies," in *European Journal of Political Research*.

Blanchard, Olivier J., et al., 1995: *Spanish Unemployment: Is There a Solution?* Madrid and London: Consejo Superior de Cámaras de Comercio, Industria, y Navegación/Center for Economic Policy Research.

Blanchard, Oliver and Justin Wolfers, 1999: "The Role of Shocks and Institutions in the Rise of European Unemployment: the Aggregate Evidence" from web.mit.edu/blanchar/

Boix, Carles, 1994: "Building a Socialdemocratic Strategy in Southern Europe: Economic Policy Under the Gonzalez Government (1982–93)." Paper prepared for discussion at the Iberian Study Group, CES: Harvard University. October 24.

Boix, Carles, 1994b: "Partisan Strategies and Supply Side Policies in Industrialized Nations, 1960–1990." Cambridge: CES. Working Paper Series #50.

Boix, Carles, 1996: *Partidos Políticos Crecimiento e Igualdad*. Madrid: Alianza Universidad.

Boix, Carles, 1998: *Political Parties, Growth and Equality: Conservative and Social Democratic Strategies in the World Economy*. New York: Cambridge University Press.

Bouza, Fermín, ed., 1989: *Perfil, Actitudes y Demandas del Delegado y Afiliado a UGT*. Madrid: Fundación Largo Caballero.

Bowman, John, 1982: "The Logic of Capitalist Collective Action," in *Social Science Information*, 21: 571–604.

Boyer, Miguel, 1983: "Opiniones," in *Papeles de Economía Española*, no. 16.

Boyer, Robert, ed., 1988: *La Flexibilité du Travail en Europe*. Paris: La Découverte.

Boyer, Robert and D. Drache, 1996: *States Against Markets: The Limits of Globalization*. New York: Routledge.

Bresser Pereira, Luis Carlos, José María Maravall, and Adam Przeworski, 1993: *Economic Reforms in New Democracies: A Social Democratic Approach*. Cambridge: Cambridge University Press.

Brunetta, Renato and Carlo Dell'Aringa, 1990: *Labour Relations and Economic Performance*. London: Macmillan.

Bruno, Michael and Jeffrey Sachs, 1985: *The Economic of Worldwide Stagflation.* Cambridge: Harvard University Press.

Burns Marañon, Tom, 1996: *Conversaciones sobre el Socialismo.* Madrid: Plaza y Janes.

Burns Marañon, Tom, 1997: *Conversaciones sobre la Derecha.* Madrid Plaza y Janes.

Burrows, Roger and Brian Loader, eds., 1994: *Towards a Post-Fordist Welfare State.* New York: Routledge.

Bustelo, Carlos, 1986: "Economic Policy in Spain's Democracy: Dilemmas and Constraints." Cambridge: CES. Working Paper Series #15.

Cabrero Morán Enrique, 1997: *La Democracia Interna en los Sindicatos.* Madrid: CES.

Calmfors, Lars, 1993: "Centralization of Wage Bargaining and Macroeconomic Performance: A Survey," *OECD Economic Studies,* 21.

Calmfors, Lars and John Driffill, 1988: "Bargaining Structure, Corporatism, and Economic Performance," in *Economic Policy,* 3: 13–61.

Calvo Sotelo, Leopoldo, 1990: *Memoria Viva de la Transición.* Barcelona: Plaza y Janes.

Cameron, David, 1978. "The Expansion of the Public Economy: A Comparative Analysis," in *American Political Science Review,* 72: 1243–1261.

Cameron, David, 1984: "Social Democracy, Corporatism, Labor Quiescence and the Representation of Economic Interest in Advanced Capitalist Society," in John H. Goldthorpe, ed., *Order and Conflict in Contemporary Capitalism.* New York: Oxford University Press.

Camiller, Patrick, 1994: "Spain: The Survival of Socialism?" in Perry Anderson and Patrick Camiller, eds., *Mapping the West European Left.* New York: Verso.

Caravaña, J., 1995: *Desigualdad y Clases Sociales.* Madrid: Fundación Argentaria.

Carlin, Wendy and David Soskice, 1990: *Macroeconomics and the Wage Bargain: A Modern Approach to Employment, Inflation, and the Exchange Rate.* Oxford: Oxford University Press.

Cerny, Philip G., 1990: *The Changing Architecture of Politics.* London: Sage.

Círculo de Empresarios, 1995: *Las Reformas de Estructuras en España.* Madrid: Círculo de Empresarios

Cohen, Benjamin, 1996: "Phoenix Risen: The Resurrection of Global Finance," in *World Politics,* 48, January: 268–290.

Collier, Ruth Berins, 1999: *Paths Toward Democracy: The Working Class and Elites in Western Europe and South America.* New York: Cambridge University Press.

Consejo Económico y Social (CES): *Economía Trabajo y Sociedad,* Various Years. Madrid: CES.

Crouch, Colin and Alessandro Pizzorno, 1978: *The Resurgence of Class Conflict in Western Europe since 1978.* London: Macmillan Press.

Crouch, Colin, 1985: "Conditions for Trade Union Wage Restrain," in Leon N. Linberg and Charles S. Maier, eds., *The Politics of Inflation and Economic Stagnation.* Washington, D.C.: The Brookings Institution.

Crouch, Colin, 1994: "Incomes Policies, Institutions and Markets: An Overview of Recent Developments," in Ronald Dore, Robert Boyer, and Zoe Mars, eds., *The Return of Incomes Policy.* London: Pinter Publishers.

Da Silva Lópes, José, 1999: El Consejo Económico y Social de Portugal," in Federico Durán López, ed., *El Dialogo Social y su Institucionalización en España e Iberoamerica.* Madrid: CES.

De la Dehesa, Guillermo, 1988: "Los Límites de la Política Económica Española," in *Leviatán,* 32: 27–37.

De la Dehesa, Guillermo, 1994: "Spain," in John Williamson, ed., *The Political Economy of Policy Reform.* Washington, D.C.: Institute for International Economics.

De la Dehesa, Guillermo, 1997: "El Mercat de Treball a Espanya. Problemaes I Propostes de Reforma," in *Revista Econòmica de Catalunya,* no. 32.

De la Villa, Luis Enrique and M. C. Palomeque, 1978: *Introduccción a la Economía del Trabajo.* Madrid: Debate.

De la Villa, Luis Enrique, 1984: *Los Grandes Pactos Colectivos A Partir de la Transición Democrática.* Madrid: Ministerio de Trabajo y Seguridad Social.

De Quinto, Javier, 1994: *Política Industrial en España.* Madrid: Ediciones Piramide.

Del Rey Guanter, Salvador, ed., 1998: *La Negociación Colectiva Tras la Reforma Laboral de 1994.* Madrid: CES.

Dettke, Dieter, ed., 1998: *The Challenge of Globalization for Germany's Social Democracy.* New York: Bergham Books.

Di Tella, Rafael and Robert MacCulloch, 1998: "The Consequences of Labour Market Flexibility: Panel Evidence Based on Survey Data." Typescript. Harvard University.

Díaz Cardiel, V., J. F. Plá, A. Tejero, and E. Triana, 1976: *Madrid en Huelga.* Madrid: Ayuso.

Díaz Güell, 1987: *Las Deudas Financieras de los Sindicatos.* Madrid: Siglo XXI.

Diamond, Larry and Marc F. Plattner, 1995: *Economic Reform and Democracy.* Baltimore: John Hopkins University Press.

Dolado J. J. y J. F. Jimeno, eds., 1995: *Estudios Sobre el Funcionamiento del Mercado de Trabajo Español.* Madrid: Coleccion Estudios FEDEA, no. 13.

Dolado, J. J., J. Felgueroso, and J. F. Jimeno, 1997: " The Effects of Minimum Bargained Wages on Earnings: Evidence from Spain," in *European Economic Review,* 1074.

Domínguez, Justo, 1990: "Diez Años de Relaciones Industriales en España" in Angel Zaragoza, comp., *Pactos Sociales Sindicatos y Patronal en España.* Madrid: Siglo XXI.

Dore, Ronald, Robert Boyer, and Zoe Mars, eds., 1994: *The Return of Incomes Policy.* London: Pinter Publishers,

Dreze, Jacques and Charles Bean, 1990: *Europe's Unemployment Problem.* Cambridge MA: MIT Press.

Dunlop, J. T., 1957: *The Theory of Wage Determination.* London: Macmillan.

Durán López, Federico, 1999: *El Dialogo Social y su Institucionalización en España e Iberoamerica.* Madrid: CES.

Encarnación, Omar G., 1997: "Social Concertation in Democratic and Market Transitions. Comparative Lessons from Spain," in *Comparative Political Studies,* vol. 30, no. 4, August: 387–419.

Escobar, Modesto, 1991: "Afiliación y Movilización Sindical en España." Paper presented at a conference held at the Universidad Internacional Menendez Pelayo, Sevilla.

Escobar, Modesto, 1995: "Spain: Works Councils or Unions?" in J. Rogers and W. Streeck, eds., *Work Councils.* Chicago: Chicago University Press.

Espina, Alvaro, (ed.) 1991: *Concertación Social, Neocorporativismo y Democracia.* Madrid: MTSS.

Espina, Alvaro, 1991b: "Los Sindicatos y la Democracia Española. La Huelga General de 1988 y sus Implicaciones Políticas," in A. Espina, A., ed., *Concertación Social Neocorporativismo y Democracia.* Madrid: MTSS.

Espina, Alvaro, 1991c: *Empleo, Democracia y Relaciones Industriales.* Madrid: Ministerio de Trabajo y Seguridad Social.

Espina, Alvaro, 1991d (1995): "Política de Rentas en España," in F. Miguelez and Carlos Prieto eds., *Las Relaciones Laborales en España.* Madrid: Siglo XXI.

Espina, Alvaro, 1994: "Una Evaluación de la Dinámica de la Negociación Salarial en España (1976–1994): del Intercambio Político a la Cooperación," in *Economía y Sociología del Trabajo,* no. 25–26, December.

Espina, Alvaro, 1995: "Política de Rentas en España," in F. Miguelez and C. Prieto, eds., *Las Relaciones Laborales en España.* Madrid: Siglo XXI.

Espina, Alvaro, 1995b: *Hacia una Estrategia Española de Competitividad.* Madrid: Fundación Argentaria.

Esping-Andersen, Gösta, 1985: *Politics Against Markets. The Social Democratic Road to Power.* Princeton: Princeton University Press.

Esping-Andersen, Gösta, 1990. *Three Worlds of Welfare Capitalism.* London: Polity Press.

Esping-Andersen, Gösta, 1996: "After the Golden Age: Welfare State Dilemmas in a Global Economy," in Esping-Andersen, Gösta, ed., *Welfare State in Transition: National Adaptations in Global Economies.* Thousand Oaks, CA: Sage.

Esping-Andersen, Gösta, 1999: "Politics Without Class: Postindustrial Change in Europe and America," in H. Kitschelt, Peter Lange, Gary Marks, and John D. Stephens eds., *Continuity and Change in Contemporary Capitalism.* New York: Cambridge University Press.

Esping-Andersen, Gösta, 1999b: *Social Foundations of Postindustrial Economies.* New York: Oxford University Press.

Estefanía, Joaquín, and Rodolfo Serrano, 1990: "Díez Años de Relaciones Industriales en España," in Angel Zaragoza, comp., *Pactos Sociales Sindicatos y Patronal en España.* Madrid: Siglo XXI.

Estefanía, Joaquín, 1996: *La Nueva Economía. La Globalización.* Madrid: Ediciones Debate.

Estevill, Jordi and Joseph de la Hoz, 1990: "Transition and Crisis: The Complexity of Spanish Industrial Relations," in G. Baglioni and C. Crouch, eds., *European Industrial Relations: The Challenge of Flexibility.* London: Sage.

Ethier, Diane, 1997: *Economic Adjustment in New Democracies: Lessons from Southern Europe.* New York: St. Martin's Press.

Evans, Peter, 1995: *Embedded Autonomy: States and Industrial Transformation.* Princeton NJ: Princeton University Press.

Evans, Peter, Dietrich Reuschemeyer, and Theda Skocpol, 1985: *Bringing the State Back In.* New York: Cambridge University Press.

Fernández, F., L. Garrido, and L. Toharia, 1991 (1995): "Empleo y Paro en España, 1976–1990," in F. Miguélez and C. Prieto, eds., *Las Relaciones Laborales en España,* Madrid: Siglo XXI, pp. 43–96.

Fernández López, María F., 1995: "El Papel del Convenio Colectivo como Fuente del Derecho tras la Reforma de la Legislación Laboral (I)," in *Actualidad Laboral*, no. 6/6, February 6–12.

Fernández López, María F., 1995: "El Papel del Convenio Colectivo como Fuente del Derecho tras la Reforma de la Legislación Laboral (II)," in *Actualidad Laboral*, no. 7, February 13–19.

Ferner A. and R. Hyman, eds., 1992: *Industrial Relations in the New Europe.* Cambridge: Blackwell.

Fishman, Robert, 1990: *Working Class Organization and the Return to Democracy in Spain.* Ithaca, NY: Cornell University Press.

Fitoussi, Jean-Paul, 1996: *El Debate Prohibido.* Barcelona: Paidós.

Flanagan, R., D. Soskice, and L. Ulman, 1983. *Unionism, Economic Stabilization, and Incomes Policies: European Experience.* Washington D.C.: Brookings Institution.

Folgado, José, 1989: *Concertación Social y Política Presupuestaria.* Doctoral Dissertation. Unpublished Manuscript. Universidad Autónoma de Madrid.

Forewaker, Joe, 1987: "Corporatist Strategies and the Transition to Democracy in Spain," *Comparative Politics,* 20, no. 1, October.

Forsyth, Douglas and Tom Notermans, 1997: *Regime Changes: Macroeconomic Policy and Financial Regulation from 1930s to the 1990s.* Providence: Bergahn Books.

Frank, Andre Gunder, 1998: *Reorient: Global Economy in the Asian Age.* Los Angeles: University of California Press.

Frankel, Jeffrey, 1991: "Quantifying International Capital Mobility in the 1980s," in B. Douglas Bernheim and John B. Shoven, eds., *National Saving and Economic Performance.* Chicago: University of Chicago Press.

Freeman, John R., 1989: *Democracy and Markets: The Politics of Mixed Economies.* Ithaca, N.Y.: Cornell University Press.

Freeman, Richard B., 1988: "Labor Market Institutions and Economic Performance." *Economic Policy,* 3: 63–80.

Freeman, Richard, 1992: "Sobre las Divergencias entre los Paises Desarrollados Desde el Punto de Vista del Sindicalismo," in R. Brunetta and C. Dell'Aringa, *Relaciones Laborales y Resultados Económicos.* Madrid: MTSS.

Freeman, Richard, 1994: *Working Under Different Rules.* New York: Russell Sage Foundation.

Freeman, R. and L. Katz, 1995a: *Differences and Changes in Wage Structures.* Chicago: The University of Chicago Press.

Freeman R. and R. Gibbons, 1995: "Getting Together and Breaking Apart: The Decline of Centralized Collective Bargaining," in R. Freeman and L. Katz, *Differences and Changes in Wage Structures.* Chicago: The University of Chicago Press.

Frieden, Jeffry, 1991: Invested Interests: The Politics of National Economic Policies in a World of Global Finance," in *International Organization,* 45.

Fuentes Quintana, Enrique, 1979: "La Crisis Económica Española," in *Papeles de Economía Española,* 1: 84–136.

Fuentes Quintana, Enrique, 1989: "Los Deberes Económicos de los Noventa," in *Economistas,* no. 41.

Fuentes Quintana, Enrique and José Barea Tejeiro, 1996: "El Déficit Público de la Democracia Española," in *Papeles de Economía Española,* no. 68.

Führer, Ilse Marie, 1996: *Los Sindicatos en España*. Madrid: CES.

Fukuyama, Francis, 1999: *The Great Disruption: Human Nature and the Reconstitution of Social Order*. New York: New York Free Press.

Gadea Rivas, María Dolores, 1996: *La Economía Política del Gasto Publico en España*, Madrid: CES.

García-Abadillo, Casimiro, 1996: *De La Euforia al Descrédito: Crónica del Dinero*. Madrid: Espasa Calpe.

García Delgado, José Luis, 1990: *Economía Española de la Transición y la Democracia, 1973–1986*. Madrid: Centro de Investigaciones Sociológicas.

García Murcia, J., R. Gutiérrez Palacios, and F. Rodríguez Sañudo, 1995: "La Incidencia de los Criterios de Representatividad en la Configuración del Sistema Sindical Español," in J. J. Dolado, and F. Jimeno, *Estudios sobre el Funcionamiento del Mercado de Trabajo Español*. Madrid: FEDEA, no. 13.

García Perea, Pilar and Ramón Gómez, 1993: "Aspectos Institucionales del Mercado de Trabajo Español, en Comparación con Otros Países Comunitarios," in *Boletín Económico*, September: 29–47. Madrid: Banco de España.

Garrett, Geoffrey, 1998. *Partisan Politics in the Global Economy*. New York: Cambridge University Press.

Garrett, Geoffrey, 1999. "Global Markets and Nacional Politics: Collision Course or Virtuous Circle?" in Peter J. Katzenstein, Robert E. Keohane, and Stephen D. Krasner, 1999. *Exploration and Contestation in the Study of World Politics*. Cambridge, MA: MIT Press.

Garrett, G., and P. Lange, 1985: "The Politics of Growth: Strategic Interaction and Economic Performance in the Advanced Industrialized Democracies, 1974–80," in *Journal of Politics*, 47: 792–827.

Garrett, G. and P. Lange, 1986: "Performance in a Hostile World: Economic Growth in Capitalist Democracies, 1974–1982," in *World Politics*, 38: 517–45.

Garrett, G. and P. Lange, 1989: "Government Partisanship and Economic Performance: When and How does 'Who Governs' Matter?" in *Journal of Politics*, 51, August, pp. 676–693.

Garrett, Geoffrey and Peter Lange, 1991: "Political Responses to Interdependence: What's 'Left' for the Left?" in *International Organization*, 45: 539–64.

Garrett, Geoffrey and Peter Lange, 1996: "The Impact of the International Economy on National Policies: An Analytical Overview," in Robert Keohane and Helen Milner, eds., *Internationalization and Domestic Politics*. New York: Cambridge University Press.

Garrett, Geoffrey and Christopher Way, 1995: "The Sectoral Composition of Trade Unions, Corporatism, and Economic Performance," in Barry Eichengreen, Jieffry Frieden, and Jürgen von Hagen, eds., *Monetary and Fiscal Policy in an Integrated Europe*. Berlin: Springer.

Giddens, Anthony, 1998: *The Third Way: The Renewal of Social Democracy*. Malden, MA: Blackwell Publishers Inc.

Gill, Stephen and David Law, 1989: "Global Hegemony and the Structural Power of Capital, " in *International Studies Quarterly*, 33: 399–424.

Gill, Stephen and David Law, 1998: *The Global Political Economy*. Baltimore: Johns Hopkins University Press.

Gillespie, Richard, 1988: *The Spanish Socialist Party.* Oxford: Oxford University Press, 1988.

Gillespie, Richard, 1991: *Historia del Partido Socialista Obrero Español.* Madrid: Alianza Universidad.

Gillespie, Richard, 1989: "Spanish Socialism in the 1980's," in T. Gallagher and A. Williams, eds., *Southern European Socialism.* Manchester: Manchester University Press.

Gillespie, Richard, 1990: "The Break-up of the 'Socialist Family': Party-Union Relations in Spain 1982–1989," in *West European Politics,* January.

Gillespie, Richard and William Paterson, eds., 1993: *Rethinking Social Democracy in Western Europe.* Special Issue of West European Politics, no.1.

Giner, S. and E. Sevilla, 1984: "Spain: from Corporatism to Corporatism," in A. Williams, ed., *Southern Europe Transformed.* London: Harper & Row.

Gobbo, Mario, 1981: *The Political, Economic, and Labor Climate in Spain.* University of Pennsylvania: The Wharton School-Industrial Research Unit.

Golden, Miriam, 1988: *Labor Divided.* Ithaca, NY: Cornell University Press.

Golden, M., 1993: "The Dynamics of Trade Unionism and National Economic Performance," in *American Political Science Review,* 87, no. 2: 439–56.

Golden, Miriam, 1998b: *Heroic Defeats: The Politics of Job Loss,* New York: Cambridge University Press.

Golden, Miriam and Jonas Pontusson, eds., 1992: *Bargaining for Change. Union Politics in North America and Europe.* Ithaca. NY: Cornell University Press.

Golden, Miriam, Peter Lange, and Michael Wallerstein, 1992: "The End of Corporatism?" Typescript. University of California Los Angeles: Institute of Industrial Relations.

Golden, Miriam, Michael Wallerstein, and Peter Lange, 1999: "Postwar Trade Union Organization and Industrial Relations in Twelve Countries," in H. Kitschelt, Peter Lange, Gary Marks, and John D. Stephens, eds., *Continuity and Change in Contemporary Capitalism.* New York: Cambridge University Press.

Goldthorpe John, ed., 1984: *Order and Conflict in Contemporary Capitalism.* Oxford: The Clarendon Press.

González, Felipe, 1991: "El PSOE, un Proyecto Renovado en Una Nueva Sociedad." Epilogue to: *Manifiesto del Programa 2000.* Madrid: Editorial Sistema.

González, Felipe, 1997: *¿Qué es el Socialismo?* Madrid: Ediciones Destino.

Goodman, John, 1992: *Monetary Sovereignty: The Politics of Central Banking in Western Europe.* Ithaca, NY: Cornell University Press.

Gould, Arthur, 1993: *Capitalist Welfare States.* New York: Longman.

Gourevitch, Peter, 1986: *Politics in Hard Times: Comparative Responses to International Economic Crises.* Ithaca: Cornell University Press.

Gual, Jordi, ed., 1996: *The Social Challenge of Job Creation: Combating Unemployment in Europe.* Brookfield, VT: Edward Elgar Publishing Company.

Guinea, J.L., 1978: *Los Movimientos Obreros y Sindicales en España de 1833 a 1978.* Madrid: Ibérico Europea de Ediciones.

Gunther Richard, Giacomo Sani, and Goldie Shabad, 1988: *Spain After Franco: The Making of a Competitive Party System.* Los Angeles: University of California Press.

Gunther, Richard, P. Nikiforos Diamandouros, and Hans-Jürgen Puhle, 1995: *The Politics of Democratic Consolidation: Southern Europe in Comparative Perspective.* Baltimore, MD: John Hopkins University Press.

Gutiérrez, Antonio, 1988: "Concertación Social y Coyuntura Política en España," in A. Zaragoxa, ed., *Pactos Sociales, Sindicatos y Patronal en España.* Madrid Siglo XXI.

Haggard, Stephen and Steven Webb, 1994: *Voting for Reform: Democracy, Political Liberalization, and Economic Adjustment.* Washington, D.C.: World Bank/Oxford University Press.

Haggard, Stephen and Robert R. Kaufman, 1995: *The Political Economy of Democratic Transitions.* Princeton NJ: Princeton University Press.

Hall, Peter, 1986: *Governing the Economy. The Politics of State Intervention in Britain and France.* Oxford: Oxford University Press, NY.

Hall, Peter, 1990: "El Impacto de la Dinámica Política y Social," in A. Espina, *Concertación Social, Neocorporatismo y Democracia.* Madrid: MTSS.

Hall, Peter, 1994: "Central Bank Independence and Coordinated Wage Bargaining: Their Interaction in Germany and Europe." Cambridge: CES. Working Paper Series #48. Also Published in 1994: *German Politics and Society,* Autumn: 1–23.

Hall, Peter, 1997: "The Role of Interests, Institutions, and Ideas in the Comparative Political Economy of Industrialized Nations," in Mark I. Lichbach and Alan Zuckerman, eds., 1997: *Comparative Politics.* New York: Cambridge University Press.

Hall, Peter and Robert Franzese, 1998: "Mixed Signals: Central Bank Independence, Coordinated Wage-Bargaining, and European Monetary Union," in *International Organization,* 52, no. 3: 505–535.

Hall, Peter, 1999: "The Political Economy of Europe in an Era of Interdependence," in H. Kitschelt, Peter Lange, Gary Marks, and John D. Stephens, eds., *Continuity and Change in Contemporary Capitalism.* New York: Cambridge University Press.

Hargreaves Heap, S., 1994: "Institutions and (Short-Run) Macroeconomic Performance," in *Journal of Economic Surveys,* 8, no. 1.

Hawkesworth, R., and Lluis Fina, 1987: "Trade Unions and Industrial relations In Spain: The Response to the Economic Crisis," in W. Brierly, ed., *Trade Unions and the Economic Crisis of the 1980s.* Aldershot: Gower, 64–83.

Helleiner, Eric, 1994: *States and the Reemergence of Global Finance.* Ithaca, NY: Cornell University Press.

Hernes, Gudmund, 1991. "The Dilemmas of Social Democracy: The Case of Norway and Sweden," in *Acta Sociologica,* 34: 239–260.

Hibbs, Douglas A. 1977. "Political Parties and Macroeconomic Policy," in *American Political Science Review,* 71: 1467–87.

Hibbs, Douglas A., 1987. *The American Political Economy: Macroeconomics and Electoral Politics in the United States.* Cambridge, MA: Harvard University Press.

Hibbs, Douglas A. 1987b: *The Political Economy of Industrial Democracies.* Cambridge, MA: Harvard University Press.

Hicks, Alexander, 1988: "Social Democratic Corporatism and Economic Growth," in *Journal of Politics,* 50: 677–704.

Hicks, Alexander, 1999: *Social Democracy and Welfare Capitalism.* Ithaca, NY: Cornell University Press.

Hicks, Alexander and Duane Swank, 1992: "Politics, Institutions and Social Welfare Spending in the Industrialized Democracies, 1960–1982," in *American Political Science Review,* 86, September: 658–674.

Hidalgo, Diego, 1996: *El Futuro de España.* Madrid: Taurus.

Hine, Robert C., 1989: "Customs Union Enlargement and Adjustment: Spain's Accession to the European Community," in *Journal of Common Market Studies,* XXVIII, no. 1, September.

Hollingsworth, Rogers J. and Robert Boyer, 1998: *Contemporary Capitalism: The Embeddedness of Institutions.* New York: Cambridge University Press.

Hyman, Richard, 1994, "Industrial Relations in Western Europe: An Era of Ambiguity?" in *Industrial Relations,* 33, no. 1: 1–24.

Iglesias, Rodrigo, 1990: "La Concertación Social desde la Perspectiva de las Organizaciones Empresariales," in A. Zaragoza, comp., *Pactos Sociales Sindicatos y Patronal en España.* Madrid: Siglo XXI.

IMF, 1991: *Determinants and Consequences of International Capital Flows,* Washington, D.C.: IMF.

Iversen, Torben, 1994: "Wage Bargaining, Monetary Regimes, and Economic Performance in Organized Market Economies: Theory and Evidence." Cambridge: CES, Working Paper Series # 59.

Iversen, Torben, 1996: "Power, Flexibility and the Breakdown of Centralized Wage Bargaining: The Cases of Denmark and Sweden in Comparative Perspective," in *Comparative Politics,* 28, July: 339–436.

Iversen, Torben, 1998: "Wage Bargaining, Central Bank Independence and the Real Effects of Money," in *International Organization,* 52, no. 3: 469–504.

Iversen Torben, 1999: *Contested Economic Institutions: The Politics of Macroeconomic and Wage-Bargaining in Organized Capitalism.* New York: Cambridge University Press.

Iversen, Torben and Anne Wren, 1996: "Equality, Employment and Fiscal Discipline: The Trilemma of the Service Economy." Paper presented at the Annual Meeting of the APSA. San Francisco, August 29-September 1.

Iversen, Torben, Jonas Pontusson, and David Soskice, eds., 1999: *Unions, Employers, and Central Banks: Wage Bargaining and Macroeconomic Regimes in an Integrating Europe.* New York: Cambridge University Press.

Janoski, Thomas and Alexander Hicks, eds., 1994: *The Comparative Political Economy of the Welfare State.* New York: Cambridge University Press.

Jimeno, J. F., 1992: "Las implicaciones macroeconómicas de la negociación colectiva: el caso español," in *Moneda y Crédito,* 195.

Jimeno, J. F., 1997: "La Negociació Collectiva: Aspectes Institucionals i les Seves Conseqències Econòmiques," in *Revista Econòmica de Catalunya,* no. 32, July 24.

Jimeno, J. F. and L. Toharia, 1993: "The Effects of Fixed Term Employment on Wage: Theory and Evidence from Spain," in *Investigaciones Económicas,* vol. XVII, no. 3: 475–494.

Jimeno, J. F. and L. Toharia, 1994: *Unemployment and Labor Market Flexibility: Spain.* Geneva: International Labour Organization.

Jordana, Jacint, 1996: "Reconsidering Union Membership in Spain, 1977–1994: Halting Decline in a Context of Democratic Consolidation," in *Industrial Relations Journal,* 27, no. 3.

Juliá, Santos, 1997: *Los Socialistas en la Política Española 1879–1982.* Madrid: Taurus.

Juliá, Santos, Javier Pradera, y Joaquín Prieto, eds., 1996: *Memoria de la Transicion.* Madrid: Taurus.

Juliá, Santos, 1988: *La Desavenencia.* Madrid: El Pais-Aguilar.

Kaldor, Nicholas, 1976: "Inflation and Recession in the World Economy," in *The Economic Journal,* no. 86, December.

Katz, Harry C., 1993: "The Decentralization of Collective Bargaining: A Literature Review and Comparative Analysis," in *Industrial and Labor Relations Review,* 47, no. 1, October: 3–22.

Katzenstein, Peter, ed., 1978: *Between Power and Plenty: Foreign Economic Policies of Advanced Industrial States.* Wisconsin: The University of Wisconsin Press.

Katzenstein, Peter, 1984: *Corporatism and Change: Austria, Switzerland, and the Politics of Industry.* Ithaca, NY: Cornell University Press

Katzenstein, Peter, 1985: *Small States in World Markets. Industrial Policy in Europe.* Ithaca, NY: Cornell University Press.

Katzenstein, Peter, Robert E. Keohane, and Stephen D. Krasner, 1999. *Exploration and Contestation in the Study of World Politics.* Cambridge, MA: MIT Press.

Kennedy, Paul, 1997: "The PSOE: Modernization and the Welfare State in Spain," in Donald Sasson, ed., 1997: *Looking Left: Socialism in Europe After the Cold War.* New York: The New Press.

Keohane, Robert, and Helen Milner, eds., 1996: *Internationalization and Domestic Politics.* Cambridge: Cambridge University Press.

King, Gary, Robert O. Keohane, and Sidney Verba, 1994: *Designing Social Inquiry: Scientific Inference in Qualitative Research.* Princeton: Princeton University Press.

Kitschelt, Herbert, 1994: *The Transformation of European Social Democracy.* Cambridge: Cambridge University Press.

Kitschelt, Herbert, 1999c: "European Social Democracy Between Political Economy and Electoral Competition," in H. Kitschelt, Peter Lange, Gary Marks, and John D. Stephens eds., *Continuity and Change in Contemporary Capitalism.* New York: Cambridge University Press.

Kitschelt, Herbert, Peter Lange, Gary Marks, and John D. Stephens, eds., 1999: *Continuity and Change in Contemporary Capitalism.* New York: Cambridge University Press.

Kitschelt, Herbert, Peter Lange, Gary Marks, and John D. Stephens 1999b: "Conclusion: Convergence and Divergence in Advanced Capitalist Democracies," in H. Kitschelt, Peter Lange, Gary Marks, and John D. Stephens, eds., *Continuity and Change in Contemporary Capitalism.* New York: Cambridge University Press.

Koelble, Thomas, 1991: "Recasting Social Democracy in Europe: 'Nested Games' and Rational Choices in Strategic Adjustment Process." Cambridge: CES. Working Paper Series #12.

Korpi, Walter and Michael Shalev, 1980: "Strikes, Power and Politics in the Western Nations, 1900–1976," in *Political Power and Social Theory,* vol. 1: 117–128.

Krieger, Mark and Joel Kesselman, eds., 1992: *European Politics in Transition.* Massachusetts: D.C. Heath and Company.

Kurzer, Paulette, 1993: *Business and Banking: Political Change and Economic Integration in Western Europe.* Ithaca, NY: Cornell University Press.

Kuttner, Robert, 1984: *The Economic Illusion: False Choices Between Prosperity and Social Justice.* Philadelphia: University of Pennsylvania Press.

Landes, David S., 1998: *The Wealth and Poverty of Nations: Why Some are So Rich and Some So Poor.* New York: W. W. Norton.

Lang, W., 1981: "Spanien Nach Franco: Von Autoritaren Zum Liberalen Korporatismus?" ("Spain after Franco: From Authoritarianism to Liberal Corporatism?") in Alemann, U., 1981: *Neocorporatismus.* Francfort/New York: Norton.

Lange, Peter, 1984: "Union, Workers, and Wage Regulation: The Rational Bases of Consent," in John H. Goldthorpe, ed., *Order and Conflict in Contemporary Capitalism.* Oxford: Oxford University Press.

Lange, P. and G. Garrett, 1985: "The Politics of Growth," in *Journal of Politics,* 47, no. 3: 792–827.

Lange, Peter and Geoffrey Garrett, 1987: "The Politics of Growth Reconsidered," in *Journal of Politics,* 49: 257–274.

Lange, P. and M. Regini, 1989: *State, Market, and Social Regulation.* Cambridge MA: Cambridge University Press.

Lange, Peter, Michael Wallerstein, and Miriam Golden, 1995: "The End of Corporatism? Wage Setting in the Nordic and Germanic Countries," in Sanford Jacoby, ed., *Workers of Nations: Industrial Relations in a Global Economy.* Oxford: Oxford University Press

Layard, Richard, 1982: "Is Incomes Policy the Answer to Unemployment?" Discussion Paper no 99. London: Centre for Labour Economics, London School of Economics.

Layard, Richard, 1997: *What Labour Can Do.* London: Warner Books

Layard, Richard, Stephen Nickell, and Robert Jackman, 1991: *Unemployment: Macroeconomic Performance and the Labour Market.* Oxford: Oxford University Press.

Leal, J. L., 1982: *Una Política Económica para España.* Barcelona: Planeta.

Lehmbruch, G., 1979. "Liberal Corporatism and Party Government," in P. Schmitter and G. Lehmbruch, eds., *Trends Towards Corporatist Intermediation.* Beverly Hills, CA: Sage.

Lehmbruch, G., 1979b: "Consolidational Democracy, Class Conflict and the New Corporatism," in P. Schmitter and G. Lehmbruch, eds., *Trends Towards Corporatist Intermediation.* Beverly Hills, CA: Sage.

Lehmbruch, Gerhard and Phillippe Schmitter, eds., 1982: *Patterns of Corporatist Policy-Making.* London: Sage.

Lehmbruch, G., 1984: "Concertation and the Structure of Corporatist Networks," in John Goldthorpe, ed., *Order and Conflict in Contemporary Capitalism.* Oxford: Clarendon Press.

Lichbach, Mark Irving and Alan Zuckerman, eds., 1997: *Comparative Politics.* New York: Cambridge University Press.

Lindblom, Charles, 1977: *Politics and Markets.* New York: Basic Books.

Lindbeck, Assar, 1993: *Unemployment and Macroeconomics.* Cambridge MA: MIT Press.

Lindbeck, Assar, et al., 1994: *Turning Sweden Around.* Cambridge MA: MIT Press.

Lindbeck, Assar and D. Snower, 1988: *The Insider-Outsider Theory of Unemployment.* Cambridge, MA: MIT Press.

Linz, Juan J., 1981: "A Century of Politics and Interests in Spain," in Suzanne Berger, ed., *Organizing Interests in Western Europe: Pluralism, Corporatism and the Transformation of Politics*. New York: Cambridge University.Press.

Liso, F., 1990: "Contenidos y Objetivos de la Concertación Social," in A. Ojeda-Aviles, ed., *La Concertacion Social tras la Crisis*. Barcelona: Ariel.

Locke, Richard and Kathleen Thelen, 1995: "Apples and Oranges Revisited: Contextualized Comparisons and the Study of Comparative Labor Politics," in *Politics and Society*, 23: 337–367.

Locke, Richard, Thomas Kochan, and Michael Piore, 1995: *Employment Relations in a Changing World Economy*. Cambridge MA: MIT Press.

López Guerra, Luis, 1984: "Partidos Políticos en España: Evolución y Perspectivas," in Eduardo García de Enterría, ed., *España: Un Presente para el Futuro*, vol. 2. Madrid: IEE.

Lynch, Lisa, ed., 1994: *Training and the Private Sector*. Chicago: Chicago University Press.

Maier, Charles, 1975: *Recasting Bourgeois Europe*. Princeton: Princeton University Press.

Malo, Miguel Angel and Luís Toharia, 1997: "El Sistema de Contratación Laboral a Espanya. De Reforma en Reforma," in *Revista Econòmica de Catalunya*, no. 32, July 24.

Maravall, José María, 1981: *La Política de la Transición, 1975–1980*. Madrid: Taurus.

Maravall, José María, 1992: "From Opposition to Government: the Politics and Policies of the PSOE," in J. M. Maravall et al., *Socialist Parties in Europe*. Barcelona: Institut de Ciences Politiques i Socials.

Maravall, José María, 1993: "Politics and Policy: Economic Reform in Southern Europe" in Luis Carlos Bresser Pereira, José María Maravall, and Adam Przeworski, eds., *Economic Reforms in New Democracies: A Social Democratic Approach*. Cambridge: Cambridge University Press.

Maravall, J. M., 1995: *Los Resultados de la Democracia*. Madrid: Alianza Editorial.

Maravall, José María, 1997: *Regimes Politics and Markets*. New York: Oxford University Press.

Marimón R. and F. Zilibotti, 1996: "Actual versus Virtual Employment in Europe: Is Spain Different?" European University Institute Working Paper, ECO no. 96/21.

Marks, Michael, 1997: *The Formation of European Policy in Post-Franco Spain*. Brookfield, VT: Ashgate Publishing Company.

Martín, Carmela, 1997: *España en la Nueva Europa*. Madrid: Alianza Editorial.

Martín Seco, Juna F., 1995: *La Farsa Neoliberal: Refutación de los Liberales que se Creen Libertarios*. Madrid: Ediciones Temas de Hoy.

Martín Valverde, A., 1985: "Congruencia de los Convenios Colectivos de Trabajo," in Borrajo, E., comp., *Comentarios a las Leyes Laborales. El Estatuto de los Trabajadores*. T. XII, vol. 2. Madrid: Edersa.

Martín Valverde, A., 1987: *La Legislación Social en la Historia de España. De la Restauración a la II República*. Madrid: Edersa.

Martínez-Alier, J., 1977: "El Pacto de la Moncloa. La Lucha Sindical y el Nuevo Corporativismo," *Cuadernos del Ruedo Ibérico*: 58–60.

Martínez-Alier, J., 1985: "Viejas Ideologías y Nuevas Realidades Corporativistas," Papers. *Revista de Sociologia*, no. 24.

Martínez-Alier J., and J. Roca, 1986: "Spain after Franco: From Corporatist Ideology to Corporatist Reality." Cambridge: CES. Working Paper Series #15.

Martínez-Alier, J. and Jordi Roca, 1986b: "El Debate sobre el Neocorporativismo," *Pensamiento Iberoamericano, Revista de Economía Política,* no. 8.

Martínez, Lucio, 1992: "Spain: Constructing Institutions and Actors in a Context of Change," in A. Ferner and R. Hyman, eds., 1992: *Industrial Relations in the New Europe.* Cambridge: Blackwell.

Martínez, Robert E., 1993: *Business and Democracy in Spain.* Westport, CT: Praeger.

Mayer, Thomas and Laurent Grillet-Aubert, 1997: "The New Dutch Model," in *Goldman Sachs European Economics Analyst.* New York: Goldman Sachs, February.

McDonough, Peter, Samuel Barnes, and Antonio López Pina, 1998: *The Cultural Dynamics of Democratization in Spain.* Ithaca, NY: Cornell University Press.

McKenzie, Richard and Dwight Lee, 1991: *Quicksilver Capital: How the Rapid Movement of Wealth has Changed the World.* New York: Free Press.

McKeown, Timothy, 1999: "The Global Economy, Post-Fordism, and Trade Policy in Advanced Capitalist States," in H. Kitschelt, Peter Lange, Gary Marks, and John D. Stephens, eds., *Continuity and Change in Contemporary Capitalism.* New York: Cambridge University Press.

McNamara, Kathleen R, 1998: *The Currency of Ideas: Monetary Politics in the European Union.* Ithaca, NY: Cornell University Press.

Merkel, Wolfgang, 1995: *¿Final de la Socialdemocracia?* Valencia: Edicions Alfons el Magnánim.

Miguelez, Faustino and Carlos Prieto, eds., 1991 (1995): *Las Relaciones Laborales en España.* Madrid: Siglo XXI.

Miguélez, Faustino, 1995: "Las Organizaciones Sindicales," in F. Miguélez and C. Prieto, *Las Relaciones Laborales en España.* Madrid: Siglo XXI.

Milner, S., 1995: "Las Relaciones Laborales en España y la Evolución Macroeconómica," in J. J. Dolado and J. F. Jimeno, eds. *Estudios Sobre el Funcionamiento del Mercado de Trabajo Español.* Madrid: Coleccion Estudios FEDEA, no. 13.

Ministerio de Trabajo y Seguridad Social, 1987: *Elecciones Sindicales. Volumen I.* Madrid: MTSS.

Ministerio de Trabajo y Asuntos Sociales, 1998: *Veinte Años de Concertación y Diálogo Social en España.* Madrid: MTAS.

Mjöset, Lars, 1987: "Nordic Economic Policies in the 1970s and 1980s," in *International Organization,* 41, no. 3: 403–456.

Moene, Karl Ove, and Michael Wallerstein, 1992: "The Decline of Social Democracy," in Karl Gunnar Persson, ed., *The Economic Development of Denmark and Norway since 1870.* Gloucester: Edward Elgar.

Moene, Karl Ove, and Michael Wallerstein, 1993: "What's Wrong with Social Democracy?" in Pranab Bradhan and John Roemer, eds., *The Current Debate.* Oxford: Oxford University Press.

Moene, Karl Ove, and Michael Wallerstein, 1995: "How Social Democracy Worked," in *Politics and Society,* 23: 185–211.

Moene, Karl Ove, and Michael Wallerstein, 1999: "Social Democratic Labor Institutions: A Retrospective Analysis," in H. Kitschelt, Peter Lange, Gary Marks, and

John D. Stephens, eds., *Continuity and Change in Contemporary Capitalism.* New York: Cambridge University Press.

Monteira, Félix, 1996: "La Huelga General," in Santos Juliá, et al., *Memoria de la Transición.* Madrid: Taurus.

Monteiro Fernades, Antonio de Lemos, 1999: "La Concertación Social y el Tripartismo: La Concertación Social en Portugal," in Federico Durán López, ed., *El Dialogo Social y su Institucionalización en España e Iberoamerica.* Madrid: CES.

Montero, J. R., 1996: "Un Terremoto Electoral," in Juliá, Santos, ed., *Memoria de la Transición.* Madrid: Taurus.

Moravcsik, Andrew, 1998: *The Choice for Europe: Social Purpose and State Power from Messina to Maastricht.* Ithaca, NY: Cornell University Press.

Moscoso, Leopoldo, 1995: "Social Democracy and Industrial Conflict: The Breakdown of Concertation in Spain, 1982–1994." Paper presented at the Harvard-Tufts Iberian Study Group, Harvard University. September.

Moses, Jonathan, 1994: "Abdication from National Policy Autonomy: What's Left to Leave?" in *Politics and Society,* 22, no. 2, June: 125–148.

Navarro, Vicente. 1997: "The Decline of Spanish Social Democracy 1982–1996," in Panitch, Leo, ed., *Socialist Register 1997: Ruthless Criticism of all that Exists.* New York: Monthly Review Press.

Navarro, Vicente, 1997a: *Neoliberalismo y Estado De Bienestar.* Barcelona: Editorial Ariel.

Navarro Arancegui, M., 1989: "La Política de Reconversión Industrial en España," in *Información Comercial Española,* no. 665.

Nickell, S., 1997: "Unemployment and Labor Market Rigidities: Europe Versus North America," *Journal of Economic Perspectives,* 3: 55–74.

North, Douglass C., 1990: *Institutions, Institutional Change and Economic Performance.* New York: Cambridge University Press.

Notermans, Ton, 1994: "The Abdication of National Policy Autonomy: Why the Macroeconomic Policy has Become so Unfavorable to Labor," in *Politics and Society,* 21.

OECD, Various Years: *Economic Surveys: Spain.* Paris: OECD.

OECD, 1995: *The Jobs Study: Taxation, Employment, and Unemployment.* Paris: OECD.

OECD, 1999: *Employment Outlook.* Paris: OECD.

Offe, Claus, 1993: *Contradictions of the Welfare State.* Cambridge: The MIT Press.

Ohmae, Keniche, 1991: *The Borderless World: Power and Strategy in the Interlink Economy.* New York: Harper Perennial.

Ojeda-Aviles, A., ed., 1990: *La Concertacion Social tras la Crisis.* Barcelona: Ariel.

Olson, Mancur, 1965: *The Logic of Collective Action: Public Goods and the Theory of Groups.* Cambridge. Cambridge, MA: Harvard University Press.

Olson, Mancur, 1982: *The Rise and Decline of Nations: Economic Growth Stagflation, and Social Rigidities.* New Haven, CT: Yale University Press.

Olson, Mancur, 1986: "A Theory of the Incentives Facing Political Organizations: Neocorporatism and the Hegemonic State," in *International Political Science Review,* no. 2.

Ortiz Lallana, M. Carmen, 1990: "Aproximación a los Objetivos y Métodos de una Nueva Política de Concertación Social en España," in A. Ojeda-Aviles, ed., *La Concertacion Social tras la Crisis.* Barcelona: Ariel.

Palacios, Juan Ignacio, 1995: "La Política de Empleo," in F. Miguelez and Carlos Prieto, eds., *Las Relaciones Laborales en España*. Madrid: Siglo XXI.

Panich, L., 1977: "The Development of Corporatism in Liberal Democracies," in *Comparative Political Studies*, no. 10.

Panitch, Leo, 1980: "Recent Theorizations of Corporatism: Reflections on a Growth Industry," in *British Journal of Sociology*, Winter.

Paramio, Ludolfo, 1992: "Los Sindicatos y la Política en España, 1982–1992," in A. Guerra and J. F. Tezanos, eds., *La Decada del Cambio: Diez años de Gobierno Socialista, 1982–1992*. Madrid: Fundación Sistema, 521–538.

Pardo Avellaneda, Rafael and Joaquín Fernández Castro, 1995: "Las Organizaciones Empresariales y la Configuración del Sistema de Relaciones Industriales," in Miguélez, Faustino and Carlos Prieto, eds., *Las Relaciones Laborales en España*. Madrid: Siglo XXI.

Pastor, Carles, 1996: "Diez Millones Para el Cambio," in Santos Juliá, Javier Pradera, y Joaquín Prieto, eds., *Memoria de la Transicion*. Madrid: Taurus.

Pérez, Sofía, 1994: "Imported Credibility and the 'Strong Peseta': Bundesbank Dominance and Spanish Economic Policy in the EMS." Paper prepared for the Ninth Annual International Conference of Europeanists, Chicago Illinois, March 31–April 2.

Pérez, Sofía, 1996: "Labor Market Institutions, Socialist Economic Policy, and Unemployment in Spain: What Exactly are the Lessons?" Paper prepared for delivery at the APSA Annual Meeting, San Francisco. August 29–September 1.

Pérez, Sofía, 1996b: "Hitching on to the DM: EMS Rules, the Southern Paradox, and the Crisis of 1992/93." Typescript. Boston: Boston University. March.

Pérez, Sofía, 1997: "From Cheap Credit to the EC: The Politics of Financial Reform in Spain," in Michael Loriaux, et al., *Capital Ungoverned*. Ithaca, NY: Cornell University Press.

Pérez, Sofía, 1997b: *Banking on Privilege: The Politics of Spanish Financial Reform*. Ithaca, NY: Cornell University Press.

Pérez, Sofía, 1997c: "Financial Liberalization and the Failure of Socialist Economic Policies in Spain." Paper prepared for delivery at the 1997 Annual Meeting of the American Political Science Association, Washington D.C., August 28–31.

Pérez, Sofía, 1998: "Yet the Century? The Return to National Social Bargaining in Italy and Spain, and Some Possible Implications." Paper prepared for delivery at the 1998 Annual Meeting of the American Political Science Association, Boston, August.

Pérez Sofía, 1999: "From Labor to Finance: Explaining the Failure of Socialist Economic Policies in Spain," in *Comparative Political Studies*, Winter.

Pérez-Díaz, Victor, 1980: "Los Obreros Españoles ante el Sindicato y la Acción Colectiva," in *Papeles de Economía Española*, no. 6.

Pérez-Díaz, Victor, 1981: *El Retorno de la Sociedad Civil*. Madrid: IEE.

Pérez-Díaz, Victor, 1984: "Políticas Económicas y Pautas Sociales en la España de la Transición: La Doble Cara del Neocorporatismo," in J. Linz, ed., *España: Un Presente Para el Futuro*. Madrid: Instituto de Estudios Económicos.

Pérez-Díaz, Victor, 1985: "Los Empresarios y la Clase Política," in *Papeles de Economía Española*, no. 22.

Pérez-Díaz, Víctor, 1986: "Economic Policies and Social Pacts in Spain During the Transition: The Two Faces of Neo-Corporatism," in *European Sociological Review,* vol. 2, no. 1, May: 1–19.

Pérez-Díaz, Victor, 1987: "Economic Policies and Social Pacts in Spain During the Transition," in Ilja Schloten, ed., *Political Stability and Neo-Corporatism.* London: Sage.

Pérez-Díaz, Victor, 1995: "El Largo Plazo y el 'Lado Blando' de las Políticas de Empleo." *ASP Research Paper 11(a).*

Pérez-Díaz, Víctor, 1996: *España Puesta a Prueba 1976–1996.* Madrid: Alianza Actualidad.

Pérez-Díaz, Víctor, 1997: *La Esfera Pública y la Sociedad Civil.* Madrid: Taurus.

Pérez-Díaz, Victor and Luís Angel Rojo, October 1983: "Economic Responses to Political Crisis: The Case of Spain," International Conference of Europeanists, Council for European Studies, Washington D.C.

Pérez Infante, José Ignacio, 1998: "Reformas Laorates y Creaciou de Empleoen la Economia Española en el Contexto de la Union Vionetaria," in Jorge Aragion Medina, ed., *Euro y Empleo.* Madrid: CES.

Pérez Royo, J., 1996: "El Mito de la Crisis del Parlamento," in Javier Tussell, ed., *Entre dos Siglos.* Madrid: Alianza Editorial.

Phelps E. H., 1980: *Las Desigualdades de Salarios.* Madrid: MTSS.

Phillips, Bill, 1958: "The Relation Between Unemployment and the Rate of Change of Monetary Wages in the United Kingdom, 1861–1957," in *Economica,* no. 25: 283–299.

Pierson, Paul, 1994: *Dismantling the Welfare State: Reagan, Thatcher and the Politics of Retrenchment in Britain and the United States.* New York: Cambridge University Press.

Pierson, Paul, 1996: "The New Politics of the Welfare State," in *World Politics,* 48, no. 2: 143–179.

Piore, M., and C. Sabel, 1984: *The Second Industrial Divide.* New York: Basic Books.

Piven, Frances Fox, ed., 1991: *Labor Parties in Postindustrial Societies.* New York: Oxford University Press.

Pizzorno, A., 1978: "Political Exchange and Collective Identity in Industrial Conflict," in C. Crouch and A. Pizzorno, eds., *The Resurgence of Class Conflict in Western Europe since 1968,* vol. 2. London: Macmillan Press.

Pontusson, J., 1992: "Sweden," in M. Krieger and J. Kesselman, *European Politics in Transition.* Massachusetts: D.C. Heath and Company.

Pontusson, J., 1992b: *Limits of Social Democracy.* Ithaca, NY: Cornell University Press.

Pontusson, Jonas, 1994: "At the End of the Third Road: Swedish Social Democracy in Crisis," in *Politics and Society,* 20, no. 3: 305–332.

Pontusson, Jonas and Peter Swenson, 1996: "Labor Markets, Production Strategies, and Wage Bargaining Institutions: The Swedish Employer Offensive in Comparative Perspective," in *Comparative Political Studies,* 29, no. 2: 223–250.

Porter, Michael, 1990: *The Competitive Advantage of Nations.* New York: Free Press

Przeworski, Adam, 1985. *Capitalism and Social Democracy.* Cambridge: Cambridge University Press.

Przeworski, Adam, 1991: *Democracy and the Market.* New York: Cambridge University Press.

Przeworski, Adam, 1995: *Sustainable Democracy.* New York: Cambridge University Press.

Przeworski, Adam and Michael Wallerstein, 1988: "Structural Dependence of the State in Capital," *American Political Science Review,* 82: 11–30.

Putnam, Robert D. 1993: *Making Democracy Work: Civic Traditions in Modern Italy.* Princeton, NJ: Princeton University Press.

Quinn, Dennis and Carla Inclan, 1997: "The Origins of Financial Openness: A 21 Country Study of its Determinants, 1950–1988," in *American Journal of Political Science,* 41, no. 3: 771–813.

Quinto, Javier, 1994: *Política Industrial en España.* Madrid: Ediciones Piramide.

Recio, Albert, 1991 (1995): "La Segmentación del Mercado de Trabajo en España," in F. Miguélez and C. Prieto, eds., *Las Relaciones Laborales en España.* Madrid: Siglo XXI.

Recio, Albert and Jordi Roca, 1988–1989: "Apuntes sobre la Política de Empleo," in *Mientras Tanto,* nos. 36–37.

Reder, Melvin and Lloyd Ulman, 1993: "Unionism and Unification," in Lloyd Ulman, Barry Eichngreen, and William T. Dickens, eds., *Labor and an Integrated Europe.* Washington, D.C.: Brookings Institution.

Redondo, Nicolás, 1990: "Informe al XXXV Congreso Confederal de la UGT," in Unión General de Trabajadores: *Boletín de la Comisión Ejecutiva Confederal,* no. 115, May: 15–26.

Regini, Marino, 1984: "The Conditions for Political Exchange: How Concertation Emerged and Collapsed in Italy and Great Britain," in John Goldthorpe, ed., *Order and Conflict in Contemporary Capitalism.* Oxford: The Clarendon Press.

Regini, Marino, 1990: "El Declinar del Intercambio Político Centralizado y la Emergencia de Nuevas Formas de Concertación," in A. Ojeda Avilés, ed., *La Concertación Social tras la Crisis.* Barcelona: Editorial Ariel.

Regini, M., 1991: *Confini Mobili. La Construzione dell'Economia Fra Politica e Societá.* Bologna: Il Mulino.

Regini, M. 1995: *Uncertain Boundaries: the Social and Political Construction of European Economies.* New York: Cambridge University Press.

Regini, Marino, 1996 (1997): "Still Engaging in Corporatism? Recent Italian Experiences in Comparative Perspective," in *European Journal of Industrial Relations,* vol. 3, no. 3: 259–278.

Regini, Marino and Ida Regalia, 1997: "Employers, Unions, and the State: the Resurgence of Concertation in Italy?," in *West European Politics,* 25, no. 1: 210–230.

Reich, Robert, 1992: *The Work of Nations.* New York: Vintage.

Richards, Andrew and Javier García Polavieja, 1997: "Trade Unions, Unemployment and Working Class Fragmentation in Spain," *Working Paper # 112.* Madrid: CEACS.

Rifkin, Jeremy, 1995: *The End of Work.* New York: Putnam.

Rigby, Mike and Rafael Serrano del Rosal, eds., 1997: *Estrategias Sindicales en Europa: Converegencias o Divergencias.* Madrid: CES.

Roca Jusmet, Jordi, 1985: "Los Pactos Sociales en El Estado Español," in *Crónica de Información Laboral,* no. 32.

Roca Jusmet, Jordi, 1987: "Neo-corporatism in Franco Spain," in Ilja Schloten, ed., *Political Stability and Neo-Corporatism.* London: Sage.

Roca Jusmet, Jordi, 1991 (1995): "La Concertación Social," in F. Miguélez, and C. Prieto, eds., *Las Relaciones Laborales en España.* Madrid: Siglo XXI.

Roca Jusmet, Jordi, 1993: *Pactos Sociales y Políticas de Rentas.* Madrid: Ministerio de Trabajo y Seguridad Social.

Rodríguez Piñero, M., 1983: "Acuerdos Interprofesionales, Centralización de la Negociación Colectiva y la Ley Estatuto de los Trabajadores," in *Revista de Política Social,* no. 137.

Rodrik, Dani, 1996: "Globalization and Labor, or: If Globalization is a Bowl of Cherries, Why are there so many Glum Faces Around the Table?" Paper presented at the CEPR Conference on Regional integration, La Coruña, Spain, April.

Rodrik, Dani, 1997: *Has Globalization Gone Too Far?* Washington, D.C.: Institute for Research Economics.

Rogers Joel, and Wolfgang Streeck, 1995: *Work Councils: Consultation, Representation, and Cooperation in Industrial Relations.* Chicago: University of Chicago Press.

Rogowski, Ronald, 1987: "Trade and the Variety of Democratic Institutions," in *International Organization,* 41: 203–223.

Rogowski, Ronald, 1989: *Commerce and Coalitions: How Trade Affects Domestic Political Alignments.* Princeton, NJ: Princeton University Press.

Rojo, Luis Angel, 1981: "Desempleo y Factores Reales" in *Papeles de Economía Española,* 8: 124–136.

Rothstein, Bo, 1992: " Labor-Market Institutions and Working-Class Strength," in Sven Steinmo, Kathleen Thelen, and Frank Longstreth, eds.: *Structuring Politics: Historical Institutionalism in Comparative Analysis.* New York: Cambridge University Press.

Rowthorn, Bob, 1992: "Corporatism and Labor Market Performance," in Jukka Pekkarinen, Matti Pohjola, and Bob Rowthorn, eds., *Social Corporatism: A Superior Economic System?* Oxford: Clarendon Press.

Royo, Sebastián, 1997: "Limits to Social Democratic Policies in Spain." Paper presented at the Iberian Study Group, Center for European Studies, Harvard University. May.

Royo, Sebastián, 1998a: *Social Democracy and the Collapse of Concertation in Spain.* Ph.D. Dissertation, Boston: Boston University.

Royo, Sebastián, 1998b: "Social Democracy and the Collapse of Concertation in Spain." Paper presented at the Annual Meeting of the New England Political Science Association, Worcester, MA, May.

Royo, Sebastián, 1998c: "The Collapse of Social Concertation and the Failure of Socialist Economic Policies in Spain." Paper presented at the Annual Meeting of the Northeastern Political Science Association, Boston, November.

Royo, Sebastián, 1998d: "Globalización y Políticas Domésticas." Paper presented at the First Congress of Social Sciences: Social Sciences Towards the Year 2000, Universidad de Puerto Rico-Mayagüez, June.

Royo Sebastián, 1999 (forthcoming): "*'Still the Century of Corporatism?* Corporatism in Southern Europe: A Comparative Analysis of Spain and Portugal." Typescript. Suffolk University.

Sagardoy Bengoechea J. A., and David León Blanco, 1982: *El Poder Sindical en España*. Barcelona: IEE/Planeta.

Salvador, I. and F. Almedros Morcillo, 1972: *Panorama del Sindicalismo Europeo*, vol. 1. Madrid: Alianza.

Sasson, Donald, 1996: *One Hundred Years of Socialism: The West European Left in the Twentieth Century*. New York: The New Press.

Sasson, Donald, ed., 1997: *Looking Left: Socialism in Europe After the Cold War*. New York: The New Press.

Scharpf, Fritz W., 1984: "Economic and Institutional Constraints of Full-Employment Strategies: Sweden, Austria, and Western Germany, 1973–1982," in John Goldthorpe, ed., *Order and Conflict in Contemporary Capitalism*. Oxford: The Clarendon Press, pp. 257–290.

Scharpf, Fritz W., 1987: "A Game-Theoretical Interpretation of Inflation and Unemployment in Western Europe," in *Journal of Public Policy*, 7, no. 3: 227–257.

Scharpf, Fritz W., 1987: "The Political Calculus of Inflation and Unemployment in Western Europe." Cambridge: CES Working Paper Series #6.

Scharpf, Fritz W., 1991: *Crisis and Choice in European Social Democracy*. Ithaca, NY: Cornell University Press.

Scharpf, Fritz W., 1997: *Games Real Actors Play: Actor-Centered Institutionalism in Policy Research*. Boulder, CO: Westview Press.

Schmidt, Manfred, 1982: "The Role of the Parties in Shaping Macroeconomic Policy," in Francis Castles, ed., *The Impact of Parties*. Beverly Hills, CA: Sage Publications.

Schmidt, Manfred, 1996: "When Parties Matter; A Review of the Possibilities and Limits of Partisan Influence on Public Policy," in *European Journal of Political Research*, 30, September: 155–183.

Schmitter, Philippe, 1974: "Still the Century of Corporatism?" in *Review of Politics*, 36, no. 1: 85–131.

Schmitter, Philippe C., 1981: "Interest Intermediation and Regime Governability in Western Europe and North America," in S. Berger, ed., *Organizing Interests in Western Europe*. Cambridge: Cambridge University Press.

Schmitter, Philippe C., 1982: "Reflections on Where the Theory of Neo-corporatism has Gone and Where the Praxis of Neo-corporatism May be Going," in G. Lehmbruch and Phillippe Schmitter, eds., *Patterns of Corporatist Policy-Making*. London: Sage.

Schmitter, Philippe C., 1990: "El Corporatismo ha Muerto, ¡Larga Vida al Corporatismo!," in A. Ojeda Avilés, ed., *La Concertación Social tras la Crisis*. Barcelona: Ariel.

Schmitter, Philippe, 1991: "La Concertación Social en Perspectiva Comparada," in A. Espina, ed., *Concertación Social, Neocorporatismo y Democracia*. Madrid: MTSS.

Schmitter, Philippe, 1995: "Organized Interests and Democratic Consolidation in Southern Europe," in Richard Gunther, P. Nikiforos Diamandouros, and Hans-

Jürgen Puhle, 1995: *The Politics of Democratic Consolidation: Southern Europe in Comparative Perspective.* Baltimore MD,: John Hopkins University Press.

Schmitter, Philippe and Gerard Lehmbruch, eds., 1979: *Trends Toward Corporatist Intermediation.* Beverly Hills, CA: Sage Publications.

Scholten, Ilja, ed., 1987: *Political Stability and Neo-Corporativism: Corporatist Integration and Societal Cleavages in Western Europe.* Beverly Hills, CA: Sage.

Schwartz, Herman, 1994: "Small States in Big Trouble," in *World Politics,* 46: 527–555.

Shonfield, A., 1965: *Modern Capitalism.* New York: Oxford University Press.

Skocpol, Theda, 1995: *Vision and Method in Historical Sociology.* New York: Cambridge University Press.

Servicio de Estudios del Banco de España, 1997: *La Política Monetaria y la Inflación en España.* Madrid: Alianza Editorial/Banco de España.

Sevilla, J. V., 1985: "La Economía Española Durante la Transición Democrática," in J. V. Sevilla, comp., *Mineros Sindicalismo y Política.* Oviedo: Fundación José Barrero.

Sevilla, Jordi, 1997: *La Economía Española Ante la Moneda Única.* Madrid: Ediciones Debate.

Share, Donald, 1989: *Dilemmas of Social Democracy: The Spanish Socialist Workers Party in the 1980s.* New York: Greenwood Press.

Simmons, Beth, 1999: "The Internationalization of Capital," in H. Kitschelt, Peter Lange, Gary Marks, and John D. Stephens eds., *Continuity and Change in Contemporary Capitalism.* New York: Cambridge University Press.

Sinn, Hans-Werner, 1996: "Social Insurance, Incentives and Risk Taking," in *International Tax and Public Finance.* Winter.

Smith, W. Rand, 1991: "Socialism and Industrial 'Adjustment': State Responses to Economic Crisis in France and Spain." Paper prepared for delivery at the 1991 Annual Meeting of the APSA, August 29 - September 1.

Solchaga, Carlos, 1988: "Presentación del Proyecto de Ley the Presupuestos Generales del Estado para 1988," in *Hacienda Pública Española,* 112: 15–44.

Solchaga, Carlos, 1997: *El Final de la Edad Dorada.* Madrid: Taurus.

Soros, George, 1998: *The Crisis of Global Capitalism : (Open Society Endangered).* Washington, D.C.: Public Affairs.

Soskice, David, 1990a: "Wage Determination: The Changing Role of Institutions in Advanced Industrial Countries," in *Oxford Review of Economic Policy,* 6, no. 4: 36–61.

Soskice, David, 1990b: "Reinterpreting Corporatism and Explaining Unemployment: Coordinated and Uncoordinated Market Economies," in Renato Brunetta and Carlo Dell'Aringa, eds., *Labour Relations and Economic Performance.* London: Macmillan.

Soskice, David, 1999: "Divergent Production Regimes: Coordinated and Uncoordinated Market Economies in the 1980s and 1990s," in H. Kitschelt, Peter Lange, Gary Marks, and John D. Stephens, eds., *Continuity and Change in Contemporary Capitalism.* New York: Cambridge University Press.

Steinmo, Sven, Kathleen Thelen, and Frank Longstreth, eds., 1992: *Structuring Politics: Historical Institutionalism in Comparative Analysis.* Cambridge: Cambridge University Press.

Steinmo, Sven, 1993: *Democracy and Taxation.* New Haven, CT: Yale University Press.

Steinmo, Sven. 1994: "The End of Redistributive Taxation: Tax Reform in a Global World Economy." *Challenge,* 37, no. 6, November - December: 9–17.

Stephens, John, Evelyn Huber, and Leonard Ray, 1999: "The Welfare State in Hard Times," in H. Kitschelt, Peter Lange, Gary Marks, and John D. Stephens, eds., *Continuity and Change in Contemporary Capitalism.* New York: Cambridge University Press.

Streeck, Wolfgang, 1992: *Social Institutions and Economic Performance: Studies of Industrial Relations in Advanced Capitalist Economies.* Newbury Park and London: Sage.

Streeck, Wolfganf, 1993: "The Rise and Decline of Neocorporatism," in Lloyd Ulman, Barry Eichngreen, and William T. Dickens, eds., *Labor and an Integrated Europe.* Washington, D.C.: Brookings Institution.

Streeck, Wolfgang, 1994: "Pay Restraint Without Incomes Policy: Institutionalized Monetarism and Industrial Unionism in Germany," in R. Dore, Robert Boyer, and Zoe Mars, eds., *The Return of Incomes Policy.* London: Pinter Publishers,

Streeck, Wolfgang and Philippe Schmitter, 1991. "From National Corporatism to Transnational Pluralism: Organized Interests in the Single European Market," in *Politics and Society,* 19, no. 2: 133–164.

Swank, Duane, 1992: "Politics and the Structural Dependence of the State in Democratic Capitalist Nations." *American Political Science Review,* 86: 38–54.

Swank, Duane, 1998: "Global Markets, Democratic Institutions, and the Public Economy in Advanced Industrial Societies." Paper presented at the Center for European Studies, Harvard University. Revised Draft, February 18.

Swenson, Peter, 1989: *Fair Shares: Unions, Pay and Politics in Sweden and West Germany.* Ithaca, NY: Cornell University Press.

Swenson, Peter, 1991: "Bringing Capital Back In, or Social Democracy Reconsidered," in *World Politics,* 43.

Swenson, Peter, 1992: "Union Politics, the Welfare State, and Intraclass Conflict in Sweden and Germany," in M. Golden, and J. Pontusson, eds., *Bargaining for Change.* Ithaca, NY: Cornell University Press.

Taboadela, Obdulia, 1993: "Clases Sociales y Acción Colectiva," in *Revista Española de Investigaciones Sociológicas,* no. 63, July - September.

Tamames, Ramón, 1993: *Estructura Económica de España.* Madrid: Alianza Universidad.

Tamames, Ramón, 1995: *La Economía Española, 1975–1995.* Madrid: Ediciones Temas de Hoy, S.A.

Tarantelli, E., 1983: "The Regulation of Inflation in Western Countries and the Degree of Neocorporatism," in *Economica,* 7.

Termes, Rafael, 1995: *Las Causas del Paro.* Madrid: Instituto de Estudios Económicos.

Thelen, Kathleen, 1993: "West European Labor in Transition: Sweden and Germany Compared," in *World Politics,* 46.

Thurow, Lester, 1992: *Head to Head.* New York: Warner Books.

Thurow, Lester, 1999: *Building Wealth: The New Rules for Companies, Individuals and Nations.* New York: Harperbusiness.

Toharia, Luis, 1981: "Un Fordismo Inacabado, entre la Transición Política y la Crisis Económica: España," in R. Boyer, ed., *La Flexibilidad de Trabajo en Europa.* Madrid: Ministerio de Trabajo.

Tortella, Gabriel, 1994: *El Desarrollo de la España Contemporánea: Historia Económica de los Siglos XIX y XX.* Madrid: Alianza Editorial, S.A.

Traxler, Franz, 1994: "Collective Bargaining: Levels and Coverage" in *OECD Employment Outlook.* Paris: OECD.

Traxler, Franz, 1995: "Farewell to Labour Market Associations? Organized versus Disorganized Decentralization as a Map for Industrial Relations," in Colin Crouch and Franz Traxler, eds., *Organized Industrial Relations in Europe: What Future?* Aldershot: Avebury.

Turner, Lowell, 1991: *Democracy at Work: Changing World Markets and the Future of Labor Unions.* Ithaca, NY: Cornell University Press.

Ulman, Barry Eichengreen, and William T. Dickens, eds., 1993: *Labor and an Integrated Europe.* Washington, D.C.: The Brookings Institution.

Valdés Dal-Re, Fernando, 1983: "Crisis y Continuidad en la estructura de la negociación colectiva," in *RPS,* no. 137.

Valdés Dal-Re, Fernando, 1994: "Notas sobre la Reforma del Marco Legal de la Estructura de la Negociacion Colectiva," in *Relaciones Laborales,* no. 5, March.

Valdés Dal-Ré, Fernando, ed., 1995: *La Reforma Del Mercado Laboral.* Madrid: Editorial Lex Nova.

Various Authors, 1992: *Sindicatos, Economía y Sociedad: Un Futuro del Sindicalismo Español.* Informes del IAE, Madrid: Ministerio de Economía y Hacienda.

Vázquez, Antonio, 1991 (1995): "Dinámica Económica y Restructuración Productiva en España," in F. Miguélez and Carlos Prieto, eds., *Las Relaciones Laborales en España,* Madrid: Siglo XXI.

Vega García, Ruben, 1995: *CC.OO. de Asturias en la Transición y la Democracia.* Oviedo: Unión Regional de CC.OO. de Asturias.

Velarde, Juan, 1996: *Hacia Otra Economía Española.* Madrid: Espasa Calpe.

Velasco, Roberto, 1996: *Los Economistas en Su Laberinto.* Madrid: Taurus.

Visser, Jelle, 1989: *European Trade Unions in Figures, 1913–1985.* Deventer: Kluwer Law and Taxation Publishers.

Visser, Jelle 1992: "The Strength of Union Movements in Advanced Capitalist Democracies: Social and Organizational Variations," in Marino Regini, ed., *The Future of Labor Movements.* London: Sage Publications.

Vogel, Steven, 1996: *Freer Markets, More Rules: Regulatory Reform in Advanced Industrial Countries.* Ithaca, NY: Cornell University Press.

Wallerstein, Michael, 1990: "Centralized Bargaining and Wage Restrain," in *American Journal of Political Science,* 34: 982–1004.

Wallerstein, Michael and Adam Przeworski. 1995: "Capital Taxation with Open Borders," in *Review of International Political Economy,* 2, Summer: 425–445.

Weaver, R. Kent, and Bert A. Rockman, eds., 1993: *Do Institutions Matter: Government Capabilities in the United States and Abroad.* Washington, D.C.: The Brookings Institution.

Weiss, Linda, 1998: *The Myth of the Powerless State.* Ithaca, NY: Cornell University Press.

Wiarda, Howard, 1974: "Corporatism and Development in the Ibero-Latin World," in F. Pike and T. Stritch, eds., *The New Corporatism. Social Political Structures in the Iberian World.* South Bend, IN: Notre Dame.

Wiarda, Howard, 1997: *Corporatism and Comparative Politics: the Other Great "Ism."* New York: M. E. Sharpe.

Williamson, John, ed., 1993: *The Political Economy of Policy Reform.* Washington, D.C.: Institute for International Economics.

World Development Report 1995. *Workers in an Integrating World.* World Development Indicators. Oxford: Oxford University Press.

Wozniak, Lynne, 1991: "The Changing Place of Labor in European Society: Spain." Paper prepared for delivery at the Workshop "The Changing Place of Labor in European Society," CES, Harvard University. November 23–24.

Zaragoza, Angel, ed., 1988 (1990): *Pactos Sociales, Sindicatos y Patronal en España.* Madrid Siglo XXI.

Zaragoza, Angel and José Varela, 1990: "Pactos Sociales y Corporatismo en España," in A. Zaragoza, ed., *Pactos Sociales Sindicatos y Patronal en España.* Madrid: Siglo XXI, 1990.

Ziegler, J. Nicholas, 1997: *Governing Ideas: Strategies for Innovation in France and Germany.* Ithaca, NY: Cornell University Press.

Zufiaur, José María, 1983: "Los Sindicatos, Elecciones Sindicales y Accion Institucional" in Various Authors, *Cambio Social y Accion Sindical en España (1975–1983).* Madrid: Fundación Largo Caballero.

Zufiaur, J. M., 1985: "El Sindicalismo Español en la Transición y la Crisis," in *Papeles de Economía Española,* no. 22.

Zysman, John, 1983: *Governments, Markets, and Growth.* Ithaca, NY: Cornell University Press.

Index

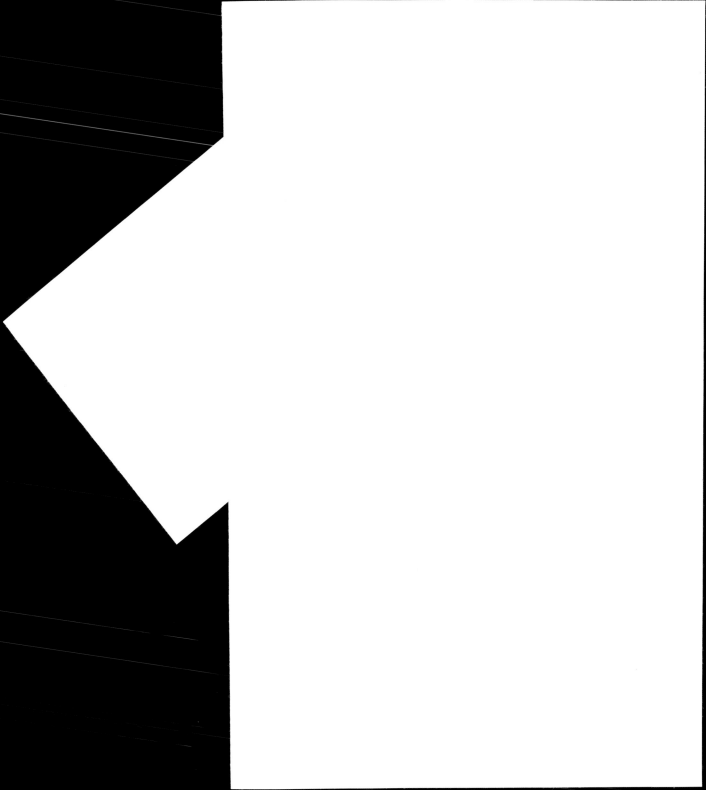

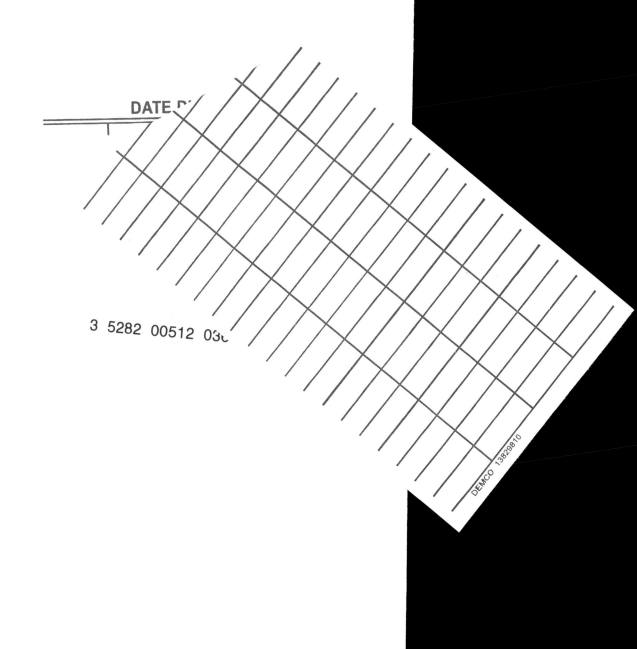

DATE D

3 5282 00512 03